The Archaeology *of* Wak'as

The Archaeology of Wak'as

Explorations of the Sacred in the Pre-Columbian Andes

edited by Tamara L. Bray

UNIVERSITY PRESS OF COLORADO
Louisville

© 2015 by University Press of Colorado

Published by University Press of Colorado
245 Century Circle, Suite 202
Louisville, Colorado 80027

 The University Press of Colorado is a proud member of
Association of American University Presses.

The University Press of Colorado is a cooperative publishing enterprise supported, in part, by Adams State University, Colorado State University, Fort Lewis College, Metropolitan State University of Denver, Regis University, University of Colorado, University of Northern Colorado, Utah State University, and Western State Colorado University.

∞ This paper meets the requirements of the ANSI/NISO Z39.48-1992 (Permanence of Paper).

ISBN: 978-1-60732-317-4 (hardcover)
ISBN: 978-1-60732-318-1 (ebook)
ISBN: 978-1-60732-731-8 (paper)

Library of Congress Cataloging-in-Publication Data

The archaeology of wak'as : explorations of the sacred in the pre-Columbian Andes / Tamara L. Bray, editor.
     pages cm
  Includes bibliographical references.
  ISBN 978-1-60732-317-4 (cloth : alk. paper) — ISBN 978-1-60732-318-1 (ebook) — ISBN 978-1-60732-731-8 (paper)
  1. Indians of South America—Andes—Antiquities. 2. Huacas. 3. Andes—Antiquities.
  4. Indians of South America—Peru—Antiquities. 5. Peru—Antiquities. I. Bray, Tamara L.
  F2229.A82 2014
  985'.01—dc23

                              2014005436

Cover illustration: Drawing by Martin de Murúa, from Códice Galvin (2004 [1590]:98r).

For Frank Salomon,
whose work has been foundational, insightful, and inspirational

And Chaupi Ñamca said: "Only this man, alone among all the other *huacas*, is a real man. I'll stay with this one forever." So she turned into stone and stayed forever . . .

HUAROCHIRÍ MANUSCRIPT, CH. 10 (CA. AD 1600)
TRANSLATED IN SALOMON AND URIOSTE (1991:78)

Figures

Acknowledgments

The idea for this edited volume evolved out of a symposium organized for the 75th Annual Meeting of the Society for American Archaeology in 2010 entitled "The Archaeology of *Huacas*: Exploring the Materiality, Meaning, and Efficacy of Sacred Objects and Places in the Andes." Given the level of interest in the topic, it was decided that deeper discussion of material approaches to Andean wak'as was merited. A proposal to convene a special colloquium was presented to the Pre-Columbian Studies program at Dumbarton Oaks and was accepted. The colloquium, "The Archaeology of Wak'as," which was held in December 2011 in Washington, DC, allowed contributors to the present volume to further hone their ideas and gain valuable feedback from colleagues and friends. I am grateful to former director of Pre-Columbian Studies, Joanne Pillsbury, and the director of Dumbarton Oaks, Jan Ziolkowski, for making the *encuentro* a warm, collegial, and highly productive one. I would also like to thank program coordinator Emily Gulick Jacobs for ably overseeing the details of the event, the Senior Fellows for their support of the colloquium agenda, and the community of scholars that attended for their thoughtful comments and input.

The process of assembling an edited volume is never an easy one, and I would like to thank all of the authors for their patience and fortitude in seeing this work through to completion. The verbal and written interactions we have shared over the course of the past few years has enriched my thinking about the subjects treated in this book and, I believe, contributed to the overall coherence and quality of the project as a whole. Many of the chapters also benefited from the careful review of two external readers for the Press who offered detailed and insightful comments. Special thanks go to Ben Alberti, who provided an enormous amount of thoughtful feedback on the manuscript. I would also like to thank my colleagues in the Department of Anthropology at Wayne State University for providing me with a supportive environment, and the University for the institutional framework that has helped sustain my research over the years. Finally, I am grateful to Boleslo Romero for his extraordinary computer skills, his thoughtful observations and insights on academia, and for his general ability to keep things on an even keel.

The Archaeology of Wak'as

PART I

Introduction

1

Andean Wak'as and Alternative Configurations of Persons, Power, and Things

Tamara L. Bray

[Wak'as] are made of energized matter, like everything else, and they act within nature, not over and outside it as Western supernaturals do.

(Salomon 1991:19)

In contrast to the plethora of archaeological studies focused on presumably secular aspects of society like subsistence practices, the economy, and political organization, investigations into the realm of the sacred have been much less common. This is not to suggest that all peoples past and present compartmentalize the sacred and secular in the way we tend to do in the West (e.g., Brück 1999; Fowles 2013). Rather, it is acknowledgment of the fact that archaeologists have tended to steer clear of anything beyond the quotidian material concerns of human societies. Yet today, a decade and a half into the twenty-first century, it remains abundantly clear that much of the world's population lead lives in which basic questions about diet, housing, education, social interaction, and so on are structured by the dictates of religion and spiritual devotion (see Hecht and Biondo 2010). As Insoll (2004) and others have argued, if we fail to consider and theorize the influence of the sacred (in a broad rather than restricted Judeo-Christian sense) on peoples in the past, then many of the questions we frame—as well as the answers we derive—are likely to be incomplete. This book on the archaeology of *wak'as* aligns with emerging theoretical interests in the role of the sacred in the past—and the

DOI: 10.5876/9781607323181.c001

insights such orientations may offer into alternative (e.g., nonwestern) ontologies and logics—within the specific context of the Andes.

Over the past twenty years, there has been a slow but steady resurgence of interest in what has generally been characterized as "the archaeology of religion" (Brown 1997; Carmichael et al. 1994; Fogelin 2008; Hall 1997; Hays-Gilpin and Whitley 2008; Hodder 2010; Insoll 2001, 2004; Lewis-Williams 2002; Renfrew 1994). During the mid- to late twentieth century, attention to the ideological realm of human experience was largely proscribed by the dictates of positivist science and processual archaeology, which emphasized the empirical, the techno-functional, and the economic. Within the dominant materialist framework of the time, religion and ideology were labeled "epiphenomenal" (Harris 1974, 1977) and essentially relegated to the status of the unknowable (Hawkes 1954). Given that archaeology inevitably responds to contemporary concerns, however, it is little surprise that research orientations have turned back to some of the more metaphysical interests that originally animated the discipline. As modern religious identities, politics and conflicts take center stage on an ever more frequent basis, it seems almost natural that archaeology would follow suit by developing parallel interests in past societies. Regardless of the ultimate reasons for the renewed interest, extending the reach of archaeological inquiry to acknowledge and encompass what we may consider nonsecular aspects of human existence adds a critical dimension to our narratives of the past that enriches and balances our understanding of premodern lifeways as well as our own.

In this book, Andean wak'as provide a point of entry for investigation of pre-Columbian notions of the sacred that lead, in turn, to considerations of the nature of beings and being. Wak'as, which may be glossed for the moment as "sacred things," constitute a fascinating point of intersection with respect to notions of materiality, agency, and personhood—concepts at the forefront of current anthropological theorizing (e.g., Fowler 2004; Gell 1998; Hodder 2012; Keane 2003; Latour 1993; Miller 2005; Watts 2013). In recent archaeological discourse, these three conceptual strands are often closely intertwined and logically entrained. Materiality is understood as the productive entanglement between humans and the material world that constitutes the basis of social life, or sociality (Meskell 2005; Tilley 2007; Watts 2013). The notion that objects or things have agency—inclusively defined as "the socio-culturally mediated capacity to act" (Ahearn 2001:110)—is a key aspect of theories of materiality (DeMarrais et al. 2004; Miller 2005; Tilley et al. 2006). Also emergent within the framework of materiality is the idea of personhood as a contingent, relational, and distributed phenomenon in which both human and nonhuman entities are implicated

(Brück 2001; Fowler 2004; Knappett 2005; Strathern 1988). These theoretical concepts are further developed and illustrated in the discussion of wak'as that follows as well as in many of the papers included in this volume.

The Andean phenomena known by the Quechua (and Aymara) term *wak'a (waqa;* also written as *huaca, guaca)* are the focal point of the present work.[1] Recognizing the cultural and presumed religious significance of the term early on, the ecclesiastical writers of the early colonial period devoted considerable effort to apprehending what it meant—not for reasons of intellectual curiosity but for purposes of eradication (Acosta 1954 [1590]; Albornoz 1984 [1581–85]; Arriaga 1968 [1621]). Their writings form the point of departure for our understanding of the concept as well as one of the principal reasons why an "archaeology of wak'as" is so necessary.

In the earliest references, which date to the latter half of the sixteenth century, the notion of wak'a was typically construed in material terms (van de Guchte 1990:239–57). In these early works, a wak'a was usually described as or associated with one of two material entities: an idol, statue, or image (*ídolo; bulto*) or an oratory or shrine-like place (*adoratorio*), with the two typically closely linked (Agustinos 1952 [1557]:55; Betanzos 1996 [1551–57]:10; Cieza 1967 [1553]:100; Pizarro 1968 [1571]:492; Sarmiento 2007 [1572]:66; Zarate 1963 [1555]:22–28). The need to employ two (or more) Spanish terms in attempts to capture the meaning of "wak'a" points to significant ontological differences regarding understandings of matter and materiality among Andeans and Europeans (see Mannheim and Salas, this volume). The notion of wak'a-as-oratory entailed spatial fixity, while wak'a-as-idol suggests a degree of motility. This combination of properties (e.g., simultaneous fixity and portability) within one entity does not fit easily within a conventional western ontology and seems to have been a source of confusion for early authors.

We can see attempts to reckon with the metaphysical conundrum of fixed place as both animate and motile expressed visually in Martín de Murúa's (2004 [1590]) illustrated manuscript wherein wak'as are depicted as landscape features (e.g., outcrops or mountains) physically conjoined with anthropomorphic beings (Figure 1.1). What the chroniclers seem to have struggled with was the apparently partible nature of wak'as—that is, the ability of a (presumed) material entity to be simultaneously spatially fixed and spatially (as well as temporally) distributed and distribute-able (see Chase, this volume). In this sense, the "wholeness" of wak'as seems to have extended beyond their corporality or materiality to encompass the broader field of relations within which they were embedded—an aspect that may, in fact, have figured into their "holiness."

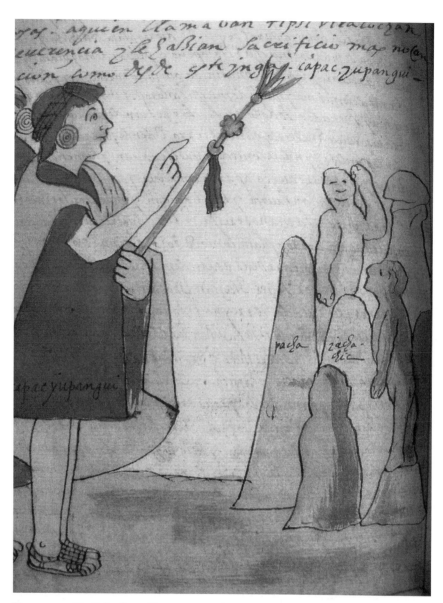

FIGURE 1.1. *The Inka Capac Yupanqui consulting with the wak'a Pachayachachic (Códice Galvin) (Murúa 2004 [1590]:96v).*

As the religious extirpators learned of ever more entities that were classified as wak'as, their definition of the term broadened even if their comprehension did not. Albornoz (1984 [1581–85]:194–97), for instance, compiled a long and seemingly disparate list of phenomena considered to be wak'as that included aphrodisiacal flies and birds, places where lightning had struck, ancestral mummies, local *pacariscas* (origin points on the landscape), ushnus, mountain passes, replicas of plants, bezoar stones, and the hallucinogen known as vilca, among other things.

In his treatise on the Inka, the mestizo writer Garcilaso de la Vega (1943 [1609]:72–73) sought to correct what he perceived to be a biased and bungled understanding of Andean wak'as (MacCormack 1991:335–39). Like Albornoz, he attempted to convey the meaning of the term by first enumerating the kinds of things considered as such by native peoples. He initiated his discussion by stating that "wak'a" referred to "sacred thing," be it idol, object, or place, through which "the devil spoke" (Garcilaso de la Vega 1943 [1609]:72). His list included "rocks, great stones or trees," as well as things made, such as "figures of men, birds, and animals" offered to the Sun, as well as places built, such as "any temple, large or small, . . . sepulchers set up in the fields, . . . and corners of houses" (ibid.). It also included things of extraordinary beauty or ugliness, and exceptional phenomena or occurrences—such as twins or ancestors. After listing the range of phenomena encompassed by the term, Garcilaso went on to state that the Inka called these things wak'as "not because they held them as gods or because they worshiped them but rather for the particular advantage they provided the community" (ibid.: 73). This is an important point that hints at an understanding of wak'as as having the capacity for personal interaction and the performance of beneficial acts—in other words, as having agency. The communicative aspect and the ability to speak included in Garcilaso's definition are also key.

Another seventeenth-century writer, the Jesuit priest Bernabé Cobo, following Acosta (1954 [1590]:141), suggested that wak'as could be divided into two categories: works of nature unaltered by human intervention, and "idols that did not represent anything other than the material from which they were produced" (Cobo 1990 [1653]:44). In the first category were natural things that differed in some significant way from other members of the same class, often in terms of size, shape, or genesis. Examples would include a peculiarly shaped potato, an exceptionally large tree, or an individual marked by a birth defect (ibid.:44–45). In the second category were statues and images made in the close likeness of the thing they represented, consisting mainly of miniature replicas of plants, animals and people (ibid.:45–46; McEwan, this volume).

With respect to these idols, the priest noted that they "*were worshiped for their own sake*" and that "the people never thought to search or use their imaginations *in order to find what such idols represented*" (Cobo 1990 [1653]:45; emphasis added). Cobo seems to suggest that native people understood wak'as as powerful in and of themselves—not as the containers of unearthly or supernatural divinities but rather as efficacious agents in their own right.

In his discussion of wak'as, Garcilaso de la Vega alluded to the fact that Inka concepts of the sacred and the holy—which he extended to Andean peoples in general—differed significantly from European notions of the same (MacCormack 1991:337; Mannheim and Salas, this volume). Many scholars have since noted that though wak'as have traditionally been construed as "sacred," they are not the kind of "abstract sacred" that characterizes western connotations of the term (Astvaldsson 1998, 2004; Rostworowski 1983; Salomon 1991). As can be seen from the lists given above, Andean wak'as were very much concrete, material phenomena, not bodiless, abstract notions. As exceptional members of their "species" or class, they were naturally more powerful, thus compelling both recognition and respect. Here power is construed not in some abstract or ideal sense but rather as a type of natural force having a specific and immediate local referent. Approaching wak'as as physical embodiments of power, rather than as representations of other-worldly beings, highlights the importance of their materiality (see Janusek, this volume). It is the physical concreteness of wak'as that enabled the concept of power to have a presence and be efficacious in the world; it is also what enabled the wak'as' participation in the network of relations that comprised the social and political worlds of Andean peoples.

Focusing on the materiality and agency of wak'as challenges western ontological assumptions and commonsense understandings of objects and subjects as discrete and essentialized entities inhabiting distinct and impermeable worlds, in the same way it challenges the division between sacred and secular. In the Andean context, various ethnographic studies suggest that "all material things (including things we normally call inanimate) are potentially active agents in human affairs" (Allen 1998:20; also Allen 1982, 1988, 1997, this volume; Bastien 1978; Gose 1994; Salomon 1998; Sillar 2009). This would suggest that native Andean people operate with a significantly different set of ontological premises than the ones we normally take for granted (see also Alberti and Marshall 2009; Bray 2009; Haber 2009). The ethnographic data point to the legitimacy of considering native Andean ontology as privileging a relational perspective. Within such a framework, following Gell (1998), the nature of something is understood to be a function of the social-relational matrix within which it is embedded. When objects or places participate in human affairs, e.g., when they become "targets for and sources of social agency" (Gell 1998:96), they must be treated as person-like,—or, if you will—as "other-than-human persons" (after Hallowell 1960). In other words, it does not matter in ascribing social agent status what a thing or a person "is" in and of itself. What matters is where it stands in a network of social relations (Gell 1998:123; also Latour 1993). Equally important within this framework is the conditional and transactional nature of the relationship between persons and things, each being necessarily constitutive of the other's agency at different moments in time (see, for example, Dean, this volume).

There are various indications throughout the ethnohistoric record that native Andean peoples understood wak'as to be persons. For instance, wak'as often shared kin relations with members of the communities with whom they were associated. There are various reports, for example, of young women being wed to local wak'as made of stone (Arriaga 1968 [1621]:36–37; Avila 1918 [1645]:69–70). Elsewhere wak'as were said to have sons and daughters who were typically identified as the mummified remains of revered community ancestors (Arriaga 1968 [1621]:89). In other cases, wak'as were known to be siblings, as in the example of Guanacauri, a stone pillar situated on a hilltop above Cuzco who was called the brother of Manco Capac, the first Inka king.

Wak'as were also able to speak, hear, and communicate—both among themselves and with human persons. That a wak'a's ability to communicate and vocalize was a key aspect of its identity is suggested by the closely related verb *wakay*, which means to cry or to wail (Santo Tomás 1951 [1560], cited in van de Guchte 1990:247). Wak'as were consulted on a regular basis—often though not always through intermediaries—by people of all ranks, from king to commoner (Curatola 2008; Gose 1996), and their function as oracles was recognized early on by the chroniclers (e.g., Cieza 1967 [1553]:98; Matienzo 1967 [1567]:129). Other aspects indicative of their personhood include the fact that they were often named, had personal biographies, and, in quintessential Andean fashion, were often clothed or dressed in woven garments (Albornoz 1984 [1581–85]:217; Arriaga 1968 [1621]:76). Sarmiento's (2007 [1572]:66) account of Guanacauri, the principal wak'a of Cuzco, offers a particularly vivid image of the agency of wak'as. In describing the Inka Ayar Uchu's encounter with Guanacauri, he states that the Inka approached the wak'a to query it regarding its presence there. "At these words," Sarmiento writes, "the huaca turned its head to see who addressed it, but was unable to see Ayar Uchu because his weight bore down upon it" (Ayar Uchu had seated himself atop the wak'a).

In an in-depth analysis of the Huarochirí manuscript—a document written in Quechua circa 1598 containing important insights into native ontologies—one of its principal exponents was led to conclude that wak'as were clearly living beings, "persons in fact" (Salomon 1991:18–19). I would suggest, though, that we are not talking here about "persons" in the familiar sense of western individualism but rather in the relational sense described above. Within such a relational framework, persons are seen as multi-authored, distributed, pluralistic entities defined on the basis of what they do rather than how they appear, conformed of their various interactions within a diverse field of social relations involving humans, animals, things, and places (Brück 2001; Chapman 2000; Fowler 2004; Strathern 1988). From this perspective, social relations can be understood to provide the grounds for and the context within which persons take (temporary) shape. Given this, it seems reasonable to suggest that a key to the recognition of "persons" within a given cultural milieu would be the identification of involvement in relations of sociality (see Allen, this volume; Bray 2012; Mannheim and Salas, this volume).

Within the Andean context, the exploration of alternative forms of personhood and types of persons articulates closely with notions of power, agency, reciprocity, and ethical obligation. Given a dominant relational ontology, the interactions and relationships that establish one's personhood entail mutual obligations of respect and reciprocity involving not only a strong moral dimension but a material one as well. The moral imperative of sharing and the ethical obligations of reciprocity are most typically realized through material transactions—be they in the form of offerings, exchanges, or some manner of caregiving. What archaeology brings to the table in terms of exploring alternative ontologies in general, and the investigation of Andean wak'as more specifically, is a retraining of the anthropological gaze on the materiality of social interactions and relations. In so doing, it offers the possibility of stretching our understandings of what constitutes the social by looking at what is assembled or gathered together at different moments in different places—an orientation that brings forward the nonessential nature and temporal contingency of the agents (or "actants," after Latour) comprising the social relational matrix.

Archaeology's necessary engagement with things and contexts arguably holds unique potential for the investigation of sociality and ontological diversity (Alberti et al. 2011; Holbraad 2009:438–40; Tilley 2007). Identifying material phenomena that defy explanation within a conventional western ontological framework is one way that archaeologists may set up productive challenges to commonly held assumptions about agency, personhood, and causation (Holbraad 2009:438). The concreteness of archaeological remains, even in

FIGURE 1.2. *A large, natural rock outcrop housed within its own structure at the Inka site of Urcos in the Urubamba Valley near Cuzco in south-central Peru (photograph by Edward Ranney, printed with permission).*

their incompleteness, constrains interpretive possibilities. Rather than hewing to mainstream anthropological aims of description and explanation (always within our own frame of reference), focusing on the materiality of the archaeological record—and in particular on the material anomalies that confront us on a fairly regular basis (think here of such things as anthropomorphic pots, the special interment of figurines, the treatment of the dead as living beings, or the cultural housing of "natural" features)—provides a point of departure for exploring novel conceptualizations that may disrupt our common sense or everyday understandings (e.g., Alberti and Marshall 2009) (Figure 1.2). Seen from this vantage, archaeological phenomena may offer unique analytical purchase for the investigation of alterity and sociality.

This volume brings together specialists in Andean studies from a variety of different backgrounds, including archaeology, art history, ethnography, linguistics, and history. The collective goal of the authors is to advance our understanding of the nature and culture of wak'as as well as contribute to larger theoretical discussions on the meaning and role of "the sacred" in ancient contexts and ways of recognizing and appreciating divergent ontologies. The assembled papers explore what a materially oriented study of wak'as can add to our current understandings of this vital Andean phenomenon that seems to conflate the boundaries between person-thing-concept. Some of the key themes addressed by the authors include how we might identify "persons" of the other-than-human variety archaeologically, how social relations are materially expressed, the ways in which identity and power are recursively constituted through human-wak'a engagement, the issue of presentation versus re-presentation, the partitive or distributed nature of wak'as, and what the study of these phenomena can contribute to our general understanding of materiality, sociality, and ontological diversity.

Several of the authors explore the notion of wak'as from an emically informed point of view though they situate their discussions within distinctly different theoretical frameworks. Allen (Chapter 2) finds utility in recuperating the notion of animism and infusing it with recent, ethnographically based insights into Amerindian ontologies. As described by Viveiros de Castro (1992, 2004), many Amerindian peoples view all beings as sharing in a universal culture and as having an interior subjectivity—the key difference among entities being the fact that they have different, bodily induced points of view that cause them to see the world differently—hence the label "ontological perspectivism." In discussing perspectivism in the Andean context, Allen highlights the reciprocal and moral aspects of "seeing" as well as the partitive nature of personhood. Mannheim and Salas in Chapter 3 take a different emically oriented approach to the analysis of "wak'a" that emphasizes both the grammatical affordances of the term within the Quechua language and social praxis. While they also advocate for the importance of reciprocal, recursive relations of sociality in recognizing wak'as as (nonhuman) persons, they prefer to work from the ground of specific material practices through which such relations are constructed and reject the generalized application of the term "animism" to describe Andean metaphysics.

Given our knowledge of sociality in the Andes, a variety of possibilities can be offered with respect to how we might identify nonhuman persons in the archaeological record. One approach would be to analyze the material evidence for social relationships as traditionally constructed via ritual commensality and the exchange or offering of gifts (Bray 2012; Mannheim and Salas, this volume). Another relates to the importance of co-residence and the notion of "domestication"—conditions of being potentially visible through architectural containment (see Figure 1.2; Dean 2010) or the spatial analysis of features and sites (Makowski, this volume). Social relations can also be expressed through their clear negation, as might be manifest in acts of violence or destruction (Janusek, this volume; Kosiba 2012). Another significant marker of social personhood in the Andes involves the use of clothing, which, in the case of other-than-human persons, we could think of approaching in a metaphorical as well as a literal sense (Cook, this volume).

As with Allen, the contributions by Dean (Chapter 7) and Meddens (Chapter 8) highlight the significance of vision—the acts of seeing and being seen—in the construction of social relations and personhood. These authors suggest that the significance of sight is materially expressed in various ways, including the construction of permanent markers on the landscape, the physical demarcation of sighted features, the creation of specific alignments, and the physical conjoining of material elements. Similar observations at Pachacamac and Pueblo Viejo-Pucará inform new interpretations of these sites, which are presented by Makowski in Chapter 5. Such specifically constructed and/or demarcated landscape features not only materially express networks of social relations but also create and instantiate these by giving them substantive existence through their material form. This key point is further developed by Kosiba in the context of Ollantaytambo (Chapter 6) and by Chase for the Huarochirí region (Chapter 4), while McEwan (Chapter 9) extends these ideas to the realm of portable wak'as.

Several of the chapters in this volume emphasize the inherently political nature of human-wak'a engagements. As suggested by various authors, the power and prestige of wak'as and the human communities to which they were linked were co-constructed, mutually dependent, and temporally contingent. Focusing on the carved monoliths at the Formative period site of Khonkho Wankane, Janusek (Chapter 11) explains the political importance of this site as a function of both the wak'a-like stones emplaced there and the people that venerated them, each reciprocally constituting the power and agency of the other through dynamic, recursive, and material articulations. In similar fashion, Chase (Chapter 4) argues for the significance of performative acts involving wak'as, people, and places in the creation of both new pasts and changing presents. All the contributors to this volume see the material acts that constituted the matrix of Andean sociality and encompassed both human and nonhuman persons as vital to the construction of new social relationships, collective identities, and political projects.

In the Andes it is clear that not every rock, tree, or mountain was considered a wak'a—that is, superlative in its class, possessed of special power, and having personhood. For us, the ability to identify such entities is dependent on identification of the material practices that constituted these as members of the social matrix. As demonstrated in this volume, archaeology as a material enterprise does have access to past relations of sociality that permit the identification of wak'as. Recognizing which entities were so construed offers a potent mechanism for reconstructing cultural landscapes of the past, furthering our understandings of community boundaries and regional politics, and gaining new insights into the social relational universe of Andean peoples and the ontological modalities within which they operated. Through the material analysis of wak'as as "sacred" substance and force, this volume contributes to the growing corpus of archaeological works concerned with the exploration of alternative ways of configuring the (social) world across both time and space, the types of entities that through their participation create this world, and the metaphysics that companion these different modalities. By focusing on wak'as as significant nonhuman members of Andean social configurations, we expand our anthropological acuity and highlight the possibilities archaeology offers for seeing into alternative worlds.

NOTE

1. In Quechua the plural form of a noun is typically indicated by the suffix -*kuna*. However, we have elected to use the English suffix -*s* when referring to wak'a in the plural to avoid unnecessary confusion.

REFERENCES CITED

Acosta, José de. 1954 [1590]. *Historia natural y moral de las Indias*. Madrid: Biblioteca de Autores Españoles, no. 73.

Agustinos. 1952 [1557]. "Religión en Huamachuco." In *Los pequeños grandes obras de historia americana*, ed. Francisco Loayza, series 1, vol. 17. Lima: Miranda.

Ahearn, Laura. 2001. "Language and Agency." *Annual Review of Anthropology* 30 (1): 109–37. http://dx.doi.org/10.1146/annurev.anthro.30.1.109.

Alberti, Benjamin, Severin Fowles, Martin Holbraad, Yvonne Marshall, and Christopher Witmore. 2011. "Worlds Otherwise: Archaeology, Anthropology, and Ontological Difference." *Current Anthropology* 52 (6): 896–912. http://dx.doi.org /10.1086/662027.

Alberti, Benjamin, and Yvonne Marshall. 2009. "Animating Archaeology: Local Theories and Conceptually Open-Ended Methodologies." *Cambridge Archaeological Journal* 19 (3): 344–56. http://dx.doi.org/10.1017/S0959774309000535.

Albornoz, Cristóbal de. 1984 [1581–85]. "Instrucción para descubrir todas las guacas del Pirú y sus camayos y haciendas." In *Albornoz y el espacio ritual andino prehispánico*, ed. Pierre Duviols. *Revista Andina* 2:169–222.

Allen, Catherine J. 1982. "Body and Soul in Quechua Thought." *Journal of Latin American Lore* 8 (2): 179–96.

Allen, Catherine J. 1988. *The Hold Life Has*. Washington, DC: Smithsonian Institution Press.

Allen, Catherine J. 1997. "When Pebbles Move Mountains." In *Creating Context in Andean Cultures*, ed. Rosaleen Howard-Malverde, 73–84. Oxford: Oxford University Press.

Allen, Catherine J. 1998. "When Utensils Revolt: Mind, Matter and Modes of Being in the Pre-Columbian Andes." *RES* 33:19–27.

Astvaldsson, Astvaldur. 1998. "The Powers of Hard Rock: Meaning, Transformation, and Continuity in Cultural Symbols in the Andes." *Journal of Latin American Cultural Studies* 7 (2): 203–23. http://dx.doi.org/10.1080/13569329809361935.

Astvaldsson, Astvaldur. 2004. "El flujo de la vida humana: El Significado de término-concepto de huaca en los Andes." *Hueso Húmero* 44:89–112.

Arriaga, Pablo Joseph de. 1968 [1621]. *The Extirpation of Idolatry in Peru*. Trans. and ed. L. Clark Keating. Lexington: University of Kentucky Press.

Avila, Francisco de. 1918 [1645]. "Prefación al libro de los sermones o homilías en la lengua castellana, y la indica general Quechua." In *Informaciones acerca de la religión y gobierno de los Incas*, ed. Horacio Urteaga and Carlos Romero, 57–89. Colección de Libros y Documentos Referentes a la Historia del Perú, vol. 2. Lima: Sanmartí.

Bastien, Joseph. 1978. *Mountain of the Condor: Metaphor and Ritual in an Andean Community*. St. Paul, MN: West Publishing Company.

Betanzos, Juan de. 1996 [1551–57]. *Narrative of the Incas*. Ed. and trans. Roland Hamilton and Dana Buchanan. Austin: University of Texas Press.

Bray, Tamara L. 2009. "An Archaeological Perspective on the Andean Concept of *Camaquen*: Thinking through Late Precolumbian Ofrendas and Huacas." *Cambridge Archaeological Journal* 19 (3): 357–68. http://dx.doi.org/10.1017/S0959774309000547.

Bray, Tamara L. 2012. "Ritual Commensality between Human and Non-Human Persons: Investigating Native Ontologies in the Late Pre-Columbian Andean World." In *Between Feasts and Daily Meals: Towards an Archaeology of Commensal Spaces*, ed. Susan Pollock. *eTopoi. Journal of Ancient Studies* (special volume) 2:197–212.

Brown, James A. 1997. "The Archaeology of Ancient Religion in the Eastern Woodlands." *Annual Review of Anthropology* 26 (1): 465–85. http://dx.doi.org/10.1146/annurev.anthro.26.1.465.

Brück, Joanna. 1999. "Ritual and Rationality: Some Problems of Interpretation in European Archaeology." *European Journal of Archaeology* 2 (3): 313–44.

Brück, Joanna. 2001. "Monuments, Power and Personhood in the British Neolithic." *Journal of the Royal Anthropological Institute* 7 (4): 649–67. http://dx.doi.org/10.1111/1467-9655.00082.

Carmichael, David L., Jane Hubert, Brian Reeves, and Audhild Schanche, eds. 1994. *Sacred Sites, Sacred Spaces*. London: Routledge.

Chapman, John. 2000. *Fragmentation in Archaeology: People, Places, and Broken Objects in the Prehistory of South-eastern Europe.* London: Routledge.

Cieza de León, Pedro. 1967 [1553]. *El señorío de los Inca* (part 2 of *La crónica del Perú*). Lima: Instituto de Estudios Peruanos.

Cobo, Bernabé. 1990 [1653]. *Inca Religion and Customs.* Trans. and ed. Roland Hamilton. Austin: University of Texas Press.

Curatola Petrocchi, Marco. 2008. "La función de los oraculos en el Imperio Inca." In *Adivinación y oráculos en el mundo andino antiguo,* ed. Marco Curatola Petrocchi and Mariusz S. Ziólkowski, 15–69. Lima: Instituto Francés de Estudios Andinos and Pontificia Universidad Católica del Perú.

Dean, Carolyn. 2010. *A Culture of Stone: Inka Perspectives on Rock.* Durham, NC: Duke University Press. http://dx.doi.org/10.1215/9780822393177.

DeMarrais, Elizabeth, Chris Gosden, and Colin Renfrew, eds. 2004. *Rethinking Materiality: The Engagement of the Mind with the Material World.* Cambridge: McDonald Institute for Archaeological Research.

Fogelin, Lars, ed. 2008. *The Archaeology of Religion.* Carbondale: Southern Illinois University Press.

Fowler, Chris. 2004. *The Archaeology of Personhood: An Anthropological Approach.* Cambridge: Cambridge University Press.

Fowles, Severin. 2013. *An Archaeology of Doings: Secularism and the Study of Pueblo Religion.* Santa Fe, NM: School of Advanced Research Press.

Garcilaso de la Vega, El Inca. 1943 [1609]. *Comentarios reales de los Incas.* Vol. 1. Ed. Angel Rosenblat. Buenos Aires: Emece Editores.

Gell, Alfred. 1998. *Art and Agency: An Anthropological Theory.* Oxford: Oxford University Press.

Gose, Peter. 1994. *Deathly Waters and Hungry Mountains: Agrarian Ritual and Class Formation in an Andean Town.* Toronto: University of Toronto Press.

Gose, Peter. 1996. "The Past Is a Lower Moiety: Diarchy, History, and Divine Kingship in the Inka Empire." *History and Anthropology* 9 (4): 383–414. http://dx.doi.org/10.1080/02757206.1996.9960887.

Haber, Alejandro. 2009. "Animism, Relatedness, Life: Post-western Perspectives." *Cambridge Archaeological Journal* 19 (3): 418–30. http://dx.doi.org/10.1017/S0959774309000602.

Hall, Robert. 1997. *An Archaeology of the Soul: North American Indian Belief and Ritual.* Urbana: University of Illinois Press.

Hallowell, A. Irving. 1960. "Ojibwa Ontology, Behavior, and World View." In *Culture in History: Essays in Honor of Paul Radin,* ed. Stanley Diamond, 19–52. New York: Columbia University Press.

Harris, Marvin. 1974. *Cows, Pigs, Wars & Witches: The Riddles of Culture*. New York: Random House.

Harris, Marvin. 1977. *Cannibals and Kings: The Origins of Cultures*. New York: Random House.

Hawkes, Christopher. 1954. "Archaeological Theory and Method: Some Suggestions from the Old World." *American Anthropologist* 56 (2): 155–68. http://dx.doi.org/10.1525/aa.1954.56.2.02a00020.

Hays-Gilpin, Kelley, and David Whitley, eds. 2008. *Belief in the Past: Theoretical Approaches to the Archaeology of Religion*. Walnut Creek, CA: Left Coast Press.

Hecht, Richard, and Vincent Biondo, eds. 2010. *Religion and Everyday Life and Culture*. New York: Praeger.

Hodder, Ian, ed. 2010. *Religion in the Emergence of Civilization: Catalhouyuk as a Case Study*. Cambridge: Cambridge University Press. http://dx.doi.org/10.1017/CBO9780511761416.

Hodder, Ian. 2012. *Entangled: An Archaeology of the Relationships between Humans and Things*. New York: Wiley-Blackwell. http://dx.doi.org/10.1002/9781118241912.

Holbraad, Martin. 2009. "Ontology, Ethnography, Archaeology: An Afterword on the Ontography of Things." *Cambridge Archaeological Journal* 19 (3): 431–41. http://dx.doi.org/10.1017/S0959774309000614.

Insoll, Timothy, ed. 2001. *Archaeology and World Religion*. London: Routledge. http://dx.doi.org/10.4324/9780203463673.

Insoll, Timothy. 2004. *Archaeology, Ritual, Religion*. London: Routledge.

Keane, Webb. 2003. "Semiotics and the Social Analysis of Material Things." *Language & Communication* 23 (3–4): 409–25. http://dx.doi.org/10.1016/S0271-5309(03)00010-7.

Knappett, Carl. 2005. *Thinking through Material Culture: An Interdisciplinary Perspective*. Philadelphia: University of Pennsylvania Press.

Kosiba, Steve. 2012. "Emplacing Value, Cultivating Order: Places of Conversion and Practices of Subordination throughout Early Inka State Formation (Cusco, Perú)." In *Constructions of Value in the Ancient World*, ed. John Papadopoulos and Gary Urton, 97–127. Los Angeles: Cotsen Institute of Archaeology, University of California, Los Angeles.

Latour, Bruno. 1993. *We Have Never Been Modern*. Cambridge, MA: Harvard University Press.

Lewis-Williams, David. 2002. *A Cosmos in Stone: Interpreting Religion and Society through Rock Art*. Walnut Creek, CA: Altamira Press.

MacCormack, Sabine. 1991. *Religion in the Andes*. Princeton, NJ: Princeton University Press.

Matienzo, Juan de. 1967 [1567]. *Gobierno del Perú*. Ed. GuillermoLohman Villena. Travaux de l'Institut Français d'Études Andines, vol. 11. Paris and Lima: Institut Français d'Études Andines.

Meskell, Lynn, ed. 2005. *Archaeologies of Materiality*. Malden, MA: Blackwell Press. http://dx.doi.org/10.1002/9780470774052.

Miller, Daniel, ed. 2005. *Materiality*. Durham, NC: Duke University Press. http://dx.doi.org/10.1215/9780822386711.

Murúa, Martín de. 2004 [1590]. *Historia de los Incas: Historia y genealogía de los reyes Incas del Perú. Códice Galvin*. Ed. Juan Ossio. Madrid: Testimonio Compañía Editorial.

Pizarro, Pedro. 1968 [1571]. *Relación del descubrimiento y conquista de los reinos del Perú*. Biblioteca Peruana, series 1, vol. 1, 439–586. Lima: Editores Técnicos Asociados.

Renfrew, Colin. 1994. "The Archaeology of Religion." In *The Ancient Mind*, ed. Colin Renfrew and Ezra Zubrow, 47–54. Cambridge: Cambridge University Press. http://dx.doi.org/10.1017/CBO9780511598388.007.

Rostworowski de Diez Canseco, María. 1983. *Estructuras andinas de poder: Ideología religiosa y política*. Historia Andina, 10. Lima: Instituto de Estudios Peruanos.

Salomon, Frank. 1991. "Introductory Essay: The Huarochirí Manuscript." In *Huarochirí Manuscript*, ed. Frank Salomon and George Urioste, 1–38. Austin: University of Texas Press.

Salomon, Frank. 1998. "How the Huacas Were." *RES* 33:7–17.

Santo Tomás, Domingo de. 1951 [1560]. *Lexicon ó vocabulario de la lengua general del Perú*. Facsimile edition. Ed. Raúl Porras Barrenechea. Lima: Instituto de Historia Gramática.

Sarmiento de Gamboa, Pedro. 2007 [1572]. *The History of the Incas*. Trans. and ed. Brian Bauer and Vania Smith. Austin: University of Texas Press.

Sillar, Bill. 2009. "The Social Agency of Things? Animism and Materiality in the Andes." *Cambridge Archaeological Journal* 19 (3): 367–77. http://dx.doi.org/10.1017/S0959774309000559.

Strathern, Marilyn. 1988. *The Gender of the Gift*. Berkeley: University of California Press.

Tilley, Christopher. 2007. "Materiality in Materials, a Response to Ingold's 'Materials against Materiality.'" *Archaeological Dialogues* 14 (1): 16–20. http://dx.doi.org/10.1017/S1380203807002139.

Tilley, Christopher, Webb Keane, Susanne Küchler, Mike Rowlands, and Patricia Spyer, eds. 2006. *Handbook of Material Culture*. London: Sage Publications Ltd.

van de Guchte, Maarten. 1990. *Carving the World: Inca Monumental Sculpture and Landscape*. Ph.D. diss., University of Illinois, Champaign-Urbana. Ann Arbor, MI: University Microfilms.

Viveiros de Castro, Eduardo. 1992. *From the Enemy's Point of View: Humanity and Divinity in an Amazonian Society*. Chicago: University of Chicago Press.

Viveiros de Castro, Eduardo. 2004. "Exchanging Perspectives: The Transformation of Objects into Subjects in Amerindian Ontologies." *Common Knowledge* 10 (3): 463–84. http://dx.doi.org/10.1215/0961754X-10-3-463.

Watts, Christopher, ed. 2013. *Relational Archaeologies: Humans, Animals, Things*. London: Routledge.

Zarate, Agustin de. 1963 [1555]. *Historia del descubrimiento y conquista del Perú con las cosas naturales que señaladamente allí se hallan*. Vol. 26. Madrid: Biblioteca de Autores Españoles.

PART II

*Contemporary
Orientations*

2

The Whole World Is Watching

New Perspectives on Andean Animism

CATHERINE J. ALLEN

INTRODUCTION

What was a *wak'a*? The word is central to our understanding of Inka culture. In colonial sources, *wak'a* (also *guaca, huaca*) referred to powerful places or to powerful objects like mummies or statues that were kept in these places. Inka society was organized in terms of wak'as situated on lines (*ceques*) radiating from the capital. Documentary sources also tell us that for native Andeans, encounters with wak'as were powerfully transformative experiences (which is why "extirpators of idolatries" were so intent on rooting them out). The mestizo chronicler Garcilaso de la Vega provided an interesting insight into wak'as when he noted that the term could refer to anything that caused surprise or fright (1943 [1609]:72–73). Indeed, these startling entities took a multitude of forms: strangely shaped potatoes, individuals born feet first or with cleft palates, mummies, springs, mountains, singular rocks, trees, caves, constellations of stars. Each of these had a distinct name, required specific kinds of offerings, and were sometimes consulted as oracles (Curatola 2008; Gose 1996). Some wak'as were manifested as hierarchically organized sets. For example, in the Huarochirí manuscript an oracular wak'a named Chaupi Ñamca is described as a five-armed stone as well as the eldest of a set of five sisters. "When people sought Chaupi Ñamca's advice on any matter, she'd respond, saying, 'I'll go and talk it over with my sisters first'" (Salomon and Urioste 1991:78).

DOI: 10.5876/9781607323181.c002

Whatever their form, wak'as were material, discrete, energetic, and communicative (van de Guchte 1990:271). They were, moreover, persons with distinct capacities, moods, and appetites who interacted with each other and with human beings. In other words, for pre-Columbian Andeans, the world was animated; the whole material universe was potentially alive and imbued with spirit. Can contemporary Andean understandings of materiality cast light on the animacy of Inka wak'as? I think they can. The following pages sketch out a broad understanding of Andean animism, drawing on a variety of ethnohistorical and ethnographic sources and noting the theoretical tracks left by forays into similar territory by other anthropologists.

I began to ponder the nature of animism while doing ethnographic research in Sonqo, a southern Peruvian community of Quechua-speaking potato farmers.[1] Participant-observation, I discovered, entailed suspending my usual assumptions about the nature of things and accepting the premise that all matter was in some sense potentially alive and imbued with agency. All material things, be they "natural" or man-made, possessed a kind of personhood (see Allen 1998, 2002a). Because everything in the world was potentially a subject with its own point of view, all activity was *inter*active—there was always the potential for a communicative response on the part of one's object.

Take, for example, the house, *wasitira*, an adobe structure fashioned from local earth, straw, and water (see also Allen 2002a:235–38). Wasitira must be treated well, for a disrespected house turns cold and unwelcoming. She is, moreover, a witness to whatever occurs within her walls, and she stands at the end of a chain of chthonic authority extending to the snow-capped mountain lords (*apu*). When a theft occurs in a house, a diviner calls upon one of the great apus who dominate the region; the apu calls on a smaller mountain who watches over a smaller region, on down to Sonqo's local guardian hill, Antaqaqa, who in turn calls on the wasitira to report the identity of the thief to the diviner.[2]

When even walls have eyes (as it were), one cannot escape being watched, even in the privacy of one's home. In my ethnography of Sonqo I wrote about the role of *watching* as an aspect of everyday life:

> Nothing seems to be more interesting [to Sonqueños] than to be situated in a high, sheltered spot watching what happens. . . . Watching is not merely a pastime; it is a form of communication among people acutely attuned to the nonverbal sign. For the watching is reciprocal; everybody watches everybody else. . . . And the Places themselves are watchers—the greatest watchers, against whom there is no concealment, who know and remember one's every move. (Allen 2002a [1988]:25)

This passage resonates strikingly with Rane Willerslev's discussion of animism among the Chukchi of Siberia: "The Chukchi live in a world full of vision, full of eyes. Every being—humans, animals, inanimate objects, and spirits— is said to have a viewpoint of its own that stares back" (Willerslev 2011:511). Willerslev finds the same concept of watching in Richard Nelson's description of the Koyukon Indians of the Alaskan boreal forest: "[They] live in a world that watches, in a forest of eyes. A person moving through nature . . . is never truly alone. The surroundings are aware, sensate, personified" (Nelson 1983:14, cited in ibid.). A person moving through the world of the wak'as, too, would not have been alone, for hills, springs, stones, even odd potatoes were "aware, sensate, and personified." It seems worthwhile, then, to explore what light contemporary research can shed on animism in the Andes.

RETHINKING ANIMISM

Long consigned to the anthropological rag-and-bone shop of nineteenth-century evolutionism, the concept of animism is undergoing a process of rehabilitation and redefinition due in part to the interest in performance and embodiment that arose in the 1990s (e.g., Descola 1992; Strathern 1996). Animism, taken seriously, poses distinct challenges for western philosophy. The attribution of mindful life to all bodies defies Cartesian categories and implies, in the words of Eduardo Viveiros de Castro (1998:470), ". . . an ethno-graphically-based reshuffling of our conceptual schemes." Reformulations of animism include Nurit Bird-David's (1999) "relational epistemology," which she describes as an interactive stance toward the nonhuman as well as the human environment, operating in the context of a relational personhood characteristic of small-scale hunter-gather societies.[3] In a carefully nuanced analysis of Amazonian ethnography, Eduardo Viveiros de Castro (1998) pro-poses the term *ontological perspectivism*, which captures very well the quality of reciprocal watching characteristic of Andean cultures. Viveiros de Castro contrasts perspectivist cosmologies with those of "the West": we "western-ers" assume that there is a world out there, a material substratum common to all creatures; human minds in different societies represent this world to themselves in different ways—thus producing a multiplicity of cultures. In contrast, according to Viveiros de Castro, Amerindian ontological perspec-tivism assumes that all beings participate in a universal culture, that is, "[a]ll beings see (represent) the world in the same way—what changes is the world that they see" (1998:477). For example, what humans see as blood, jaguars see as chicha; what humans see as a mud holes, tapirs see as ceremonial houses.

The key here is to avoid considering these descriptions as mistaken meta-phoric projections of human imagination onto animal nature—and to respect different ontological premises that privilege *viewpoint* (also see Sándor 1986; Willerslev 2007:20–22). Viewpoint has a deictic function; that is, it defines the context in which a creature lives (e.g., blood for humans is chicha for jaguars); ". . . such deictic attributes are immanent in the viewpoint, and move with it" (Viveiros de Castro 1998:477).

Willerslev develops a related concept, *mimesis*, in his ethnography of Siberian elk hunters. Drawing on Taussig's *Mimesis and Alterity* (1993), Willerslev describes mimesis as the meeting point of engagement and reflex-ivity, a simultaneous experience of difference and sameness. When a hunter takes the viewpoint of an elk in order to seduce and kill her, he is both elk and not-elk, or more precisely, not-elk and yet not not-elk. Thus,

> . . . meaning is inherent in the relational contexts of people's direct perceptual engagement with the world . . . [P]ersonhood, rather than being an inherent property of persons and things, is constituted in and through the relationships into which they enter . . . [T]he relational context in which [something] is placed and experienced determines its being. (Willerslev 2007:20–21)[4]

Viveiros de Castro, Willerslev, Bird-David, and others worked out their ideas in the context of hunting societies, and their discussions concen-trate mainly on human relationships with wild animals. Fernando Santos-Granero's edited volume, *The Occult Life of Things: Native Amazonian Theories of Materiality and Personhood*, expands on their work by focusing on mate-rial objects rather than animals, exploring the ways in which "things, or at least some things, are considered to be subjectivities possessed of a social life" (2009:2).[5] Some of these studies of human-object relationships in Amazonian societies resonate with certain Andean relationships between humans and artifacts that I describe in this chapter: ". . . 'things,' rather than being con-ceived as *independent subjects*, seem to be considered as semi-autonomous *subordinates*. In other words, 'things' seem to be less perceived as full subjects than as fully subjected . . . [as] submitted to an 'overt life' as 'obedient things'" (Erikson 2009:188, emphasis in the original). While human/animal relation-ships are important in assessing Andean "animism," landscape and artifact are at least equally important players; they are players, moreover, in the con-text of highly stratified, expansive societies with centralized governments and economies. "Obedient things" include humans as well as artifacts and places, joined in hierarchical chains of authority always in danger of rupture and reversal.

The landscape of sacred places, so important to Andean cultures, does not figure much in studies of Amazonian animism, although Santos-Granero (2009) includes landmarks in his discussion of "ways of being a thing" among the Arawakan Yanesha, who live in a more rugged environment.[6] He classes landmarks as "metamorphosed objects" because they were originally people who were petrified by a creator divinity (ibid.:108). In the Andes, too, many sacred places are identified as people who turned to stone in very ancient times—with the difference that the transformation is seldom attributed to a divinity. Moreover, a given landmark may be only one manifestation of a multiplex being, as we saw above in the example of Chaupi Ñamca. Similarly, the wak'a Pariacaca figures in the Huarochirí manuscript variously as a mountain, five falcon eggs, and five brothers.

THE WORLD AS VIEWPOINT

In what sense do places (e.g., hills, caves, ravines, springs) and artifacts (e.g., houses, textiles) have viewpoints and enter into relationships? *Pacha*, the world we live on and within, is a complex configuration of matter, activity, and moral relationship.[7] Frank Salomon (1991:14) comments that pacha "is an untranslatable word that simultaneously denotes a moment or interval in time and a locus or extension in space—and does so, moreover, at any scale." I translate the word as "world" in an attempt to convey its meaning as both spatial and temporal. Pacha can denote the whole cosmos as well as a specific moment. Pacha is also the prototypical body, a material order of concrete nature, the stuff we grow potatoes in and build houses out of. Finally, she is a moral order, for matter and morality are inseparable aspects of each other.

Can a perspectivist approach help us get a handle on this "untranslatable word"? Can we perhaps understand the world as a viewpoint? Ethnographic and linguistic data support this conclusion. For example, a belief that is widespread in both the Andes and Mesoamerica holds that worlds appear and disappear as one kind of sun follows another. In Sonqo I was told repeatedly that in a different sun there would be a different world and a different kind of people. To participate in a pacha—a living moment—is to share in its *sut'i*, its clarity (Allen 1994, 2011). Sut'i has as synonyms *kunan* ("now") and *chiqaq* ("true" or "straight"). In the immediate moment one sees clearly and truly. In a different pacha there would be different light, and we would see differently.

To have an object within sight is to have direct knowledge of it. That which is outside one's vision (even just around the corner) can be known only indirectly, through the mediation of other sources (Howard 2002). Thus the first and last spots from which one can see important places are marked by ritual greeting and leave-taking. Travelers blow coca leaves with words of greeting or parting; processions stop while musicians play a short *alabaru* (prayer; from the Spanish *alabado*).[8]

The intrinsic relationship between "that which is seen" and "that which is known" is borne out by linguist Rosaleen Howard's research on Quechua evidential suffixes that indicate whether a statement is based on direct or indirect knowledge. Howard observed that a person with firsthand experience of a place can use direct witness validation when speaking of events that happened there, even if the events happened in the very distant past (Howard 2002:45). This kind of witness-validation communicates a point of view that originates in the place and for which the speaker can vouch as a participant in the place's sphere of influence.

ARTIFACT, AGENCY, AND RECIPROCAL APPROPRIATION

From this world-as-viewpoint perspective, how do places (hills, caves, ravines, springs) and artifacts (houses, textiles) have viewpoints and enter into relationships with each other and with human beings? How do all these viewpoints communicate and affect each other? In a sensitive exploration of Apache language and landscape, Keith Basso (1996) describes the interactive relationship between humans and places as *reciprocal appropriation*. This term applies very well in an Andean context. Andean "ritual" is basically reciprocal appropriation among beings of different ontological status, as when human diviners, through configurations of coca leaves, appropriate the earth's witnessing presence. By bad behavior, you may unwittingly appropriate the hills' poor opinion, provoking an unpleasant commentary (or counter-prestation) of heavy fogs, sleet, or rolling rocks. We've seen that family and house share a reciprocal commitment: if you don't take proper care of your house, she'll respond by getting "turned off" and cold (see also Sillar 2004:180–82). The "Revolt of the Utensils" is a persistent Andean theme: it appears in the iconography of Moche ceramics (Lyon 1981; Quilter 1990, 1997), and, about a thousand years later, it resurfaces in the myths related in the Huarochirí manuscript. The latter tells of an apocalypse when the sun went out for five days, llamas herded men, and mortars and pestles ate people (Salomon and Urioste 1991:53). In the 1980s villagers in Apurimac told Peter Gose that after death one's soul has to journey through villages whose inhabitants punish him or her for mistreatment they suffered during life. One of these villages is Pot Town (*Mank'allaqta*; Gose 1994:124–25). (Imagine being mobbed by all the dishes you ever broke!)

Interestingly, the emphasis on reciprocal appropriation is built into Quechua grammar, which requires that verbal suffixes specify an interaction of persons (e.g., I-to-you; you-to-me; he-to-you, etc.). Mannheim argues that reciprocity is fundamental to Quechua grammar because it is an ontological principle. "Reciprocity saturates the organization of the Quechua lexicon and grammar . . . the axioms of reciprocity do not exist in an abstract nether-world; rather they are latent in every act of speaking" (Mannheim 1991:90–91).

All activity thus has a discursive element, glancing sideways "at others' languages, at other points of view and other conceptual systems, each with its own set of objects and meanings" (Bakhtin 1981:376). In a very complex sort of heteroglossia, the range of "languages" informing any utterance must be extended to include, for example, the changing weather. The witnesses and "shadow participants" to be taken into account in any particular speech event are multiplied. Human language is embedded within a larger communicative context that includes a myriad of nonhuman participants.

In this context, technology becomes a type of discourse, not only *about* the world but *with* the world. The technological minimalism so characteristic of Andean cultures derives from the inherently social nature of artisanry; a craftsperson needs to interact directly and personally with his or her materials. Heather Lechtman (1977) addresses the mechanical simplicity of Andean technology in what she calls "technological style," emphasizing the way Andean technology accommodates itself to the material world, as in Inka landscape architecture and wall-building where stones retained their own shapes (Lechtman 1993:246; also Lechtman 1996).

Because technology is a kind of discourse, one does not so much act upon the world as with, and within, it; through the interactive process, artifacts develop a distinct personhood. In Sonqo, people who have mastered a skill are described as *santuyuq* which, roughly translated, means "possessing the saint." Every important human skill—weaving, plowing, spinning, coca chewing—is said to have originated with a specific saint and is only attainable through contact with that saint. People become santuyuq by maturing into their skills through practice and observation while opening themselves to the saint's influence. Figure 2.1 shows don Erasmo Hualla and his son making "flowers" (yarn tassels) for their horses' ears for the feast day of Santiago, patron saint of horses. Their purpose is not simply decorative, as the tassels will protect the animals throughout the coming year (also see Abercrombie 1998:383). The men are chewing coca and whispering to Santiago as they work with great concentration to draw the saint's protective virtue into the "flowers."

FIGURE 2.1. *Don Erasmo Hualla (right) and his son making tassel "flowers" to adorn their horses during the Feast of Santiago. They are chewing coca leaves and whispering prayers to Santiago as they work (photograph by author, Allen 1984).*

A similar process takes place every time a weaver works at her loom. Before setting to work, she whispers over her coca leaves to *Awaq Mamacha* (Weaving Mother), the patron saint of weaving, "Little Mother, let me weave with your hands." As she weaves, the paired warp threads interact to reciprocally "appropriate" each other's positions, producing "a dialogue of colors" (Cereceda 1986:150). If the textile is a poncho or mantle, it will be sewn to its other half, a mirror image folding around its "heart" (also see Franquemont et al. 1992). According to Cereceda, weavers in Isluga, Bolivia, refer to broad dark bands as "mother" and narrower stripes as "offspring." The finished textile is a creature with a body, heart (the central seam), and two mouths (the outer seams). Side seams are "mouths" because of what they *do*—open and close as the weft passes back and forth between the warp threads. Asked about the light border on a woven sack (*talega*), the weaver spoke into the interior of the sack itself: "What might you be saying in there, talega?" The shading of light into dark was understood as a kind of speaking. The finished textile is a derivative creature, beholden to the force of the weaver who drove its threads into relationship with each other; who appropriated the Weaving Mother's energizing force and impressed it into the cloth. The Weaving Mother, for her part, appropriates the weaver's offerings in the fragrance of coca leaves and alcohol. And the completed textile-creature has its own wants and needs—in a continuing cycle of reciprocal appropriation, it receives a libation from the weaver, who asks it to stay strong, to keep the wearer warm, and to not wear out (also see Allen 1998).

This is not symbolism. The textile's personhood is not a symbolic correspondence in which textile stands for the person. It is more useful to think of the relationship in terms of "distributed personhood." This term was proposed by Alfred Gell, who held that the living quality of art objects derives from being "enmeshed in a texture of social relationships" (1998:17): ". . . as social persons, we are present, not just in our singular bodies, but in everything in our surroundings which bears witness to our existence, our attributes, our agency" (ibid.:103). Gell does not ascribe life force to artifacts, and in this his viewpoint differs from the one I am discussing here. "Distributed personhood" nevertheless is a useful phrase with which to express Andean understandings of the relationship between artisans and artifacts. The woven garment participates in a *distributed personhood* because it becomes a locus of creative agency (the saint), transmitted by the weaver in a kind of personhood that extends into multiple sites beyond the boundaries of the body.

The importance of this embodied communication was poignantly expressed during an ultimately successful lawsuit brought by the Bolivian community of Coroma against a San Francisco art dealer who had bribed community custodians into selling ancient textiles in their charge. "These weavings," the Coromeños testified, "are our grandfathers and our grandmothers. They are our inheritance from those who left us. They show us the path we have to follow" (Bubba 1997:40). The weavings are "the ones who choose"; they select the political authorities through a rite called *kanchaku*, or "illumination," and they are consulted for advice about community problems.

TRANSFORMATIVE COMMUNICATION

The *santuyuq* person has acquired the ability to coax materials (threads, rocks, clay) into new configurations—a new body, the locus of a new perspective. While much has changed in the half millennium since the Spanish conquest of the Andes, there are continuities between these concepts and practices and those of the Inka. I've suggested elsewhere (Allen 1982; 2002a:34) that santuyuq is probably a reformulation of *kamayuq*, the Inka term for "master artisan." The root of this word, *kamay* (usually translated as "to create"), implies authority to reorder matter into new configurations (Taylor 1974). A person or thing that has been reordered by an outside force is termed *kamasqa* (subject to kamay). For example, there was a class of Inka priests who were called kamasqa because they had been struck ("terror-stricken") by Thunder (MacCormack 1991:306). In other words, this terrifying encounter had fundamentally changed their perspective. Reconfigured as participants in Thunder's "distributed personhood," the kamasqa priests had special knowledge and powers not available to normal people.

In contemporary and pre-Columbian times, powerful light, especially flashing or reflected light, is the hallmark of transformative experience. The best diviners and curers in contemporary communities are those who, like the kamasqa priests, have been struck or had close encounters with lightning. A different kind of encounter with light comes about on June 24, the feast of St. John the Baptist, when the Sun is said to "come up dancing." His rays momentarily turn the streams to "holy water" said to have healing qualities. At the very moment of daybreak fortunate persons may find *enqaychus*, small but powerful objects that encapsulate health and prosperity.

While the context differs, St. John's Day recalls Molina's account of Pachakuti Inka's initiation into kingship. Resting by a spring at dawn, the prince saw a shining crystal fall into the water, and at that moment the Sun appeared in blinding radiance to instruct him how to defeat his enemies and build an empire. Throughout his life he consulted the crystal when he needed advice about governing his realm (Steele 2004:64, 230–32). As MacCormack observes, the possession of such a crystal was a prerequisite of sovereignty, critical to the ruler's enactment of economic and political power (1991:306). As a refractor of light, the crystal linked the king with the Sun's world-shaping perspective, informing and enlarging his authoritative vision.

Kingship and artisanry are similar processes. Like Pachakuti Inka and his successors, who opened their subjectivity to that of the Sun in order to master surrounding peoples, the contemporary potter or weaver opens her subjectivity to that of the saint in order to master that of her material. Eventually that mastery is bound to falter: the potter or custodian dies, kingship is challenged, a sun goes out and is replaced by another.[9] Organization of any kind is held in place by a mastering viewpoint and persists only as long as the viewpoint maintains its dominance.

DISTRIBUTING PERSONHOOD

Another expression of distributed personhood that has survived the centuries is ritual forced-feeding. Based on the premise that bodies separated in space and time may yet be interconnected, this practice—ubiquitous today as it was in the pre-Columbian Andes[10]—entails consuming vast quantities of food and/or alcoholic beverage in order to share it with ancestors and sacred places:

> . . . mourners overeat at funerals and during the feast of Todos los Santos, saying that they are eating for the dead person's stomach (Gifford and Hoggarth 1976; Candler 1993). Similarly, when I couldn't finish my dinner, I was instructed to send the food from my stomach to that of my absent husband. The food could not have been sent to just any stomach—it had to be the stomach of someone connected to me in an intrinsic way, just as the stomach of the deceased is intrinsically connected to his living kinsmen who comprise the funeral mourners. (Allen 1998:23)

In these examples, ritual forced-feeding addresses a poignant dilemma in the participants' lives, namely the separation of bodies (viewpoints) that hitherto belonged together. I was directed to eat food for the stomach of my spouse who, my hosts felt, *should* have accompanied me. Similarly, ritual forced-feeding for the dead addresses the problem of kinsmen who *should* be a unified group, but who include dead members as well as living ones. The common practice of keeping and feeding ancestral skulls or other bones (e.g., Délétroz Favre 1993:80) expresses the same attitude, for bones remain a locus of ancestral "affects and dispositions." These contemporary practices resonate with the

Inkas' treatment of their mummified ancestors, whom they fed and clothed. High-ranking mummies even owned large estates administered by a corporation (*panaca*) of descendants (see Ramírez 2005; Zuidema 1973).

Early documents include other accounts of distributed personhood as well. During the "extirpation of idolatries," many wak'as were burned or smashed but continued, nevertheless, to be objects of veneration. In one case, for example, the extirpator Avendaño burned twin wak'as and erected a cross in their stead. To his dismay, people returned to the place to feed and commune with their wak'as, who, they felt, still consumed their sacrifices and reciprocated with well-being (Duviols 1986). In spite of the terrible transformation—for the wak'as had gone up in smoke—potential for communication with them still existed in the place itself (now conveniently marked with the inquisitor's cross). As MacCormack comments, "In the Andes, identity could be conceptualized as continuous even when its expression or representation changed" (1991:408). Although their destruction was a traumatic loss, it did not terminate the wak'a's personhood, which still had the potential for redistribution. "The huacas have, in some contexts, individuality and properties, but in others they are seemingly imagined as long-term overarching sequences of phenomena or deeds" (Salomon 1998:9).

DISTRIBUTED PERSONHOOD AND ORACULAR AUTHORITY

I began this chapter with the example of a humble adobe house that is part of a chain of communication extending through progressively higher and more powerful mountains until it reaches one of the great regional mountain lords, in this case Apu Ausangate. Sonqueños explained that, at each level, higher places are *kamachikuq* (authorities) over the lower ones. Kamachikuq is an agentive form of kamay; it more literally means, "one who makes things happen." Power and authority of places expand as their vision expands, with the greatest authority literally being the highest snowcapped peaks, who can see and be seen over the widest region; lower hills are visible over a smaller territory, and so forth, until one reaches the house (*wasitira*) at the most localized level. The house provides a particularly interesting and complex case of distributed personhood that is very similar to that described for many Inka wak'as. The house is a product of human agency; she depends on her family for upkeep and continued existence. Without human intervention, the spot of earth on which, and out of which, the house is fashioned lies inert and without identity. Because humans animate that substance by building the house, the house participates in their distributed personhood. Eventually she will be abandoned (for these adobe houses are seldom occupied for more than a couple of generations) and will sink back into the earth from which she was fashioned. Yet she is not exactly an "obedient thing." Her personhood is very special because she is a Place and thus belongs to an ontological category that transcends human beings. Elsewhere (Allen 2002a:235–36; 2002b) I have described how the house is also a self-contained microcosm. She defines a unique spatial orientation; within her walls east is defined by the door, "the Sun's entering place" (*Intiq haykuna*), even if, from an outside perspective, the door faces a different direction. In other words, east inside the house could be south outside the house.

She not only watches over the behavior of her inhabitants, making their lives comfortable or miserable as she sees fit, but she may also report what she sees. Her inhabitants cannot make her speak; for this they need the services of a diviner who intercedes with Mount Ausangate, the very highest power in the topological chain of command. Ausangate sends the message through his subordinates until it reaches Antaqaqa, a local Place and the house's immediate superior. The house then speaks through the voice of the diviner, and/ or through coca leaves that fall in configurations that the diviner interprets. These divination sessions take place at night, so speech and hearing are the salient modes of communication. The Places speak to each other in modes not intelligible to human beings until the Wasitira finally speaks through the diviner-medium. Platt comments, when describing a similar kind of divinatory session in Bolivia, that "[g]esture is available only in aural form: actions are etched on the darkness. Intonations, murmurs and rustles, hesitations, the clinking and blowing of bottles . . . all combine with distant background noises to make an overwhelmingly aural field of meaning that dispenses with all visual cues . . ." (1997:201). Perspective should thus be understood as aural as well as visual. That which human beings hear as distant thunder, Places may hear as intelligible speech.

To participate in this conversation of Places, normal human beings employ a diviner (*qawaq* or *misayuq*), an extra-ordinary individual whose encounter with *Rayu* (Lightning) has rendered him (or, less frequently, her) able to transit ontological perspectives, a quality he shares with some Amazonian shamans (e.g., Miller 2009:62, 69). The diviner is a contemporary counterpart of the Thunder-struck kamasqa priests of Inka times—and, furthermore, contemporary divining sessions seem to operate on essentially the same principles as oracular wak'a-to-human communication described for Inka society (see, e.g., Curatola 2008; Gose 1996; MacCormack 1991; Rostworowski 1988).

By "oracle," I mean a thing that reveals, through speech or other modes of communication, information that is hidden from normal human perception. The range of things that could function as oracles was very broad, including, for example,

> ... a standing stone [*huanca*] identified as the mythic founder of a lineage or group, the mummified bodies [*mallquis*] of ethnic lords [*curacas*], or simply a natural landmark ... called *paqarina,* from which the first pair of mythic ancestors was thought to have emerged. All these sacred entities, and whatever other object, image or place of worship ... were called generically *huacas* [wak'as] and all of them were, at least potentially, oracles. (Curatola 2008:17; my translation)

Chaupi Ñamca, the five-armed stone of Huarochirí, was an oracle; so was Inka Pachakuti's crystal. In this context, the adobe house who reports on events within her walls can also be called an oracle; unlike a wak'a's, however, her political reach is negligible. Inka oracles played a central role in the political organization of an immense empire in "a distinctive genre of political representation" (Gose 1996:1). In this respect, the textile bundles that "illuminate" policy for the community of Coroma (see above) are closer to the Inka oracles, for no important political decision is taken without consulting them.

Gose (1996) and, more recently, Curatola (2008) offer complex and nuanced interpretations of the Inka state as a segmentary system with the divine ruler, the Sapa Inka, at its apex, governed through networks of oracular communication. Remarkably, the Inka empire (and presumably earlier Andean states as well) seems to have been based on a cultural modus operandi more typical of societies with localized, face-to-face, social practice and relational personhood, like those studied by Viveiros de Castro in Amazonia and Willerslev in the Arctic. Developed on a scale of great complexity, the Inka state consisted of "an immense and delicate meshwork of personal relations woven by the Inka ruler, the impalpable and fragile strands of which had to be constantly reinforced and renewed" (Curatola 2008:57; my translation).

Local communities at the provincial level also had their wak'as, which apparently functioned much like Coroma's ancestral bundles. During the period of Inka expansion, these communities were forced into a highly centralized *ceque* system, a wheel-like system of lines radiating from the sacred center of Cuzco (Zuidema 1964, 1990; Bauer 1998). As the central hub of the empire, Cuzco held the authoritative viewpoint, which emanated via the divine king from the Sun itself (Ramírez 2005). Although "the subjectivity of the sovereign tended to engulf and obliterate that of his subjects" (Gose 1996:2), each of these subject communities had initially had its own viewpoint. In other words, each of them was a center with the potential—if Cuzco's "gaze" were to weaken—to overwhelm their neighbors' subjectivities and become a defining center of power.

Even in defeat, subject communities retained their wak'as, whose pronouncements voiced their interests and concerns. About once a year the Sapa Inka called all the regional wak'as together in Cuzco and publically consulted them on policy matters "in what amounted to a congress of oracular deities" (Gose 1996:6). Gose argues that this mode of communication through the voice of the wak'a gave indirect expression to subaltern opinions and concerns, avoiding direct confrontation with the king.

The divine king had direct access to the Sun, in the form of a golden statue housed within the Temple of the Sun, whom he consulted on a daily basis. The Sun also had an elite priesthood whose high priest was one of the empire's most powerful figures. The aristocracy of Cuzco was basically composed of corporate groups who served the mummies of deceased rulers. These mummies, like Coroma's ancestral bundles, were consulted by the ruler regarding important decisions. During festivals, these royal mummies spent the day in the main plaza of Cuzco, accompanied by retainers who danced and drank chicha for them until the plaza literally ran with urine. In this forced-fed communion of bodies, alive and dead, the mummies' retainers would enter "an oracular trance"[11] and speak with the ancestral voices.

The Sapa Inka governed his immense empire through a system of delegated authority whose complexity goes beyond the scope of this chapter. The highest administrators, called *Inkap rantin* (the Sapa Inka's substitute, or stand-in), were his close kinsmen. Another Inkap rantin was elected by the priesthood of the Sun to serve as the Sapa Inka's mouthpiece (*yncap rantin rimac*)[12] and relay his proclamations, much as a priest communicated the pronouncements of a wak'a. The Sapa Inka's person was also extended through a statue that he called his brother (*wawqe*). This wawqe traveled to the provinces where people gave it obeisance and sacrifices exactly as they did for the Sapa Inka. At other times the wawqe traveled along with the Sapa Inka, who often sought its advice. Through these "substitutes" the Sapa Inka in effect distributed himself through his kingdom:

> By working through the multiple embodiments of "substitutes," statues, and
> mediums, a ruler extended his influence in space and time and delegated
> enough authority to govern effectively. At the same time, he demonstrated his
> divinity by "animating" these far-flung subdivisions of himself, thereby making
> an ideological virtue out of administrative necessity. (Gose 1996:21)

In addition to the wawqe, other artifacts were agents of imperial authority as well. Acceptance by local chiefs of the Sapa Inka's fine textiles and drinking cups indicated surrender to Cuzco's rule (Cummins 2002). This is, of course, a classic example of the way "gifts" create obligations and can be used strategically for political purposes. These gifts, moreover, were extensions of the Sapa Inka himself, presentations (not representations) of the imperial distributed person. They extended the ruler's person into the local context. To accept them was to acknowledge the overpowering of local subjectivity; to possess and care for these royal gifts was to acknowledge Cuzco's viewpoint as dominant over one's own.

CONCLUDING THOUGHTS

I have tried to sketch out a preliminary overview of Andean animism with special attention to what light the ethnography of contemporary Andean people can shed on our understanding of Inka wak'as. Although I have moved around in time with apparent impunity, I did so not on the assumption that "nothing changed" over the centuries but in order to show that the discourse and practices of contemporary Andeans sometimes illuminate information we have about earlier periods, and vice versa. Santuyuq is not the same as kamayuq, but the two are related conceptually and, I suggest, historically.

Drawing on recent studies of animism, I argue that a perspectivist approach can help us get a handle on discourse and practice among contemporary Andean people and, indirectly, on those of their Inka predecessors. I emphasized the role of vision partly because "watching" and "seeing" are culturally salient activities that lend themselves to a perspectivist account—we naturally associate perspective with vision. Implicit, however, in much of the material discussed here is the world-changing power of sound, especially speech. A fuller discussion would give equal time to aural perspectives.[13]

Of course, abstractions like *perspectivism* and *distributed personhood* are only conceptual tools. I am not necessarily arguing that this is the only "right" way to understand information from Andean cultures.[14] I simply suggest that these tools can help us "reset" our thinking so as to better apprehend another human way of being. For example, a perspectivist approach illuminates the practices of contemporary Andean artisans and opens a way for a more nuanced understanding of material culture left behind by Andean people long dead. It helps us understand what *kind* of things Andeans artifacts are, and puts the "technological style" perceived by Lechtman into an ontological framework that explains its differences from technological style elsewhere in the world.

Finally, "resetting" our thinking helps us recognize presentation rather than representation, predication rather than symbolism. Coroma textile bundles are not symbolic of the ancestors—they *are* the ancestors. Feeding and eating is not an idiom through which a group of people symbolically communicates with the dead—it *is* communication, and the corporate unity of living and dead thus achieved is corporeal.

ACKNOWLEDGMENTS

As this paper draws upon fieldwork and writing carried out over a space of many years, I am beholden to more individuals and institutions, and in more ways, than I can enumerate here. I am most grateful, of course, to the people of Sonqo who opened their homes and shared their lives with me. My colleagues in the Department of Anthropology at George Washington University provided a supportive home base, and the university provided several small grants for travel and research in Peru, most recently in 2008. I began to rethink my understanding of creative process in Andean culture during a residential fellowship with the Center for the Advanced Study of the Visual Arts at the National Gallery of Art (2001), followed by a Guggenheim Foundation Fellowship (2001–2). For five weeks in 2011, I had the privilege of participating in a visiting lecturership with the Andean Studies Program of the Pontificia Universidad Católica del Perú, supported by the Fulbright Specialist Program, and I profited greatly from stimulating discussion with colleagues and students there. I am grateful to Dumbarton Oaks for sponsoring the colloquium that gave rise to this volume; to Tamara Bray for conceiving and organizing it; and of course to my fellow participants for their lively and constructive comments. Finally, I thank two anonymous peer reviewers for their careful reading and helpful commentary. Any errors of fact or interpretation are, of course, my own.

NOTES

1. I carried out research in Sonqo for about a year in 1975–76 and have returned nine times since then (most recently in 2011) for stays of varying lengths.

2. Among many references to similar place hierarchies in Andean ethnographic literature are Earls (1969), Gose (1994), Martínez (1989), and Núñez del Prado (1970).

3. Bird-David replaces the term *animism* with *relational epistemology*. I prefer Viveiros de Castro's term *ontological perspectivism* because at issue is a theory of being (ontology), not a theory of knowledge (epistemology). See also Viveiros de Castro 2004.

4. Here Willerslev also follows Ingold (2000). The concept of mimesis is employed to good effect by Stensrud (2011) in her interesting study of working-class Cuzqueños' relationship with local and regional saints.

5. Also see *Animism in Rainforest and Tundra: Personhood, Animals, Plants and Things in Contemporary Amazonia and Siberia,* edited by Brightman, Gould, and Ulturgasheva (2012), which became available too late to include in this discussion. Previous work on the agency of material objects in Amazonian cultures includes Gow (1999), Guss (1989), and Whitten and Whitten (1993).

6. Santos-Granero (2004:100) suggests that this may be related to the difference in environment: most of the Amazon Basin is flat and forested with few landmarks and long-distance vistas.

7. I provide a much more extended discussion of *pacha* in Allen 2002a [1988] and 1998; also see Bastien (1978), Harris (2000).

8. This practice is reported many times in the ethnographic literature; e.g., Abercrombie (1998), Sallnow (1987).

9. While it goes beyond the scope of this paper, we can see the relation here to a pervasive sense in Andean cultures of the fragility of social and cosmological order: ". . . [harmony] will not remain suspended in a static equilibrium but will be thrown back [in] . . . a continual flux of reordering" (Platt 1987:98). Also see, among others, Gose (1996), Urton (1997).

10. On Inka forced-feeding, see, among others, Zuidema (1980).

11. Gose (1996:8) and Curatola (2008:28) also note the importance of excessive drinking in producing oracular communication.

12. *Yncap rantin rimac*: the Inka's substitute speaker, or the speaker who stands in for the Inka (Guaman Poma de Ayala 2006 [1615]:950; also see Gose 1996:18).

13. The creative power of sound is perceptively explored in Henry Stobart's *Music and the Poetics of Production in the Bolivian Andes* (2006) and in Denise Arnold's *Rio de Vellón, Rio de Canto* (1998).

14. The "wrong" way to interpret Andean and other "animistic" cultures is to assume that they are expressions of pathological, childish, or primitive mentalities. To assume, for example, that pre-Columbian elites cynically manipulated their oracles to control a gullible populace simply means that one cannot imagine sharing such a belief. (This is not to say that oracles were never manipulated, but this would have occurred within a culturally Andean context in which oracles were a powerful reality; see Curatola's argument on this point [2008:27–28, 37–49].) Calling it all metaphor and symbolism is a version of the same stance, although modified and more appreciative of animism's subtleties.

REFERENCES CITED

Abercrombie, Thomas A. 1998. *Pathways of Memory and Power: Ethnography and History among an Andean People*. Madison: University of Wisconsin Press.

Allen, Catherine J. 1982. "Body and Soul in Quechua Thought." *Journal of Latin American Lore* 8 (2): 179–96.

Allen, Catherine J. 1984. "Patterned Time: The Mythic History of a Peruvian Community." *Journal of Latin American Lore* 10 (2): 151–73.

Allen, Catherine J. 1994. "Time, Place and Narrative in an Andean Community." *Bulletin de la Société Suisse des Américanistes* 57–58:89–95.

Allen, Catherine J. 1998. "When Utensils Revolt: Mind, Matter, and Modes of Being in the Pre-Columbian Andes." *RES* 33:18–27.

Allen, Catherine J. 2002a [1988]. *The Hold Life Has: Coca and Cultural Identity in an Andean Community*. 2nd ed. Washington, DC: Smithsonian Institution Press.

Allen, Catherine J. 2002b. "The Incas Have Gone Inside: Pattern and Persistence in Andean Iconography." *RES* 42:180–203.

Allen, Catherine J. 2011. *Foxboy: Intimacy and Aesthetics in Andean Stories*. Austin: University of Texas Press.

Arnold, Denise Y. 1998. *Río de Vellón, Río de Canto: Cantar a los animales, una poética andina de la creación*. La Paz: Universidad Mayor de San Andrés.

Bakhtin, Mikhail M. 1981. *The Dialogic Imagination*. Austin: University of Texas Press.

Basso, Keith H. 1996. *Wisdom Sits in Places: Landscape and Language among the Western Apache*. Albuquerque: University of New Mexico Press.

Bastien, Joseph. 1978. *Mountain of the Condor: Metaphor and Ritual in an Andean Ayllu*. Prospect Heights, IL: Waveland Press.

Bauer, Brian S. 1998. *The Sacred Landscape of the Inca: The Cusco Ceque System*. Austin: University of Texas Press.

Bird-David, Nurit. 1999. "'Animism' Revisited: Personhood, Environment, and Relational Epistemology." *Current Anthropology* 40 (S1): S67–91. http://dx.doi.org /10.1086/200061.

Brightman, Marc, Vanessa Elisa Gould, and Olga Ulturgasheva, eds. 2012. *Animism in Rainforest and Tundra: Personhood, Animals, Plants and Things in Contemporary Amazonia and Siberia*. New York: Berghan Books.

Bubba Zamora, Cristina. 1997. "Collectors versus Native Peoples: The Repatriation of the Sacred Weavings of Coroma, Bolivia." *Museum Anthropology* 20 (3): 39–44.

Candler, Kay. 1993. Place and Thought in Quechua Household Ritual. Ph.D. diss., University of Illinois at Urbana-Champaign. University Microfilms, Ann Arbor, MI.

Cereceda, Verónica. 1986. "The Semiology of Andean Textiles: the Talegas of Isluga." In *Anthropological History of Andean Polities*, ed. John V. Murra, Nathan Wachtel, and Jacques Revel, 149–73. Cambridge: Cambridge University Press. http://dx.doi.org/10.1017/CBO9780511753091.015.

Cummins, Thomas B.F. 2002. *Toasts with the Inca: Andean Abstraction and Colonial Images on Quero Vessels*. Ann Arbor: University of Michigan Press.

Curatola Petrocchi, Marco. 2008. "La función de los oráculos en el imperio Inca." In *Adivinación y oráculos en el mundo andino antiguo*, eds. Marco Curatola Petrocchi and Mariusz S. Ziólkowski, 15–69. Lima: Instituto Francés de Estudios Andinos and Pontificia Universidad Católica del Perú.

Délétroz Favre, Alain. 1993. *Huk kutis kaq kasqa . . . relatos del distrito del Coaza (Carabaya-Puno)*. Cuzco: Instituto de Pastoral Andina.

Descola, Philippe. 1992. "Societies of Nature and the Nature of Society." In *Conceptualizing Society*, ed. Adam Kuper, 107–26. London: Routledge.

Duviols, Pierre. 1986. *Cultura andina y represión: Procesos y visitas de idolatrías y hechicerías, Cajatambo siglo XVII*. Cuzco: Centro de Estudios Rurales Andinos "Bartolomé de las Casas."

Earls, John. 1969. "The Organization of Power in Quechua Mythology." *Journal of the Steward Anthropological Society* 1:63–82.

Erikson, Philippe. 2009. "Obedient Things: Reflections on the Matis Theory of Materiality." In *The Occult Life of Things: Native Amazonian Theories of Materiality and Personhood*, ed. Fernando Santos-Granero, 173–91. Tucson: University of Arizona Press.

Franquemont, Edward M., Christine Franquemont, and Billie Jean Isbell. 1992. "Awaq ñawin: El ojo del tejedor. La práctica de la cultura en el tejido." *Revista Andina* 10 (1): 47–80.

Garcilaso de la Vega, El Inca. 1943 [1609]. *Comentarios reales de los Incas*. Vol. 1. Buenos Aires: Emece Editores.

Gell, Alfred. 1998. *Art and Agency: An Anthropological Theory*. Oxford: Oxford University Press.

Gifford, Douglas, and Pauline Hoggarth. 1976. *Carnival and Coca Leaf: Some Traditions of the Peruvian Quechua Ayllu*. New York: St. Martin's Press.

Gose, Peter. 1994. *Deathly Waters and Hungry Mountains: Agrarian Ritual and Class Formation in an Andean Town*. Toronto: University of Toronto Press.

Gose, Peter. 1996. "Oracles, Divine Kingship and Political Representation in the Inka State." *Ethnohistory* 43 (1): 1–32. http://dx.doi.org/10.2307/483342.

Gow, Peter. 1999. "Piro Designs: Painting as Meaningful Action in an Amazonian Lived World." *Journal of the Royal Anthropological Institute* 5 (2): 229–46. http://dx.doi.org/10.2307/2660695.

Guaman Poma de Ayala, Felipe. 2006 [1615]. *Nueva coronica y buen gobierno*. http://www.kb.dk/permalink/2006/poma/964/en/text/.

Guss, David. 1989. *To Weave and Sing: Art, Symbol, and Narrative in the South American Rain Forest*. Berkeley: University of California Press.

Harris, Olivia. 2000. *To Make the Earth Bear Fruit: Ethnographic Essays on Fertility, Work and Gender in Highland Bolivia*. London: Institute of Latin American Studies, University of London.

Howard, Rosaleen. 2002. "Spinning a Yarn: Landscape, Memory, and Discourse Structure in Quechua Narratives." In *Narrative Threads: Accounting and Recounting in Andean Khipu*, ed. Jeffrey Quilter and Gary Urton, 26–49. Austin: University of Texas Press.

Ingold, Tim. 2000. *The Perception of the Environment: Essays in Livelihood, Dwelling and Skill*. London, New York: Routledge. http://dx.doi.org/10.4324/9780203466025.

Lechtman, Heather. 1977. "Style in Technology—Some Early Thoughts." In *Material Culture: Styles, Organization, and Dynamics of Technology*, ed. Heather Lechtman and Robert S. Merrill, 3–20. 1975 Proceedings of the American Ethnological Society. St. Paul, MN: West Publishing Company.

Lechtman, Heather. 1993. "Technologies of Power: The Andean Case." In *Configurations of Power in Complex Societies*, ed. Patricia Netherly and John Henderson, 244–79. Ithaca, NY: Cornell University Press.

Lechtman, Heather. 1996. "Cloth and Metal: The Culture of Technology." In *Andean Art at Dumbarton Oaks*, vol. 1, ed. Elizabeth H. Boone, 33–43. Washington, DC: Dumbarton Oaks.

Lyon, Patricia J. 1981. "Arqueología y mitología: La escena de 'los objetos animados' y el tema de 'el alzamiento de los objetos.'" *Scripta Etnológica* 6:103–8.

MacCormack, Sabine. 1991. *Religion in the Andes: Vision and Imagination in Early Colonial Peru*. Princeton: Princeton University Press.

Mannheim, Bruce. 1991. *The Language of the Inka since the European Invasion*. Austin: University of Texas Press.

Martínez, Gabriel. 1989. *Espacio y pensamiento*. La Paz: HISBOL.

Miller, Joanna. 2009. "Things as Persons: Ornaments and Alterity among the Mamaindê (Nambikwara)." In *The Occult Life of Things: Native Amazonian Theories of Materiality and Personhood*, ed. Fernando Santos-Granero, 60–80. Tucson: University of Arizona Press.

Molina, Cristóbal de (del Cuzco). 1947 [1573]. *Ritos y fabulas de los incas*. Colección Eurindia 14. Buenos Aires: Editorial Futuro. Downloaded from https://www.scribd.com/doc/50568715/MOLINA-Cristóbal-de-del-Cuzco-1573-1947-Ritos-y-fabulas-de-los-incas.

Nelson, Richard K. 1983. *Make Prayers to the Raven: A Koyukon View of the Northern Forest*. Chicago: University of Chicago Press.

Núñez del Prado, Juan Victor. 1970. "El mundo sobrenatural de los Quechuas del sur del Perú, a través de la comunidad de Qotabamba." *Allpanchis Phuturinqa* 2:57–120.

Platt, Tristan. 1987. "Entre Ch'axwa and Muxsa. Para una historia del pensamiento político Aymara." In *Tres reflexiones sobre el pensamiento andino*, ed. Thérèse Bouysse-Casagne, Olivia Harris, Tristan Platt, and Verónica Cereceda, 61–132. La Paz: HISBOL.

Platt, Tristan. 1997. "The Sound of Light: Emergent Communication through Quechua Shamanic Dialogue." In *Creating Context in Andean Cultures*, ed. Rosaleen Howard-Malverde, 196–226. Oxford: Oxford University Press.

Quilter, Jeffrey. 1990. "The Moche Revolt of the Objects." *Latin American Antiquity* 1 (1): 42–65. http://dx.doi.org/10.2307/971709.

Quilter, Jeffrey. 1997. "The Narrative Approach to Moche Iconography." *Latin American Antiquity* 8 (2): 113–33. http://dx.doi.org/10.2307/971689.

Ramírez, Susan Elizabeth. 2005. *To Feed and Be Fed: The Cosmological Bases of Authority and Identity in the Andes*. Stanford: Stanford University Press.

Rostworowski de Diez Canseco, María, 1988. *Historia del Tahuantinsuyu*. Lima: Instituto de Estudios Peruanos.

Sallnow, Michael. 1987. *Pilgrims of the Andes: Regional Cults in Cuzco*. Washington, DC: Smithsonian Institution Press.

Salomon, Frank. 1991. "Introductory Essay." In *The Huarochirí Manuscript: A Testament of Ancient and Colonial Andean Religion*, ed. and trans. Frank Salomon and George L. Urioste, 1–38. Austin: University of Texas Press.

Salomon, Frank. 1998. "How the *Wak'as* Were: The Language of Substance and Transformation in the Huarochirí Quechua Manuscript (1608)." *RES* 33:5–17.

Salomon, Frank, and George L. Urioste, eds. 1991. *The Huarochirí Manuscript: A Testament of Ancient and Colonial Andean Religion*. Austin: University of Texas Press.

Sándor, András. 1986. "Metaphor and Belief." *Journal of Anthropological Research* 42 (2): 101–22.

Santos-Granero, Fernando. 2004. "Arawakan Sacred Landscapes." In *Kultur, Raum, Landschaft. Zur Bedeutung des Raumes en Zeiten der Globalitat*, ed. Ernst Halbmayer and Elke Mader, 93–122. Frankfurt am Main: Brandes & Apsel Verlag.

Santos-Granero, Fernando. 2009. "Ways of Being a Thing in the Yanesha Lived World." In *The Occult Life of Things: Native Amazonian Theories of Materiality and Personhood*, ed. Fernando Santos-Granero, 105–27. Tucson: University of Arizona Press.

Sillar, Bill. 2004. "Acts of God and Active Material Culture: Agency and Commitment in the Andes." In *Agency Uncovered: Archaeological Perspectives on Social Agency, Power, and Being Human*, ed. Andrew Gardner, 153–90. London: UCL Press.

Steele, Paul R. 2004. *Handbook of Inca Mythology*. Santa Barbara, CA: ABC/Clio.

Strathern, Andrew. 1996. *Body Thoughts*. Ann Arbor: University of Michigan Press.

Stensrud, Astrid. 2011. "'Todo en la vida se paga': Negotiating Life in Cusco, Peru." Ph.D. diss., University of Oslo, Norway.

Stobart, Henry. 2006. *Music and the Poetics of Production in the Bolivian Andes*. London: Ashgate Press.

Taussig, Michael T. 1993. *Mimesis and Alterity*. New York: Routledge.

Taylor, Gerald. 1974. "Camay, camac et camasca dans le manuscrit Quechua de Huarochirí." *Journal de la Société des Américanistes* 63 (1): 231–44. http://dx.doi.org /10.3406/jsa.1974.2128.

Urton, Gary. 1997. *The Social Life of Numbers*. Austin: University of Texas Press.

van de Guchte, Maarten. 1990. "'Carving the World': Inca Monumental Sculpture and Landscape." Ph.D. diss., University of Illinois at Urbana-Champaign. Ann Arbor, MI: University Microfilms.

Viveiros de Castro, Eduardo. 1998. "Cosmological Deixis and Amerindian Perspectivism." *Journal of the Royal Anthropological Institute* 4 (3): 469–88. http:// dx.doi.org/10.2307/3034157.

Viveiros de Castro, Eduardo. 2004. "Exchanging Perspectives: The Transformation of Objects into Subjects in Amerindian Ontologies." *Common Knowledge* 10 (3): 463–84. http://dx.doi.org/10.1215/0961754X-10-3-463.

Whitten, Dorothea, and Norman E. Whitten Jr. 1993. "Creativity and Continuity: Communication and Clay." In *Imagery and Creativity: Ethno-aesthetics and Art Worlds in the Americas*, ed. Dorothea Whitten and Norman E. Whitten Jr., 309–56. Tucson: University of Arizona Press.

Willerslev, Rane. 2007. *Soul Hunters: Hunting, Animism, and Personhood among the Siberian Yukaghirs*. Berkeley: University of California Press. http://dx.doi. org/10.1525/california/9780520252165.001.0001.

Willerslev, Rane. 2011. "Frazier Strikes Back from the Armchair: A New Search for the Animist Soul." *Journal of the Royal Anthropological Institute* 17 (3): 504–26. http://dx.doi.org/10.1111/j.1467-9655.2011.01704.x.

Zuidema, R. Tom. 1964. *The Ceque System of Cuzco: The Social Organization of the Capital of the Inca*. Leiden: E. J. Brill.

Zuidema, R. Tom. 1973. "Kinship and Ancestor Cult in Three Peruvian Communities: Hernández Príncipe's Account of 1622." *Boletín del Instituto Francés de Estudios Andinos* 2 (1): 16–33.

Zuidema, R. Tom. 1980. "El Ushnu." *Revista de la Universidad Complutense de Madrid.* 28 (117): 317–62.

Zuidema, R. Tom. 1990. *Inca Civilization in Cuzco.* Austin: University of Texas Press.

3

Wak'as

Entifications of the Andean Sacred

Bruce Mannheim and
Guillermo Salas Carreño

What is, or what was, a *wak'a?* If you ask the question that way, you already assume a certain kind of answer, one in which a wak'a is a substance. But the assumption, which tends to characterize much anthropological treatment of "wak'a" today, is not innocent. It belongs to a specific ontology of the sacred—a Christian rather than an indigenous Andean one—and has a specific history. It is also the wrong kind of question to ask because it is posed as top-down, as if archetypes of Andean wak'as, of Andean sacrality, and of the nature of agency in Andean cultures can be defined apart from the social practices that they engage. In this chapter, we address three related questions that approach Andean sacrality: First, what does wak'a mean in Quechua and what are the origins of current scholarly practices in using the word wak'a—be it in Spanish or in English? Second, what are the social sources of attributions of sacrality in modern Andean practices, be they in indigenous communities or mestizo, and within these contexts, how does sacrality engage local conceptions of social agency? And third, does it even make sense to speak of sacrality when the practices we consider sacred are imbricated in the profane and the quotidian realms of Andean life? In doing so, we engage three distinct fields—linguistics, ethnography, and history—but our goal is to provide a firmer conceptual footing for understanding social practices that have substantial material bases and repercussions. Hence our ultimate target is to provide archaeologists with a material foundation for exploring Andean ontology.

DOI: 10.5876/9781607323181.c003

PRELIMINARIES: HOW TO THINK ABOUT
MEANING AND AGENCY

Bound up in any discussion of wak'a is the nature of social agency and the ways in which it is embedded in a specifically Quechua ontology—that is, specifically Quechua ideas of the kinds of objects that exist in the world and their interaction with each other. (Alfred Gell [1998] argued persuasively that social notions of agency are central to any understanding of material objects whatsoever; also see Keane [2010]). A standard way to approach the subject of wak'a is to ask what it means and to provide a list of words in another language, say English, which correspond to objects or concepts in English. To follow this format is to buy into what the philosopher W.V.O. Quine (1961, 1969:27) called "the myth of a museum in which the exhibits are meanings and the words are labels." Under a museum exhibit theory of meaning, translation between languages is a simple matter of changing the labels; a museum exhibit theory of meaning assumes that the things in the exhibits—conceptual frameworks and ontologies—are identical from language to language and from culture to culture, a claim that is demonstrably false (see Keane 2006 for an updated version of this argument). For example, in the language of the Inka capital Cuzco, until the middle of the nineteenth century, two different words were used for "water," *unu* and *yaku*. *Unu* designated the substance water, *yaku* the flowing water of irrigation. *Yaku* was understood to flow under its own agency. An irrigation canal, then, could not "carry" water (as it does in English, but not in French); rather the canal "guided" or "led" water (as it does in French, but not in English). Both the conceptual framework around the verbs and the ontological assumptions about the nature of water are different enough that a museum exhibit theory of meaning cannot hold water.

Over the fifty or so years since Quine published *Word and Object*, substantial parts of its argument have been falsified, particularly its famous core example: Two individuals meet in a remote rain forest. They speak different languages, unrelated and never before in contact. In order to communicate with each other, the two engage in what Quine called "radical translation." A rabbit hops by, and one of them points to it and says, "gavagai." How does his interlocutor know that the person who pointed meant "rabbit" rather than, say, "undetached rabbit parts"? Quine used this as the pivot of a general theory of ontological relativity—that one cannot merely assume that "what there is" in the world is the same for speakers of two distinct languages—and across the book argues that this is true even for speakers of (ostensibly) "the same" language. "Entification," says Quine (1969:1), "begins at arm's length".

There is now substantial evidence of an innate bias toward identifying objects holistically even in very young children (roughly on the principle of "if it moves together it is a single object"[Spelke 1988]). In other respects, however, Quine's objections to a museum exhibit theory of meaning (and concomitant ontological relativity) have become more robust over the years. Words and concepts do not develop in isolation from each other but are embedded in overarching, domain-specific theories (Medin 1989; Gelman 1996), and linguists have long observed that syntactic categories (noun, verb, and so forth) and the grammatical reactances that words have with each other are critical determinants of their meanings and ontological status.[1] What can count as the agent of an event is determined by—and transmitted through—the grammatical constructions within which it occurs. For example, in Quechua *Intiqa ruphayashan* "The sun is [becoming] hot" *explicitly* treats the sun as the agent of the warmth that the speaker is experiencing; the English counterpart can only be the agentless "It is hot" (for reasons peculiar to English syntax)—a word-for-word translation from Quechua to English would only be understood in an inchoative sense, as a statement about the temperature of the sun, not as the speaker's experience. In both these senses—of concepts as parts-of-theories and of concepts as partly determined grammatically—the conceptual differences between the languages reflect *systematic* practices rather than idiosyncratic figures of speech. We will call these two determinants of concepts together the *affordances* of a word, using a term that the psychologist Gibson (1966:285) first coined for material objects. Like material objects (really we should say "like *other* material objects"), words have specific structurally endowed conceptual properties that allow them to be used in specific ways.

For example, there are three common systems of agreement in languages of the world, each of which handles agency in distinct ways. In simple terms, for nominative-accusative agreement systems, like the dominant system in English, the subject of a transitive verb (e.g., "eat") is treated like the subject of an intransitive verb (e.g., "walk"), and differently from the object of a transitive verb; in ergative-absolutive agreement systems, the object of a transitive verb is treated like the subject of an intransitive verb (the absolutive) and different from the agent of a transitive verb (the ergative). Languages with ergative-absolutive agreement also have nominative-accusative agreement, with agreement "split" depending on the nature of the subject noun phrase, the nature of the verb in question, or both, according to the relative agency of the noun or the relative volitionality of the action denoted by the verb. In addition, the split can be used tactically to attribute social agency to the subject (Ahearn

2001; Duranti 1994). In short, the type of agreement system and the agreement options available in a language provide affordances for the attribution of agency, some rigid and some tactical. A third type of agreement system—the active—assigns agency in transitive verbs through a poly-person system that marks both the agent of an action and a second noun phrase that can be the object, but can also be a noun phrase that is affected by the action in some other way.

Where does Southern Quechua stand in this typology? Though it has commonly been described as a nominative-accusative language (perhaps because of observer bias; e.g., it has normally been described through the medium of nominative-accusative languages, like Spanish and English), it has strong traces of the other two agreement systems as well. Consider the following examples:

(ia) Qusayki-Ø puñukushan.

"Your husband (nominative) is sleeping."

(ib) Qusayki-Ø aycha-ta mihushan.

"Your husband (nominative) is eating the meat (accusative)."

The examples in (i) have garden-variety nominative-accusative agreement, in which the agent of the action specified in the verb can be "read off" of the subject.

Consider now the examples in (ii):

(iia) Qayniwanchay sipas-warmillan-Ø ñak'aqpa ñak'asqan wañuran (Cusihuamán and Solá 1967:8.1).

"Just the other day, a young woman-Ø died, butchered by the *phistaku* ['fat stealer']."

(iib) Qanpa papa mihusqaykita yachani (Ebina 2010:63).

"I know that you ate potatoes."

This is a two-clause construction. In the main clause the woman dies; in the subordinate clause the phistaku (or *ñak'aq*) is identified as the agent of her death. As in (i), the woman is the subject of the intransitive main clause (a standard example nominative-accusative agreement), but the woman is also the object of the action of the ñak'aq—a straightforward ergative-absolutive construction in which the ñak'aq is the agent and marked by the genitive *-pa*, the woman is the absolutive and marked by the absolutive zero (Ø), and the verb is nominalized with *-sqa*, used for an action that is completed or placed in the background of the main clause action.

In (iia) the agent in subordinate clauses is specified by the genitive (possessive) *-pa*, and the affected noun by a morphological zero (Ø),[2] essentially an ergative-absolutive distinction. Similarly, in (iib) the agent of the subordinate clause (the eater of potatoes) is marked with the genitive and the affected noun (the potatoes) with zero (Ø). The linguist Daisuke Ebina (2010) has proposed a novel analysis of nominalized verbs ending in *-sqa* in which all begin syntactically as ergative constructions and when promoted to main-clause status ("insubordination") change to a nominative-accusative case marking.

The third set of syntactic affordances for agency follows a pattern more typical of active languages, in which the agent of an action is marked by the inflection of the verb. Consider the utterances in (iii):

(iiia) Cervezata munani.

    "I (agent) want (or like) beer."

(iiib) Cervezata munashani.

    "I (agent) am wanting beer."

(iiic) Cervezata uhyanayashani.

    "I (agent) am about to drink beer."

(iiid) Cerveza uhyanayawashan.

    "I (object) want to drink beer (agent)"; (literally: "the beer wants to be drunk by me").

(iiie) Cerveza uhyanayakuwashan.

    "I (object) want to drink beer (agent)"; (i.e., single-mindedly— you would not want to interrupt someone who says this).

(iiif) Cervezanayawashan.

    "I (object) want to drink-beer (verb)."

In (iiia–c) the agent of the action is "I," marked on the verb by the first-person inflection *-ni*. Notice that this is so even with the affix *naya*, whose interpretation depends on the verbal inflection—in this case it marks imminence of the action. But in (iiid–f) "I" is imbued with a desire over which "I" have no volitional control. The desire comes from elsewhere, from the beer itself, and is marked with the third-person inflection on the verb. The beer, which was marked as the object of desire in (iiia–c) is now the agent (and so marked with a nominative zero). "I" is in the thrall of the agent, and so "I" is marked with the affix -*wa* on the verb. And finally in (iiif) "beer" is completely dematerialized so as to be the action itself.

Examples (iiid–f) are difficult to translate into English or Spanish because they so completely violate the ontology of agency grounded in English or Spanish grammar. It isn't that we cannot express the notion that we are in thrall of the volitionality of another—consider, for example "The devil made me do it" or "It's not me, it's the beer that's talking." It is rather that attributions of agency of the sort marked in (iiid–f) have routine affordances in Southern Quechua grammar, whereas in English or in Spanish they require explicit—and nonroutine—cancellation of the default assumptions about agency. Example (iiid) is unremarkable in Quechua, but translating it into Spanish with Quechua-dominant bilinguals produces giggles.

How do the different syntactic affordances for agency affect everyday ideas of agency and volition? How do Quechua speakers use these resources to attribute agency and volition in concrete social situations? At this point, no systematic research has been done on these various constructions, apart from anecdotes in reference grammars. In a remarkable comparative study of Australian languages, Michael Silverstein (1976) showed that splits between nominative-accusative and ergative-absolutive agreement patterns conditioned culture-specific ontologies of agency against the background of a universal hierarchy of agentive possibilities; similar splits were conditioned by the types of verbs in play, again as culturally specific splits against a universal hierarchy of possibilities. In order to understand how Quechua speakers construct an ontology of agency we need similar systematic work on these grammatical constructions. What kinds of agencies are available to Quechua speakers? Where do they split types of agency and with which types of verbs? We simply don't know how this works systematically (apart from the purely syntactic condition of clause structure), but absent that knowledge, it is not possible to make claims about the nature of agency outside of specific ethnographic contexts, such as the place-persons discussed in the final section.

In addition to the systematic affordances of words, they also form parts of less systematic open networks of associations. Two such open networks that have been studied in Southern Quechua are structurally aligned concepts (reflected in the semantic parallelism of poetry and popular song [see Mannheim 1998]) and associative networks of form—through which it has been argued that the ejective and aspirate stops historically spread through the lexicon, sometimes based on conceptual similarity and sometimes based on contiguities of practice. As an example of the former, consider the words *qaqa* and *rumi,* "rock" (the substance) and "stone" (individual rocks), respectively. For Quechua speakers, rock flows like water; stones maintain that motion, though it might be individual and segmented (Cummins and Mannheim 2011). *Qaqa* and *rumi* frequently appear aligned in Quechua folk poetry, with *qaqa* always the first, more general term, and *rumi* the second, more specific term. Similarly, *rit'i,* "frozen water, whether snow or ice," aligns with *chhullunku,* "pieces of snow or ice." In the annual pilgrimage to the Señor de Quyllu-rit'i—the Lord of Pure Snow—ritual dancers, *ukukus* or Pawluchas, ascend to a glacier, *rit'i,* and return with pieces of the glacier, *chhullunku.*³ A last example, familiar to most Inka scholars, concerns the geography of Cuzco. The main plaza of Inka Cuzco was divided in half by the Saphi River (running approximately under the Café Extra today). The half of the plaza to the southeast was called *Hawk'aypat*a and the half to the northwest, *Kusipata,* names that translate approximately as "the plaza of pleasure" and "the plaza of joy," respectively. In all these cases, the concepts are aligned—mutually defining, not individual, atomistic notions. To understand one, it is necessary to understand both and their mutually defining relationship. It is not possible to define just one concept in isolation from the other.

As an example of an associative network of form, consider the vocabulary of twists and bends (Figure 3.1), all of which have historically acquired glottalization (Mannheim 1991, chap. 8, esp. 291–92).

In Figure 3.1, *Q'iwi* (1) is a crook or bend, with its derivatives *q'iwiy* "to twist, to turn aside" and *q'iwi-q'iwi* "zigzag"—which if entangled or interleaved is *q'inqu. T'iksu* (2) is "twisted, inclined." *T'ikray* (3) "to reverse, to turn inside out, to change, to translate." *K'ullku* or *k'illku* "very twisted" (4), denotes the twist in spun yarn or thread (which if tangled becomes *ch'arwi). K'uyuy* "to twist, to roll up" (as a belt or a coiled rope) (5) reframes twistedness as circularity. *K'umu* (6) restricts the notion of 'rolling' to a single bend as "bent over." Another chain of traces extends the constellation into twistedness in a particular medium or context. *Q'apñuy* "dent" (7) is a bend in a surface. The stems of the chains from (8) to (10) denote crookedness in the legs. *Wisq'u* (11) and *lirq'u* (12) are both "cross-eyed," the former a loanword from Spanish. *Wit'ititiy* (13) denotes "to flip around, to convulse, to thrash," while the stems of (14) to (15) are the twists that join entities together.

The key in both of these cases—the alignment of conceptually related forms like "rock" and "stone" and the associative network—is that, contrary to what we would expect from a "museum exhibit theory of meaning" and contrary to the ways in which we represent words in dictionaries (which are basically one

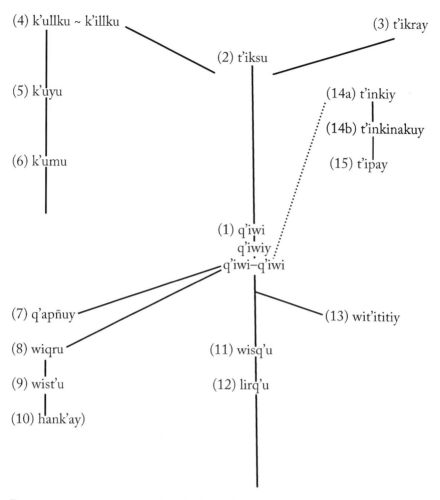

FIGURE 3.1. *Semantic constellation of twists and turns.*

instantiation of a museum exhibit theory of meaning), words are not merely labels for meanings or concepts but together with their meanings form structured assemblages. To explore the meaning of wak'a, then, does not involve asking what classes of objects it applies to. Rather, it is to explore the syntactic affordances and assemblages of meaning from which it derives its value. Grammatical and lexical relations—like any other material assemblage—provide affordances through which meaning is locally constructed.

THE MEANING AND ITINERARY OF WAK'A

The first question to ask is "How does wak'a work syntactically?" Like many (and potentially any) Quechua word stems, it is ambivalent as to part of speech. Without further modification, it can be a noun, an adjective, and a verb (though not an adverb). As a verb, wak'a involves a change-of-state, from domestic to wild: *Chay michi wak'akushan* "That cat's gone wild"; or from a domestic species to a conceptually related species, such as a chicken turning into a condor or a cat turning into a (mythically significant) *quwa* (ocelot). In rural southern Peru today it can be used to denote a cleft, a fissure, a cavern, or a crevice, as in *riru* wak'a, "the crevices between the fingers," *siki* wak'a "butt crack," or in the phrase *makiyqa wak'ashanmi* to refer to the development of cracks in the skin of the hand (as, for example, occurs due to continual manipulation of nearly frozen water). It is ambivalent as to grammatical category; as a verb it can mean "to furrow," as one does when plowing. It also refers to deformities: a cleft-lipped or hare-lipped person or animal is wak'a, as is a person with six fingers. Wak'a is also used in the community of Hapu (Paucartambo) for referring to places that are empty of human or livestock presence, as in *wak'a wayku* (an empty ravine). Another use of wak'a that we heard in Paucartambo, Quispicanchis, and the city of Cuzco, and closer to "sacredness," shows the imprint of dialogue with Christianity (including Roman Catholics and Evangelical Protestants): Wak'a is used to qualify places—such as rock formations, springs, prehispanic cemeteries—as dangerous, risky, and associated with an evil agency toward humans that is aligned with Satan. These places—many of which are difficult to get to—eat humans who dare to get close to them (see also Casaverde 1970:176). Wak'a is also used by urban *curanderos* to characterize, in derogatory tone, rural *paqus*.[4] In both the deformity and sacred senses of wak'a, it is an attribute. But it is important to recognize that in Quechua, unlike English, attributes are also ambivalent as to grammatical category, so wak'a can modify a noun, but it can also be used in place of a noun. Wak'a alone would thus mean "a wak'a thing."

In all of these senses of wak'a, it is important to locate them in their Quechua lexical contexts. The senses of crevice and of a physical deformity both tie closely into the lexical network diagrammed in the first section of this paper, in which glottalization spread diachronically through the lexicon of twists, turns, and physical deformities.[5] (There is a related network involving things breaking into smaller parts, also marked by glottalization.) As to more tightly woven alignment relations, wak'a is the unmarked term in semantic couplets with *willk'a*. Willk'a is narrower semantically and more rare contextually, perhaps used only for sacred objects. It may well be a loanword from

Aymara, but the evidence there is quite limited.[6] Since Quechua—like other languages that have used semantic couplets as a poetic device—can complete a couplet with a loanword (and as indeed Quechua does today with Spanish loanwords), it is possible that the semantic couplet was a vehicle for borrowing willk'a into the vocabulary of Southern Quechua. In any case, it is narrower semantically than wak'a; in the Inka heartland it is willk'a—not wak'a—that appears in place-names and personal names.

A second question is a bit more complex: If we grant that wak'a has a much broader semantic range in Quechua as it is spoken in the central Andes today and, indeed, had the same broad semantic range before the European invasion in 1532, where does the use of wak'a by modern scholars—to mean "sacred object" come from? In order to answer that question, we need to follow the itinerary of the word wak'a across languages and across specific groups of speakers of the languages. Languages acquire different shapes among differently positioned speakers, especially when we are speaking about a word as ontologically and theologically charged as wak'a.

Here it is especially important to pay attention to shifts in the syntactic affordances of the word as it moves across linguistic boundaries. In Quechua, wak'a is ambivalent as to syntactic category and can be used as any part of speech without modification (as indeed is true of far more of the Quechua lexicon than one would expect from the entries in Quechua-Spanish or Quechua-English dictionaries). Once wak'a is transported into Spanish, however, it must fit the syntactic affordances of Spanish, and so in Spanish it is a "substantive," that is, ambivalent between noun and adjective only. And when it is moved into English-language contexts, which happens when it is used in archaeological or other anthropological writing, it is fit onto the syntactic affordances of English, which require a distinction between adjectives and nouns. In this context, wak'a is used strictly as a noun, never as an adjective. What is striking, however, is that the path from Quechua to Spanish to English is not unidirectional: When wak'a is used in archaeological writing, or indeed in local travel writing in Spanish, it is used within the affordance restrictions of English—that is, as a noun, never as an adjective. This suggests that the use of wak'a as a technical term in the Spanish-language archaeology of the Andes is borrowed back from its use in English, namely as a material object.

There is a second story to be told, however, whose results converge with the transit of the word wak'a across languages, from Quechua to Spanish to English back to Spanish. The missionary priests of the sixteenth and seventeenth centuries took up the indigenous languages in their own ways and in their own discourse contexts, shaping a second, parallel linguistic register of Quechua, which has been the subject of Alan Durston's masterful book, *Pastoral Quechua* (2007).[7] The formation of the colonial Quechua attested in sermonals, grammars, and dictionaries from the sixteenth and seventeenth century is not a post-conquest version of the Quechua spoken in the rural hinterlands nor of the "lengua general" of the Inkas but a distinctive variety of Quechua formed for evangelical purposes within the crucible of Romance (mainly Spanish and Italian) conceptual frameworks and ways of speaking—and in critical ways, articulated within expository frameworks that were grounded in European textual traditions. Wak'a is an excellent case in point.

Consider the *Doctrina christiana*, published by the Third Council of Lima in 1584. The *Doctrina*, a handbook for instructing the faithful in Spanish, Quechua, and Aymara, including a standardized short catechism and long catechism, was written with a precise eye toward concepts—especially theologically relevant concepts—that did not translate well among the three languages. A set of linguistic annotations explaining the treacheries of translation into Quechua and Aymara was appended to the *Doctrina*. Willk'a appears near the end of the Quechua annotations as "y huaca idem [,] ydolo" (Tercer Concilio Limcnse 1584:77v). A similar entry appears in the Aymara annotation, with wak'a defined simply as "ydolo" (ibid.:81v).

The central figure around which colonial evangelists configured their notion of idolatry was the golden calf of the Hebrew Bible, the calf constructed as an idol in the impatience of the ancient Hebrews after Moses was summoned to Mount Sinai to receive the Ten Commandments (see Cummins 2009). Wak'a and willk'a are introduced in both the *Doctrina* and the accompanying *Cathecismo por sermones* (1585) in the context of enumeration of the commandments as they were "delivered to these peoples' most learned one, named 'Moses'" (Tercer Concilio Limcnse 1585:102r; for alternative translations see the Spanish text of the sermonal and Taylor 2003:81). The *Doctrina* and the *Cathecismo por sermones* typologically reproduce Moses's act of transmitting the commandments—the preacher assuming the voice of Moses—at the same time as they reproduce the opposition between the material idol and the one true God, conveyed in Quechua by the words *Dios* (borrowed from Spanish, per explicit instruction of the Third Council) and wak'a~willk'a, placing the material idol at the semantic center of the latter two words, as multiple referents are enumerated in the penumbra: "'Ama wakakta willkakta imatapas Diostahina muchankichu' ninmi" "'Don't adore wak'a or willk'a or whatever as you would God' He says [means]" (Tercer Concilio Limcnse 1585:103v; Taylor 2003:82, orthography and translation ours). And now the enumeration of wak'a: Sun, Moon, Venus, stars, the Pleiades, other constellations, the dawn, lightning, rainbow, mountains, springs, rivers, lakes, ravines, shrubs, stones, rock, the places where the old ones have been kept, the serpent, the puma, the bear, other four-legged animals, fertile land. And then: "Don't keep wak'a or willk'a," here mentioning portable objects: anything made of stone in the likeness [Quechua word with Spanish semantics used] of a person or animal or made of *mullu* shells. This list is followed by a list of prohibited offerings, burial practices, and ritual appeals. "Chay chaykunaqa manam ari Dios" "These are not God," with the final "Chay chay" fully materializing the list, although in the passage we cited and in others in the *Doctrina* and *Cathecismo* the words wak'a and willk'a are used in their Spanish-language affordance, that is, ambivalent between noun and adjective, but never as a verb.[8]

The use of these words in sixteenth- and seventeenth-century religious contexts, then, repurposes them so that they fit the Christian religious contexts of "idolatries." They are not so much descriptions of the indigenous sacred as they are placeholders for the projection of the ontology of the golden calf story in which a fully material idol is set in opposition to a specifically Roman Catholic monotheism. That the earliest description of a material "idol" used the Arawakan *cimin* to describe it (1534, two years after the Spanish arrival in Cajamarca [van de Guchte 1990:242]) underscores the extent to which even in sixteenth-century Quechua "wak'a" was repurposed to fit a theological interpretation and cultural ontology that preexisted the Spanish appearance in Peru. Intersecting with the theological configuration of wak'a was a blatantly material one: If the wak'as were plainly religious in nature and not burials, they could be mined and were subject to Spanish law regarding mining claims on unclaimed lands. (If they were burials, on the other hand, grave goods were the private property of the descendants of the individual whose grave it was, a legal distinction that could be litigated or ignored.) Both religious and lay colonists had stakes in the materialization of wak'a, distinct but intersecting (Ramírez 1996:121–51). And as Kenneth Mills (1997:39–74) has shown, the idea of "wak'a" was central to the Spanish religious project in Peru.

Frank Salomon (1991:19) insightfully identifies lists like that of the Third Council of Lima and a similar one in Garcilaso's seventeenth-century history of the Inkas as "things the English language forces us to call 'deities,'" but this is only one turn in a complexly interwoven, double itinerary for the word "wak'a," which in one stream takes us from Quechua to Spanish to English, back to Spanish; and in another stream through the rhetorical and theological filters of colonial pastoral Quechua. Why should these matters philological be of concern to archaeologists? If our goal is not merely to label specific places and structures as "wak'as" but to understand the nature of religiosity in the late prehispanic Andes, then we have to be as careful with the historiography of key notions like wak'a as we would with the formation of a site. The materialization of wak'a is ours, as is the tendency we have to define it top-down, much as the missionary priests of the Third Council did, through a notional core that is also ours and a penumbra that attempts—in vain—to take in the range of social practices encompassed by wak'a. In the following section, we move into ethnographic terrain to develop an account of how places specifically are sacralized, as a way of approaching the problem from the "bottom up."

WAK'A AS PERSON

In his introduction to the English translation of the Huarochirí manuscript, Salomon (1991:19) observes that "huacas are living beings, persons in fact." Traditionally, ethnographers have approached the personhood of wak'a in top-down fashion by positing a "cosmology" in which sacred entities have specific powers ascribed to them. In order to enable this view, they tacitly accept the entification of wak'a as a given. In order to account for the social powers—the personhood—possessed by wak'as (here as entities), they must make recourse to the hoary notion of "animism" and assert that Quechuas ascribe agency to entities, like mountains, that *we* know are nonagentive. But as we saw in the first section of this chapter, ascriptions of agency are not that simple. In Quechua, as in English, agency is constrained by the grammatical affordances of the language, and many things—and actions—can be ascribed agency without having to claim that Quechua (or English) speakers live in an animistic universe.[9] As we saw, when one has a strong desire for a drink of beer, both the beer and the act of drinking can be agentive—as can any desire—but this should not lead us to assume that any thing and any action can have the same kinds of social powers as do wak'a entities and actions.

Far from being a relic of nineteenth-century armchair anthropologists, the notion of "animism" has gained new currency among social anthropologists, sometimes as a warrant for rethinking the relationships among humans and material objects (Ingold 2012, chap. 5) and sometimes as a form of totalistic classification of societies (see the extended discussion by Allen, this volume).[10] Here we propose rather that the personhood of wak'a—and its concomitant social agency—is a consequence of social practices that define personhood more broadly. As these practices must be accounted for independently of the question of the agency of wak'a, it is more parsimonious to attribute the agency of wak'a to the practices than to stipulate, top down, a cosmology in which particular entities, such as mountains (or even drinks of beer), have agentive powers. In the next section, we discuss a specific class of (entified) wak'as—place-persons—and show how their social character is determined by practices of feeding.

FOOD, COHABITATION, AND RELATIONSHIPS
WITH POWERFUL PLACES

Notions of food circulation and cohabitation are at the foundations of Quechua sociality. Commensality and the serving of food are among the most structured of domains of everyday life at every scale of social life—from the chanciest of encounters between individuals to the interactions of the state with other like entities (Rostworowski 1976; Weismantel 1988; see esp. Bray 2012)—and with every kind of entity (or being) that can be ascribed social-ity, including parents and children, affines, guests and hosts, people and their herds, people and their fields, people and places (though not people and "place" as much of the anthropological literature would have it—places are named social individuals [Allen 2002:41].) The ascription goes beyond mere offerings or exchanges with these beings or entities. Rather they instantiate a Quechua "theory of mind" (*sensu stricto*) in which the beings and entities are attrib-uted the thoughts, capacities of action, emotions and intentions of all social beings—the ability to continue the relationship or to spurn it unrequited, and, with the right physical capacity, the ability to nurture or destroy. This is a fundamental fact of Quechua social life, an assumption that trumps all others, including "etiquette" (on one end of the hospitality continuum) and consan-guinity (at the other).[11] Humans emerge as persons—in a material as well as in a moral sense—through this web of social interactions with beings and enti-ties, including places. By contributing to the material constitution of human bodies, providing support where they live and work, and actively watching and judging human moral behavior, places participate in quotidian human existence (see also chapters by Allen and Dean, this volume).

Recent research in different Quechua communities shows that the relations between parents and their children do not rest primarily on ties established by parturition. As Van Vleet (2008:58) puts it in her ethnography of Sullk'ata, a Bolivian Quechua community, "who gives birth to whom is in itself insuf-ficient for understanding Sullk'ata relatedness. Silveria claims to be Javier's mother because she *raised* him: fed him and cared for him, carried him on her back, laughed with him, and comforted his cries." At the other end of the Andes, in Zumbaga, Ecuador, nonbiological parents "by taking a child into their family and nurturing its physical needs through the same substances as those eaten by the rest of the social group, can make of that child a son or a daughter who is physically as well as jurally their own" (Weismantel 1995:695).

Food is the substance that constitutes and relates Quechua bodies: "Flesh is made from food. . . Those who eat together in the same household share the same flesh in a quite literal sense: they are made of the same stuff" (ibid.). In Sullk'ata, Bolivia, sexual procreation and agriculture are iconic of each other: "A child is born nine or ten months after a man plants seed in a woman. A child ripens during pregnancy through the *actions* of the woman who nourishes her child, just as Pacha Mama [Mother Earth] nourishes the seed of corn or potatoes, allowing those seeds to ripen" (Van Vleet 2008:59). Even before birth, the notion of feeding is already important in the construction of relatedness. The new person is in the semen as a potentiality, just as plants are potentially in their seeds.[12] Hence, pregnancy is framed as a crucial stage that initiates the process of caring and feeding, which continues postnatally with breastfeeding. Critical to forming the infant into a *particular* person are commensality and co-residence. By sharing food and physical space one does not become a generic or normative person. Rather a person is constituted over time through particular relationships that are brought into being through the provision of care and food as part of a wider process of continuous cohabitation (Leinaweaver 2008:135; Walmsley 2008).

Humans interact with places in exactly the same ways, through food sharing and continuous cohabitation. Persons share substance with their place of birth, much as they do with their procreative parents, but must renew it routinely by feeding—not as the making of generic "offerings to the place" but as part of an ongoing set of relationships with particular, named places. Just as the circulation of children across households supersedes the procreative relationship through ongoing practices of feeding and cohabitation, so, too, do humans circulate through the named landscape, establishing new relationships with particular local places through routine feeding and cohabitation. Every request, cure, or plea to the places has to be accompanied with food (see Fernández 1997; Gose 1994; Tomoeda 1992). The preparation and deliverance of food offerings (called, among other things, *despacho*, *haywarisqa*, *alcanzo*, *pago*, and *pagapu*) are the most known of practices centered in feeding places.[13]

Such food offerings are done in the cities and in the countryside on specific calendrical occasions, such as for Carnival, on the opening of the Earth on August 1, or at the animal increase rites that take place on San Juan or Santiago feast days, as well as when there is a new project to initiate or a calamity or illness to cure. Among such offerings there is a wide range of variability. Every individual—especially every ritual adept—who carries out a food offering does so in his or her own style. A food offering in the region of Cuzco usually consists of a package containing many different ingredients, some of which are edible by humans (such as corn, coca leaves, llama fat, cookies, different types of candies, etc.) and others which are not (e.g., small lead figurines, starfish, llama fetuses, cotton, small pieces of gold and silver paper, etc.).

The preparation and deliverance of food offerings on celebratory occasions is also a time of joy, and alcohol and food consumption among humans. People knowledgeable in the preparation of these types of offerings, both in the city of Cuzco and in rural communities, have stressed how at the very moment an offering is placed upon the embers outside a house, the places to whom it is dedicated begin to congregate around it and start eating, talking among themselves and enjoying themselves just as the people are doing inside their houses.

Humans give these offerings to places of personal interest as a form of limited repayment for the sustenance and resources that they enjoy from places. Places are the owners of their fertility and, thus, the owners of all types of life sustained by them. Places give food to humans—food that constitutes the substance of their bodies and their social relations. Without the generous gift of the fertility of places, human labor is absolutely useless and life impossible.

These offerings are given to places that are not only providers of food but entities with whom, and under whose power, it is possible to live. As humans cohabit with places and receive and give food to them on a regular basis, it should not be surprising that Quechua people use kin terms to refer to the places that are important to them. For example, the *apu*,[14] or mountain peaks, are called fathers (*taytakuna*) in Sonqo (Paucartambo) (Allen 2002:49) or grandparents in Ocongate (Quispicanchis) (Harvey 1991:6). In a similar way, several experts in giving food to the places with whom we talked in Cuzco consistently said "dear father"[15] before the name of any mountain. So, too, with "Mother Earth." As a Quechua woman from Sonqo explained to Allen in the 1970s, these kin relations are established through food: "We owe our lives to her. . . She nurses the potatoes lying on her breast, and the potatoes nourish us" (Allen 2002:29).[16]

Thus the relationships and interactions that Quechua peoples have with places are not different in kind from the interactions they have with each other. It is through these practices that Quechuas attribute sentience and intentionality to each other *and to places*. The places to which agency is ascribed are exactly the same as the places that are fed routinely. Which comes first? The assertion that Quechua people are animists must still identify the set of entities that they view as animated. After all, one does not feed just any place or any object or any being. If we reverse that argument and say that the named places with which Quechuas interact have social agency and intentionality, for the very same reasons that any being with which one interacts—be it you or me or Maria next door has social agency and intentionality—then we identify exactly the correct set of beings as agentive, including places such as streams, rock outcroppings, and mountains. Using Occam's razor, we would be forced to discard the animist account—which overgeneralizes the attribution of agency—in favor of one in which all attributions of agency are grounded in habitual social practices.[17] Animacy and sentience, as social constructs in Quechua culture, are based not upon a set of abstract beliefs that attribute them randomly to some beings and not others, but rather upon practices of co-residence and the provisioning of food that are grounded in the quiddities of face-to-face interaction.[18]

This web of relatedness involving humans and places is inscribed in the evidence of the very existence of life. It is honored and cultivated not only through complex food offerings, but inscribed in the routine of everyday etiquette. This is the case, for example, in the exchange of coca leaves in the community of Hapu (Paucartambo) that occurs during the breaks in agricultural work or after meals. After receiving a *k'intu*[19] and before chewing it, one dedicates it to the main mountains and plains of the locality and then blows it toward them so they will consume some of its essence beforehand.[20] Likewise, it is common in any corn beer brewery in the city of Cuzco to see people spilling a few drops of their beverage on the soil before drinking it in order to share first with the land.

What kinds of places constitute persons? Allen (2002:41) has pointed out that any feature of the landscape that could be considered a landmark has personhood. We would add that the personhood of a place hangs critically on a very specific element, namely, its name. All named places are persons.[21] Named places have a fractal quality, as it is possible to find more and more names within a given named place. A place may thus contain many places, which in turn can contain more places, all depending on the social and spatial context in which people might refer to places. Each particular place has a sphere of influence that is subsumed within a bigger and more encompassing place.[22] These different scopes of influence are related to power differentials. In Quechua terms, there are neither sacred places nor profane ones. There are powerful places, vastly more powerful than humans, and as such they receive privileged attention. Conversely, there are places that do not have great power and consequently do not receive much attention. Power and sphere of influence are associated with altitude. The higher the mountain, the stronger its power and the larger its sphere of influence. (Gose [2008] suggests that the relative power of place-persons has to do with tribute relationships among them.)

Powerful places willfully intervene in human affairs and punish or reward humans according to their somewhat opaque criteria. As Earls (1969) and Harvey (1991) have stressed, places are capricious and their behavior ambiguous. They can grant special petitions to a human depending on the affection demonstrated through food offerings. Illness, a poor harvest, a business failure, or any other misfortunes are outcomes of improperly feeding, or neglecting to feed, some place. It is difficult to know which place has been offended and why. Humans have relationships with many places through their lives, and, as such, there is always a possibility for some place to be resentful (Ricard 2007). Places have particular personalities: some are generous and caring; others anger easily without clear reasons. There is always a level of uncertainty regarding how places will act.

Hence, through the processes of caring and feeding, relatives emerge jointly and interdependently related to one another at their most primary constitution. Ultimately, human bodies are produced through the incorporation of the materiality of places, mediated through the consumption of food, which is cultivated and cooked by human relatives. Contributing to the material constitution of human bodies, providing support where they live and work, and actively watching and judging human moral behavior, places participate in quotidian, human existence. In this sense, even entified wak'as, such as place-persons, derive their social capacities from social practices (see also Bray 2012). A specific take-away for archaeologists is that understanding the Andean sacred does not require recourse to unobservables; the social practices that constitute the sacred are material and (given appropriate preservation) materially observable.

CONCLUSIONS

In this chapter, we proposed three related methodological propositions about the nature of wak'as: that wak'as, linguistically and conceptually, must be understood within broader lexical and grammatical fields; that the current use by anthropologists of the term wak'a to denote *entified* wak'as alone is a consequence of its historical and social itinerary; and that the social agency of wak'as must be understood in terms of the social and grammatical practices through which Quechua speakers constitute social agency rather than as the precipitate of an abstract cosmology. (Inter alia, we explored the ways in which social agency is constituted grammatically in the Quechua language and found it to be much broader and more complex than a simple extension of social agency to places would suggest. But this is a point to which we must return in a future work.) There are similarly three empirical take-aways.

The first is that wak'a is far broader in its conception than simply "sacred entity" and can encompass attributes and events as well as things. It is critical that scholars of Andean cultures disengage themselves from the colonial impulse to reduce wak'as to the "merely" material on the one hand or to an abstract spiritual essence on the other, both of which have much more to do with the institutionalized theologies of European Christian tradition than they do with any Andean social practices. Not only is the reduction of wak'a to material artifacts and to mountain "deities" tendentious, but even the identification of Quechua wak'a with the "sacred" of European modernism is problematical. Both must be held at arm's length as wak'a is explored linguistically, ethnographically, and archaeologically in all its aspects.

Second, though the word wak'a itself is of Quechua origin, its current use by anthropologists owes more to its uses in Spanish and English than Quechua. We have traced two routes that it has taken historically: The first was a colonial-era reduction of scope, in which it was understood primarily within Christian ideas of idolatry, mediated through the account of the golden calf in the Hebrew Bible. The second is the use of wak'a in the modern anthropology of the Andes, which owes itself in part to the colonial-era reduction of wak'a, but which has been further interpreted and reified through the filter of South American archaeology. Archaeologists frequently used wak'as as a label for a feature of the (often built) landscape, whence it was borrowed into Anglophone archaeology as a technical term and then borrowed back into Hispanophone archaeology, still as a term of art. Both these routes—the religious and the scientific—have left traces in the grammatical affordances of the word wak'a, in the first case reducing its grammatical affordances to those of a Spanish-language *sustantivo* (an adjective/noun) and in the second by reducing its affordances to those of an English noun (even when it is used in Spanish).

Third, on grammatical and ethnographic evidence, it is clear that notions of social agency extend more broadly in Quechua culture than to just "persons" as understood in our ordinary sense of the word (indeed more broadly than persons and material objects). While many aspects of a broadened view of agency are shared with North Americans and coastal Peruvians, for example, others are not. Differences such as these have been the concern of many anthropologists over the past decade, but they have often been approached taxonomically by characterizing entire societies as having a specific agentive orientation (e.g., "animistic"). This is both politically dangerous and analytically short-sighted. For example, in his last months in office, Peruvian president Alan García argued that it was inconceivable that native Peruvians be granted the right to prior consultation with respect to the sale of mineral rights to their traditional lands because they were "animistic" and so beyond the bounds of rational judgment (Gamio 2011). (Never mind that weeks later President García himself was to attribute the death of Osama bin Laden to a miracle performed posthumously by Pope John Paul II.) It is analytically short-sighted because it explains neither the range of social agency nor the social ontology taken for granted by Quechua speakers, and so is inadequate ethnographically. We have argued that the sources of social agency surrounding wak'a are to be found not in abstract cosmological principles but in quotidian social practices identifiable ethnographically at a local level. Wak'a is as wak'a *does*.

ACKNOWLEDGMENTS

Dr. Salas's research was supported by the National Science Foundation under Doctoral Dissertation Improvement Grant NSF-0817712. We are grateful to Rodolfo Cerrón-Palomino, Susan A. Gelman, Margarita Huayhua, Joyce A. Marcus, Erik Mueggler, Warren Thompson, and Howard Tsai for their comments on earlier drafts of this chapter and to María Eugenia (Ch'aska) Carlos Rios, Adela (Urpi) Carlos Rios, and Kathryn Hobbs for discussing the Quechua syntactic examples.

NOTES

1. The notion of "grammatical reactance" is from Whorf's (1945) posthumous paper on grammatical categories. For succinct statements of "the new Whorfianism," see Hill and Mannheim (1992), Lucy (1992), Bowerman and Levinson (2001), and Gentner and Goldin-Meadow (2003).

2. A morphological zero is a morpheme that is realized by a phonologically null affix. It is identified by contrast with other, phonologically substantial morphemes that can occur in the same position.

3. Since 2003, *ukukus* no longer bring ice from the glacier. This was forbidden by the Brotherhood of the Señor de Quyllurit'i and the Council of Nations (the umbrella organization of all dancers attending the pilgrimage) as a reaction to the glacial retreat affecting the Qulqipunku (Silvergate) glacier.

4. In this context, both *curanderos* and *paqus* should be understood as people particularly knowledgeable in giving food offerings to powerful places.

5. Just to be clear, while the semantic network motivated the spread of ejectivity diachronically, it is not a biunique marker of the semantic network, that is, not a morphological classifier, much as the *sl* at the beginning of words in English like *slip, sleet,* and *sleaze* ties them together semantically without becoming a true morphological feature of English. See Bolinger (1940) for this well-attested phenomenon. The diachrony of this and other lexical networks in Quechua is discussed in Mannheim (1991, chap. 8). A similar spread of a single phonological feature, retroflexivization, took place in the Indic languages under similar semantic circumstances (Turner 1924), suggesting that the semantic relationships in question are relatively natural in human languages.

6. The Jesuit grammarian Bertonio (1612, Spanish to Aymara section, 435) suggested that it was the word for "Sun" used by the elderly in Juli (*Inti* being the word used more commonly in his day), and this factoid has been repeated by Aymara specialists ever since. *Willka* (no ejective) is used as an honorific today in Aymara, but we do not know whether this is an older usage in Aymara or a back-borrowing from Spanish.

7. Also see Taylor (2000, 2002, 2003). This process was not unique to Quechua, of course. For comparable cases in Nahuatl and in Quiche Mayan, see Burkhart (1989) and Hanks (2010), respectively.

8. Van de Guchte (1990, chap. 9) discusses the colonial historiography of wak'a in the material senses, including an exhaustive taxonomy of its uses in the primary sources.

9. Though constrained by the grammatical affordances of the language, it should be noted that agency is not *uniquely* constrained by grammar.

10. See especially Descola's (2013) typology of relationships between humans and the "natural world": naturalism, animism, indexicality, totemism, etc., and Viveiros de Castro's (1998) of "perspectivism." The use of "animism" and "perspectivism" to characterize entire societies and even entire regions of the world, as opposed to practices, is especially pronounced in the ways in which these have been taken up by other scholars.

11. By "consanguinity" we mean relationships with all beings and entities with whom one shares substance, including parent-child relationships, but also one's relationships with the place in which you were born and expect to return to at death. When you are introduced to someone, you ask where they are from before you ask their name. Mannheim is *from* Ann Arbor or Cuzco, but he *is* New York. Salas is *from* Ann Arbor, or Lima, or Montreal, but he *is* Cuzco. Also see Oxa (2005: 239) and de la Cadena (2015:102).

12. On the analogy between the mother's womb and Mother Earth, see Platt (2002).

13. The terms that appear in the literature for the practice of feeding places are rarely contextualized linguistically or ethnographically. They differ in language (*alcanzo*

being a direct translation of *haywarisqa* "that which was tendered"; *despacho* arguably a loan from Spanish with a more active approximation of *haywarisq*; *pagu* a loan from Spanish; and *pagapu* a Quechua portmanteau incorporating *pagu*). In the Spanish of urban Cuzqueños, the practice is usually referred to as a *pago a la tierra*, though to our knowledge this is rarely used in the countryside; rather one can (in Spanish) *pagar la chakra* (pay the [particular] field) and *pagar la casa* (pay one's own house) in rituals requiring that a field or a house be fed. (On this point see, among others, Casaverde 1970; Dalle 1969; Fernández 1997; Ricard 2007).

14. *Apu* (Quechua), an honorific usually translated as "lord."

15. *Papacito* (Spanish); the Spanish diminutive is an index of affection.

16. While it is usually stated that *Pachamama* refers to the Earth as a total unity, this word is also used as an honorific to refer to the agricultural lands or places that people inhabit.

17. There is an added benefit to this bottom-up social account in that it allows us to identify the attribution of agency to places in Quechua culture as an instance of a general cognitive phenomenon that is relatively well understood by psychologists, namely theory of mind (Wellman 1992).

18. Keane (2010:194) uses a similar argument to refute the traditional distinction between material and religious activities, which, he says, "becomes problematic when it also leads us to ignore the implications of [the] materiality [of religious activities], and to assume that things function *in order to* express concepts, rather than as indexical entailments like those left by *any* mode of activity, no matter how mundane and utilitarian." Here agency functions not only as the indexical entailment of food provisioning, but as the interactional presupposition.

19. *K'intu* (Quechua) refers to a set of coca leaves that are carefully arranged.

20. Similar etiquettes were described by Allen (2002) for Sonqo (Paucartambo) in the 1970s.

21. Related claims about the role of the places' names were made by Ødegaard 2011.

22. It is not surprising that similar recursivity has also been noted regarding the use of the word *ayllu*, which can be applied to a family, a community, or a whole country (Allen 2002:107; Earls 1996).

REFERENCES CITED

Ahearn, Laura. 2001. "Language and Agency." *Annual Review of Anthropology* 30 (1): 109–37. http://dx.doi.org/10.1146/annurev.anthro.30.1.109.

Allen, Catherine J. 2002. *The Hold Life Has: Coca and Cultural Identity in an Andean Community*. 2nd ed. Washington, DC: Smithsonian Institution Press.

Bertonio, Ludovico. 1612. *Vocabulario de la lengua Aymara*. Juli: Francisco del Canto.

Bolinger, Dwight. 1940. "Word Affinities." *American Speech* 15 (1): 62–73. http://dx.doi
.org/10.2307/452731.

Bowerman, Melissa, and Steven Levinson, eds. 2001. *Language Acquisition and
Conceptual Development.* Cambridge: Cambridge University Press. http://dx.doi
.org/10.1017/CBO9780511620669.

Bray, Tamara L. 2012. "Ritual Commensality between Human and Non-Human
Persons: Investigating Native Ontologies in the Late pre-Columbian Andean
World." In *Between Feasts and Daily Meals: Toward an Archaeology of Commensal
Spaces,* ed. Susan Pollock. *eTopoi* (special volume) 2: 197–212.

Burkhart, Louise. 1989. *The Slippery Earth: Nahua-Christian Moral Dialogue in
Sixteenth-Century Mexico.* Tucson: University of Arizona Press.

Casaverde, Juvenal. 1970. "El mundo sobrenatural de una comunidad." *Allpanchis
Phuturinqa* 2:121–243.

Cummins, Thomas B.F. 2009. "The Golden Calf in America." In *The Idol in the Age
of Art: Objects, Devotions and the Early Modern World*, ed. Michael W. Cole and
Rebecca Zorach, 77–104. Farnham, UK: Ashgate.

Cummins, Thomas B.F., and Bruce Mannheim. 2011. "The River around Us, the
Stream within Us: The Traces of the Sun and Inka Kinetics." *RES* 59/60:5–19.

Cusihuamán Gutiérrez, Antonio, and Donald F. Solá. 1967. *Spoken Cuzco Quechua.*
Ithaca, NY: Department of Modern Languages and Linguistics, Cornell University.

Dalle, Luis. 1969. "El despacho." *Allpanchis Phuturinqa* 1:139–54.

de la Cadena, Marisol. 2015. *Earth Beings. Ecologies of Practice across Andean Worlds.*
Durham: Duke University Press.

Descola, Philippe. 2013. *Beyond Nature and Culture.* Chicago: University of Chicago Press.

Duranti, Alessandro. 1994. *From Grammar to Politics: Linguistic Anthropology in a
Western Samoan Village.* Berkeley: University of California Press.

Durston, Alan. 2007. *Pastoral Quechua.* South Bend, IN: University of Notre Dame
Press.

Earls, John. 1969. "The Organisation of Power in Quechua Mythology." *Journal of the
Steward Anthropological Society* 1 (1): 63–82.

Earls, John. 1996. "Rotative Hierarchy and Recursive Organization: The Andean
Peasant Community as a Viable System." In *Structure, Knowledge, and
Representation in the Andes: Studies Presented to Reiner Tom Zuidema on the Occasion
of his 70th Birthday*, ed. Gary Urton. Special issue of *Journal of the Steward
Anthropological Society* 24 (1, 2): 297–320.

Ebina, Daisuke. 2010. クスコ・ケチュア語における名詞化節の脱従属節化
[Insubordination of nominalized clauses in Cuzco Quechua]. *Asian and African
Languages and Linguistics* 5: 59–77.

Fernández Juárez, Gerardo. 1997. *Entre la repugnancia y la seducción: Ofrendas complejas en los Andes del sur*. Cuzco: Centro de Estudios Regionales Andinos "Bartolomé de Las Casas."

Gamio Gehri, Gonzalo. 2011. "El extirpador de idolatrías." *Revista Ideele* 209 (July): 2.

Gell, Alfred. 1998. *Art and Agency: An Anthropological Theory*. Oxford: Oxford University Press.

Gelman, Susan A. 1996. "Concepts and Theories." In *Perceptual and Cognitive Development*, ed. Rochel Gelman and Terry Kit-Fong Au, 117–49. San Diego, CA: Academic Press. http://dx.doi.org/10.1016/B978-012279660-9/50022-1.

Gentner, Dedre, and Susan Goldin-Meadow, eds. 2003. *Language in Mind: Advances in the Study of Language and Thought*. Cambridge, MA: MIT Press.

Gibson, James J. 1966. *The Senses Considered as Perceptual Systems*. Boston: Houghton Mifflin.

Gose, Peter. 1994. *Deathly Waters and Hungry Mountains: Agrarian Ritual and Class Formation in an Andean Town*. Toronto: University of Toronto Press.

Gose, Peter. 2008. *Invaders as Ancestors: On the Intercultural Making and Unmaking of Spanish Colonialism in the Andes*. Toronto: University of Toronto Press.

Hanks, William F. 2010. *Converting Words: Maya in the Age of the Cross*. Berkeley: University of California Press. http://dx.doi.org/10.1525/california/9780520257702 .001.0001.

Harvey, Penelope. 1991. "Drunken Speech and the Construction of Meaning: Bilingual Competence in the Southern Peruvian Andes." *Language in Society* 20 (1): 1–36. http://dx.doi.org/10.1017/S0047404500016055.

Hill, Jane H., and Bruce Mannheim. 1992. "Language and World View." *Annual Review of Anthropology* 21 (1): 381–406. http://dx.doi.org/10.1146/annurev.an.21 .100192.002121.

Ingold, Tim. 2012. *Being Alive: Essays on Movement, Knowledge, and Description*. London: Routledge.

Keane, Webb. 2006. "Signs are Not the Garb of Meaning: On the Social Analysis of Material Things." In *Materiality*, ed. Daniel Miller, 182–205. Durham, NC: Duke University Press.

Keane, Webb. 2010. "Marked, Absent, Habitual: Approaches to Neolithic Religion at Çatalhöyük." In *Religion in the Emergence of Civilization: Çatalhöyük as a Case Study*, ed. Ian Hodder, 187–219. Cambridge: Cambridge University Press.

Leinaweaver, Jessaca B. 2008. *The Circulation of Children: Kinship, Adoption, and Morality in Andean Peru*. Durham, NC: Duke University Press. http://dx.doi.org /10.1215/9780822391500.

Lucy, John. 1992. *Language Diversity and Thought: A Reformulation of the Linguistic Relativity Hypothesis.* Cambridge: Cambridge University Press. http://dx.doi.org/10.1017/CBO9780511620843.

Mannheim, Bruce. 1991. *The Language of the Inka since the European Invasion.* Austin: University of Texas Press.

Mannheim, Bruce. 1998. ""Time, not the Syllables, Must Be Counted": Quechua Parallelism, Word Meaning, and Cultural Analysis." *Michigan Discussions in Anthropology* 13:245–87.

Medin, Douglas L. 1989. "Concepts and Conceptual Structure." *American Psychologist* 44 (12): 1469–81. http://dx.doi.org/10.1037/0003-066X.44.12.1469.

Mills, Kenneth. 1997. *Idolatry and Its Enemies: Colonial Andean Religion and Extirpation, 1640–1750.* Princeton, NJ: Princeton University Press.

Ødegaard, Cecilie Vindal. 2011. "Sources of Danger and Prosperity in the Peruvian Andes: Mobility in a Powerful Landscape." *Journal of the Royal Anthropological Institute* 17 (2): 339–55. http://dx.doi.org/10.1111/j.1467-9655.2011.01683.x.

Oxa Diaz, Justo. 2005. "Vigencia e la cultura andina en la escuela." In Arguedas y el Perú de hoy, edited by Carmen María Pinilla, Gonzalo Portocarrero Maisch, Cecilia Rivera, and Carla Sagástegui, pp. 235–242. Lima: SUR, Casa de Estudios del Socialismo.

Platt, Tristan. 2002. "El feto agresivo: Parto, formación de la persona y mito-historia en los Andes." *Estudios Atacameños* 22:127–55.

Quine, Willard van Orman. 1961. *Word and Object.* Cambridge, MA: MIT Press.

Quine, Willard van Orman. 1969. "Ontological Relativity." In *Ontological Relativity and Other Essays*, ed. Willard van Orman Quine, 26–68. New York: Columbia University Press.

Ramírez, Susan E. 1996. *The World Upside-Down: Cross-Cultural Contact and Conflict in Sixteenth-Century Peru.* Palo Alto, CA: Stanford University Press.

Ricard, Xavier. 2007. *Ladrones de sombra: El universo religioso de los pastores del Ausangate (Andes Peruanos).* Cusco: Centro de Estudios Regionales Andinos "Bartolomé de Las Casas."

Rostworowski de Diez Canseco, María. 1976. "Reflexiones sobre la reciprocidad Andina." *Revista del Museo Nacional* (Lima). 42:341–54.

Salomon, Frank. 1991. "Introductory Essay." In *The Huarochirí Manuscript*, ed. and trans. Frank Salomon and George L. Urioste, 1–38. Austin: University of Texas Press.

Silverstein, Michael. 1976. "Hierarchy of Features and Ergativity." In *Grammatical Categories in Australian Languages*, ed. R.M.W. Dixon, 113–71. Australian Institute of Aboriginal Studies Linguistic Series, no. 22. Canberra: Australian Institute of Aboriginal Studies.

Spelke, Elizabeth S. 1988. "The Origins of Physical Knowledge." In *Thought without Language*, ed. Lawrence Weiskrantz, 168–84. Oxford: Oxford University Press.

Taylor, Gérald. 2000. *Camac, camay y camasca y otros ensayos sobre huarochirí y yauyos*. Cusco. Centro de Estudios Regionales Andinos "Bartolomé de las Casas."

Taylor, Gérald. 2002. *Sermones y ejemplos: Antología bilingüe castellano-quechua, siglo XVII*. Lima: Institut Français d'Études Andines.

Taylor, Gérald. 2003. *El sol, la luna y las estrellas no son dios: La evangelización en Quechua (Siglo XVI)*. Lima: Institut Français d'Études Andines.

Tercer Concilio Limense. 1584. *Doctrina christiana y cathecismo para instrucción de los indios, y de las demas personas q' le han de ser enseñados en nuestra sancta fe*. Lima: Antonio Ricardo.

Tercer Concilio Limense. 1585. *Tercero cathecismo y exposición de la doctrina christiana, por sermones*. Lima: Antonio Ricardo.

Tomoeda, Hiroyasu. 1992. "Mestizos y curanderos: Salud y ritual en el cusco contemporáneo." In *500 años de mestizaje en los Andes*, ed. Hiroyasu Tomoeda and Luis Millones, 221–31. Osaka: Museo Etnológico Nacional del Japón.

Turner, Ralph Lilley. 1924. "Cerebralization in Sindhi." *Journal of the Royal Asiatic Society* 3:555–84.

van de Guchte, Maarten J.D. 1990. "'Carving the World': Inca Monumental Sculpture and Landscape." Ph.D. diss., Department of Anthropology, University of Illinois at Urbana-Champaign. Ann Arbor, MI: University Microfilms.

Van Vleet, Krista E. 2008. *Performing Kinship: Narrative, Gender, and the Intimacies of Power in the Andes*. Austin: University of Texas Press.

Viveiros de Castro, Eduardo 1998. "Cosmological deixis and Amerindian perspectivism." *Journal of the Royal Anthropological Institute* 4 (3): 469–88. http://dx.doi.org/10.2307/3034157.

Walmsley, Emily. 2008. "Raised by Another Mother: Informal Fostering and Kinship Ambiguities in Northwest Ecuador." *Journal of Latin American and Caribbean Anthropology* 13 (1): 168–95. http://dx.doi.org/10.1111/j.1548-7180.2008.00008.x.

Weismantel, Mary. 1988. *Food, Gender, and Poverty in the Ecuadorian Andes*. Philadelphia: University of Pennsylvania Press.

Weismantel, Mary. 1995. "Making Kin: Kinship Theory and Zumbagua Adoptions." *American Ethnologist* 22 (4): 685–704. http://dx.doi.org/10.1525/ae.1995.22.4.02a00010.

Wellman, Henry. 1992. *The Child's Theory of Mind*. Cambridge, MA: MIT Press.

Whorf, Benjamin Lee. 1945. "Grammatical Categories." *Language* 21 (1): 1–11. http://dx.doi.org/10.2307/410199.

PART III

Wak'as in the Time of the Inkas

4

What Is a Wak'a?
When Is a Wak'a?

Zachary J. Chase

INTRODUCTION

Perhaps no aspect of indigenous Andean life vexed colonial Spanish clerics as severely or in as many ways as *wak'as*. Spanish clergy and other state actors grasped at wak'as, attempting to apprehend them both intellectually and physically. However, with few exceptions, the chauvinism informing the eradication of non-Christian cult among Indians constrained the parameters of these exploratory endeavors, which focused primarily on inquiring about, defining, describing, explaining, and uncovering wak'as as a means to destroying them (Duviols 1977, 1986, 2003; García Cabrera 1994; Griffiths 1996; Huertas Vallejos 1981; Mills 1997; Ramos and Urbano 1993; Silverblatt 1987). The present volume provides sympathetic foil to Peruvian intellectual Porras Barrenechea's characterization of these colonial extirpators as "reverse archaeologists" ("*arqueólogos al revés*") (Duviols 1977:429–30). Moreover, it offers movement beyond the purely "practical" constraints of identification and description of wak'as by exploring their modes of existence and operation, and the different contexts within which these obtained and to which they contributed.

Despite an antiquated "treasure-hunting" tint to Porras Barrenechea's depiction of archaeology, one aspect of his evocation of wak'as as a nexus between Spanish colonial extirpation and modern archaeology is more than superficially apt: the material complexities of Andean numina defied both Spanish colonial

DOI: 10.5876/9781607323181.c004

75

and modern explanation. This is due in large part to historically deep and persistent semiotic concepts of the referential and representational function of symbols, as well as to ontological notions of the ultimately incommensurable natures of the agentive and the material. The currency of these issues is evinced by numerous recent studies spanning a number of academic disciplines (Allen 1998; Brown 2003; Daston and Galison 2007:17–53; Dobres and Robb 2000; Gell 1998; Gosden 2004:33–40; Harvey 2006; Ingold 2007:1–38; Küchler 2005; Latour 2005; Meskell 2005; Miller 2005:11–15). Similar concerns have prompted archaeologists to reexamine "animism and other ontologies" (VanPool and Newsome 2012:244) in order to interpret the material record more completely (Alberti and Bray 2009; Brown and Walker 2008). I propose that wak'as defy the dualism of the unmarked (but not unstated), putative Cartesian ontology discussed in much of this recent literature by circumventing the spirit/matter dichotomy altogether.

In his study comparing wak'as to the images, idols, and icons of Europe and the ancient Mediterranean, Henrique Urbano (1993:15–16) addressed these semiotic and ontological concerns simultaneously, concluding that, unlike the former representations of some separate "higher" reality, "*huaca* is reality itself." Exploring the "cultural ontology" of wak'as—the emic reality to which Urbano refers—should be a primary focus of the study of wak'as. Further, the reality of wak'as is amenable to archaeological and historical analyses. That is, precisely because they were dense centers of social, historical, and cultural gravity, wak'as have the potential to be singularly revelatory in archaeological investigation of the Andean past. Human life bent around and pivoted on wak'as *both* in perception *and* in effective historical fact.

In this chapter, I make the case for exploring the "ontology" of wak'as in terms of their temporality, or through their associations both with and in time (cf. Salomon 1998). Temporality here includes concepts of origins and "pastness," historicity, tradition, time reckoning (e.g., calendrics), and genealogy. Not only is this temporal orientation required by the nature of wak'as, but it provides insight into historical events and processes and also aids in the conceptualization of "temporal *perception*[s]" (Lucas 2005:70, italics in original; Bradley 1998:87) in the Andean past. As demonstrated by studies of the Andes' most famous wak'a assemblage—the Inka *ceque* system—time and temporality have long been recognized as important explanatory aspects of wak'as (Bauer 1998; Cobo 1990 [1653]; Rowe 1979; Zuidema 1964, 2011). Here I propose additional types of temporal inquiry that expand our understanding of what wak'as were, by investigating what they *did* and *meant* in the Andean past, and suggest how this understanding assists archaeological research.

The approaches and suggestions submitted here are necessarily interdisciplinary: historical and archaeological sources are used together in a dialectical fashion to define, identify, and explore the various facets of wak'as (cf. Wernke 2003:95). After discussing the basic practical and theoretical aspects of my analysis, I address the "what" together with the "when" of wak'as by presenting a specifically historicized characterization of these entities. I then discuss two ethnohistoric cases in order to flesh out the historically and socially interactive constitution of wak'a agency. Finally, turning to newly gathered archaeological data, I discuss three different wak'as associated with the Huarochirí region of central highland Peru. Throughout this chapter, the data and attendant interpretations from any one case combine to inform possible interpretations for the others. The idea of wak'as as a kind of Andean "history" (in the sense suggested by Trouillot [1995:3]) is repeatedly touched upon, as is an argument for a performative approach to the pasts that wak'as produced and in which they were involved.

BACKGROUND TO STUDY

The research presented here is concentrated on Huarochirí, though I have also drawn material from neighboring areas to the north and from Cuzco. Huarochirí is a highland region on the western side of the central Peruvian Andes, east of the capital city of Lima (see Figure 4.2). It comprised one half of the Inka district registered in Spanish colonial records by the macro-ethnic moniker "Yauyos" (Dávila Brizeño 1965 [1586]). This study spans the Late Intermediate period ([LIP], ca. AD 1000–1470), the Late Horizon (Inkaic) ([LH], ca. AD 1470–1532), and the early Spanish colonial period (AD 1532–ca. 1700).

Huarochirí is famous among Andean scholars for its Quechua manuscript offering a "history" of the region. This text was narrated by one or more indigenous members of the Checa kin group in the early seventeenth century at the behest of parish priest Francisco de Avila (Arguedas and Duviols 1966; Durston 2007; Salomon and Urioste 1991; Taylor 1999). The "Huarochirí manuscript" is a complex combination of mythical and historical accounts referencing the battles and marriages between wak'as and humans, which created sociopolitical hierarchies and alliances; it also details the indigenous rituals that marked these affairs. The text has often been used as a surrogate primary historical source or interpretive aide (in many cases to cogent effect) for a variety of time periods and geographic areas in the Andes, despite the fact that it was compiled decades after the Spanish arrival to Peru (see Bourget 2001; Cornejo 2002; Eeckhout 2004a, 2004b, 2004c; Feltham 1983; Isbell 1997; Makowski 2002; Marcone and López-Hurtado 2002; Patterson 1985; Quilter 1990, 1997; Spalding 1984; Stern 1993). These treatments far outnumber archaeological investigations into the content of the manuscript itself (though these have been carried out; see, for example, Astuhuamán 1999, 2007; Bonavia et al. 1984; Farfán 2001, 2010; Spalding 1984:98–101). The archaeological field data discussed in this chapter are among the first to be gathered through systematic archaeological research in the areas of central concern to the Huarochirí manuscript's narrators.

Why "When" with "What"?

In a very basic sense, the importance of asking "When was a wak'a?" becomes obvious when the historical trajectory of the term is considered (Chase n.d.; Mannheim and Salas, this volume; Ramírez 1996:121–51). Certainly, a great deal would be lost with respect to our understanding of wak'as in the past if, for instance, we considered only the limited range of objects referred to colloquially as wak'as in modern-day Lima (wak'a generally referring to any of the monumental ruins that dot the capital city). There are also sound theoretical reasons for historicizing wak'a research. Elucidating the ontologies of wak'as and other agentive materials is important to the anthropological goal of understanding different times, peoples, perceptions, and practices. But to ensure that our expositions are not simply playing epistemological host to the asserted or accepted ideologies that our very data helped constitute, we must also investigate the specific contexts within which phenomena such as wak'as obtained cogency, and the realities to which they contributed (see Smith 2004). I suggest that the lenses of performance and performativity are particularly well suited for the investigation of wak'as. More specifically, I focus on performances of the past in the past, together with their performative efficacy (Austin 1962). By "performativity," I mean semiotic acts that bring about, or are intended to bring about, changes in the world, as opposed to those which merely describe or reflect current realities.

Performances of ritual and mythical narrative can mark or correspond to times that are important to the reproduction of society in physical, social, political, and cosmological ways. Performances also produce their own kinds of time in both micro- and macro-cosmic realms and may also be socially transformative (Babcock 1984; Bell 1997:160–62; Inomata and Coben 2006; Kertzer 1988; Swenson 2007, 2011; Turner 1969:166–203; Van Gennep 1960). This alteration of time may last only for the duration of the performance, or may actually establish new collective eras (Hughes 1995:5). As discussed by J. L. Austin (1962), when performative actions conform to established, collectively

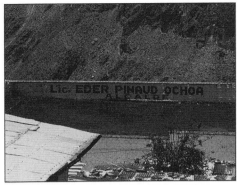

FIGURE 4.1. *Performative semiotics, politics, and temporality: (a) a painted statement on the inner wall of San Damián's soccer stadium declaring the fact of Eder Pinaud's status as mayor (photograph taken November 10, 2010); (b) the grammatically equivalent statement on a store wall near Peru's central highway (photograph taken November 11, 2010) declaring a desired future state of affairs in terms of a fait accompli in the present—an attempted performative utterance (photographs by author).*

understood social institutions and practices, they are "felicitous"; conversely, they are considered "infelicitous" when the utterance or the action and the external social world do not correspond. However, because performative actions by their nature may alter the world, I suggest that it is necessary to consider them on a continuum between felicity and infelicity *over time.*

Two modern Peruvian inscriptions illustrate this point nicely. The painted inscription observed in Figure 4.1a was a statement of fact: Eder Pinaud was indeed (municipal) mayor of San Damián at the moment this picture was taken. However, despite the simple declarative form of the second "inscription" (Figure 4.1b), Eder Pinaud was *not* regional mayor, as the text reads (nor did he win the position in 2011). Instead, this was a statement intended to perform a fact into existence through assertion—i.e., an attempted performative act that in time became definitively infelicitous. The ubiquity of such statements in political campaigns and any automatic or seemingly natural ability to interpret and categorize these as political propaganda only serve to underscore the intended point: material, verbal, and spatial performative acts are part and parcel of political struggles. And yet, if these inscriptions became the object of study hundreds or thousands of years from now, surely knowledge of the temporal performativity in play and of the signs' specific historical contexts would be crucial elements in more accurately reconstructing the past.

While in this example, the intention was to bring into reality a desired state of affairs by declaring a present objective as a future fait accompli—essentially a performance of the future, the focus in the present chapter is on the performative efficacy of wak'a-centered presentations of the *past* during the late prehispanic and early Spanish colonial periods in Huarochirí.

HISTORICIZED CHARACTERIZATION OF WAK'AS

On the basis of the combined ethnohistoric and archaeological data, I propose a definition for one specific type of wak'a associated with the central Peruvian highlands and coast pertaining to the specific time period mentioned (i.e., the late fifteenth to mid-seventeenth centuries). This definition is not meant to be comprehensive, but rather derives from a preponderance of local and historically specific evidence that supports a characterization of wak'as as sharing a core set of traits: wak'as were (1) agentive superhuman entities, though not inexorably separate from humans in a qualitative sense; (2) intrinsically material; and (3) not restricted by or to any particular thing—that is, wak'as were materially partitive but did not conform to any sharp semiotic division between signifier and signified.[1]

Again, this answer to the question "What is a wak'a?" is historically and regionally specific, and the particularities of this context must be taken into consideration. Historical documents dealing with wak'as were produced as an integral part of the antagonistic and aggressive religious campaigns intended to eradicate them. It is also true that Spanish Catholic influence on the practices and religious views of the indigenous can be detected in many of these texts (Salomon 1991; see also Mannheim and Salas, this volume). Nevertheless, it seems extremely unlikely that all of these basic, common aspects of wak'as were sui generis products of the Spanish colonial era.

Still, even provisional acceptance of such a unified characterization of wak'as from this time period requires further exploration of the temporal conditions and productive effects of specific wak'as. In order to do so, the different ways agency is discussed with respect to wak'as in this chapter must be briefly considered. In the first instance, wak'a agency is characterized by the activities of these entities as perceived and described by the native population. But, as mentioned earlier, "wak'a reality" was not limited to the subjective perception of indigenous Andeans. Because this agency was the emergent product of sociopolitical interactions between wak'as and human groups, wak'as were sociopolitically generative (Astuhuamán 2007; Bauer 1991, 1992; Gose 2008; Janusek, this volume; Patterson 1985; Salomon 1991; Topic et al. 2002; Urton

1990; van de Guchte 1999; Zuidema 1964, 1977–78) and were also temporally originary (discussed below).

As apical ancestors of kin groups, many of the mythical/historical deeds of wak'as served to win territories and create group identities and alliances. Their material presence in the living landscape marked complex residential patterns and corporate rights to land and other resources. In short, because wak'as and their attendant rituals frequently demarcated boundaries of various types (Bauer 1991, 1992, 1998; Isbell 1997; Meddens, this volume; Rostworowski 1988; Salomon 1991:19–24, 2004:68–69; Urton 1990; Zuidema 1964, 1977–78:149), temporal issues that may be archaeologically discernible (such as the history of a group's recognition of and cultic performance to geopolitically salient wak'as) should prove potent in reconstructing the past. With this approach, "the landscape of the gods becomes as informative as that of men" (to use Susan Alcock's [1993:172] expression), and the "transconquest Andes" (Wernke 2007) become more amenable to comparison with other areas of the world (e.g., Alcock 1993; Munn 1996; Polignac 1995; Sahlins 1985:58).

TEMPORAL IMPLICATIONS OF THE MATERIALITY AND INTERACTIVE AGENCY OF WAK'AS

Two examples of the temporal processes of the material emergence and recognition of wak'as demonstrate how their agency was as real and intrinsic to their existence as their materiality. This agency emerged from the *interaction* between wak'as and humans, even when the agentive action was held to have occurred between wak'as only (because such could only be known through human accounts).

The first example concerns the wak'as associated with the north-central highland region of Ancash and comes from the report of Rodrigo Hernández Príncipe's 1621 extirpation tour (Hernández Príncipe 2003 [1621]). The report is well-known among Andeanists for its description of an Inka *capacocha* (or *capac hucha*) ceremony from a provincial viewpoint (Duviols 2003:732–46; cf. McEwan, this volume). Hernández Príncipe's report details the genealogies of four groups descended from Carhua Huanca, a lithified regional wak'a associated with lightning. He focuses in particular on the lineage of Carhua Huanca's second son, the wak'a Caha Yánac, reporting that the elite governors of Ocros "worshipped" him "as their progenitor" (Duviols 2003:734). However, in Hernández Príncipe's rendering, this lineage's right to rule was not inherited from a pre-Inkaic,[2] apical ancestor-wak'a but rather was based upon the sacrifice of Tanta Carhua by her father Caque Poma. This capacocha sacrifice occurred perhaps a century prior to Hernández Príncipe's visit (Duviols 2003:734–35) and transformed Tanta Carhua into a wak'a. The ceremonial-political event earned Caque Poma Inka recognition as *kuraka* among his kin and within the larger community. Upon returning from Cuzco, the daughter Tanta Carhua was said to have been willingly entombed alive, perhaps atop a preexisting local wak'a (Zuidema 1977–78:739, 744). The tombs of both father and daughter became centers of ritual veneration.

The reciprocal interaction between the Inka and Caque Poma that led to the creation of a new wak'a and cemented Caque Poma's political station marked the beginning of a new era in Ocros (Duviols 2003:734–36).[3] It also produced what could be construed as "temporal feedback," whereby the past and the present informed one another recursively (cf. Bender et al. 1997; Clendinnen 1987; Farriss 1995; Gell 1992:37–53, 149–89, 221–41; Gillespie 1989, 2001; Gose 1996a, 2008; Hamann 2002, 2008; McAnany 1995; Munn 1992; Sahlins 1981, 1985:47, 104–35). Hernández Príncipe's description of the arrangement of deceased males of Caque Poma's lineage in their multi-chambered tomb structure is interpreted by Zuidema as being centered around Caque Poma's mummy: "It was Caque Poma's change of rank that awarded him the central position *with reference to his ancestors and descendants*" (1977–78:145; italics added).[4] In Ocros the creation of this wak'a coincided with a rearrangement of the "corporate history" to pivot on the transcendent figure who brought right of rule to the lineage. Hernández Príncipe warns that Caque Poma's was not a unique case and that there were other Indian leaders who had acquired their status in the same way (Duviols 2003:745; Kolata 2013:193–97).

In the second example, local-imperial political interaction and the inextricable relation between wak'as and kin groups are also important features, though here the exercise of agency by animate wak'as is more clearly on display. The example concerns how the wak'a Llocllay Huancupa revealed himself to the woman Lanti Chumpi while she was digging in her highland field. In their first encounter, the wak'a's form was so unremarkable that she "just threw it right back down on the ground" (Salomon and Urioste 1991:101). It was only after a second identical encounter with the same object that Lanti Chumpi considered that she might be dealing with a wak'a. The relation continues:

And so, thinking, "I'll show it to my elders and the other people of my ayllu," she brought it back. At that time there existed in the village named Llacsa Tampu another *huaca*, called Cati Quillay, an emissary of the Inca. Cati Quillay was . . . one who could force any *huaca* that wouldn't talk to speak. Saying, "Who are you?" "What is your name?" "What have you come for?" he started to make the *huaca* called Llocllay Huancupa talk. Llocllay Huancupa answered, saying, "I am a child of Pacha Camac ... My name is Llocllay Huancupa. It was my father who sent me here, saying "Go and protect the Checa village!" The people rejoiced exuberantly, exclaiming, "Good news! Let him live in this village and watch over us." (Salomon and Urioste 1991:101–2; italics in original)

Salomon provides crucial insight into the particularities of Llocllay's ratification as a wak'a, pointing out that the delivery of "this oracle was mediated by an Inca-sponsored wak'a [Cati Quillay]" and that Llocllay's father "Pacha Camac was also a heavily Inca-subsidized cult" (Salomon and Urioste 1991: 102n473).

Once the wak'a's identity, affiliation, and mission were confirmed, Lanti Chumpi's courtyard was enlarged to house it. But subsequent problems apparently arose:

[a]t one time, maybe because people didn't take good care of him, Llocllay Huancupa went back to his father Pacha Camac and disappeared. When the people saw this happen, they grieved deeply and searched for him, adorning the place where Lanti Chumpi had first discovered him, and building him a step-pyramid. But when they still couldn't find him, all the elders readied their llamas, guinea pigs, and all kinds of clothing, and went to Pacha Camac. So by worshipping his father again, they got Llocllay Huancupa to return. People served him even more, with renewed fervor, endowing him with llama herders ... declaring "These are llamas of Pacha Camac." The Inca also ratified this practice. ... As for maize offerings, they gave him maize belonging to the Inca from the common granaries, to provide for his drinks. (Salomon and Urioste 1991:102–3)

The account raises important temporal questions about wak'a agency and ontology. In terms of the material thing itself—that is, the twice-excavated object—when was it a wak'a? Was it a wak'a the whole time it was buried in the field? Was it only a wak'a following its (first or second) disinterment? Or was it only a wak'a once it had been identified by Lanti Chumpi and/or ratified by a politically important, state-sponsored wak'a? These are not merely rhetorical questions; timing in the process of Llocllay Huancupa's revelation, in the "commissioning" of the object as a wak'a, as well as its subsequent history suggest how wak'a agency emerged and operated within and among human individuals and groups (cf. Salomon 1998:8). The strong indication of Inka brokerage between regional wak'as and local groups is nuanced in the account by Llocllay's initial and insistent revelation to a common woman, and her initiating the process of his identification. The resulting impression is one of the emergence of wak'as as mediators at precise moments in Andean geopolitical relations.

When Else Is a Wak'a?

Further considerations of waka characteristics show them to be "originary" entities (cf. Moore 1995; Squair 1994) whose "intransigent" but partitive materiality and agency made them potent forces in the Andean past, as well as potentially unique avenues for developing archaeological understanding of that past. Here I apply the term "originary" in a broad sense to encompass a range of debates about the ways the past and present are materially and conceptually related. The drive to connect with the material past for any variety of present ends is virtually ubiquitous in human societies (see, e.g., Barkan 1999; Bradley 2002; Dietler 2005; Hamann 2002, 2008; Johnson 2006; Mayne 2008; Schnapp 1997). In politically charged processes like the production of social identity and claims of rights to natural resources, the ponderous "aura of naturalness that comes from deep historicity" (Smith 2004:3) is a powerful force, making the past itself a valuable "cultural resource." As originary entities, wak'as, together with their narratives or "histories," ordered the past and present for those who venerated them.

This originary character suggests that an archaeology of wak'as may hold great potential for understanding temporality and temporal perceptions in the Andean past. For example, the fact that wak'as of the Huarochirí manuscript were at once the beings that conquered and consorted in the originary past, possessed or exercised ongoing agency (Tello 1999:40), and were also particular material entities present in the living landscape, made experiences of "temporal collapse" possible through encounters between humans and wak'as. These powerful moments could occur spontaneously and unexpectedly (Taylor 1999:105, 349–57). But, as Salomon (1999:20) explains, there were also "methods of remembrance" and other activities that "accompanied an idea of the past as a parallel reality into which one could enter by ritual means, retrieving powerful knowledge and thereby influencing the future." In this sense, the materiality of wak'as meant that the causal and organizing principles of the present order (as derived from an originary past) were in many cases continually present and accessible to people. The agency of wak'as meant that this access could go both ways, providing avenues for the "invention of tradition" (Hobsbawm and Ranger 1983), whereby the present and the foundational, orienting past could be harmonized. These emic insights regarding the temporal significance of wak'as may be viewed in relation to historical events and processes. For instance, archaeological research directed toward uncovering the historical duration of ritual practices at or associated with a wak'a site may aid in detecting sociopolitical events and processes such as site and regional settlement, or the establishment of group alliances and collective identities (e.g., Astuhuamán 2007; Bauer 1991; Bauer and Stanish 2001; Reinhard and Ceruti 2011; Topic et al. 2002; Topic 1992, 2007). In turn, the wak'a characteristics explored up to this point—their agency, partitive materiality, and originary nature—provide new insights into how such entities figured in the creation of transregional community alliances during the Late Horizon. Such changes, expressed in narrative form as wak'a "biographies" or "pasts," were constructed over time, and their genealogical rankings adjusted with the shifting political fortunes and relations of the groups that venerated them.

Consideration of the temporal nature of wak'as permits archaeologists to explore how people in the Andean past made cultural order from the chaos of history. It should also lead to new discoveries and interpretations of extant archaeological data. The significance of such a focus can be seen in recent work at the site of Pueblo Viejo-Pucará (Makowski 2002; Makowski and Vega Centeno 2004; Makowski et al. 2005; see also Makowski, this volume). The site was a *mitmaqkuna* settlement of the Caringa who were relocated to the coast from the highlands of Huarochirí to guard the valley and the Inka flocks offered to Pachacamac (Rostworowski 2002b [1999]:181–83). Among the site's several ceremonial structures is a naturally occurring modified rock outcrop identified as a wak'a (see Makowski, this volume).

The highland Caringa's recognition of this mid-lower-valley wak'a, in contrast to the other entirely anthropogenic ritual structures at Pueblo Viejo-Pucará, offers a fascinating archaeological counterpart to the originary narratives characteristic of wak'as (see Arriaga 1968 [1621]:117–18; Castro de Trelles 1992 [1560]; Chase 2004; Duviols 1973:159, 1986, 2003; García Cabrera 1994; Gose 2008; Mills 1994, 1997; Salomon and Urioste 1991; Sánchez 1991; Topic 1992, 2007; Topic et al. 2002), and the data correspond exceedingly well to the specific ethnohistoric cases discussed above. Landscape-feature wak'as ostensibly carried autochthonous associations linking people to territory (Arriaga 1968 [1621]; Duviols 2003; García Cabrera 1994:163–65; but see Bauer 1998:25). In Pueblo Viejo-Pucará, it appears that the Caringa either recognized a new wak'a or identified the modified outcrop as a partitive manifestation of a preexisting wak'a from their homeland. In either case, in a new, imperially mandated situation, the people of this colony identified or adopted and united with this wak'a and were thus cosmologically situated within their new geographic and political setting. The archaeological data from this site vividly illustrate the indispensable nature of wak'as to human territorial inhabitation. Indeed, organized, collective being in the world without wak'as seems to have been inconceivable, which is perhaps why the absence of wak'as (whether stolen, lost, captured, or destroyed) is recorded as causing such grief, anxiety, and unease.[5]

These phenomena are indicative of a broader sociality than that between human actors only. The insistence on importing wak'as, adopting autochthonous wak'as, or having "epiphanous" wak'as (Makowski et al. 2005:310) revealed seems inherent to this sociality and should inform archaeological analysis of late prehispanic territorial expansion or colonization. Indeed, Pueblo Viejo's wak'a evinces the "expanded sociality" inherent to a *llacta*. Salomon (1991:23) defines this complex term as "the union of a localized *huaca* (often an ancestor-deity), with its territory and with the group of people whom the *huaca* favored." Because wak'as were material, agentive, and social, human settlement activities in the form of llactas "implie[d] both being possessor of a local *huaca*'s sanctum *and being possessed by it*" (Salomon 1991:23, emphasis added) as well as being enmeshed in the inherent territorial and genealogical adjuncts mentioned.

Pueblo Viejo-Pucará gives tangible testament to the generative, originary, and interactive dynamics referenced in the ethnohistoric observations discussed above. It shows archaeologists that the presence and involvement of wak'as in the sociopolitical and geographic production of landscape was not just an ideal or a verbal tradition. Indeed, late prehispanic settlements (qua llactas), in material fact and cosmological understanding, were wak'as (Salomon 1991:24). For example, the Checa narrators of the Huarochirí manuscript claimed that their ancestors conquered the llacta Llacsatambo and became "settlers" (*llactayucuna*) by adopting and being adopted by the local wak'as (*llactahuacacuna*) (Salomon 1991:24; Salomon and Urioste 1991:79–81, 117–19; Taylor 1999:160–71, 302–17).[6] This idea enhances traditional archaeological settlement analysis by infusing it with new cultural and historical meaning, while understanding of these wak'a characteristics should, in turn, lead to the generation of new data on settlements, sociopolitical alliances, even ethnogenesis.

Despite the illumination that Pueblo Viejo-Pucará's archaeological data provide, there are particular "biographical" details of its wak'a (as the Caringa understood and would have related them) that will likely remain unknown. How did the wak'a manifest within the newly ordered llacta of Pueblo Viejo-Pucará, and how and when was it recognized or commissioned as such? What was this wak'a's narrative past? Did the Caringa know this outcrop as

Pariacaca (Salomon and Urioste 1991:68–69, 75)? Or did they identify it as one of Pariacaca's kin, comparable to Tutayquiri or the wounded Chuqui Huampo, who stayed down-valley and was the first to receive offerings of coca from Sisicaya (Salomon and Urioste 1991:69, 80; Salomon and Grosboll 2009)? There is also the possibility that the wak'a was Chaupi Ñamca (Salomon and Urioste 1991:85), Pachacamac (Rostworowski 1992), or the offspring of one of these wak'as. As the case of Llocllay Huancupa shows, it is possible the outcrop was a completely new son or daughter of any of these wak'as. Discussion of comparable (but not hypothetical) scenarios is the subject of the next section.

Performing the Past in Huarochirí (ca. AD 1400–1700)

The Proyecto Arqueológico Huarochirí–Lurín Alto (PAHLA), which officially began in 2010, was organized to conduct archaeological and historical research in the Huarochirí region (Figure 4.2). The project was designed to investigate the different semioses—sign "actions" or "processes" (see Peirce 1998 [1907]:411)—involved in the ways the past was understood, codified, communicated, and made politically and socially operative through two phases of colonization in the area (i.e., by the Inka and the Spanish). The project involved full-coverage archaeological survey, surface collection, mapping, excavation, materials analysis, and historical research. To date, PAHLA has registered several dozen archaeological sites, mapped and excavated at four primary sites in Huarochirí (Llacsatambo, a series of Inka colcas, Cerro San Cristóbal, and the reducción pueblo of San Damián), and begun development of the first ceramic classification for the area (Chase et al. 2011).

The remaining portion of this chapter will discuss some of PAHLA's findings in the context of the prevalent historiography of the Huarochirí area (especially the sites the manuscript's narrators called home) and in relation to the ontological and temporal characteristics of the wak'a sites established thus far. In this analysis I have been able to draw from mythology, history, and the archaeological data to examine the temporal claims associated with wak'as in Huarochirí. This recent archaeological research in the epicenter of the region described in the Huarochirí manuscript has provided particularly important temporal information about Tutayquiri, the famous tutelary wak'a of the manuscript's Checa narrators. Before this research, scholarly knowledge of Tutayquiri was limited to manuscript narratives of his originary actions in a chronologically unspecified time, and some intriguing but conjectural information from historical documents (Ayala in Arguedas and Duviols 1966:252; Salomon and Urioste 1991:70, 79–83, 119–20, 128, 143, 152–53).

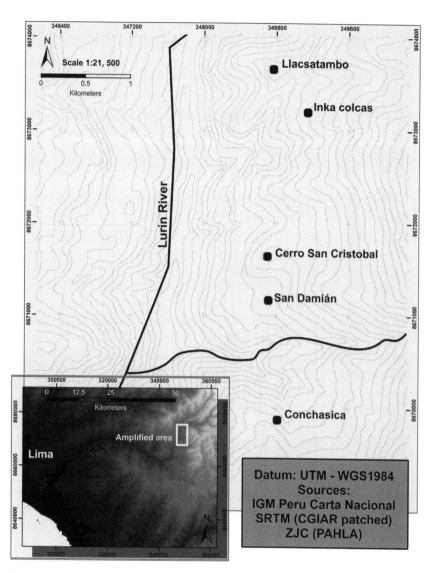

FIGURE 4.2. *The Proyecto Arqueológico Huarochirí–Lurín Alto (PAHLA) study area (2010–13) with major sites of investigation indicated.*

When Were the Wak'as of Huarochirí?

The idea that "[t]he past must be subjugated and harnessed in order to create the social order of the present" (Yoffee 2007:1) pervaded both the Inka and Spanish expansions. In such pursuits, "the past" was a potent and invaluable cultural resource (Appadurai 1981; Chase 2004; D'Altroy 2001:210; Flores Galindo 1987; MacCormack 1991; Patterson 1997; Silverblatt 1988; Urton 1990). Wak'as were such an important focal point for the agents of expansive polities and their "would-be subjects" (Comaroff and Comaroff 1992:236) precisely because of their originary associations. Cosmologies and political power were both the means and the stakes of these colonial struggles over the practical and interpretive control of the past. These dynamics, of course, complicate the task of reconstructing the "history" of these pasts. The preceding analysis indicates that a wak'a's past did not "just happen" but rather was performed. Wak'as were intrinsically tied to performative histories and collective identities. Such performative presentations constructed pasts that resonated with a desired present. However, this is not to suggest a wholly constructivist invention of tradition. As discussed earlier, while it is true that the efficacy of efforts to "perform the past" depend on creative appropriations of the past in the present (Kolata and Ponce Sangines 1992; Schnapp 1997:11–37; Smith 2004), it is also true that whatever the desired "present order" may be, it, too, is informed and conditioned by the lived past.

Chronological categorization of the Huarochirí manuscript's wak'as comprises a large part of the scholarship on the text and region (e.g., Astuhuamán 1999; Bueno 1992; Dávila Brizeño 1965 [1586]; Farfán 2010; Mejía Xesspe 1947; Rostworowski 2002a [1978], 2002b [1999]; Salomon 1991; Spalding 1984; Sykes 1990; Taylor 1999; Tello 1999:39–41). The periodization of the manuscript's contents has a long and complex history that cannot be fully discussed here. For our purposes it is sufficient to acknowledge María Rostworowski as having pioneered the historical reading of this text. In her ethnohistorical work she placed the manuscript in its local context, historicized the myths instead of considering them "eternal Andeanisms," and treated wak'as as temporal indicators (Rostworowski 1988, 2002a [1978]). For Rostworowski, the manuscript's myths encoded the history and prehistory of the central Peruvian highlands and coast. They were reflections of the pre-Inkaic Yauyos from the mountains to the south and east of Lima's Pacific coast, who had invaded Huarochirí's fertile river valleys, conquering and occupying new territories "in waves" for centuries prior to Inka and Spanish colonization of the area (Rostworowski 2002a [1978]:205).

In order to situate it historically, Rostworowski fit data from the manuscript and other early colonial documents into the established archaeological Intermediate period/Horizon model. Thus, wak'a narratives lacking reference to, or detectable traces of, Inka or Spanish colonial times are generally interpreted as *post hoc* explanations of occurrences in the Late Intermediate period or the late Middle Horizon (ca. AD 600–1100). These interpretations have become the virtually canonical version of the settlement history of the area.[7] Waldemar Espinoza Soriano, a historian whose influence on this topic approaches that of Rostworowski, sums up this "canonical" history in superlatives:

> When the Cusqueños arrived, the population of Huarochirí . . . had a long presence in these territories: hundreds of years of experience and a perfect knowledge of their ecology, traditions, legends, and myths. *Thus, the Inkas found this territory totally occupied, organized and being governed by leaders of Yauyo origin for centuries.* The aymara (aru) speaking ayllus and the other ayllus—yungas, or natives of Huarochirí enjoyed a well-known sedentary existence *of many centuries' duration.* Their constructions, fields and artisanal activities were so well managed under administrative control so efficiently exercised by their *curacas* and *capacuracas*, that the Inkas were impressed. . . . As pastors and agriculturalists, masters over multitudes, [the yauyos] ruled over the "yungas" population, *whom they had invaded four centuries earlier,* propagating themselves across a considerable area which almost reached the coast itself. This is why the Inkas respected them and acknowledged their rights over the fields, houses, water, and pasturage over which they had ruled ever since they defeated and had run the ancient yungas inhabitants out of the area . . . . The Inkas were not about to intervene in this internal organization of sayas, huarangas, and ayllus. *Everything remained intact.* (1992:120–21; translation mine; emphasis added)

A tripartite chronological classification (pre-Inka, Inka, and Spanish colonial periods) of settlement and activity in the area based on the ethnohistoric model has been adopted and applied by archaeologists who have published preliminary observations of sites central to the manuscript's redaction (Bueno 1992; Coello Rodríguez 2000; Coello Rodríguez and Díaz Arce 1995; INC 2008; Patrocinios and Tapia 2002). Given the rigor of the ethnohistoric research, the richness and detail of the Huarochirí text, the striking toponymic correspondence between the manuscript and sites on the ground, and even the apparent correspondence between ethnohistoric periodization and the surface architecture at sites, this ratification by archaeologists is understandable but unfortunate. Ethnohistorians like Rostworowski and Espinoza were making innovative interpretations by reaching beyond the limits of the historical data. Instead of investigating these interpretations with rigorous field research, archaeologists seemed content to overlay the ethnohistoric model onto the archaeological record of the region.

In general, I am in agreement with Rostworowski's instinct to treat the wak'as as historical, or even as "history" of their own sort. A historical and historicizing approach seems best suited to understanding wak'as and the Huarochirí manuscript. Wak'as have long been interpreted as allegorically representing long-term, telluric processes (Tello 1999:40).[8] And it is telling that Garcilaso's (1991 [1609], bk.I:76–77) detailed list of things that could be wak'as included "events" that were sufficiently anomalous or exceptional to be considered outside the flow or course of natural occurrences (though still materially so, as in the examples of an egg with two yolks or an unusually large Amazonian serpent). As Bauer (1998:23) has stated: "Most, if not all, of the huacas in the Cuzco ceque system represented contact points with important chthonic powers that were thought to have shaped the lives of the inhabitants of the region."

As may already be evident from what has been discussed, my argument is that wak'as like Tutayquiri emerged from, and in a sense were, historical events and/or processes. Further, I view Rostworowski's reading of the manuscript in terms of culturally specific idioms for communicating sociopolitical processes and events as the fundamentally correct interpretive approach. However, in my view, these cultural idioms are active tools of social and political construction, not merely reflections of sociopolitical processes. As we have established and will explore further below, the ethnohistoric and archaeological data challenge the unidirectional causality wherein wak'as and their narratives and rituals are mere post hoc reflections of history.

This predominant way of asking and answering the question "When were the wak'as of Huarochirí?" draws on and perpetuates a unidirectional model of time, history, tradition, and causality. However, once the originary, agentive, and material aspects of wak'as, their power in generating collective identities and their role in creating the sociality that united peoples, settlements, and territories are understood, this "traditional" historiography is exposed as insufficient. If wak'as were agents, they must be more than just vestigial expressions of the historical past. In short, if we are willing to take wak'as seriously, there must be other ways of asking "When?" If wak'a were originary entities, we should expect to pursue and find a plurality of temporal threads, as performative acts involving wak'as, people, and places created new pasts together with changing presents.

As mentioned, the Huarochirí manuscript was collaboratively composed by, and centers around, the Checa, a kin-based social and political group. At the time of the manuscript's composition, the Checa were politically situated as the "fifth of five" *waranqas* (or groupings of a thousand) in the Lower Yauyos "cluster" of Huarochirí (Salomon 2004:56–57). Mythological homology of this structure

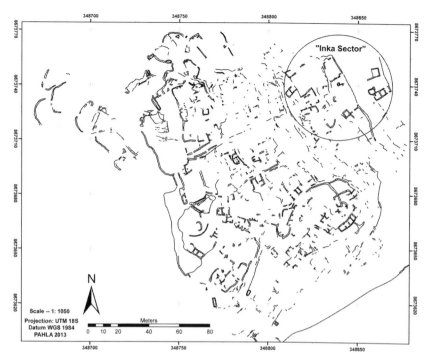

FIGURE 4.3. *Map of the architectural center of Llacsatambo.*

is found in descriptions of the partitive unity of Pariacaca, the snowcap mountain and apical ancestor-deity of these groups: though a single wak'a, Pariacaca was born as "five eggs that became five falcons that became five men, [who were in turn] the founders of" these five waranqas (Salomon 1991:6). The Checa tutelary deity Tutayquiri was one of Pariacaca's sons (Salomon and Urioste 1991:79).

In the 1580s, the Checa were forcefully resettled into the Spanish colonial *reducción* pueblo of San Damián, which, like all reducciones, was constructed specifically to "civilize," evangelize, and exploit indigenous populations by moving them from their "scattered" settlements into nucleated towns, thereby also severing their ties to pre- or non-Christian sacred places. But even two decades after the resettlements, i.e., by the ca. 1608 redaction of the Huarochirí manuscript, its Checa narrators still identified the hilltop site of Llacsatambo (2.5 km north of San Damián) as their social, political, temporal, and ritual focal point (Figure 4.3) (i.e., as their llacta).

Archaeological investigation of Llacsatambo reveals architecture, construction techniques, and spatial patterning at the site that seem, for the most

FIGURE 4.4. *Example of one of the many multi-chambered tombs at Llacsatambo (photograph by author).*

part, typical of Late Intermediate period occupations in the central Peruvian Andes, particularly in the areas of Yauyos, Huarochirí, and Canta (Casana 1976; Dillehay 1976; Lane and Luján Dávila 2012; Sykes 1990; Villar Córdova 1982 [1935]). The site seems to have housed ritual and periodic domestic/craft production activities: much of the standing architecture consists of single or multi-chambered tomb structures surrounded by walled patio or court spaces. There are, in fact, mortuary structures or elements in a majority of the site's sectors (see also Kosiba, this volume). In many cases the tombs have a domestic-like structure conjoined or situated nearby, though these are found most frequently within the walled patio space. The highest areas of the site are occupied by large, well-built, multi-chambered tombs (Figure 4.4).

The central area of Llacsatambo's apex comprises a large plaza flanked on two sides by retainer terraces. The northern end of the flat plaza abruptly abuts a rock outcrop that forms the highest spot on the site and that housed a tomb structure with a single large, framed opening. Though the outcrop gradually tapers down toward the east to meet the level of the plaza, a stone staircase

Figure 4.5. *Examples of Inka fineware sherds excavated and collected from Llacsatambo (photographs by author).*

was constructed upon this part of the slope, creating a two-sided step platform that leads to the highest tomb.

Surface collection and excavation at the site has produced hundreds of ceramic sherds representing medium- to large-sized food and liquid storage and serving vessels. The ceramic assemblage includes several pieces of typical Inka form and style (e.g., neck fragments and *"asas falsas"* from the Inka *urpu* [aríbalo] vessels used for serving *aqha*, or corn beer)[9] (Figure 4.5). Handles associated with food storage, serving, or preparation vessels make up more than 20 percent of the assemblage. Though analysis is still ongoing, broad patterns consistent with the collective feasting of shared ancestors are already apparent. Both archaeological and ethnohistoric evidence indicates that the site at times contained a concentration of ancestral remains and wak'as corresponding to (or being the necessary constituents of) various social and political relations (Chase et al. 2011; cf. Coello Rodríguez 2000; Patrocinios and Tapia 2002; Taylor 1999:247–65).[10]

In addition to feasting evidence, carbonized coca (*Erythroxilum* sp., *Erythroxilum coca*) remains were recovered in flotation samples from three of the excavation units at the site. Two of these units were set within domestic-like structures, and the third was placed directly in front of the access "window" to one of the prominent standing tombs at the top of the site.[11] Coca was a ritual substance sine qua non in the Andes and is referenced throughout the Huarochirí manuscript in the context of wak'a rituals at Llacsatambo (Salomon and Urioste 1991:67, 69, 71, 73, 99, 108). It is even once mentioned directly in connection with Llacsatambo (ibid.:74).

Llacsatambo was also the center for more overt performances of the past and political and social allegiances. These were performative acts that—in time—established a "new era" for the Checa. The Checa narrators of the manuscript did not immediately claim Llacsatambo as their place of origin. Rather, after providing a brief account of their place of origin at (the still geographically unspecified) Vichi Cancha, the narrators explain that once their wak'a Tutayquiri had conquered the Yunca ("yunga"; the lowland valley dwellers who ostensibly occupied the llacta prior to the Checa), they divided up the fields, houses, and villages that were left behind. Even extant wak'as were allocated, or "received" by the invaders (Salomon and Urioste 1991:119–20; cf. Gose 2008). One wonders if something similar may have happened or been said to have happened at Pueblo Viejo-Pucará. Following Tutayquiri's expulsion of the Yunca, the Checa gathered there and "danced their dance of origin, just as they'd once danced it in [their previous place of origin] Vichi Cancha" (Salomon and Urioste 1991:120). This act indicates the performative creation of an origin or "new past" whereby a people and a wak'a-conquered place were recursively defined and identified.[12] Tutayquiri's conquests were also the basis for broader Checa territorial claims in the early seventeenth century. Each November, a Checa pilgrimage beginning and ending at Llacsatambo ostensibly commemorated these conquests by imitating Tutayquiri's original movement through their territory (Figure 4.6).

In the ethnohistoric periodization mentioned above, this pilgrimage is interpreted as the ritual counterpart of the conquest myth, both of which were seen as reflections of actual invasions by ancestors of the Checa. In the "canonized" regional chronology that grew out of Rostworowski's study, Tutayquiri's conquest of Llacsatambo and of Checa territory would have taken place sometime between the Middle Horizon and the Late Intermediate period. This interpretation is likely based on two factors: (1) the apparent failure of the Checa narrators to place Tutayquiri's originary events in an explicit chronological framework, or at least in such a way that readily conforms to the

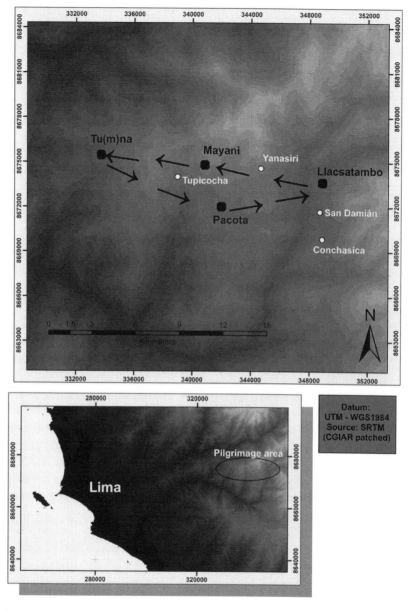

FIGURE 4.6. *Map of the Checa pilgrimage route based on Chapter 11 of the Huarochirí manuscript. While performing the annual ritual, the participants declared: "We go in Tutayquiri's steps. We go in the path of his power" (Salomon and Urioste 1991:80), ostensibly repeating their wak'a's originary territorial conquest.*

FIGURE 4.7. *Examples of Inka architectural features at Llacsatambo (photographs by author).*

intermediate period/horizon model, and (2) the 1611 Jesuit report of a mummy recovered in Santiago de Tumna (modern-day Santiago de Tuna, about 15 km west of San Damián) called "Tarayquiri," which was reported to be 600 years old (Arguedas and Duviols 1966:252). This periodization is problematic, as will be seen below.

References in the Huarochirí manuscript to Inka-Checa relations are generally phrased in terms of a loose, informal alliance based on Checa military service to the Inka, and the Inka fearing and feting the ancestors and wak'as of Huarochirí (Salomon and Urioste 1991:94–106). As they did in many areas, the Inka were said to have validated and even aggrandized the cultic activities of the locally situated population and built special spaces for the Checa's ancestors and wak'as. Indeed, preliminary archaeological examinations of Llacsatambo and the surrounding area seem to confirm this. The structures at Llacsatambo displaying the most characteristic Inka architectural traits (e.g., double-jamb windows and niches, orthogonal wall alignment, and trapezoidal access and communication points; Figure 4.7) cluster primarily on the northeastern slope of Llacsatambo's hill at a lower elevation than most of the other architecture. Unlike at other sites, the Inka-style buildings were not constructed in the most prominent spaces, as seen, for example, at Pachacamac (Uhle 2003 [1903]), nor were they placed over destroyed, local Late Intermediate period structures, as seen at Wat'a, near Cuzco (Kosiba 2010). As has been postulated elsewhere (Coello Rodríguez and Díaz Arce 1995; Coello Rodríguez 2000; Patrocinios and Tapia 2002), this pattern would seem to confirm Late Intermediate period occupation prior to the Inka arrival and the imperial additions to the site. This apparent architectonic "grafting" onto an extant site has been taken to suggest that the Inka colonization here involved alliance-building with the Checa. In this rendering, the Inka would seem to have reinforced Checa group identity by valorizing their llacta, just as they honored their wak'as.

Drawing on the architectural and spatial patterns of local, Late Intermediate period architecture recorded through systematic survey of the area around

FIGURE 4.8. *Panoramic photograph of Inka colcas (foreground) and Llacsatambo (background); both sites were excavated by PAHLA (photograph by Teddy Abel Traslaviña Arias).*

Llacsatambo, as well as information from other studies in adjacent areas (Casana 1976; INC 2008; Lane and Luján Dávila 2012; Thatcher and Hellmuth 1968–71; Villar Córdova 1982 [1935]), excavation units at Llacsatambo were strategically placed in what were thought to be representative Late Intermediate period built spaces and Late Horizon–Inka spaces at the site, as well as in the nearby Inka colcas (Figure 4.8), and the Spanish colonial pueblo of San Damián.[13] The objective was to investigate changes and continuities in practices related to performing the past at this Checa "place of origin" through the aforementioned episodes of colonization in the area. The focus was on architecture and other uses of space, practices of consumption and production, and (given the lack of previous archaeological work in the area) overall site and regional history.

Not surprisingly, excavations of the most obviously Late Horizon–Inka-influenced structures (Figure 4.9) yielded clear evidence of single occupations. It was sometimes difficult to detect whether the excavated structures had even been used due to the lack of stratigraphic deposition and artifacts. This evidence of a late and brief Inka presence in the area conformed to expectations. However, in every excavation unit associated with presumed local, Late Intermediate period Checa areas—even in mortuary sectors associated with ancestor veneration—the stratigraphic pattern was similar or identical to that of the units in the Inka structures, i.e., what we found was a single occupation situated directly atop bedrock. In fact, the two shallowest units were those placed in areas previously thought to have been the longest occupied based on architectural morphology (Figure 4.10). The only excavated evidence of secondary use or occupation was associated with the Spanish colonial period or later.[14]

FIGURE 4.9. *Stratigraphy in PAHLA excavation units in Late Horizon–style structures at Llacsatambo. The shallow deposition evincing a single, brief occupation of these structures conforms to accepted ethnohistorical interpretations of Llacsatambo and matched research expectations (photographs by author).*

These findings cannot be considered definitive, and, as always, more research and analysis is needed. We await, in particular, the dating of the carbon samples recovered from nearly every locus. However, the evidence as it stands does correspond well with the broad patterns posited in this chapter vis-à-vis llactas, wak'as, and the originary generation of collective, territorially connected identities. As opposed to the dominant chronological interpretations of Checa activity in the upper Lurín, it currently appears unlikely that there was a long Late Intermediate period occupation of Llacsatambo prior to the Late Horizon. The fact that this interpretation rests on (for the most part) simple stratigraphic evidence makes it more straightforward and reliable, as periodization based on ceramic or architectural style is proving to be increasingly problematic for the late periods in this area (Feltham and Eeckhout 2004; Feltham 2009; Makowski 2009).

While the possibility of activity at the site prior to the Inka arrival certainly still exists, all evidence thus far suggests a primarily Late Horizon construction and occupation of Llacsatambo. In addition to site stratigraphy, architecture, and ceramics, there is other evidence for Inka involvement with the site. The series of rectangular Inka colcas located about 600 m to the southeast of Llacsatambo were standard features at Inka provincial settlements (D'Altroy and Hastorf 1984; Hyslop 1990; Levine 1992; Morris and Thompson 1985; Topic and Topic 1993:30–33). The colcas were built on a terraced hillside at a

FIGURE 4.10. *Stratigraphy in PAHLA excavation unit in front of a large, Late Intermediate period–style tomb opening on the apex of Llacsatambo. The shallow deposition evinces a single, brief occupation of what were previously assumed to be Late Intermediate period structures (photograph by author).*

slightly lower elevation than the structures on Llacsatambo's apex. The main access point to the site faces the colcas nearly directly, and the storage structures can be seen from about 70 percent of the built space at Llacsatambo. It would have been very difficult for any at Llacsatambo to miss the architectural symbol of state subsidies for the ritual activities carried out at the site (see Salomon and Urioste 1991:113, 115–16). The colcas may in fact have provisioned those who built Llacsatambo.

Aside from a rustically elegant stone floor and a handful of plainware sherds used as fill, excavations in the Inka colcas yielded little cultural material. Flotation samples did turn up some very scant evidence of their possible use for potato storage.[15] In addition to these structures, there is also a magnificently preserved section of Inka road near Llacsatambo (Figure 4.11), with the longest sections running between the upper Lurín Valley and Llacsatambo (Coello Rodríguez 2000; Coello Rodríguez and Díaz Arce 1995; Hyslop

Figure 4.11. *Section of Inka road below Llacsatambo and Cerro San Cristóbal showing Late Horizon construction in and around the primary sites discussed (photograph by author).*

1984). While these features reinforce the diagnosis of Inka involvement with Llacsatambo, the stratigraphy is the most compelling evidence for the llacta being of Late Horizon origins.

Application of these data to the "traditional" Checa past presented by the narrators of the Huarochirí manuscript is similarly problematic. The stratigraphy does not support a historically literal reading of these narratives. If there had been a conquest and ousting of the site's previous inhabitants, we would expect some evidence of multiple occupations, even within structures that the narrators claimed were simply reoccupied. The "archaeological expectations" of "post holes or cane fragments to indicate Yunga houses" (Feltham 2005:133–34) have not been met at any of the four sites where PAHLA excavations were carried out.

The disjuncture between the seventeenth-century Checa account of their ancestors' past and the archaeological data likewise raises many questions. This represents an opportunity for reinterpretation of traditional histories of the region in light of the new ways of exploring and understanding wak'as and temporality presented in this chapter. The evidence strongly suggests that Tutayquiri, as associated with the Checa and Llacsatambo, was possibly a Late Horizon phenomenon, analogous to Pueblo Viejo-Pucará's wak'a (see Makowski, this volume). Was Checa identity as linked to Tutayquiri and Llacsatambo directly or indirectly a product of Inka imperialism (cf. Kolata 1992:217; 2013)? Can Checa insistence on their role as inheritors of the conquests of Tutayquiri and their nonautochthonous status in and around Llacsatambo be traced not to a "deep" history, but to the ripple-effect Late Horizon movements of Inka expansion (similar to the effects of the "Iroquois Hammer") (see White 1991), or perhaps even to colonization/settlement in service of the Inka? Both the archaeology and the documentary evidence make this explanation very compelling. In sixteenth-century court documents (Rostworowski 1988:148, 178), the Inka are clearly credited with "driving" the Yauyos' conquest of the Collique area—the precise terms the Checa used in narrating Tutayquiri's conquest of Llacsatambo. This prompts further questions into why (ca. AD 1600) the San Damián Checa told their originary story of Llacsatambo as they did in the Huarochirí manuscript.

If, as it appears, the ancestors of the Checa built Llacsatambo, the construction was a performative ritual that, together with the repetition of the other rituals and myths mentioned above, became "felicitous" over time. These performances of the past were reinforced in the present and reverberated into the future. They welded the Checa to Llacsatambo and the adjoining territory, to Tutayquiri, and to a new past—remembered and memorialized a century later as the conquest of an already inhabited llacta. But then, as we have seen, this is the way the cosmos "worked": wak'as were originary. Together with their llactas and people, they were the makers and markers of late prehispanic "history."

The possibility that the wak'a Tutayquiri emerged out of Late Horizon interactions between the Inka and the ancestors of the Checa should be seriously considered. Taken together, Tanta Carhua, Llocllay Huancupa, Pueblo Viejo-Pucará's wak'a, and the new archaeological data from Llacsatambo combine to make the case compelling. It may be that the relationship between the Inka and the Checa was mediated by the manifestation of a son of Pariacaca, one of the most prominent wak'as of the late prehispanic Andes.

THE ARCHAEOLOGY OF PARIACACA AT SAN CRISTÓBAL

Before concluding, I present one more archaeological case that builds on the preceding arguments and evidence. The originary, agentive, and partitive nature of wak'as is inseparable from cultural, social, and political existence in the late prehispanic Andes. As in the case of oracles associated with

FIGURE 4.12. *Cerro San Cristóbal with path spiraling around and up to the hilltop's stone platforms, topped with massive andesite boulders; one 2 × 2 m excavation unit was opened on one of the platforms (photograph by author).*

the Late Horizon studied by Gose (1996b; also Curatola and Ziółkowski 2007), the simultaneous existence of provincial and imperial wak'as in the Late Horizon allowed changing relations to be mediated through them. For example, Pariacaca was a wak'a already widely venerated across the central Peruvian highlands in the prehispanic period (Astuhuamán 2007). Insofar as this wak'a was adopted and promoted by the Inka, it was also able to serve as a "nodal" figure through whom both the Checa and the Inka were able to construct and navigate the "broad sociality" between peoples, wak'as, and territory discussed above.

With these ideas foregrounded, the evidence for the late origins and occupation of Llacsatambo and other sites in the PAHLA study area may shed light on finds at the 32 ha hilltop site of San Cristóbal and vice-versa (see Figure 4.12). This site directly overlooks the post-Toledan reducción of San Damián de Checa and is also roughly equidistant from, and within view of, Llacsatambo and Conchasica. The latter is the prehispanic llacta of the Concha, a group with whom the Checa seem to have had a tolerant, if condescending kin relationship under the apical ancestor Pariacaca. The manuscript narrators declare that "the Concha were the very last of Paria Caca's and Tutayquiri's offspring to be born, and the least prestigious of them" (Salomon and Urioste 1991:143).[16] But this claim comes after the explanation that of Pariacaca's children "the *Checa were born last*" (ibid.:79; emphasis added).[17] This may be an illustration of the ongoing negotiation of a mutually unsatisfactory union in an existence where llactas and lands were closely situated and connected. Conchasica's architecture and site layout are comparable to that of Llacsatambo, but it has an even lower density of surface artifacts,[18] giving cause to suggest that, like its Checa counterpart, it may also represent a primarily Late Horizon occupation.

San Cristóbal was not located on the basis of any clear reference given in the Huarochirí manuscript but rather through the PAHLA's systematic survey. The morphology of the site and its features suggest ritual functions of a periodic nature (e.g., there is no evidence of dense domestic architecture). Beginning at the hill's upper east side is an inclined causeway (averaging 3–4 m wide) that is supported by a retaining wall. The causeway spirals around and leads to the top of the hill. At about 220 m from its start, the path bifurcates. One branch leads to a platform constructed of medium- to large-sized fieldstones and earth. This platform is roughly rectangular in shape and is demarcated by five large andesite boulders. The other continues to spiral up the hill for another 50 m or so from where it divides. It is flanked by more stone platforms as it leads up and around to the roughly planed hilltop. This area forms something of a plaza space surrounded by five rustic, mostly single-tiered platforms. One of the platforms supports a green wooden cross measuring 8 m tall, which links with the hill's Christian name.

In addition to surface collections made at the site, the easternmost platform (with the five andesite boulders) was partially excavated, with a 2 × 2 m test pit placed over the structure's western edge (Figure 4.13). This edge of the platform, which faces the plaza, may have been the only side made of cut stones (or ones that were at least aligned) to create a planar exterior face. This side included, if not a second tier, then at least a second step leading up to the platform's top and center. The platform's interior structure was designed to embed and buttress it against the hill's disintegrating, granular bedrock. Among the fieldstone, earth, and ash comprising the platform structure fill were high densities of pottery sherds (n = 3,110; wt. = 12.07 kg) and faunal remains (n = 1,812; wt. = 2.49 kg) far exceeding the weights and counts of materials from any of the excavation units at the other three sites examined within the project area.

Figure 4.13. *Stone platform excavation unit (2 × 2 m) on Cerro San Cristóbal that yielded the copper hand and egg artifact and "egg-stone ancestor" as well as other evidence of the platform having been built in a single construction event (photograph by Teddy Abel Traslaviña Arias).*

The excavation unit at San Cristóbal reached a depth of 1.7 m, at which point an immense boulder that seems to have served as a foundation for the platform was found abutting bedrock.

Within this excavation unit, in a locus that contained very compact soil suggestive of heavy foot traffic—presumably of those who would have been approaching the platform—an item of finely crafted metal was uncovered at a depth of about 30 cm below the original ground surface (Figure 4.14). The artifact, measuring about 3 cm in length by 2.3 cm in height by 1.3 cm in width, is in the form of a hand grasping what appears to be an egg. It appears to be either the hook for a projectile rod ("spear thrower") or a crafted object comparable to naturally occurring *illas*, which were thought "to contain the fecundating essence of the good they represented" According to González Holguín's definition from the same time as the Huarochirí manuscript's composition (cited in Taylor 1999:139n87), illas were believed to produce general wealth for

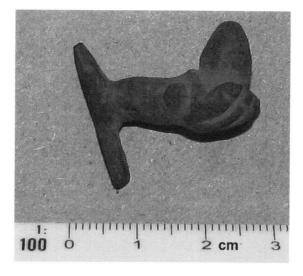

FIGURE 4.14. *Copper "hand with egg" from 30 cm below the surface immediately adjacent to the stone platform on Cerro San Cristóbal; the piece could be the hook of a "spear thrower" or a fecundity amulet (photograph by author).*

the owner. Interestingly for the case presented here, González Holguín mentions "vn hueuo" as an example of the shape these illas could take. The results of X-ray fluorescence have shown the amulet to be made of copper.[19]

Further down, at a depth of about 1.5 m below surface in the same unit, a stone worked into the shape of a large egg was uncovered at the interface between the bedrock and the immense foundation boulder (Figure 4.15). The stone measures approximately 20 × 16 cm and has a pecked and flattened base that allows it to stand upright. Significantly, unlike the bedrock underlying the rest of the hill, the stone egg appears to be made of the same white andesite as the boulders on the upper surface of the platform. Further, the egg was accompanied by large flakes that preliminary refitting suggests match the cortex scarring observed on the surface of these boulders.

The intentional burial of the stone egg and the large flakes and the site's location relative to San Damián as well as to the prehispanic llactas are equal parts compelling and vexing. The platform at San Cristóbal could represent the burial of a wak'a to protect it against extirpation during the colonial period, or it could have been a shared or even mediating boundary marker for the pre-reducción era Checa and Concha. Of course, it is also possible that both scenarios could be correct. Faunal evidence makes it clear that the site has been used in modern times, but the presence of goat, pig, and cow bones ceased in the lower loci, where only alpacas, deer, and llama could be positively identified.[20]

FIGURE 4.15. *White andesite "egg–stone ancestor" excavated from Cerro San Cristóbal platform; the artifact recalls other "stone ancestors" recently excavated from a Late Horizon stone platform as well as the egg morphology associated with apical wak'a Pariacaca (photograph by author).*

Among the many connections these finds evoke, the majority of the data suggest Late Horizon associations. The stone egg may be included among the "stone ancestors" made of white and red andesite recently discovered and presented by Meddens et al. (2010; see also Meddens, McEwan, this volume). Like the egg stone, these stone ancestors were found buried within high-altitude platforms. Meddens et al. (2010:177) explain that their stone platform is one of a class that is "closely associated with the notion of *boundary* or *liminal space*" (emphasis added). This observation resonates with the location of the San Cristóbal platform between Llacsatambo and Conchasica. It is important to note here that the platform sites and stone ancestors reported by these investigators were Inka and not Huari (see Cook 1992), further suggesting that San Cristóbal's stone egg should be associated with the Late Horizon and not projected into earlier periods. Of equal significance for understanding the past in this area of Huarochirí is the egg morphology of the artifacts and the imagery related to Pariacaca.

The fact that the stone egg and the flakes from the andesite boulders topping the platform were interred almost directly upon the local bedrock constitutes evidence of a single construction episode. In general, the basic morphology, material, composition, and location of the egg stone all seem characteristically

Inka (cf. Meddens et al. 2010:182–83). But these aspects also seem to correspond to the wak'a Pariacaca, who "was born" and "dwelled as five eggs." Stone eggs (*runtu*) alone or in sets feature prominently in the seventeenth-century documents as "idols" in areas where Pariacaca's cult had spread, most probably during the Late Horizon (Archivo Arzobispal de Lima, Leg. III, exp. 10 [1656], 6v, 8r; Astuhuamán 2007:109–10; Duviols 1973:168; 2003; Polia Meconi 1996 [1611–13]:213; Salomon and Urioste 1991:54, 57, 92).

Other data suggesting a Late Horizon association for this site include the Inka road noted above, which leads to the point on the hill where the causeway would have been accessed. In addition, fragments of a spouted zoomorphic bottle of the kind Topic and Topic (1993:25) associate with the Late Horizon were excavated from the platform at San Cristóbal, and a surprising 40 percent of excavated ceramic fragments from the platform consisted of strap handles, which is also consistent with a Late Horizon occupation of San Cristóbal (ibid.:36). In addition, the copious amount of ash, carbon, and faunal materials mentioned (including an entire deer antler) are comparable, though on a much smaller scale, to excavated contexts at other Late Horizon platforms (see Ziółkowski 2007:141).

These data suggest the possibility that San Cristóbal constituted a shared Concha-Checa boundary that was mediated by Pariacaca in the same way that their kinship, their relation with the Inka, and their llactas were. Various scholars have demonstrated that the Inka promotion of Pariacaca throughout Chinchaysuyu was part of their imperial expansion (Astuhuamán 1999, 2007; Salomon 1991). If Llacsatambo and Conchasica were settled as part of an Inka-associated Late Horizon push into the upper Lurín, it was surely as "Pariacaca's children" (Salomon and Urioste 1991:143). The view of and from San Cristóbal is one of the development and operation through time of kin-related wak'as like Tutayquiri and Pariacaca, and wak'a-related kin like the Concha and Checa, in regional settlement and in the creation and maintenance of sociopolitical relations during the Late Horizon.

CONCLUSIONS

The most basic argument of this chapter is, very simply, that wak'as can best be understood ontologically when considered temporally. There are many reasons for this, which have been reviewed and examined above, but the primary thrust is that wak'as of the central Peruvian highlands during the late fifteenth to mid-seventeenth centuries comprised a set of characteristics that make them not only amenable to archaeological and historical investigation, but downright revelatory with respect to the Andean past, if approached and understood in the right ways. Wak'as were agentive, material, partitive, and originary. Sociopolitically, and in terms of cosmic and geographic belonging, wak'as were indispensible. Researching them with the temporal dynamics of performativity in mind offers a more complete and accurate understanding of the Andean past. Indeed, this chapter has reviewed several exciting new developments that have come about from the probing of the temporal aspects of wak'as and the consideration of the attendant implications of their temporality to various spheres of life.

Several of the wak'a characteristics presented in this chapter—e.g., their territorial, material, and ontological divisibility, their originary cosmological and sociopolitical nature, and their role in expansive territorial, social, and political networks—echo and reinforce the conclusions of other Andean scholars, such as Astuhuamán (1999, 2007) on Pariacaca and Pachacamac and Topic (1992, 2007, this volume) on Catequil in Huamachuco, among others (see also Bauer 1998:25; Topic et al. 2002; Ziółkowski 2007). In addition, PAHLA's findings thus far in Huarochirí coincide remarkably with Topic's (1992, 1998) conclusions regarding the relationship between the Inka province of Huamachuco, its inhabitants' creation myth, and the wak'a Catequil. As Topic et al. (2002:308) note, the "very close correspondence between the creation myth [involving Catequil] and the boundaries of the Inkaic province of Huamachuco may only date to the Late Horizon."

In comparison, I have argued that the archaeological data indicate that the collective identity of the seventeenth-century Checa as a *unified* llacta (i.e., as an amalgam of social relations/kin group/ceremonial center/ territory/wak'a) began in the Late Horizon, and suggest the possibility that, by implication, the wak'a Tutayquiri emerged in the context of Late Horizon interactions that placed the Checa at Llacsatambo. Through various performative actions (e.g., migration, building Llacsatambo, the dancing of the origin dance, housing and serving wak'as and ancestors at Llacsatambo, and the production of cultural landscape through pilgrimage and oral tradition), the new imperial order was codified within a regionally cogent, idiomatic-vernacular structure (i.e., as invading highlands ancestor-deities conquering villages and territory by driving out the "previous" chthonic inhabitants with whom the wak'a's descendants share complementary but oppositional geographic, economic, sociopolitical, temporal, and religious relationships). In the decades preceding the composition of the Huarochirí manuscript (as well as contributing to numerous other civil-religious "writing events"), these performative practices became "felicitous" in Checa consciousness, history, and cosmology as they worked to "concretize" (Urton 1990:126) the group's identity by virtue of its shared, spatially and materially identifiable past.

Archaeological investigation of wak'as, as they have been presented and explored in this chapter, will continue to illuminate our understanding of Andean pasts and the history of these pasts. In pairing "wak'a ontology" with questions of wak'a temporality, whole new lines of inquiry emerge, which can be followed to important new findings "on the ground" and which will, in turn, continue to provide new interpretive possibilities. In time we may come to understand and appreciate wak'as for the "reality" that they were and continue to be.

ACKNOWLEDGMENTS

I am most grateful for my advisor Alan Kolata's initial suggestion that I undertake the archaeology of Huarochirí and for his continued guidance, inspiration, support, and friendship, which are all invaluable. The research upon which this chapter is based could not have been carried out without the legal co-directorship and generous friendship of Lic. José Luis Pino Matos. I also wish to thank Teddy Abel Traslavña Arias, Lic. Abraham Magno Imbertis Herrera, Lic. Giovanna P. Bravo Castillo, Alexander Menaker, Diego Agustín Rebatta Gómez, as well as all of the other archaeologists who contributed so much to PAHLA. Further thanks go to Victor Falcón Huayta and Amalia Ibáñez Caselli, who generously worked on the figures, and to Thomas Patterson for his sharing of the 1968–71 field notes. The project was carried out under Resolución Directoral Nacional no. 1559. Licenciada Mónica de la Vega Romero carried out the Acta de Supervisión and Lic. Claudia Bastante reviewed the materials for custody. I thank Peru's Ministry of Culture for working to facilitate this ongoing research. Special gratitude is also expressed to Dain Borges, Adam Smith, Shannon Dawdy, Frank Salomon, Krzysztof Makowski, Juan Ossio, Marco Curatola, Karen Spalding, and the Programa de Estudios Andinos and the Departamento de Ciencias Sociales of the Pontificia Universidad Católica del Perú.

The project has been funded by Fulbright Hays, the Mellon Foundation, the Tinker Foundation, the University of Chicago's Center for Latin American Studies and Social Sciences Division, and the Workman, Maycock, Fuller, and Chase families. My gratitude also goes to Tamara Bray for organizing the events that led to this volume as well as to the events' participants for their intellectual inspiration and feedback. All errors are, of course, my own.

NOTES

1. On the notion of wak'as as agentive, see Salomon and Urioste 1991:50–62, 67, 101, 113–28; Arriaga 1968 [1621]:49; Archivo Arzobispal de Lima, Leg. IV, exp. 24; on "ontological continuity" between wak'as and humans, see Arriaga 1968 [1621]:23–24, 31; Duviols 1973:158, 162; Garcilaso 1991 [1609]:77; Gose 2008; Salomon 1991, 1995, 1998; Salomon and Urioste 1991:46n44, 125–28; Taylor 1999:324–27; on the materiality of wak'as, see Arguedas and Duviols 1966:252; Arriaga 1968 [1621]:83–84, 85, 88, 89; Hernández Príncipe 2003 [1621]:735, 745; Misión de los jesuitas a las provincias de Ocros y Lampas in Duviols 2003:721–30; also cf. Cabello Balboa 1951 [1586]:328–29; Demarest 1981; Gose 2008:94–117; MacCormack 1991; Millones 1990; Salomon and Urioste 1991:79–80; Topic 2007:80; Urbano 1993; on the partitive nature of wak'as, see Astuhuamán 2007; Dean 2010:40–41; Polia Meconi 1996 [1611–13]: 213; Salomon 1991:6; Salomon and Urioste 1991:59, 61–62, 66, 68, 80, 115, 127; also cf. Strathern 1988; on the lack of division between signifier and signified in relation to wak'as, see Astuhuamán 2007; Cabello Balboa 1951 [1586]:328–29; Topic et al. 2002:207; Topic 2007:80.

2. In the genealogy, Caque Poma (alive during the Inka expansion around the end of the fifteenth/ beginning of the sixteenth centuries) was five generations from apical ancestor and lightning wak'a Carhua Huanca (Duviols 2003:734).

3. While Tanta Carhua is not explicitly referred to as a wak'a in Hernández Príncipe's report, I maintain that treating her *Capacocha* burial site as a wak'a is justified on many counts (cf. Salomon 1995:332). For example, there was kin-based and other priestly cultic and oracular practice carried out at the tomb (Duviols 2003:744–45; Zuidema 1977–78:141) as well as regional worship of Tanta Carhua (Zuidema 1977–78:146), an ushnu was constructed at the site (Duviols 2003:745), and there were Inka state fields kept for the maintenance of her cult (ibid.:742).

4. Though not altering the principal elements of my interpretations, I note potential problems with Zuidema's reading and exposition of this document, which will be addressed in an upcoming work (Chase n.d.).

5. For destroyed wak'as see Arguedas and Duviols 1966; Cabello Balboa 1951 [1586]:328–29; Duviols 2003; García Cabrera 1994; Griffiths 1996; Mills 1997; Millones 1990; Salomon and Urioste 1991:126; Topic 2007:80. For lost wak'as, see Salomon and Urioste 1991:102. For stolen, sequestered, or vanished wak'as see Cobo 1990 [1653]:91–95; D'Altroy 2002:142, 222–23; 2005; Hernández Príncipe 1919 [1613]:184; Salomon and Urioste 1991:100, 120; Sarmiento 1999 [1572]:165–66; Spalding 1984:63.

6. See Taylor (1999:314, 482) for instances in the Huarochirí manuscript where "the gloss 'local *huaca*'. . . corresponds to the Quechua term *llacta*" (cf. Duviols 2003:733). See also Taylor (1999:20; emphasis added) for an instance of "*huacas locales*" being translated from the compound plural "*llactahuacacunapas*."

7. Note, however, the careful language of Salomon and Grosboll (2009:21; emphasis added) in referring to the Huarochirí manuscript myths as "allegorically representing the *protohistoric* movements of Yauyos . . . towards the coca fields and the coast." Though they note (ibid.:22) that these movements have been periodized *by archaeologists* as spanning the Late Intermediate period and Late Horizon, they leave open the possibility that these "incursions" took place later than has frequently been asserted.

8. There has been a long, if intermittent tradition of viewing the Huarochirí wak'as this way. Dávila Brizeño (1965 [1586]:161) interpreted the oral tradition of the titanic clash between the telluric, fiery Huallallo Caruinco and the stormy, aquatic Pariacaca as mythical description of a geological process in the high, snowy western cordillera. For the Spanish bureaucrat, what was described as Pariacaca's extinguishing of Huallallo's infernal flames was actually the creation of a highland lake (Mullu Cocha) as the result of an extinguished volcano's caldera being inundated with the water from snow runoff. It is difficult not to make comparable geological interpretations of the story of the female wak'a Caui Llaca fleeing from Anchi Cocha in the mountains towards Pachacamac on the coast, with male wak'a Cuni Raya in pursuit (Salomon and Urioste 1991:47–50). Because the Lurín Valley and river run between Anchi Cocha and Pachacamac, the myth presents the female wak'a as valley and the male wak'a as fluid, combining in the creation of a fecund, fertile river valley. In these examples wak'as seem to correspond to activity in the realm of the geological *longue durée* (Braudel 1995 [1966]).

9. The paste of these sherds is a single, well-fired type that is so far associated only with Inka wares at Llacsatambo. The paste type and inclusions match that described by Feltham (2009:96) as typically Cusqueño ("Tanto la cocción como la pasta son diferentes de las del Intermedio Tardío, pues la alfarería cusqueña tiene color naranja vivo o beige claro, con inclusiones redondas, rojas y negras"). This description of Late Horizon Inka wares from Sisicaya, located lower down in the Lurín Valley from Llacsatambo, serves as well for the Late Horizon Inka wares recovered at Llacsatambo.

10. In the Huarochirí manuscript, Llacsatambo is associated with at least five different wak'as: Pariacaca, Tutayquiri, Maca Uisa, Llocllay Huancupa, and Cati Quillay (Salomon and Urioste 1991:74, 79, 99, 101, 103).

11. While the author was responsible for soil processing, sample flotation and macrobotanical analysis was supervised by Lic. Gabriela C. Bertone and Paula Espósito.

12. Taylor (1999:319) discusses the implications of the Quechua terms used in this section (variants on the root *pacari-* which denote emergence, origins, dawning, the moment of appearance, etc.) and their undeniable connection to specific places (*pacarinas*), not of occupation but original emergence of a social collective. See also Santo Thomas 2006 [1560]:391–92; González Holguín 1989 [1608]:266–67.

13. A total of ten test units were excavated at these sites. Seven of these units measured 2 × 2 m, while three measured 1 × 2 m. Six of the 2 × 2 m units were placed at Llacsatambo, while one was placed inside the Inka colcas (located about 600 m southeast of Llasatambo). The six Llacsatambo units were located on the plaza (*n* = 2), in Inka-style small administrative or domestic structures (*n* = 2), and in what were thought to be local, Late Intermediate Period domestic structures (*n* = 2). One of the 1 × 2 m units was placed in the Inka colcas, and two were placed on the plaza of San Damián.

14. In one unit, half of a blue Nueva Cádiz glass bead and the bottom of a well-fired, wheel-thrown sherd were recovered.

15. Carbonized potato (*Solanaceae, Solanum* sp.) remains were found in both colca excavation units, but the counts were low (*n* = 5 ; *n* = 19). Each also had negligible counts of quinoa (Chenopodium quinoa; *n* = 1), and one possibly had *ají* (*Capsicum* sp.; *n* = 1).

16. The Concha were also reduced into San Damián de Checas.

17. I write "after" based on my impression that the thirty-first and final full chapter of the Huarochirí manuscript, the only chapter to treat the Concha as the primary subject, was composed after the rest of the manuscript by assignment of Francisco de Avila.

18. This is a perfunctory determination as Conchasica has not yet been systematically examined by PAHLA.

19. The XRF procedure and analysis was carried out by Mirian Mejia of the Facultad de Ciencias Físicas and Dr. Jorge Bravo of the Laboratorio de Arqueometría at the Universidad Nacional Mayor San Marcos.

20. The faunal analysis was carried out by Víctor Vásquez Sánchez and Theresa Rosales Tham of ARQUEOBIOS laboratory in Trujillo, Peru, in August 2013.

REFERENCES CITED

Archivo Arzobispal de Lima, Sección de Hechiceriás e Idolatriás, Leg. III, exp. 10 [1656], 6v, 8r.

Alberti, Benjamin, and Tamara L. Bray. 2009. "Introduction: Special Section: Animating Archaeology: of Subjects, Objects and Alternative Ontologies." *Cambridge Archaeological Journal* 19 (3): 337–43. http://dx.doi.org/10.1017/S09597 74309000523.

Alcock, Susan. 1993. *Graecia Capta: The Landscapes of Roman Greece*. Cambridge: Cambridge University Press.

Allen, Catherine. 1998. "When Utensils Revolt: Mind, Matter, and Modes of Being in the Pre-Columbian Andes." *RES* 33:18–27.

Arguedas, José María (translator) and Pierre Duviols (editor). 1966. *Dioses y hombres de Huarochirí: Narración quechua recogida por Francisco de Avila [¿1598?].* Lima: Instituto Francés de Estudios Andinos and Instituto de Estudios Peruanos.

Appadurai, Arjun. 1981. "The Past as a Scarce Resource." *Man* 16 (2): 201–19. http://dx.doi.org/10.2307/2801395.

Arriaga, Pablo José de. 1968 [1621]. *The Extirpation of Idolatry in Peru.* Trans. and ed. L. Clark Keating. Lexington: University of Kentucky Press.

Astuhuamán Gonzáles, César W. 1999. "El Santuario de Paricaca." *Alma Mater, Revista de investigación de la Universidad Mayor de San Marcos* 17:127–47.

Astuhuamán Gonzáles, César W. 2007. "Los otros Pariacaca: Oráculos, montañas, y parentelas sagradas." In *Adivinación y oráculos en el mundo andino antiguo,* ed. Marco Curatola Petrocchi and Mariusz S. Ziółkowski, 97–119. Lima: Fondo Editorial, Pontificia Universidad Católica del Perú.

Austin, John L. 1962. *How to Do Things with Words.* Cambridge, MA: Harvard University Press.

Babcock, Barbara. 1984. "Arrange Me into Disorder: Fragments and Reflections on Ritual Clowning." In *Rite, Drama, Festival, Spectacle: Rehearsals toward a Theory of Cultural Performance,* ed. John MacAloon, 102–28. Philadelphia: Institute for the Study of Human Issues.

Barkan, Leonard. 1999. *Unearthing the Past: Archaeology and Aesthetics in the Making of Renaissance Culture.* Princeton, NJ: Princeton University Press.

Bauer, Brian. 1991. "Pacariqtambo and the Mythical Origins of the Inca." *Latin American Antiquity* 2 (1): 7–26. http://dx.doi.org/10.2307/971893.

Bauer, Brian. 1992. "Ritual Pathways of the Inca: An Analysis of the Collasuyu Ceques in Cuzco." *Latin American Antiquity* 3 (3): 183–205. http://dx.doi.org/10.2307/971714.

Bauer, Brian. 1998. *The Sacred Landscape of the Inca: The Cuzco Ceque System.* Austin: University of Texas Press.

Bauer, Brian, and Charles Stanish. 2001. *Ritual and Pilgrimage in the Ancient Andes: The Islands of the Sun and the Moon.* Austin: University of Texas Press.

Bell, Catherine. 1997. *Ritual: Perspectives and Dimensions.* Oxford: Oxford University Press.

Bender, Barbara, Sue Hamilton, and Christopher Tilley. 1997. "Leskernick: stone worlds; alternative narrative; nested landscapes." *Proceedings of the Prehistoric Society* 63:147–78. http://dx.doi.org/10.1017/S0079497X00002413.

Bonavia, Duccio, Fabiola León Velarde, Monge C. Carlos, María Inés Sánchez-Griñan, and José Whittembury. 1984. "Tras las huellas de Acosta 300 años después. Consideraciones sobre su descripción de "mal de altura."." *Histórica* 8 (1): 3–31.

Bradley, Richard. 1998. *The Significance of Monuments: On the Shaping of Human Experience in Neolithic and Bronze Age Europe*. London: Routledge.

Bradley, Richard. 2002. *The Past in Prehistoric Societies*. London: Routledge.

Braudel, Fernand. 1995 [1966]. *The Mediterranean and the Mediterranean World in the Age of Phillip II*, vol. 1. Berkeley: University of California Press.

Brown, Bill. 2003. *A Sense of Things: The Object Matter of American Literature*. Chicago: University of Chicago Press. http://dx.doi.org/10.7208/chicago/9780226076317 .001.0001.

Brown, Linda A., and William H. Walker. 2008. "Prologue: Archaeology, Animism and Non-Human Agents." *Journal of Archaeological Method and Theory* 15 (4): 297–99. http://dx.doi.org/10.1007/s10816-008-9056-6.

Bourget, Steve. 2001. "Rituals and Sacrifice: Its Practice at Huaca de la Luna and its Representations." In *Moche Art and Archaeology in Ancient Peru*, ed. Joanne Pillsbury, 89–110. New Haven, CT: Yale University Press.

Bueno Mendoza, A. 1992. "Arqueología de Huarochirí." In *Huarochirí: Ocho mil años de historia*, vol. I, 13–66. Lima: Municipalidad de Santa Eulalia de Acopaya.

Cabello Balboa, Miguel 1951 [1586]. *Miscelánea Antártica*. Lima: Facultad de Letras, Instituto de Etnología, Universidad Nacional Mayor de San Marcos.

Casana Robles, Teodoro. 1976. *Restos arqueológicos de la Provincia de Canta*. Lima: Colegio Militar Leoncio Prado.

Castro de Trelles, Lucila, ed. 1992 [1560]. *Relación de la religión y ritos del Perú hecha por los Padres Agustinos*. Lima: Fondo Editorial, Pontificia Universidad Católica del Perú.

Chase, Zachary James. 2004. "Materiality and Meaning: Views of the Spiritual Life of Things in the Seventeenth-Century Archdiocese of Lima." Master's thesis, University of Chicago.

Chase, Zachary James. n.d. "Pasts Present and Future: Andean Wak'as in History and Time." Unpublished manuscript.

Chase, Zachary J., Magno Imbertis Herrera Abraham, and Enrique Paredes Sánchez Luis. 2011. *Informe técnico: Proyecto arqueológico huarochirí–lurín alto*. Archived at the Ministry of Culture, Lima, Peru.

Clendinnen, Inga. 1987. *Ambivalent Conquests: Maya and Spaniard in Yucatan, 1517–1570*. Cambridge: Cambridge University Press.

Cobo, Bernabé. 1990 [1653]. *Inca Religion and Customs*. Ed. and trans. Roland Hamilton. Austin: University of Texas Press.

Coello Rodríguez, Antonio. 2000. "El Camino inca en el distrito de san damián (provincia de huarochirí) Perú." In *Caminos precolombinos: Las vías, los ingenieros y los viajeros*, ed. Leonor Herrera y Marianne Cardale de Schrimpff, 167–93. Bogotá: Instituto Colombiano de Antropología e Historia.

Coello Rodríguez, Antonio, and Ernesto Díaz Arce. 1995. "Un tampu inka en San Damián (Huarochirí-Perú)." *Sequilao: Revista de historia, arte y sociedad* 8: 125–40.

Comaroff, John, and Jean Comaroff. 1992. *Ethnography and the Historical Imagination.* Boulder, CO: Westview Press.

Cook, Anita. 1992. "The Stone Ancestors: Idioms of Imperial Attire and Rank among Huari Figurines." *Latin American Antiquity* 3 (4): 341–64. http://dx.doi.org/10.2307/971953.

Cornejo, Miguel. 2002. "Sacerdotes y tejedores en la provincia Inka de Pachacamac." *Boletín de Arqueología PUCP* 6:171–204.

Curatola Petrocchi, Marco, and Mariusz Ziółkowski, eds. 2007. *Adivinación y oráculos en el mundo andino antiguo.* Lima: Pontificia Universidad Católica del Perú.

D'Altroy, Terence. 2001. "Politics, Resources, and Blood in the Inka Empire." In *Empires: Perspectives from Archaeology and History*, ed. Susan Alcock, Terence D'Altroy, Kathleen Morrison, and Carla Sinopoli, 201–26. Cambridge: Cambridge University Press.

D'Altroy, Terence, and Christine Hastorf. 1984. "The Distribution and Contents of Inca State Storehouses in the Xauxa Region of Peru." *American Antiquity* 49 (2): 334–49. http://dx.doi.org/10.2307/280022.

Daston, Lorraine, and Peter Galison. 2007. *Objectivity.* New York: Zone Books.

Dávila Brizeño, Diego. 1965 [1586]. "Descripción y relación de la provincial de los yauyos." In *Relaciones geográficas de Indias*, vol. 1, ed. Marcos Jiménez de la Espada, 155–65. Madrid: Ediciones Atlas.

Dean, Carolyn. 2010. *A Culture of Stone: Inka Perspectives on Rock.* Durham, NC: Duke University Press. http://dx.doi.org/10.1215/9780822393177.

Dietler, Michael. 2005. "The Archaeology of Colonization and the Colonization of Archaeology: Theoretical Challenges from an Ancient Mediterranean Colonial Encounter." In *The Archaeology of Colonial Encounters: Comparative Perspectives*, ed. Gil Stein, 33–68. Santa Fe, NM: SAR Press.

Dillehay, Tom D. 1976. "Competition and Cooperation in a Prehispanic Multi-Ethnic System in the Central Andes." PhD diss., Department of Anthropology, University of Texas, Austin. Ann Arbor, MI: University Microfilms.

Dobres, Marcia, and John Robb, eds. 2000. *Agency in Archaeology.* New York: Routledge.

Durston, Alan. 2007. "Notes on Authorship of the Huarochirí Manuscript." *Colonial Latin American Review* 16 (2): 227–41. http://dx.doi.org/10.1080/10609160701644516.

Duviols, Pierre. 1973. "Huari y llacuaz: Agricultores y pastores, un dualismo prehispánico de oposición y complementaridad." *Revista del Museo Nacional (Lima)* 39:153–91.

Duviols, Pierre. 1977. *La destrucción de las religiones andinas (Conquista y Colonia)*. Mexico City: Universidad Nacional Autónoma de México.

Duviols, Pierre. 1986. *Cultura andina y represión: Procesos y visitas de idolatrías y hechicerías, cajatambo, siglo XVII*. Cuzco: Centro de Estudios Rurales Andinos Bartolomé de Las Casas.

Duviols, Pierre. 2003. *Procesos y visitas de idolatría, Cajatambo siglo XVII*. Lima: Instituto Francés de Estudios Andinos and Fondo Editorial, Pontificia Universidad Católica del Perú.

Eeckhout, Peter. 2004a. "Relatos míticos y prácticas rituales en pachacamac." *Bulletin de l'Institut Français d'Études Andines* 33 (1): 1–54.

Eeckhout, Peter. 2004b. "La Sombra de ychsma: Ensayo introductorio sobre la arqueología de la costa central del Perú en los periodos tardíos." *Bulletin de l'Institut Français d'Études Andines* 33 (3): 403–23.

Eeckhout, Peter. 2004c. "Pachacamac y el proyecto ychsma (1999–2003)." *Bulletin de l'Institut Français d'Études Andines* 3 (3): 425–48.

Espinoza Soriano, Waldemar. 1992. "Huarochirí y el Estado Inca." In *Huarochirí: Ocho mil años de historia*, vol. I, 117–94. Lima: Santa Eulalia de Acopaya.

Farfán Lovatón, Carlos. 2001. "Investigaciones arqueológicas en la cordillera del pariacaca." In *XII congreso peruano del hombre y la cultura andina "Luis G. Lumbreras,"* ed. Ismael Pérez, Walter Aguilar, and Medado Purizaga, 102–7. Lima: Universidad Nacional de San Cristóbal de Huamanga.

Farfán Lovatón, Carlos. 2010. "Poder simbólico y poder político del estado inca en la cordillera del pariacaca." In *Arqueología en el Perú: Nuevos aportes para el estudio de las sociedades andinas prehispánicas*, ed. Rubén Romero Velarde and Trine Pavel Svendsen, 377–413. Lima: Universidad Nacional Federico Villareál.

Farriss, Nancy. 1995. "Remembering the Future, Anticipating the Past: History, Time, and Cosmology among the Maya of Yucatan." In *Time: Histories and Ethnologies*, ed. Diane Owen Hughes and Thomas R. Trautman, 107–38. Ann Arbor: University of Michigan Press.

Feltham, Jane. 1983. "The Lurín Valley, Peru, AD 1000–1532." PhD diss., University of London.

Feltham, Jane. 2005. "Yungas and Yauyos–The Interface between Archaeology and Ethnohistory as Seen from the Lurín Valley." In *Wars and Conflicts in Prehispanic Mesoamerica and the Andes*, ed. Peter Eeckhout and Geneviève Le Fort, 128–45. BAR International Series 1385. Oxford: BAR.

Feltham, Jane. 2009. "La arqueología de sisicaya." In *La revisita de Sisicaya, 1588. Huarochirí veinte años antes de dioses y hombres*, ed. Frank Salomon, Jane Feltham, and Sue Grosboll, 57–101. Lima: Fondo Editorial de la Pontificia Universidad Católica del Perú.

Feltham, Jane, and Peter Eeckhout. 2004. "Hacia una definición del estilo Ychsma: Aportes preliminares sobre la cerámica Ychsma Tardía de la Pirámide III de Pachacamac." *Boletín del Instituto Francés de Estudios Andinos* 33 (3): 643–79.

Galindo, Flores. Alberto. 1987. *Buscando un inca: Identidad y utopía en los andes.* Lima: Instituto de Apoyo Agrario.

García Cabrera, Juan Carlos. 1994. *Ofensas a dios, pleitos e injurias: causas de idolatrías y hechicerías, Cajatambo, siglos XVII–XIX.* Cusco: Centro de Estudios Regionales Andinos Bartolomé de Las Casas.

Garcilaso de la Vega, El Inca. 1991 [1609]. *Comentarios reales de los Incas,* book I. Mexico City: Fondo de Cultura Económica.

Gell, Alfred. 1992. *The Anthropology of Time: Cultural Constructions of Temporal Maps and Images.* Oxford: Berg.

Gell, Alfred. 1998. *Art and Agency: An Anthropological Theory.* Oxford: Oxford University Press.

Gillespie, Susan D. 1989. *The Aztec Kings: The Construction of Rulership in Mexica History.* Tucson: University of Arizona Press.

Gillespie, Susan D. 2001. "Body and Soul among the Maya: Keeping the Spirits in Place." *Archaeological Papers of the American Anthropological Association* 10:67–78.

González Holguín, Diego. 1989 [1608]. *Arte y diccionario qquechua–español.* Lima: Imprenta del Estado.

Gosden, Chris. 2004. *Archaeology and Colonialism: Cultural Contact from 5000 BC to the Present.* Cambridge: Cambridge University Press.

Gose, Peter. 1996a. "The Past is a Lower Moiety: Diarchy, History, and Divine Kingship in the Inka Empire." *History and Anthropology* 9 (4): 383–414. http://dx.doi.org/10.1080/02757206.1996.9960887.

Gose, Peter. 1996b. "Oracles, Divine Kingship, and Political Representation in the Inka State." *Ethnohistory* 43 (1): 1–33. http://dx.doi.org/10.2307/483342.

Gose, Peter. 2008. *Invaders as Ancestors: On the Intercultural Making and Unmaking of Spanish Colonialism in the Andes.* Toronto: University of Toronto Press.

Griffiths, Nicholas. 1996. *The Cross and the Serpent: Religious Repression and Resurgence in Colonial Peru.* Norman: University of Oklahoma Press.

Hamann, Byron. 2002. "The Social Life of Pre-Sunrise Things: Indigenous Mesoamerican Archaeology." *Current Anthropology* 43 (3): 351–82. http://dx.doi.org/10.1086/339526.

Hamann, Byron. 2008. "Chronological Pollution: Potsherds, Mosques, and Broken Gods before and after the Conquest of Mexico." *Current Anthropology* 49 (5): 803–36. http://dx.doi.org/10.1086/591274.

Harvey, Graham. 2006. *Animism: Respecting the Living World*. New York: Columbia University Press.

Hernández Príncipe, Rodrigo. 1919 [1613]. "Idolatrías de los indios huachos y yauyos." *Revista Histórica* 6:180–97.

Hernández Príncipe, Rodrigo. 2003 [1621]."Visita de Rodrigo Hernández Príncipe a Ocros (1621)." In *Procesos y visitas de idolatría, Cajatambo siglo XVII*, ed. Pierre Duviols, 731–46. Lima: IFEA & Fondo Editorial de la Pontificia Universidad Católica del Perú.

Hobsbawm, Eric, and Terrence Ranger, eds. 1983. *The Invention of Tradition*. Cambridge: Cambridge University Press.

Huertas Vallejos, Lorenzo. 1981. *La religión en una sociedad rural andina*. Ayachucho: Universidad Nacional de San Cristóbal.

Hughes, Diane Owen. 1995. "Introduction." In *Time: Histories and Ethnologies*, ed. Diane Owen Hughes and Thomas R. Trautman, 1–18. Ann Arbor: University of Michigan Press.

Hyslop, John. 1984. *The Inka Road System*. New York: Academic Press.

Hyslop, John. 1990. *Inka Settlement Planning*. Austin: University of Texas Press.

Ingold, Tim. 2007. "Materials against Materiality" (and responses). *Archaeological Dialogues* 14 (1): 1–38. http://dx.doi.org/10.1017/S1380203807002127.

Inomata, Takeshi, and Lawrence Coben, eds. 2006. *Archaeology of Performance: Theaters of Power, Community, and Politics*. Walnut Creek, CA: Alta Mira Press.

Instituto Nacional de Cultura (INC). 2008. *Proyecto de inventario y registro del patrimonio cultural arqueológico de la nación. Programa qhapaq ñan. Macro región centro*. Lima: Instituto Nacional de Cultura, Lima.

Isbell, William H. 1997. *Mummies and Mortuary Monuments: A Postprocessual Prehistory of Central Andean Social Organization*. Austin: University of Texas Press.

Johnson, Matthew. 2006. "On the Nature of Theoretical Archaeology and Archaeological Theory." *Archaeological Dialogues* 13 (2): 117–82. http://dx.doi.org/10.1017/S138020380621208X.

Kertzer, David. 1988. *Ritual, Politics, and Power*. New Haven, CT: Yale University Press.

Kolata, Alan. 1992. "In the Realm of the Four Quarters." In *America in 1492: The World of the Indian Peoples Before the Arrival of Columbus*, ed. Alvin M. Josephy Jr., 215–47. New York: Random House.

Kolata, Alan. 2013. *Ancient Inca*. Cambridge: Cambridge University Press.

Kolata, Alan, and Carlos Ponce Sangines. 1992. "Tiwanaku: The City at the Center." In *The Ancient Americas: Art from Sacred Landscapes*, ed. Richard Townsend, 317–35. Chicago: Art Institute of Chicago.

Kosiba, Steven B. 2010. "Becoming Inka: The Transformation of Political Place and Practice during Inka State Formation (Cusco, Peru)." PhD diss., University of Chicago. Ann Arbor, MI: University Microfilms.

Küchler, Susanne. 2005. "Materiality and Cognition: The Changing Face of Things." In *Materiality*, ed. Daniel Miller, 206–30. Durham, NC: Duke University Press. http://dx.doi.org/10.1215/9780822386711-009.

Lane, Kevin, and Milton Luján Dávila, eds. 2012. *Arquitectura prehispánica tardía: construcción, y poder en los Andes centrales*. Lima: Universidad Católica Sedes Sapientiae.

Latour, Bruno. 2005. *Reassembling the Social: An Introduction to Actor-Network-Theory*. Oxford: Oxford University Press.

Levine, Terry, ed. 1992. *Inka Storage Systems*. Norman: University of Oklahoma Press.

Lucas, Gavin. 2005. *The Archaeology of Time*. London: Routledge.

MacCormack, Sabine. 1991. *Religion in the Andes: Vision and Imagination in Early Colonial Peru*. Princeton, NJ: Princeton University Press.

Makowski, Krzysztof. 2002. "Arquitectura, estilo e identidad en el horizonte tardío: el sitio de Pueblo-Viejo-Pucará, Valle de Lurín." *Boletín de Arqueología PUCP* 6:137–70.

Makowski, Krzysztof. 2009. "Prefacio." In *La revisita de Sisicaya, 1588: Huarochirí veinte años antes de dioses y hombres*, ed. Frank Salomon, Jane Feltham, and Sue Grosboll, 9–14. Lima: Fondo Editorial de la Pontificia Universidad Católica del Perú.

Makowski, Krzysztof, and Milena Vega Centeno. 2004. "Estilos regionales en la costa central en el horizonte tardío. Una aproximación desde el Valle del Lurín." *Bulletin de l'Institut Français d'Études Andines* 33 (3): 681–714.

Makowski, Krzysztof, María Fe Córdova, Patricia Habetler, and Manuel Lizárraga. 2005. "La plaza y la fiesta: reflexiones acerca de la función de los patios en la arquitectura pública perhispánica de los Períodos Tardíos." *Boletín de Arqueología PUCP* 9:297–333.

Marcone, Giancarlo, and Enrique López-Hurtado. 2002. "Panquilma y Cieneguilla en la discusión arqueológica del Horizonte Tardío de la Costa Central." *Boletín de Arqueología PUCP* 6:375–94.

Mayne, Alan. 2008. "On the Edges of History: Reflections on Historical Archaeology." *American Historical Review* 113 (1): 93–118. http://dx.doi.org/10.1086/ahr.113 .1.93.

McAnany, Patricia. 1995. *Living with the Ancestors: Kinship and Kingship in Ancient Maya Society*. Austin: University of Texas Press.

Meddens, Frank, Colin McEwan, and Cirilio Vivanco Pomacanchari. 2010. "Inca 'Stone Ancestors' in Context at a High-Altitude Usnu Platform." *Latin American Antiquity* 21 (2): 173–94. http://dx.doi.org/10.7183/1045-6635.21.2.173.

Mejía Xesspe, M. Toribio. 1947. *Historia de la antigua provincia de Anan Yauyo.* Lima: N.p.

Meskell, Lynn. 2005. "Objects in the Mirror Appear Closer Than They Are." In *Materiality*, ed. Daniel Miller, 51–71. Durham, NC: Duke University Press. http://dx.doi.org/10.1215/9780822386711-002.

Miller, Daniel. 2005. "Materiality: An Introduction." In *Materiality*, ed. Daniel Miller, 1–50. Durham, NC: Duke University Press. http://dx.doi.org/10.1215/9780822386711-001.

Millones, Luis, ed. 1990. *El retorno de las huacas: estudios y documentos sobre el taki onqoy, siglo XVI.* Lima: Instituto de Estudios Peruanos y Sociedad Peruana de Psicoanálisis.

Mills, Kenneth. 1994. *An Evil Lost to View? An Investigation of Post-Evangelisation Andean Religion in Mid-Colonial Peru.* Liverpool: Institute of Latin American Studies, University of Liverpool.

Mills, Kenneth. 1997. *Idolatry and Its Enemies: Colonial Andean Religion and Extirpation, 1640–1750.* Princeton, NJ: Princeton University Press.

Moore, Henrietta. 1995. "The Problem of Origins: Poststructuralism and Beyond." In *Interpreting Archaeology: Finding Meaning in the Past*, ed. Ian Hodder, Michael Shanks, Alexandra Alexandri, Victor Buchli, Jonathan Last, and Gavin Lucas, 51–53. London: Routledge.

Morris, Craig, and Donald Thompson. 1985. *Huánuco Pampa: An Inca City and Its Hinterland.* London: Thames and Hudson.

Munn, Nancy. 1992. "The Cultural Anthropology of Time: A Critical Essay." *Annual Review of Anthropology* 21 (1): 93–123. http://dx.doi.org/10.1146/annurev.an.21.100192.000521.

Munn, Nancy. 1996. "Excluded Spaces: The Figure in the Australian Aboriginal Landscape." *Critical Inquiry* 22 (3): 446–65. http://dx.doi.org/10.1086/448801.

Patrocinios, Pedro, and Liliana Tapia. 2002. "Proyecto: Determinación de sectores y tipología de arquitectura funeraria en Llaquistampu (San Damián)." Technical report archived with Ministry of Culture, Lima, Peru.

Patterson, Thomas C. 1985. "Pachacamac—an Andean Oracle under Inca Rule." In *Recent Studies in Andean Prehistory and Protohistory*, ed. D. Peter Kvietok and Daniel H. Sandweiss, 159–76. Ithaca, NY: Latin American Studies Program, Cornell University.

Patterson, Thomas C. 1997. *The Inca Empire: The Formation and Disintegration of a Pre-Capitalist State.* Oxford: Berg Publishers.

Peirce, Charles S. 1998 [1907]. *The Essential Peirce: Selected Philosophical Writings.* Vol. 2, *1893–1913*. Ed. Peirce Edition Project. Bloomington: Indiana University Press.

Polia Meconi, Mario. 1996 [1611–13]. "Siete cartas inéditas del Archivo Romano de la Compañía de Jesús (1611–1613): huacas, mitos y ritos andinos." *Antropológica* 14:209–59.

Polignac, François de. 1995. *Cults, Territory, and Origins of the Greek City-State.* Chicago: University of Chicago Press.

Quilter, Jeffrey. 1990. "The Moche Revolt of the Objects." *Latin American Antiquity* 1 (1): 42–65. http://dx.doi.org/10.2307/971709.

Quilter, Jeffrey. 1997. "The Narrative Approach to Moche Iconography." *Latin American Antiquity* 8 (2): 113–33. http://dx.doi.org/10.2307/971689.

Ramírez, Susan Elizabeth. 1996. *The World Upside Down: Cross-Cultural Contact and Conflict in Sixteenth-Century Peru.* Palo Alto, CA: Stanford University Press.

Ramos, Gabriela, and Henrique Urbano, eds. 1993. *Catolicismo y extirpación de idolatrías, siglos XVI–XVIII.* Cusco: Centro de Estudios Regionales Andinos Bartolomé de las Casas.

Reinhard, Johan, and Maria Constanza Ceruti. 2011. *Inca Rituals and Sacred Mountains: A Study of the World's Highest Archaeological Sites.* Los Angeles: Cotsen Institute of Archaeology, University of California.

Rostworowski de Diez Canseco, María. 1988. *Conflicts over Coca Fields in XVIth-Century Peru.* Ann Arbor: University of Michigan, Museum of Anthropology.

Rostworowski de Diez Canseco, María. 1992. *Pachacamac y el señor de los milagros: una trayectoria milenaria.* Lima: Instituto de Estudios Peruanos.

Rostworowski de Diez Canseco, María. 2002a [1978]. "Señoríos indígenas de Lima y Canta." In *Pachacamac. Obras completas II*, ed. Maria Rostworowski de Diez Canseco, 193–373. Lima: Instituto de Estudios Peruanos.

Rostworowski de Diez Canseco, María. 2002b [1999]. "Estudio introductorio al informe de Rodrigo Cantos de Andrade. In *Pachacamac. Obras Completas II*, ed. Maria Rostworowski, 173–87. Lima: Instituto de Estudios Peruanos.

Rowe, John H. 1979. "An Account of the Shrines of Ancient Cuzco." *Ñawpa Pacha* 17: 1–80.

Sahlins, Marshall. 1981. *Historical Metaphors and Mythical Realities: Structure in the Early History of the Sandwich Islands Kingdom.* Ann Arbor: University of Michigan Press.

Sahlins, Marshall. 1985. *Islands of History.* Chicago: University of Chicago Press.

Salomon, Frank. 1991. "Introductory Essay; The Huarochirí Manuscript." In *The Huarochirí Manuscript: A Testament of Ancient and Colonial Andean Religion*, trans. and ed. Frank Salomon and George L. Urioste., 1–38. Austin: University of Texas Press.

Salomon, Frank. 1995. "'The Beautiful Grandparents': Andean Ancestor Shrines and Mortuary Ritual as seen through Colonial Records." In *Tombs for the Living: Andean Mortuary Practices*, ed. Tom Dillehay, 315–53. Washington, DC: Dumbarton Oaks.

Salomon, Frank. 1998. "How the Huacas Were: The Language of Substance and Transformation in the Huarochirí Quechua Manuscript." *RES* 33: 7–17.

Salomon, Frank. 1999. "Testimonies: The Making and Reading of Native South American Historical Sources." In *The Cambridge History of the Native Peoples of the Americas*, vol. 3, *South America*, ed. Frank Salomon and Stuart Schwartz, 19–95. Cambridge: Cambridge University Press. http://dx.doi.org/10.1017 /CHOL9780521630757.003.

Salomon, Frank. 2004. *The Cord Keepers: Khipus and Cultural Life in a Peruvian Village*. Durham, NC: Duke University Press. http://dx.doi.org/10.1215 /9780822386179.

Salomon, Frank, and George L. Urioste, eds. and trans. 1991. *The Huarochirí Manuscript: A Testament of Ancient and Colonial Andean Religion*. Austin: University of Texas Press.

Salomon, Frank, and Sue Grosboll. 2009. "Una visita a los hijos de Chaupi Ñamca en 1588: Desigualdad de género, nombres indígenas y cambios demográficos en el centro de los Andes pos-incas." In *La revisita de Sisicaya, 1588: Huarochirí veinte años antes de dioses y hombres*, ed. Frank Salomon, Jane Feltham, and Sue Grosboll, 17–55. Lima: Fondo Editorial de la Pontificia Universidad Católica del Perú.

Sánchez, Ana. 1991. *Amancebados, hechiceros y rebeldes (Chancay, siglo XVII)*. Cusco: Centro de Estudios Regionales Andinos Bartolomé de las Casas.

Santo Tomás, Domingo de. 2006 [1560]. *Lexicon o vocabulario de la lengua general del Peru*. Ed. Jan Szemiński. Cusco, Warsaw, and Jerusalem: Convento de Santo Domingo–Qorikancha, Sociedad Polaca de Estudios Latinoamericanos, Universidad Hebrea de Jerusalén.

Sarmiento de Gamboa, Pedro. 1999 [1572]. *History of the Incas*. Trans. Roland Hamilton. Austin: University of Texas Press.

Schnapp, Alain. 1997. *The Discovery of the Past*. London: British Museum.

Silverblatt, Irene. 1987. *Sun, Moon, and Witches: Gender Ideologies and Class in Inca and Colonial Peru*. Princeton, NJ: Princeton University Press.

Silverblatt, Irene. 1988. "Imperial Dilemmas, the Politics of Kinship, and Inca Reconstructions of History." *Comparative Studies in Society and History* 30 (1): 83–102. http://dx.doi.org/10.1017/S001041750001505X.

Smith, Adam T. 2004. "The End of the Essential Archaeological Subject (and responses)." *Archaeological Dialogues* 11(1): 1–20, 27–30.

Spalding, Karen. 1984. *Huarochirí: An Andean Society under Inca and Spanish Rule*. Palo Alto, CA: Stanford University Press.

Squair, Robert. 1994. "Time and the Privilege of Retrospect." In *Archaeological Theory: Progress or Posture?* ed. Ian M. MacKenzie, 92–113. Aldershot, UK: Avebury.

Stern, Steve. 1993. *Peru's Indian Peoples and the Challenge of Spanish Conquest: Huamanga to 1640*. Madison: University of Wisconsin Press.

Strathern, Marilyn. 1988. *The Gender of the Gift: Problems with Women and Problems with Society in Melanesia*. Berkeley: University of California Press. http://dx.doi.org/10.1525/california/9780520064232.001.0001.

Swenson, Edward. 2007. "Local Ideological Strategies and the Politics of Ritual Space in the Chimú Empire." *Archaeological Dialogues* 14 (1): 61–90. http://dx.doi.org/10.1017/S138020380700219X.

Swenson, Edward. 2011. "Stagecraft and the Politics of Spectacle in Ancient Peru." *Cambridge Archaeological Journal* 21 (2): 283–315. http://dx.doi.org/10.1017/S095977431100028X.

Sykes, Kathleen. 1990. "Symbolic Structure, Social Strategies, and the Built Environment of an Ancient Andean Village: A.D. 1250–1460." PhD diss., Simon Fraser University. Ann Arbor, MI: University Microfilms.

Taylor, Gerald. 1999. *Ritos y tradiciones de Huarochirí*. Lima: Instituto Francés de Estudios Andinos.

Tello, Julio C. 1999. *Arqueología del valle de Lima. Cuadernos de investigación del archivo Tello, No. 1*. Lima: Museo de Arqueolgía y Antropología, Universidad Nacional Mayor de San Marcos.

Thatcher, John, and Nicholas Hellmuth. 1968–71. Field notes and "A Seriation of the Ceramics of Huarochirí." In author's possession, courtesy of Dr. Thomas Patterson.

Topic, John R. 1992. "Las huacas de Huamachuco: Precisiones en torno a una imagen indígena de un paisaje andino." In *La persecución del demonio. Crónica de los primeros agustinos en el norte del Perú (1560)*, by Fray Juan de San Pedro, 41–99. Malaga, Spain / Mexico City: Algazara / Centro Andino y Mesoamericano de Estudios Interdisciplinarios.

Topic, John R. 1998. "Ethnogenesis in Huamachuco." *Andean Past* 5: 109–27.

Topic, John R. 2007. "El santuario de Catequil: Estructura y agencia: Hacia una comprensión de los oráculos andinos." In *Adivinación y oráculos en el mundo andino antiguo*, ed. Marco Curatola Petrocchi and Mariusz S. Ziółkowski, 71–95. Lima: Fondo Editorial, Pontificia Universidad Católica del Perú.

Topic, John R., and Theresa Lange Topic. 1993. "A Summary of the Inca Occupation of Huamachuco." In *Provincial Inca: Archaeological and Ethnohistorical Assessment of the Impact of the Inca State*, ed. Michael Malpass, 17–43. Iowa City: University of Iowa Press.

Topic, John R., Theresa Lange Topic, and Alfredo Melly. 2002. "Catequil: The Archaeology, Ethnohistory and Ethnography of a Major Provincial Huaca." In *Andean Archaeology I: Variations in Sociopolitical Organization*, ed. William H. Isbell and Helaine Silverman, 303–36. New York: Kluwer Academic–Plenum Press. http://dx.doi.org/10.1007/978-1-4615-0639-3_11.

Trouillot, Michel-Rolph. 1995. *Silencing the Past: Power and the Production of History*. Boston: Beacon Press.

Turner, Victor. 1969. *The Ritual Process: Structure and Anti-Structure*. New York: Aldine de Gruyter.

Uhle, Max. 2003 [1903]. *Pachacamac: Informe de la expedición peruana William Pepper de 1896*. Lima: Universidad Nacional Mayor de San Marcos.

Urbano, Henrique. 1993. "Ídolos, figuras, imágenes: La representación como discurso ideológico." In *Catolicismo y extirpación de idolatrías, siglos XVI–XVIII*, comp. Gabriela Ramos and Henrique Urbano, 7–30. Cusco: Centro de Estudios Regionales Andinos Bartolomé de las Casas.

Urton, Gary. 1990. *The History of a Myth: Pacariqtambo and the Origin of the Inkas*. Austin: University of Texas Press.

van de Guchte, Maarten. 1999. "The Inca Cognition of Landscape: Archaeology, Ethnohistory, and the Aesthetic of Alterity." In *Archaeologies of Landscape: Contemporary Perspectives*, ed. Wendy Ashmore and A. Bernard Knapp, 149–68. Malden, MA: Blackwell Publishers.

Van Gennep, Arnold. 1960. *The Rites of Passage*. Chicago: University of Chicago Press.

VanPool, Christine S., and Elizabeth Newsome. 2012. "The Spirit in the Material: A Case Study of Animism in the American Southwest." *American Antiquity* 77 (2): 243–62. http://dx.doi.org/10.7183/0002-7316.77.2.243.

Villar Córdova, Pedro. 1982 [1935]. *Las culturas prehispánicas del departamento de Lima*. Lima: Ediciones Atusparia.

Wernke, Steven. 2003. "An Archaeo-History of Andean Community and Landscape: The Late Prehispanic and Early Colonial Colca Valley, Peru." PhD diss., University of Wisconsin, Madison. Ann Arbor, MI: University Microfilms.

Wernke, Steven. 2007. "Negotiating Community and Landscape in the Peruvian Andes: A Transconquest View." *American Anthropologist* 109 (1): 130–52. http://dx.doi.org/10.1525/aa.2007.109.1.130.

White, Richard. 1991. *The Middle Ground: Indians, Empires, and Republics in the Great Lakes Region, 1650–1815*. Cambridge: Cambridge University Press. http://dx.doi.org/10.1017/CBO9780511584671.

Yoffee, Norman. 2007. "Peering into the Palimpsest: An Introduction to the Volume." In *Negotiating the Past in the Past: Identity, Memory, and Landscape in Archaeological Research*, ed. Norman Yoffee, 1–9. Tucson: University of Arizona Press.

Ziółkowski, Mariusz. 2007. "Coropuna y solimana: Los oráculos de condesuyos." In *Adivinación y oráculos en el mundo andino antiguo*, ed. Marco Curatola Petrocchi and Mariusz Ziółkowski, 121–59. Lima: Pontificia Universidad Católica del Perú.

Zuidema, R. Tom. 1964. *The Ceque System of Cuzco: The Social Organization of the Capital of the Inca*. Leiden: Brill.

Zuidema, R. Tom. 1977–78. "Shaft Tombs and the Inca Empire." *Journal of the Steward Anthropological Society* 9 (1–2): 133–78.

Zuidema, R. Tom. 2011. *El calendario inca: Tiempo y espacio en la organización ritual del Cuzco: La idea del pasado*. Lima: Fondo Editorial del Congreso del Perú; Fondo Editorial de la Pontificia Universidad Católica del Perú.

5

Pachacamac—Old Wak'a or Inka Syncretic Deity?

Imperial Transformation of the Sacred Landscape in the Lower Ychsma (Lurín) Valley

INTRODUCTION

KRZYSZTOF MAKOWSKI

The Spanish chroniclers referred to the Lurín Valley by several names, including Ychsma or Irma, both Spanish transcriptions of an Aymara word, and Pachacamac, which is a Quechua word. This south-central coastal valley is one of the relatively few regions in Peru where it is possible to study across the boundaries of protohistoric and colonial period archaeology. The number of written sources pertaining to this region is relatively large, and many were published during the sixteenth century by the first Spanish conquerors and priests (Eeckhout 1999b; Rostworowski 1972, 1999, 2002a, 2002b; Salomon et al. 2009; Spalding 1984). However, what may seem like a blessing can also be a hindrance to archaeological investigation. The simple comments made by the chroniclers are often uncritically accepted as truth with the archaeological data serving only to illustrate the historian's interpretations.

In this chapter I intend to show how our reading changes when the results of systematic excavations of considerable extension are taken as a starting point and written sources are subject to rigorous internal scrutiny. The archaeological results suggest that Inka imperial policies completely transformed the landscape of the Lurín Valley. The reorganization involved not only the construction of new urban settlements for populations moved from elsewhere in the highlands and possibly the coast, but also the creation of new sacred sites—or *wak'as*—and new ceremonial spaces. As expected, the

DOI: 10.5876/9781607323181.c005

127

largest building activities were conducted in Pachacamac proper. This local ceremonial center, which was originally relatively modest, was transformed during the Late Horizon by the construction of walled streets, new enclosed space, and large plazas, in addition to the erection of substantial new temples and an *acllahuasi* (house of chosen women). New ramped pyramids were also built during this time period.

Studies on the distribution of wak'as and their ceremonial functions in the imperial capital of Cuzco (e.g., Bauer 1998, 2004; Rowe 1979; Zuidema 1980, 2008, 2010) indicate that the main rituals associated with the Inka ceremonial calendar were not restricted to the monumental urban core of the city but rather were conducted throughout the sacred valley. The empire's religious doctrine and history were inscribed upon the state-modified landscape (van de Guchte 1990; Kosiba, this volume). Rocks, both carved and natural, springs, caves, fountains, and architectural elements were transformed by the Inka into "wak'as," or sacred places, serving as points of reference for socially shared memory. I believe that imperial strategies in the Lurín Valley followed the same pattern and procedures. Both Pachacamac and the site of Pueblo Viejo–Pucará were part of a new sacred geography created by the Inka to legitimize their right to rule the coast. The two case studies that will be presented in this chapter are based on field research conducted at the sites of Pachacamac and Pueblo Viejo–Pucará and will serve to substantiate the hypothesis outlined above.

Our investigations in the Lurín Valley have focused on issues related to the nature of Inka administration in this zone. They have been carried out as part of the archaeological program Lomas de Lurín, and subsequently the Valle de Pachacamac program, both of which were field-school projects of the Pontificia Universidad Católica del Perú (PUCP) conducted with the support of the Peruvian-based company Cementos Lima S.A. Investigations began here in the 1990s with excavations of the monumental entrance to Pachacamac from the north, which is referred to as the "Third Wall," undertaken in 1994–95 by Hernán Carrillo and Daniel Guerrero and the commencement of long-term excavations in Pueblo Viejo–Pucará in 1999 (Figure 5.1). Judging by the ethnohistoric evidence, the burial rites, and the typical highland architecture, Pueblo Viejo–Pucará, located near the ceremonial center of Pachacamac, was a major settlement of the Caringa of Huarochirí (see Chase, this volume) and the principal abode of the lords of this moiety.

The comparative analysis between Pachacamac proper and Pueblo Viejo–Pucará proves that the rigid architectural classifications often used to distinguish between political and religious functions, which typically counterpose

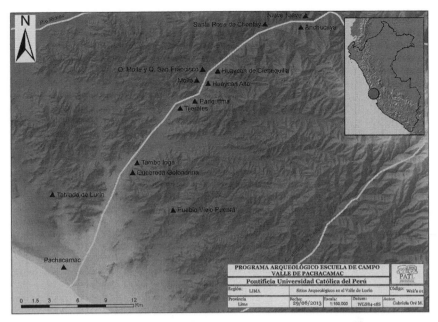

Figure 5.1. *Map of the Lurín Valley, south coast of Peru (produced by Gabriela Oré).*

palaces and temples, fail to explain the variety of forms and uses of the sacred places and things. Unlike in the Greek Hellenistic, Roman, and Christian traditions, it is the landscape, transformed or not, rather than buildings or iconography, that comprises the sacred and ritual spaces of the Andes. The concept of wak'a, somewhat equivalent to the notion of numen, relates primarily (in its material form) to rocks, fountains, lakes, and other landscape features (for further discussion, see Bray, this volume; van de Guchte 1990).

In Pachacamac and Pueblo Viejo–Pucará, ceremonial architecture is found associated with sacred landscape features like rock outcrops, hills, and promontories located near the sea or lakes. The monumental architecture associated with these sacred places fulfilled multiple functions that were as much political and economic as religious in nature. Plazas and enclosures were used for mass gatherings. Ramped platforms served in some cases as *ushnus* (see Meddens, this volume) and in others as elevated spaces that overlooked enclosures from which the representatives of power and sometime officiates of particular rituals appeared before the assembled audiences. The frequent association of these features with storage areas as well as the absence of spaces with clear residential functions suggest that these various-sized structures served as a stage for both tax payments and festival gatherings (Eeckhout 1999b, 2003a; López-Hurtado 2011; Villacorta 2004, 2010).

In Pachacamac, ceremonial roads enclosed between parallel walls directed the movements of parishioners who came to pay taxes, to deposit offerings, to fast, or to celebrate. Pachacamac is no different in this respect from two of the most important extant temples of the imperial Inka cult: the Coricancha and the Temple of Lake Titicaca (Stanish and Bauer 2004). In Pueblo Viejo–Pucará two large enclosed plazas attached to both the ushnu and the main palace served as a stage for celebrations. In both of these cases, the sharp differentiation between secular and ceremonial spaces turns out to be difficult and ultimately inoperative.

IMPERIAL INKA TRANSFORMATIONS OF THE PACHACAMAC SACRED LANDSCAPE

Throughout the twentieth century, from Max Uhle (2003 [1903]) to Arturo Jiménez Borja (1985), Thomas Patterson (1966, 1985), María Rostworowski (1999, 2002a), and Peter Eeckhout (1995, 1998, 1999a, 1999b, 2003a, 2003b, 2004a, 2004b, 2004c, 2005, 2008, 2009, 2010), multiple interpretive scenarios have been presented for the monumental complex of Pachacamac. Uhle (2003 [1903]), for instance, argued that the planned organization and erection of the major monumental buildings at the site were associated with the imperial Inka administration. Other scholars subsequently assumed instead that the orthogonal layout of Pachacamac had its origin in the Middle Horizon (Shimada 1991; Lumbreras 1974:154, 165). These interpretations undoubtedly stemmed from Dorothy Menzel's (1964, 1968, 1977) important work on the stylistic chronology of the Middle Horizon and her convictions regarding the role of this ceremonial center during this time period. Some scholars, like Régulo Franco (1993a, 1993b; also Franco and Paredes 2000), went even further, positing that the foundations of Pachacamac dated back to the Formative period and that the ceremonial complex had developed continuously since then.

In recent decades, new interpretive proposals supported by new archaeological evidence have joined the previous ones. Considering both old and new proposals, we now have four completely different interpretations of Pachacamac, which include the following:

1. That it was a ceremonial center with a major temple and several secondary temples, built by faithful communities comprising ethnic groups from both the coast and the highlands (e.g., Jiménez Borja 1985; Rostworowski

1999, 2002a; also Eeckhout 1999b:405–8), with implicit comparisons drawn between the site of Pachacamac and those of Mecca and Delphi that derive, in large measure, from the comments of the early Spanish chroniclers.

2. That it was a planned urban administrative and ceremonial center whose layout was defined in the Middle Horizon or slightly earlier (e.g., Bueno 1970, 1974–75; Patterson 1985).

3. That it was the capital city of one of the major coastal chiefdoms in the Late Intermediate period, where many palaces of rulers were successively built, one alongside the other on the sandy open field that lies to the northeast of the temple of the god Pachacamac, on the valley's high edge (e.g., Eeckhout 1999b, 2003a; Uhle 2003 [1903]; and Tello 2009 [1940–41] had already made similar statements). For Eeckhout (1999b, 2003a), each king was buried in his palace in similar fashion to Chanchan, the capital of the north coast state of Chimor.

4. That it was the result of a long, discontinuous development wherein each of the successive stages of monumental construction was separated by breaks of different duration and each was seen as having a different origin and characteristics. The perceived spatial organization was actually due to the superimposed phases corresponding to the late periods, and particularly to the Late Horizon (Uhle 2003 [1903]). This view can be seen in Hyslop's (1990:255–61) statement that "Pachacamac is probably the most monumental example of Inka planning that coordinated and adjusted its design to a pre-existing layout."

I believe that the fourth scenario best fits the results of the archaeological excavations undertaken by Eeckhout (1995, 1999a, 2004b, 2010; Makowski 2007; also Shimada, 2003, 2004, 2007; Shimada et al. 2004, 2010). Clearly, all the interpretations of Pachacamac's layout offered to date start from three presumably key material features of the complex: (1) the presence of a road network with the two main thoroughfares intersecting at right angles and running between two walls; (2) the presence of two monumental alignments on the north side, known as the Second and Third Walls, that closed off the entrance to the *temenos* delineated by the First Wall; and (3) the impressive contrast in the archaeological elements contained within the spaces between the First and the Second Walls, as well as the Second and Third ones, in comparison to elsewhere at the site. The later observation relates to the fact that the pyramids with ramps and other adobe-brick complexes of a monumental nature are aligned along the outskirts of the First Wall, while in contrast, the dense concentrations of materials indicative of human occupation outside the Second Wall are not associated with any trace of monumental architecture. It

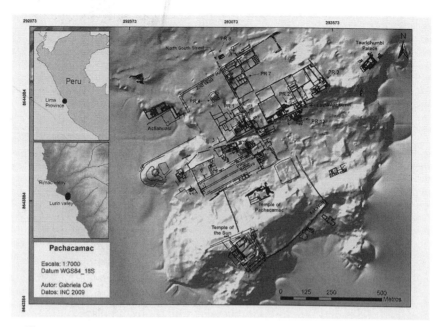

FIGURE 5.2. *Map of Pachacamac in the lower Lurín Valley showing the principal architectural features at the site (produced by Gabriela Oré).*

was on the basis of this contrast that Uhle had speculated about the presence of residential precincts having been built of perishable materials in this area.

One assumption whose validity was never proven affects most of the interpretations of the architectural development of Pachacamac: namely, that evidence of the Inka presence at this famous site would have been limited to a single occupation level—the last—in the complex stratigraphy. Another is that there had been only a few constructions built by the Inka and that all of them were exclusively distributed around the peripheries of the monumental core comprising the Painted Temple and various of the pyramids with ramps (Eeckhout 1998, 1999b, 2010; Shimada 1991). Among the long-recognized Inka buildings at Pachacamac are the Sun Temple, the Pilgrim's Square, the Acllahuasi, and the Taurichumbi Palace (Figure 5.2).

Since 2005, when I began systematic excavations at Pachacamac, abundant and strong evidence has mounted against the above-mentioned assumption about the relatively restricted degree of Inka intervention at the site. We have also accumulated considerable evidence that the planned appearance of monumental Pachacamac, with its three massive walls, primary streets, and

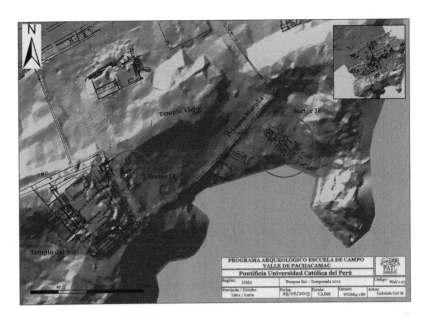

FIGURE 5.3. *Map showing the location of excavation areas I-E (northeast facade of the Temple of the Sun) and I-F in the Pampa Sur sector of Pachacamac (produced by Gabriela Oré).*

walled enclosures, was created under the aegis of the Inka administration. These major construction works, involving the movement of massive amounts of soil, clay, and bricks, as well as some catastrophic natural events such as earthquakes and heavy rains, have resulted in the presence of more than one layer and many superimposed structures in the stratigraphy associated with the Late Horizon. The various overlapping layers containing Late Horizon materials, which reflect the leveling of surfaces, the dismantling of walls, the creation of floors, and the compacting of colluvial sediments, were found to be almost 2 m thick in some areas of the site.

Our most powerful evidence to this effect comes from the 2010–11 and 2011–12 excavation seasons, which focused on the northeast facade of the Pyramid of the Sun and the First Wall (Sector I-E) (Figure 5.3). Our excavation units at the Pyramid of the Sun were placed within the deep cavity previously created by looters at the center front of the structure that cut through the first and second terrace of the northeast facade of the temple.[1] The looters took advantage of the collapsed retaining wall associated with the lower (first) terrace and perhaps also an ancient passageway with stairs located right in the middle of the temple facade. This wall, almost completely buried by sand, is omitted from the map of Uhle as well those made by subsequent investigators.

Our excavations at the Pyramid of the Sun were located a few meters south of Strong and Corbett's (1943) early trench. The First Wall, which partially encircles the Pyramid of the Sun and the two temples supposedly dedicated to Pachacamac (e.g., the Ancient Temple and the Painted Temple), attaches to the front of the retaining wall of the lower terrace of the Temple of the Sun. It should be stressed that our excavation is in the middle of the northeast facade of the temple where Max Uhle located the main entrance to the courtyard situated atop the pyramid. The stratigraphy exposed in the reexcavation of this area parallels the profile published by Strong and Corbett (ibid.) both in terms of orientation and composition. Our unit, however, exposed an area of direct contact between the natural and cultural layers and the Inka architecture that provides significant insight into the depositional sequence. Similar profiles are found in various other parts of Pachacamac, as well, particularly inside and outside the walled courtyard of the ramped pyramids.

The uppermost layers in our excavation correspond to well-preserved organic waste (Figure 5.4). In excavating them, we realized that these layers were composed of mats from ceilings and walls made of perishable materials that had originally been associated with the first or second terrace of the Temple of the Sun. Those who had been charged with throwing out this material had probably descended by the staircase that had been destroyed by the looters. They would have gone to the bottom of the terrace and deposited the waste on the left (to the northwest) over the walls that were already partially destroyed at this time. Along with the discarded mats we also found quantities of fine Inka-Lurín-style ceramic fragments (Figure 5.5), other organic waste, and weaving and spinning tools. If this profile had been found elsewhere within the site of Pachacamac, it would have been interpreted as evidence of the reoccupation of an older Ychsma ceremonial building for domestic purposes during the Late Horizon. However, in this case it is clear that the wall segments, partially destroyed and covered with Inka period trash, were also built during the Inka occupation. Nevertheless, these walls clearly correspond to a second phase of construction and the use of the first terrace of the Temple of the Sun.

During the first phase of construction, the adobe walls were carefully faced with cut stone. These walls served to retain the fill of one of the two short terraces that project outward at the two ends of the northeast facade of the stepped pyramid-like bastions. Possibly the main entrance to the Sun Temple originally opened to the walls of the second terrace from the east-facing courtyard that was formed by the bastion-shaped projections of the first terrace. We

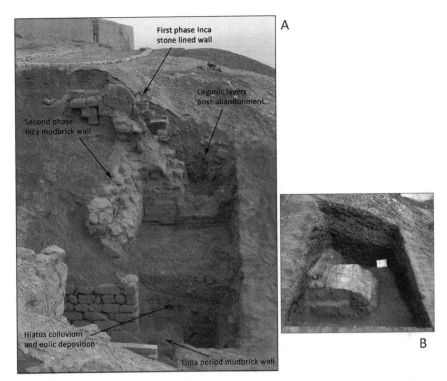

FIGURE 5.4. *Excavation units Nos. 3 and 4 in Sector I-E near the northeast facade of the Temple of the Sun: (a) excavation profiles indicating complex depositional sequence and contacts between Inka architecture and other natural and cultural layers; (b) Sector I-E, Unit 3, showing layers of stratified organic waste covering Inka wall of the second phase (photographs by author and Alaín Vallenas).*

were able to define the stratigraphic level for the foundation of the walls of the first phase as existing well below those of the wall of the second phase. In both levels we found diagnostic Inka ceramic fragments, though in smaller quantities in comparison to the upper layers with the remnant organic mats.

The second phase of adobe wall construction is not lined with cut stone, such as seen in the first phase, but rather is thinner and made of low-quality bricks. Layers of sand and fragments of archaeological adobe separate this level from the lower one. Late Horizon ceramics and some adobe fragments are also found in the levels that lie beneath the foundations of both walls mentioned above. These profiles provide strong evidence of four successive episodes, all of which appear to be associated with the Inka presence in the Pachacamac

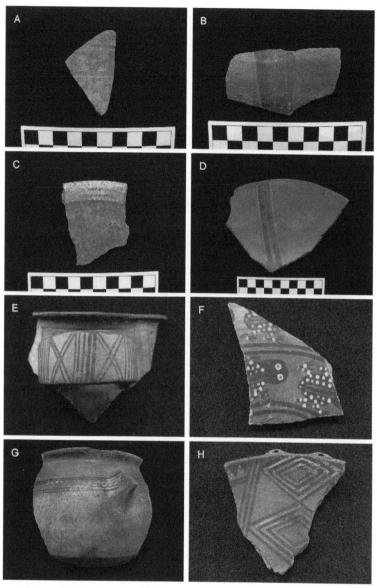

Figure 5.5. *Fragments of identifiable vessel forms of provincial Inka polychrome pottery recovered from the northeast facade of the Temple of the Sun in Sector I-E: aríbalos (a, f), shallow plates (c, d, h), and wide-mouthed ollas with horizontal handles (e, g); provenience of sherds: (a) Unit E-3, Layer 1; (b–d) Unit E-3, Layer 3; (e–g) Unit 5, Layer C; (h) Unit 5, Layer D (photographs by author).*

sanctuary. Some of these episodes appear to be separated by fairly significant amounts of time. For instance, the analysis of the micro-stratigraphy indicates that the walls of the second construction phase were destroyed, subjected to erosion by rain and weathering, and then covered over by sand before the trash and rush mats were subsequently deposited on top of them.

A relatively thin, colluvial layer of sand and a layer containing fragments of adobe representing an episode of destruction were found below the Late Horizon levels. These layers cap the construction of the Lima period (AD 300–600) architecture that was found at the bottom of our excavation. During the reexcavation of Strong and Corbett's trench, we also encountered several layers containing both negative-decorated and plain pottery dating to the Early Intermediate period between the level of the Middle Lima architecture and the sterile stratum.

The First Wall of the Pachacamac sanctuary is attached to the retaining wall of the lower terrace of the Pyramid of the Sun. It is little wonder, therefore, that we found evidence in several segments of the First Wall that it was a very late construction built at the end of the Late Horizon. Trenches and test pits were placed along sections of this wall where it would have been feasible to have gates (Figure 5.6). We were not successful in locating any entrances, however, nor are any known from any other part of this enclosure. The excavations made clear that the construction was never completed and that only the foundations had been consolidated in several sections (Figure 5.7). Beneath the wall foundations, which were found to contain fragments of fine Inka polychrome pottery (Figure 5.8), we encountered several sterile colluvial layers and one of alluvial origin. We discovered no traces of a parallel older wall in our investigations. The wide trenches excavated inside this wall produced evidence of occupation only during the Lima 4 and 5 periods (AD 300–600). We were also able to pinpoint the founding date of the only two monumental adobe structures located in the area outside of the First Wall. Neither of these was ramped. The structure near the Pyramid of the Sun labeled as the Southwest Building was certainly built at the same time as the First Wall (see Figure 5.6).

The results of our investigations in the remaining structures (e.g., the Northeast Buildings) found on the lower slopes of Cerro Gallinazo in Sector I-F have been a surprise (see Figures 5.3 and 5.6). Based on the surveys of Max Uhle (2003 [1903]) and Go Matsumoto (2005), we expected to find one or two large structures potentially correlated with a path registered on Uhle's original map. This path is still in use today and may have had an early prehispanic origin. If so, it would have connected the beach facing the island group of Cahuillaca

FIGURE 5.6. *Map of the southern sector of Pachacamac indicating location of the First Wall and excavation units from 2009 and 2012 field seasons (produced by Gabriela Oré).*

with the temples of the Sun and Pachacamac. However, more detailed survey and excavations showed that the path did not exist in ancient times. Instead of a single large rectangular building, we uncovered at least nine independent residential structures aligned in two rows that can be seen in Sector I-F in Figure 5.6. These houses were built during the later part of the Late Horizon; during the colonial period these buildings were reused as stables.

In the area of the Second Wall, we excavated four large units in strategic locations. One of the excavation units (SW-E1) trenched through the final section of the main North-South Street (Figure 5.9). This unit allowed us to record the stratigraphic associations of the road and the packed earth surfaces and mud floors associated with the western lateral wall. This wall is an extension of one of the two that line the street along its length. The results of these excavations were again surprising.

We had expected to find a complex stratigraphic sequence similar to the profiles documented by Eeckhout (2005) and Shimada (2003, 2004; Shimada et al. 2004, 2010) below the Painted Temple and in the Pilgrim's Plaza.[2] Instead, we found clear evidence that this part of the North-South Street

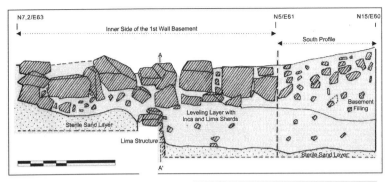

SECTOR: I	U. Exc: B3	TIPO: Perfil Sur	CONTEXTO: Cara Interior, 1ra Muralla		CAPA / NIVEL:

PROYECTO ARQUEOLÓGICO -TALLER DE CAMPO- "LOMAS DE LURIN" - PATL

PONTIFICIA UNIVERSIDAD CATÓLICA DEL PERÚ - CEMENTOS LIMA

SITIO: PACHACAMAC	FECHA: 07/04/2009	CÓDIGO: IB-3-028	N° Inv 0252
DIRECTOR: Dr. Krzysztof Makowski	DIB: Gabriela Oré M.	CAD: Gabriela Oré	
RESPONSABLE: Lic. Milagritos Jimenez / Lic. Gabriela Oré	COORDENADAS: N: 17.2 / E60-63		ESCALA: 1:20

FIGURE 5.7. *Profile of wall segment indicating that wall construction was aborted at point at which foundation was being prepared (drawing by Gabriela Oré).*

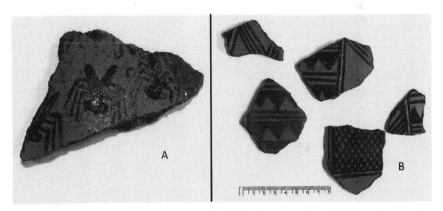

FIGURE 5.8. *Provincial Inka polychrome sherds found associated with the foundations of the First Wall (photographs by author).*

had been built in the early part of the Late Horizon. A solid floor associated with the foundations of one of the lateral walls was constructed upon sterile soil or an intentionally leveled layer bearing traces of heavy wear from foot traffic. This floor, composed of coarse clay, the canal lined with slabs of stone that cuts the floor in the middle of the street, and the west wall were all built

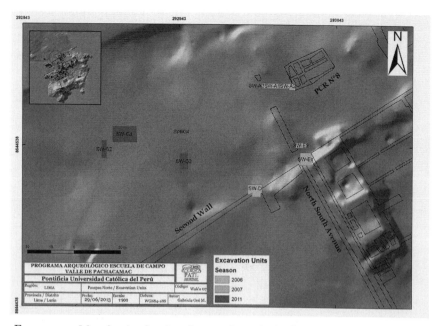

FIGURE 5.9. *Map showing location of excavation units in the area of the Second Wall (produced by Gabriela Oré).*

at the same time (Figure 5.10). The east wall had been remodeled by attaching a jamb that created a monumental entrance through the Second Wall. On the solid floor we recorded many layers of accumulation of wind-driven sand and some slight traces of the packed earth indicative of heavy traffic. Over time, the ground level rose, making it necessary to construct wells to reach the canals for cleaning.

In another trench we registered the partial dismantling of the lateral walls of the road after a catastrophic earthquake and before the construction of Pyramids V and VIII and the enclosure that connects them. The erection of the first of these pyramids entailed the destruction of the lateral eastern wall of the road, judging by the surface evidence. These two ramped pyramids are the only ones that were built outside the Second Wall. The back (west) wall of Pyramid VIII is situated 5 m from the northeast edge of the road (see Figure 5.9). Once the walls had been dismantled, the area where the road had once been located was built over with domestic wattle-and-daub structures. This latter occupation clearly dates to the Late Horizon, producing diagnostic materials such as Cuzco Provincial Polychrome *aríbalos* and dishes.

FIGURE 5.10. *East-west profile across the entrance to the North-South Street through the gate in the Second Wall, showing the floor of coarse clay and the stone-lined canal cutting through the floor in the middle of the street (photograph by author).*

These findings required us to revise our understanding of the role of the North-South Street. I am convinced that the major function of both it and the eastern extension of the East-West Road (see Figure 5.2) was to ensure access to Ramped Pyramid No. 2 (Paredes 1988) and thus, indirectly, to the Plaza of the Pilgrims. As both Paredes (1991) and Ravines (1996) correctly noted, however, the East-West Road differs significantly from the North-South Street. From its junction with the latter, the western end of the East-West Road lacks the formal characteristics of a street; rather it consists of irregular segments partially covered with piles of prehispanic refuse. The eastern extension of the East-West Road does, however, end at the entrance to the ramped pyramid (No. 2). A depression of nearly 4 m in depth recorded by Uhle (2003 [1903]; Shimada 1991) extends from the junction of the two roads and the possible sunken patio entrances to the Plaza of the Pilgrims.

Both streets also gave access to the storehouse area and the secondary patios at the rear and sides of Ramped Pyramids Nos. 1 and 12 (see Figure 5.2). The eastern part of the East-West Road only reaches the back door of the complex of Ramped Pyramid No. 1. Here a large depression opens onto a triangular-shaped field that is partially enclosed by tall piles of refuse. The stratigraphic sequence we recorded suggests the possibility that the intersecting road system was modified after Ramped Pyramid No. 2 was constructed (Franco 1998). The gateway in the Second Wall was also filled in with sand, and the entrance segment of the North-South street was dismantled and later partially covered over by wattle-and-daub constructions.

Given these findings, we had to ask ourselves the following question: where was the main entrance to the sanctuary of Pachacamac? People who entered the shrine from the north, through the gateway in the Third Wall, would have had to pass through the Second Wall at some point. Besides the access to the North-South Street, the Second Wall has only one more opening on the northern periphery of the monumental complex. This opening corresponds fairly closely to the visual axis that extends from the gateway in the Third Wall to the main ramp of Pyramid No. 1 (Figure 5.11a). It also has an inner buttress on the eastern side, similar to the one seen on the gateway in the Third Wall. Its shape is currently amorphous, as if it were simply a part of the wall that had collapsed due to either human or natural causes. At this location, we excavated two large areas on either side of the Second Wall (Figure 5.11b). The results proved very insightful. We were able to ascertain that this was actually the main entrance to the monumental complex of Pachacamac on the north side during the Late Horizon. The gateway was specifically designed as such and was built at the same time as the Second Wall. This is clear because the wide threshold of the doorway is a part of the wall's plinth; both were built together with two levels of large, interlocking, parallelepiped adobe bricks. The entrance to the inner patio was carefully prepared for heavy traffic. A thick floor of cast clay was built over an adobe brick platform affixed to the plinth. The fill used to level the floor contains a good deal of diagnostic Late Horizon material.

These results match the conclusions of the still-unpublished report of Ponciano Paredes, who excavated Ramped Pyramid No. 1 (Ramos 2011). Paredes believes that the monumental phase of this complex—now reconstructed—dates to the Late Horizon. Pyramids Nos. 1 and 4—which have different orientations—formed the hypothetical entrance-complex to the sanctuary complex of Pachacamac. Their ramps opened onto the same sequence of patios, one of which contained a large *puquio* (spring); now covered by sand; these patios were entered through the gateway in the Second Wall. I find the presence of a puquio—an essential element for the required ablutions prior fasting and other ritual acts—most significant.

A

B

FIGURE 5.11. *Gateway opening in the Second Wall opposite Ramped Pyramid No. 1 after the entrance to the North–South Street was destroyed by earthquake and abandoned: (a) before and (b) after excavation (photographs by author and Gabriela Oré).*

At the beginning of the first season of excavations in 2005, we considered several possible scenarios with respect to the role or possible roles of the area between the Second and Third Walls. The first idea was that it might have been a residential urban area that housed artisans and low-ranking officials; a second idea was that it might have been a complex with areas where goods and food were produced related to the pyramids with ramps and the large walled enclosures, or *canchones*. Third was the possibility that it could have been an encampment area meant to house the large numbers of laborers required to build the walls and structures ordered by the imperial administration, and also produce the cultural paraphernalia necessary for foundational rites and other ceremonial requirements. In this latter case, the complex would not have been expected to exhibit a planned organization. However, spatial relations of a functional nature might be expected given such a scenario linking control stations, communal areas of manufacture, the areas where food was prepared, and the relatively ephemeral residential areas distributed about the peripheries.

The results of our excavations on the north side of the Second Wall provided important evidence to support the third scenario (see Figure 5.9). Small reed and wattle-and-daub structures were found situated above and between the piles of refuse that surrounded a large rectangular structure subdivided into various rooms and built within a relatively short time period. Activities conducted in this large structure included food preparation and low-intensity craft production. The remarkable thickness and complex stratigraphy of the refuse piles in this area indicate the intensity of production processes that took place here. This organization of space seems to correspond to specific tasks entrusted to several nuclear family groups under a single command. The results of the ground-penetrating-radar (GPR)[3] and magnetometer survey (Figure 5.12) conclusively confirmed that the entire eastern expanse of the open field between the Second and Third Walls was given over to temporary activities and residences similar to what was found in the area excavated nearby by Daniel Guerrero and Hernán Carrillo (Guerrero, n.d.). The residential structures in the peripheries were not aligned with the roads, nor was any other planning criteria perceivable. But the architecture located close to the Second Wall was partially planned, with the main axis oriented along this feature. While we had anticipated finding a straight road between the gateways in the Third and the Second Walls that would have continued on to the north, this was not confirmed. Instead of a road or an area of packed earth lined by stones, excavations revealed a dense occupation area where activities and dwellings similar to those mentioned above were recorded.

FIGURE 5.12. *Map of grid of remote sensing survey conducted in 2006 and 2009 in the area of the Second Wall (produced by Gabriela Oré).*

All occupation levels in this area contained Late Horizon diagnostic materials. The stratigraphy in the excavation units matched that obtained through the GPR survey; in other words, we found only one level with architecture that went no deeper than 1 m below the current ground level. Below this Late Horizon level is the natural sandy soil. Through a series of test pit excavations, it was established that the sterile soil levels have a complex natural stratigraphy with multiple layers of saltpeter and alluvial sediments that correspond to episodes of unusual humidity or rain, such as occurred in the seventh or twelfth century AD. In 2010 this initial study was complemented with magnetometer studies.[4] The remote-sensing data from the open area around the Second Wall yielded conclusive negative results regarding the presence of residential agglomerations of an urban nature. To the contrary, a patchwork of relatively brief, and often unrelated, events was recorded in this sector, all dating to the Late Horizon.

The implications of the excavation results presented here are as follows. First, the monumental site of Pachacamac, the great temple and oracle of regional notoriety, was created by the Inka Empire. Indeed, it is likely that this special place on the edge of the fertile valley, in front of the guano islands, next to a freshwater lagoon and various other water sources, had previously been a wak'a, or a traditional place of worship, for the local people. But a careful review of the arguments of Maria Rostworowski (1999, 2002a) and other historians does not necessarily confirm that Pachacamac was a local cult for 1,000 years or more. This idea, which has also been championed by various archeologists (e.g., Franco 1993a, 1993b, 2004; Franco and Paredes 2000; Paredes and Franco 1988; Shimada 1991), arises from only one ambiguous material fact: the sloping sides of a pyramid built in the Lima period (approximately AD 300–600) served to support the Step Pyramid of the Late Intermediate period, whose outermost facades were painted during Inka times. However, it has never been demonstrated that the decision to build the Painted Temple on the side of the pyramid called the "Old Temple," which would have been in ruins and abandoned for at least two hundred years prior to the Inka intervention, was deliberate. The overlap of later Ychsma buildings on earlier Lima period ruins is common on the central coast of Peru, as seen, for example, at Maranga and Cajamarquilla, and does not necessarily imply continuity in use of architectural spaces. The decision to build one structure on or near another that has been abandoned for centuries or even decades can be due to any number of factors, ranging from random selection to convenience of location vis-à-vis natural features like water sources or high ground to vague perceptions of the sacredness of a site. To suggest that two temples built next to one another in two different periods were dedicated to the same deity would require evidence of continuity in architectural design or religious iconography, and no such evidence has yet been found at Pachacamac.

The Step Pyramid is usually called the Temple of Pachacamac, although neither the mural decoration nor the iconographic program of the two-faced idol matches the presumed personality traits of the "organizer of the universe," or "the god who remains in the bowels of the earth," to whom the temple was believed to have been dedicated (Dulanto 2001). The sculpture at the top of the pyramid represents two independent figures. Each of these deities differs in important details of dress and attributes from the other. One appears to represent a god associated with the land and the growth of corn, and the other a being of opposite nature, e.g., a god of the heavens. The mural decoration of the pyramid from the Inka period (see Bonavia 1985) becomes the symbolic image of an island with corn, surrounded by the sea full of fish. These figurative designs would appear to have been inspired by the myths of two other ancient gods worshiped at Pachacamac: Cuniraya Viracocha and his lover,

Cahuillaca, who became an offshore island (visible from the sanctuary) in an attempt to flee the persecution of the supernatural father of her child.

Structures of later periods built over those of the Lima period are very common on the central coast and don't represent positive proof of the continuity of worship in any given place. On the other hand, the Pachacamac idol's decoration (see Dulanto 2001) appears to be closely linked with northern traditions—particularly as seen at the Huaca del Dragon in the Moche Valley, Chotuna in Lambayeque (Donnan 2011:233–44), and in the motifs associated with the ceramic tradition of the Casma Valley (Shimada 1991). Perhaps it is no coincidence that the Huaca de la Luna in Trujillo bore the name of Pachacamac (Rostworowski 2002a). In the myths recorded by the chroniclers, Pachacamac is portrayed as a foreign deity in contrast to the goddesses Cahuillaca and Urpaihuachac and the god Cuniraya Viracocha. The hypothesis that the cult of Pachacamac was brought by the Inkas from the north to the central coast and merged with local cults is a tempting one.

In any case, it is evident that the Inka administration appropriated the sacred landscape of Pachacamac and transformed it completely. It seems that every Sapa Inka added another set of buildings to the site, including Ramped Pyramids Nos. 1, 2, 4, and 8 and perhaps many others. Enclosing perimeter walls were also being continuously erected during the Late Horizon. There are signs that ramped pyramids and other secondary buildings were used briefly and then essentially abandoned. There is no single or permanent road system that links the large walled enclosures (canchones) and ramped pyramids to the Pilgrim's Plaza, the Painted Temple, the Pyramid of the Sun, or the Acllahuasi. Each building had its own separate entrance system and reception area for visitors. As a hypothesis, we can suggest that the visitors to the temple oracle were housed, perhaps according to their place of origin, in the courtyards in front of the ramped pyramids and were allowed to access the Pilgrim's Plaza after fasting.

As noted above, the pyramids with ramps were fully in use during Inka times and many of them were constructed during the Late Horizon (Pavel Svendsen 2011:155–56). At least three of them (Nos. 1, 2, and 4) played a key role in the hypothetical reception given to pilgrims who entered the shrine from the north (see Figure 5.2). It is therefore reasonable to postulate that they never functioned as permanent or principal residences of Ychsma lords, as has been previously suggested, at least during the period of Inka occupation of the site. There are several arguments for this line of thinking, with some of the evidence for this supposition coming from excavations at the site of Pueblo Viejo–Pucará—another striking example of the Inkaic creation of a new sacred landscape and new landscapes of power.

THE WAK'AS OF THE MITMAQKUNA
SETTLEMENT OF PUEBLO VIEJO-PUCARÁ

The site of Pueblo Viejo–Pucará was the abode of the lords of Caringa, the major chiefdom on the left bank of the Ychsma Valley (Makowski 2002). The site lies less than 15 km from the ceremonial center of Pachacamac in the *lomas* grazing zone (400–600 m a.s.l., which is still used today by the highland herders of Santo Domingo de los Olleros (see Figure 5.1). It is located in the labyrinthine system of lateral ravines that crisscross the first spurs of the Andes. It is worth noting that Pueblo Viejo–Pucará visually dominates the access to Pachacamac from the south and east. Archaeological excavations at the site produced ceramics diagnostic of the Inka period in all stratigraphic levels, and our investigations conclusively demonstrate that it was built during the Late Horizon and abandoned shortly after first contact with the Spaniards, around 1560 AD (Makowski 2002).

The site is situated in a naturally fortified location. Recurring evidence of weapons manufacture and camelid husbandry suggest that Pueblo Viejo–Pucará was occupied by allies of the Inka, perhaps a military detachment, which may have been charged with the management of the herds pertaining to Pachacamac as well. This Late Horizon urban center, or *llacta*, is about 12 ha in size (not counting the agricultural terraces or minor activity areas noted on the peripheries, which would increase the size of the site to approximately 26 ha in total).

Excavations at the site encompassed an area of more than 11,000 m² and uncovered two palatial dwellings, a small temple, and portions of four residential precincts (Figure 5.13). Each of the residential precincts comprise several courtyard units containing from three to five groups of houses whose entrances open onto a common area of irregular shape that may be partially enclosed. The architecture of both the common houses and the elite dwellings has the same modular design. A module comprised two rectangular rooms connected by a passageway that usually contained two, two-story storage units. Areas with human burials were found within most of the residential groups. Some of the storerooms were turned into mortuary chambers to receive various of individuals. The bodies were seated in a flexed position; they had probably been buried fully dressed but with no other wrappings, to judge by the position of the bone elements. The types and amounts of associated funerary objects correspond to the highland tradition (Isbell 1997; Salomon 1995). The spatial organization of the Pueblo Viejo–Pucará settlement also suggests a form of social organization common to the highlands involving division into upper and lower halves, each of which contained a palace-like house as seen in Sectors II and IV.

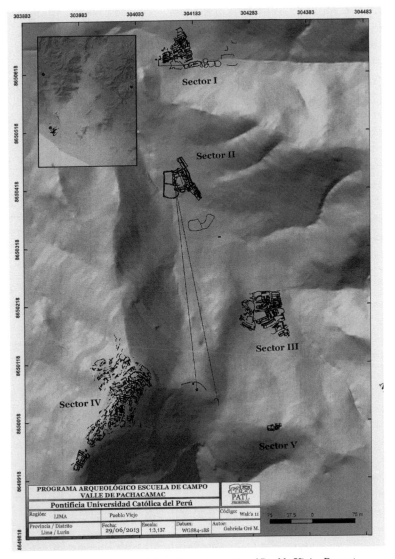

FIGURE 5.13. *General plan of the mitmaqkuna site of Pueblo Viejo–Pucará, located above and to the northeast of Pachacamac. The palatial complexes are associated with Sectors II and IV; the small temple is located between Sectors IV and V; and distinct residential precincts are found in Sectors I, III, IV, and V. The two straight lines indicate the visual field, which extends from the ushnu platform in Sector II to the space between two sukanka-like circular structures located on the top of the summit temple platform (produced by Gabriela Oré).*

Many of the structures found in the four residential areas were clearly elite dwellings. These contained from two to six modules, each with porch-terraces that opened onto a common internal patio. Access to the interior patio space from the outside was restricted (Makowski et al. 2005, 2008). As mentioned, two dwellings at the site are clearly palace-like in size and composition. They have large double kitchens associated with the courtyard, along with evidence of food and drink having been prepared for a large number of people. Several outbuildings, including various domestic enclosures and large corrals, are associated with the largest of the two palaces, which also had three ample patios and a general monumental character (Figure 5.14). Two of the patios are not connected with the domestic sectors and appear to have had a ceremonial function to judge by the finds of *Spondylus* and the presence of a large, wak'a-like rock in the center of one.

The palaces are neither Inka in design nor made of cut stone masonry, but the principal palace in the lower half of the settlement includes two ceremonial courtyards with a typical Inka altar-ushnu that was likely given periodic libations. The material culture, the residential and public architecture, and apparent customs of the former residents of Pueblo Viejo–Pucará are very similar to those known for the peoples living near the headwaters of the Lurín Valley, and from Huarochirí itself, where Avila recorded the traditions of the Checa (Salomon and Urioste 1991; Chase, this volume).

Thanks to the high degree of preservation, three sacred places containing several probable wak'as in their original contexts were documented at the Pueblo Viejo–Pucará settlement. These include an ushnu-altar, the summit temple comprising a monumental platform with staircase and two *sukanka*-like circular structures,[5] and a *huanca*-altar. The features identified here as potential wak'as correspond closely with the descriptions provided by both Avila (see Salomon and Urioste 1991) and Polo de Ondegardo (1916 [1571]), among other early colonial sources. For instance, the offerings found in the crevices of the sacred rock on the summit temple and around it consisted of gold beads, pieces of gold and silver sheet metal, fragments of *Spondylus princeps,* and a *sara conopa* (Figure 5.15a, b). These items are similar to those received by the highest-ranking wak'as in Cuzco (Rowe 1979).

We suggest that the element referred to as an ushnu at Pueblo Viejo–Pucará warrants this name for several reasons in spite of the fact that it is not part of an architectural complex as seen at other classic Inka sites. The ushnu at Pueblo Viejo–Pucará consists of an elevated platform containing a loose gravel fill that dominates two ceremonial plazas where *Spondylus princeps* and other fragmented mollusk shells were found. Excavations around the base of

FIGURE 5.14. *Palatial compound in Sector II in the lower part of Pueblo Viejo–Pucará (photograph by author).*

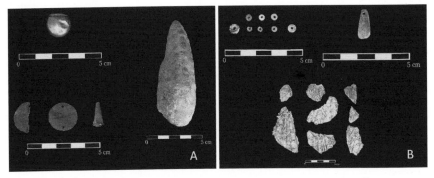

FIGURE 5.15. *Offerings found in association with the stone outcrop and wak'a comprising part of the summit temple at Pueblo Viejo–Pucará: (a) spherical gold bead, perforated silver discs, propitiatory amulet, and carved corn (Zea mays) conopa; (b) Spondylus princeps shell fragments, a pendant, and eight beads made of Spondylus shell (photographs by Manuel Lizárraga).*

this elevated platform produced a vessel decorated with modeled corncobs (Makowski et al. 2008). The platform is accessed by staircases from the two ceremonial plazas and a ramp from the central patio of the palace where evidence of banquets with abundant consumption of corn beer, deer meat, and camelids was recovered.

From the ushnu platform, the visual axis extends toward the south and is demarcated by the space between two circular, turret-like structures built on the summit temple platform (see Figure 5.13). One of these structures contains a sacred rock (Figure 5.16a) to which gold and silver had been offered, as noted above, while the other had contained a huanca-idol originally located in the interior center of the structure (Figure 5.16b). Viewed from the ushnu, these two round structures stood out against the horizon like sukankas. A second huanca-idol with an associated altar is found along the same visual axis in the middle of a large corral at the foot of the mountain.

Unlike the settlement, the summit temple of Pueblo Viejo–Pucará exhibits signs of systematic and intentional destruction, which was performed, in all likelihood, by the extirpators of idolatries in the early colonial period. Only the retaining wall of the platform, with its monumental staircase of nine steps, remains intact. The walls of the two circular structures were dismantled down to their foundations. It is estimated that they may have originally reached 3 m in height, based on a comparison of their average width with the better-preserved structures at the site. Both structures had two narrow doors, the widths of which varied between 0.56 m to 0.85 m; the interior space within each, however, was so small that one could not have easily walked around either the huanca or the rock outcrop contained inside the two enclosures. The location of the double apertures in both circular structures is best explained by the play of light. Tracking the progress of light and shadows projected through a narrow entrance over the surface of niches or small rooms was one of the principal methods used to define ceremonial time in Inka architecture (Ziólkowski and Sadowski 1992:46–64, fig. 10).

The one huanca preserved in situ in Pueblo Viejo–Pucará is found in the middle of the livestock corrals located to the south of the main palace in the lower moiety. The monolith is attached to a small stone platform, which may constitute an altar. As attested by Duviols (1973, 1979), huancas were typically found in pairs, and marked the center of the two halves that comprised the sacred space of highland communities in the sixteenth and seventeenth centuries (see also Dean, this volume). One of the two huancas, which was linked to the founding ancestor and protector of the community (the huanca marcayoc), was erected at the spring, canal, or cave from which the founding

FIGURE 5.16. *The summit temple at Pueblo Viejo–Pucará with two circular structures: (a) circular structure with two narrow entrances and sacred rock outcrop inside; (b) circular structure with two narrow entrances and hole in center where monolith, or huanca, would have originally been placed (photographs by Manuel Lizárraga).*

ancestor had originally emerged (Arriaga 1999 [1621]:128). The other huanca was called huanca chacrayoc, and, as its name suggests, it was located in the middle of the community's cultivated fields, or at the boundary between fields and pasture (Arriaga 1999 [1621]:128). In the Andean highlands, the settlement area—which in Quechua is *marca*—is generally located near sources of water in the valley bottoms or near the edge of terraces that overlook deep valleys. Conversely, the cultivated fields (*chakras*) climb up the slopes almost to the edge of the pasture lands. A natural opposition thus arises between the center of the productive half above and the center of the populated half below.

Within a classificatory scheme that is recurrent in Andean cultural reality, one of these centers relates to the male ancestors, e.g., the marcayoc, considered the colonizer and proprietor of a village, and the other to the female ancestors, e.g., the chacrayoc, the tiller and owner of the productive fields (Dean 2001; Duviols 1979). In imperial Cuzco the main male ancestor known as Huanacauri dominated the landscape from the summit of a nearby mountain. Huanacauri purportedly merged with the huanca marcayoc of Cuzco (associated with the third of the Ayar brothers, the founders of Inka Cuzco) and Zañu (the local, non-Inka ancestor) (Urbano 1981). In Pueblo Viejo–Pucará, the huanca within the circular structure on the summit temple would be classified as the huanca chacrayoc while the huanca located in the heart of the settlement near the corrals would likely have constituted the huanca marcayoc.

The main symbolic and ceremonial axis for important sacred places in the Andean highlands is the north-south alignment. The people of Pueblo Viejo–Pucará chose to construct their main temple at a site on the visual horizon very close to the south celestial pole as seen from the ushnu platform (see Figure 5.13). All the evidence suggests that this choice of location, as well as the specific rock outcrop, was carefully selected. At the opposite end of this axis, to the north, is Cerro Botija—the highest peak in the area—on the summit of which has been found offerings of shell (Figure 5.17). Investigations on the slopes of this mountain have revealed a facility to condense fog that would have produced water for irrigation and a reservoir; we believe these features were likely constructed by the people of Pueblo Viejo–Pucará (Makowski 2008).

The location of the summit temple wak'as do not correspond to astronomically relevant orientations related to calendric calculations (Makowski and Ruggles 2011). Rather there seems to have been a different intention behind their placement. We believe the aim of the builders of the summit temple and the ushnu was to create a proper frame for the ritual activities carried

FIGURE 5.17. *Cerro Botija, the highest peak in the area, seen from the summit temple looking north in the dry season when the vegetation grows thanks to fog condensation (e.g., the loma phenomenon); structures seen below in center of photo comprise the palatial compound and associated ceremonial plazas and ushnu in Sector II (photograph by author).*

out in the ceremonial space defined by the wak'as adjacent to the palace of the principal ethnic lord. In this area of the coast, the dry season comes to an end at the beginning of November when the thick fog known as *garua* disappears (except during anomalous years). At this time of year, a portion of the starry sky becomes visible from the ushnu in the broad pass between two local peaks named Lomas de Pucará. It is on the top of this broad pass that the summit temple with the two sukanka-like circular structures was built. In a recent archaeoastronomical study, Makowski and Ruggles (2011) demonstrated that these two structures frame astronomical south and point to where the Andean constellation Yacana-Llama appears in the night sky in the corresponding months of the rainy season in the mountains. Local people from colonial times to the present have believed that the longer this constellation can be viewed through this pass, the more intense will be the summer heat in the coast and the more water will fill the Lurín riverbed.

The observation of dark constellations within the Milky Way, together with the tracking of bright constellations such as the Pleiades (known as Catachillay in Quechua), played a substantial role in both Andean calendrical calculations (Zuidema 1982) and weather prediction. For the people of Huarochirí in the sixteenth century, the constellations were particularly important for the forecasting of rain. The well-being of many Andean communities was highly dependent on the volume of rain predicted, and the rains were believed to be related to the behavior of the Yacana, the mythical llama who drinks water from the Mayu river (Milky Way) in the night sky (Salomon and Urioste 1991, chap. 29). The reappearance of the mythical llama's head and eyes, e.g., the star clusters Alfa and Beta Centauri, located near the South Pole, in the months of November and December signaled the beginning of the new agricultural cycle for Andean communities (Zuidema and Urton 1976). Farmers predicted the intensity and duration of the rains from the intensity of the trajectory of the Yacana and other dark constellations, like H'anpatu, the Toad, near the Southern Cross.[6]

The features of the summit temple discussed above suggest that it (re)constituted the *paqarina*, or ancestral wak'a, of the Caringa mitmaqkuna from Huarochirí (see also Chase, this volume). This mitmaq population, resettled by imperial mandate to guard the flocks of Pachacamac and defend the oracle site, would appear to have moved their wak'a with them to their new location. In reconstituting their llacta within this new setting, the Caringa reestablished their native wak'a precisely where it belonged in the new, imperially ordered landscape—to the south of the ushnu.

CONCLUSIONS

This chapter presents some of the results of archaeological investigations conducted at two landmark settlements in the Lurín (Ychsma) Valley that have long been recognized for their importance and complexity. The field research undertaken at the sites of Pachacamac and Pueblo Viejo–Pucará by the author over the past two decades invites us to reconsider the standard interpretations of Inka political strategies on the central coast that have traditionally privileged the documentary sources (see also Chase, this volume). Based on her reading of the historical materials, Rostworowski (1972, 1999, 2002a, 2002b) suggested that the imperial footprint on the central coast was both discrete and limited, with local political and religious structures as well as economic organization left largely intact by the Inka out of deference to the power and prestige of the god Pachacamac. As a consequence of this view, it has typically been assumed that all late-period structures and sites in the Lurín Valley that lack clear sign of Cuzco-style masonry or form must predate the Inka conquest, e.g. that they must pertain to the Late Intermediate period or earlier.

The results of our investigations show that this is not the case. Most buildings constructed during the Late Horizon, to judge by associations with provincial Inka pottery, lack diagnostic features of Cuzco's imperial architecture of stone and adobe. It is also evident from our research that the Inka administration completely appropriated the existing sacred landscape of Pachacamac, encompassing the sacred islands of Cahuillaca, the lagoon of Urpaihuachac, and the temples of Cuniraya Viracocha, and fully transformed it. The Inka clearly established a new military urban settlement with mitmaqkuna from Huarochirí who were relocated to Pueblo Viejo–Pucará, and made the *yunga* people from the left bank of the Ychsma (Lurín) River submit to the power of this highland population, who had become allies of the Cuzqueños. The Pachacamac area was but one component of a larger overall plan whose apparent purpose was to reorganize the economic management of the lands and resources of the Lurín Valley, turning it into the "pantry" of the Punchao and Pachacamac wak'as. Other new settlements like Huaycán de Cieneguilla (Álvarez Calderón 2008; Marcone and López-Hurtado 2002) certainly formed part of this plan. Many of these late-period sites are distinct from one another in terms of both public and domestic architecture—an aspect that likely reflects the different origins of the communities relocated to these sites by the imperial administration.

The question of whether the settlements containing platforms with ramps found in the Lurín and other central coast valleys were established by the Inka administration or whether they were simply expanded during the Late Horizon with the construction of new areas of residential and public architecture remains open (Eeckhout 1999b, 2009, 2010; Makowski 2002; Makowski et al. 2008). At Panquilma, for example, López-Hurtado (2011) found Inka sherds in association with both earlier and later phases of occupation in excavations around the platforms with ramps at the site. In any case, it is clear that the distribution of settlements with residential occupation dating to the Late Horizon correlates closely with the main farming and herding areas in the valley and the lomas zone.

It is likely that the construction and/or reuse of platforms with ramps in the Lurín Valley and elsewhere on the central coast during the Late Horizon was related to the special status of the resident populations of these settlements as those who paid tribute to the Inka-sponsored deity Pachacamac. We have shown in the previous discussion that visitors to Pachacamac during the Late

Horizon arrived through a gate in the facade of the Second Wall, after which they entered enclosed plaza spaces in front of the ramped pyramids. During the excavations, abundant evidence of large-scale food and drink preparation was recovered in these plaza spaces, suggesting ritual feasting activity (Eeckhout 2010).

It is reasonable to suggest that the buildings that served to bring together the faithful at the beginning and end of their hypothetical pilgrimages, e.g., the platforms with ramps, would have been an appropriate setting for the appearance of the local ethnic lords, or *kurakas*, who served as intermediaries for the Inka. From atop the raised platform, the kuraka and his subordinates, or *mandones,* could preside over ceremonial acts after the pilgrims had deposited their gifts and tribute in the form of foodstuffs in the warehouses at the rear of the building complex. A similar platform in miniature likely served for comparable tributary or offering purposes in the context of the festivities held at each of the outlying settlements in the Lurín and other central coast valleys such as Panquilma (see López-Hurtado 2011). This does not necessarily mean that the platform or pyramid with ramp was conceived as the main or even secondary residence of the kurakas. Neither the ramped pyramids nor the platforms with ramps have produced unambiguous evidence of domestic habitation (Villacorta 2004). On the other hand, there is plenty of indication of the sacredness of these architectural spaces (Farfán 2004). The buildings whose palatial function was clearly indicated, such as found at Puruchuco (Villacorta 2004, 2010) or Pueblo Viejo–Pucará (Makowski et al. 2005), differ significantly from the ramped pyramids insofar as they contain large residential areas, as well as areas for reception, ceremonial activities, and depository functions.

In the context of the evidence presented, it should be clear that the typological distinctions embedded in the division of architectural spaces into secular versus ceremonial, as seen in the use of such common terms as "palace" and "temple," are both mistaken and inappropriate. The whole landscape, with or without monumental architecture, was most likely the setting for Andean ceremonialism, simultaneously retaining both its sacred character and its economic significance. The transformation of the ceremonial landscape via the construction of new wak'as at Pachacamac, such as the Temple of Sun, the new lagoon, and the acllahuasi (Tello 2009), as well as the creation of monumental architectural spaces where people could both worship and pay tribute, was undoubtedly a principal instrument of imperial policy and an effective tool of ideological domination. In this way, the submission of the local deities to the imperial gods in the collective religious consciousness was probably achieved, and the acceptance of the power of Cuzco over the local yunga lands and peoples of the coast materially realized.

ACKNOWLEDGMENTS

The author takes this opportunity to express his gratitude to all members of the Archaeological Program, the Field School "Pachacamac Valley" of the Pontifical Catholic University of Peru, and, in particular, to Milagritos Jimenez, Gabriela Oré, Cynthia Vargas, Carla Hernandez, María Fe Córdova, Lucia Watson, Alain Vallenas, Gonzalo Presbítero, Manuel Lizárraga, and Tomasz Lapa. Special thanks goes, as well, to UNACEM Association (formerly Cementos Lima). Thanks to their generous support, our research in the Lurín Valley has been able to continue without interruption from 1991 to the present.

NOTES

1. The illegal activity of the looters took place mostly in the years between 1919 and 1924 (Daggett 1988:13; Tello 2009:357–58, fig. 295).

2. This was because we expected that several road levels and various road layouts would have been superimposed on the place where the main entrance to the shrine of Pachacamac was likely located. Patterson (1985; see also Bueno 1970, 1974–75, 1982; Shimada 1991) believed the main road had been in use since the Lima period, i.e. for almost a thousand years, since the North-South Street seems to head toward the pyramid made with small adobe bricks like those found in the Old Temple.

3. The excavations were supplemented with a ground-penetrating-radar survey (GPR) in 2006 using the ZOND 12E geo-radar of Finnish manufacture; this instrument had a bipolar antenna as well as two external 500 and 700 MHz antennae; Jaroslaw Jaworski was in charge of the study.

4. Two types of magnetometers, fluxgate and cesium gradiometer, as well as a differential GPS were used by Dr. Krzysztof Misiewicz from the Ptolemais Warsaw University in this investigation.

5. "*Sukanka*" is mentioned in colonial sources as being a two-pillar device that was built on the Cuzco visual horizon to enable the determination of the position of the sun and provide the reference for the calculation of calendrical dates and events. Because of the presumed distance from the point of observation, scholars agree that *sukanka* must have been somewhat turret-like in form and appearance (Williams 2001; Zuidema 1988, 2010:171–91).

6. It is interesting that both of these creatures (the llama and the toad) appear to be embroidered into the famous Brooklyn mantle in which they are depicted with

crops growing out of the their bodies; this mantle, which dates to the period AD 1–300, is housed in the Brooklyn Museum (Makowski 2000:304, fig. 52; 2005).

REFERENCES CITED

Álvarez Calderón, Rosabella. 2008. "El uso de espacios comunitarios en un asentamiento del horizonte tardío: El caso de huaycán de cieneguilla en el valle de Lurín." Master's thesis, College of Letters and Human Sciences, Pontificia Universidad Católica del Perú, Lima.

Arriaga, Pablo Joseph de. 1999 [1621]. *La extirpación de la idolatría en el Pirú*. Ed. Henrique Urbano. Cusco: Centro de Estudios Regionales Andinos "Bartolomé de Las Casas."

Bauer, Brian S. 1998. *The Sacred Landscape of the Inca: The Cuzco Ceque System*. Austin: University of Texas Press.

Bauer, Brian S. 2004. *Ancient Cuzco: Heartland of the Inca*. Austin: University of Texas Press.

Bonavia, Duccio. 1985. *Mural Painting in Ancient Peru*. Bloomington: Indiana University Press.

Bueno, Alberto. 1970. "Breves notas acerca de Pachacamac." *Arqueología y Sociedad* 4: 13–24.

Bueno, Alberto. 1974–75. "Cajamarquilla y Pachacamac: Dos ciudades de la costa central del Perú." *Boletín Bibliográfico de Antropología Americana* 37 (46):171–93.

Bueno, Alberto. 1982. "El antiguo valle de Pachacamac: Espacio, tiempo y cultura." *Boletín de Lima* 24: 10–29.

Daggett, Richard E. 1988. "The Pachacamac Studies: 1938–1941." *Michigan Discussions in Anthropology* 8: 13–22.

Dean, Carolyn. 2001. "Andean Androgyny and the Making of Men." In *Gender in Pre-Hispanic America*, ed. Cecelia F. Klein, 143–82. Washington, DC: Dumbarton Oaks Research Library and Collection, Trustees for Harvard University.

Donnan, Christopher. 2011. *Chotuna and Chornancap: Excavating an Ancient Peruvian Legend*. Monograph 70. Los Angeles: Cotsen Institute of Archaeology, University of California, Los Angeles.

Dulanto, Jahl. 2001. "Dioses de Pachacamac: El idolo y el templo." In *Los dioses del antiguo Perú*, vol. 2, ed. Krzysztof Makowski, 159–84. Lima: Banco de Crédito del Perú.

Duviols, Pierre. 1973. "Huari y llacuaz, agricultores y pastores: Un dualismo prehispánico de oposición y complementariedad." *Revista del Museo Nacional(Lima)* 39:153–91.

Duviols, Pierre. 1979. "Un symbolisme de l'occupation, de l'aménagement et de l'exploitation de l'espace: Le monolithe "huanca" et sa fonction dans les andes préhispaniques." *L'Homme* 19 (2): 7–31. http://dx.doi.org/10.3406/hom.1979.367954.

Eeckhout, Peter. 1995. "Pirámide con rampa N° 3 de Pachacamac, costa central del Perú: Resultados preliminares de la primera temporada de excavaciones (Zona 1 y 2)." *Bulletin de l'Institut Français d'Études Andines* 24 (1): 65–106.

Eeckhout, Peter. 1998. "Le temple de Pachacamac sous l'empire Inca." *Journal de la Société des Americanistes* 84 (1): 9–44. http://dx.doi.org/10.3406/jsa.1998.1768.

Eeckhout, Peter. 1999a. "Pirámide con rampa N° III, Pachacamac: Nuevos datos, nuevas perspectivas." *Bulletin de l'Institut Français d'Études Andines* 28 (2): 169–214.

Eeckhout, Peter. 1999b. *Pachacamac durant l'intermédiaire récent: Étude d'un site monumental prehispánique de la côte centrale du Pérou.* BAR international series, No. 747. Oxford: Hadrian Books Ltd.

Eeckhout, Peter. 2003a. "Diseño arquitectónico, patrones de ocupación y formas de poder en Pachacamac, costa central del Perú." *Revista Española de Antropología Americana* 33:17–37.

Eeckhout, Peter. 2003b. "Ancient Monuments and Patterns of Power at Pachacamac, Central Coast of Perú." *Beiträge zur allgemeinen und vergleichend archäologie* 23: 139–82.

Eeckhout, Peter. 2004a. "La sombra de Ychsma: Ensayo introductorio sobre la arqueología de la costa central del Perú en los periodos tardíos." *Bulletin de l'Institut Français d'Études Andines* 33 (3): 403–23.

Eeckhout, Peter. 2004b. "Pachacámac y el proyecto Ychsma (1999–2003)." *Bulletin de l'Institut Français d'Études Andines* 33 (3): 425–48.

Eeckhout, Peter. 2004c. "Reyes del sol y señores de la luna: Inkas e Ychsmas en Pachacámac." *Chungara, Revista de Antropología Chilena* 36 (2): 495–503.

Eeckhout, Peter. 2005. "Ancient Peru's Power Elite." *National Geographic* 207 (3): 52–57.

Eeckhout, Peter. 2008. "El oráculo de Pachacamac y los peregrinajes a larga distancia en el mundo andino antiguo." In *Adivinación y Oráculos en el Mundo Andino Antiguo*, ed. Marco Curatola Petrocchi and Mariusz S. Ziólkowski, 161–80. Lima: Fondo Editorial de la Pontificia Universidad Católica del Perú.

Eeckhout, Peter. 2009. "Poder y jerarquías Ychsmas en el valle de Lurín." *Arqueología y Sociedad* 19: 223–40.

Eeckhout, Peter. 2010. "Las pirámides con rampa de Pachacamac durante el horizonte tardío." In *Arqueología en el Perú: Nuevos aportes para el estudio de las sociedades andinas prehispánicas*, ed. Romero Velarde Rubén and Trine Pavel Svendsen, 415–34. Lima: Anheb Impresiones.

Farfán, Carlos. 2004. "Aspectos simbólicos de las pirámides con rampa. Ensayo interpretativo." *Bulletin de l'Institut Français d'Études Andines* 33 (3): 449–64.

Franco, Régulo. 1993a. "Los dos templos principales de Pachacamac." *Revista del Museo de Arqueología* 4: 55–77.

Franco, Régulo. 1993b. "El centro ceremonial de Pachacamac: Nuevas evidencias en el Templo Viejo." *Boletín de Lima* 86:45–62.

Franco, Régulo. 1998. *La pirámide con rampa Nº 2 de Pachacamac: Excavaciones y nuevas interpretaciones.* Trujillo: N.p.

Franco, Régulo. 2004. "Poder religioso, crisis y prosperidad en Pachacamac: Del horizonte medio al intermedio tardío." *Bulletin de l'Institut Français d'Études Andines* 33 (3): 465–506.

Franco, Régulo, and Ponciano Paredes. 2000. "El templo viejo de Pachacamac: Nuevos aportes al estudio del horizonte medio." *Boletín de Arqueología* 4:607–30.

Guerrero, Daniel. N.d. "La portada del santuario de Pachacamac, valle de Lurín: Excavaciones en la tercera muralla (periodo horizonte tardío, 1470–1533)." Manuscript in possession of the author.

Hyslop, John. 1990. *Inka Settlement Planning.* Austin: University of Texas Press.

Isbell, William H. 1997. *Mummies and Mortuary Monuments: A Postprocessual Prehistory of Central Andean Social Organization.* Austin: University of Texas Press.

Jiménez Borja, Arturo. 1985. "Pachacamac." *Boletín de Lima* 38:40–54.

López-Hurtado, Luis Enrique. 2011. "Ideology and the Development of Social Hierarchy at the Site of Panquilma, Peruvian Central Coast." PhD diss., Department of Anthropology, University of Pittsburgh. Ann Arbor, MI: University Microfilms.

Lumbreras, Luís Guillermo. 1974. *The Peoples and Cultures of Ancient Perú.* Washington, DC: Smithsonian Institution Press.

Makowski, Krzysztof. 2000. "Los seres sobrenaturales en la iconografía Paracas y Nasca." In *Los dioses del antiguo Perú*, vol. 1, ed. Krzysztof Makowski, 277–307. Lima: Banco de Crédito del Perú.

Makowski, Krzysztof. 2002. "Arquitectura, estilo e identidad en el horizonte tardío: El sitio de Pueblo Viejo-Pucará, valle de Lurín." *Boletín de Arqueología* 6:137–70.

Makowski, Krzysztof. 2005. "La imagen de la sociedad y del mundo sobrenatural en el manto de Brooklyn." In *Tejiendo sueños en el cono sur: Textiles andinos, pasado, presente y futuro*, ed. Victoria Solanilla Demestre, 102–23. Proceedings of the 51st Congreso Internacional de Americanistas, Santiago de Chile. Barcelona: Grupo d'Estudios Precolombinos, Universidad de Barcelona.

Makowski, Krzysztof. 2007. "The Transformation of Pachacamac's Layout during Inca Occupation and the Network of Entrances to the Pyramids with Ramps."

Paper presented at the 47th Annual Meeting of the Institute for Andean Studies Meeting, Berkeley, CA.

Makowski, Krzysztof. 2008. "Fog Facility at Pueblo Viejo-Pucará." Paper presented at the conference "Taller Interdisciplinario sobre Cambios Socioambientales en la Agricultura del Sur Andino desde hace 1,000 años." Institut de Recherche pour le Développement (IRD), La Paz, Bolivia, October 28–30, 2008.

Makowski, Krzysztof, María Fe Córdova, Patricia Habetler, and Manuel Lizárraga. 2005. "La plaza y la fiesta: Reflexiones acerca de la función de los patios en la arquitectura pública prehispánica de los periodos tardíos." *Boletín de Arqueología* 9:297–333.

Makowski, Krzysztof, Iván Ghezzi, Daniel Guerrero, Héctor Neff, Milagritos Jimenez, Gabriela Oré, and Rosabella Álvarez Calderón. 2008. "Pachacamac, Ychsma y los Caringas: Estilos e identidades en el valle de Lurín Inca." In *Arqueología de la Costa Centro Sur Peruana*, ed. Omar Pinedo and Henry Tantaleán, 267–316. Lima: Avqi.

Makowski, Krzysztof, and Clive Ruggles. 2011. "Watching the Sky from the Ushnu: The Sukanka-like Summit Temple in Pueblo Viejo-Pucará (Lurín Valley, Peru)." In *Archaeoastronomy and Ethnoastronomy Building Bridges between Cultures. (Proceedings of International Astronomical Union Symposia and Colloquia)*, ed. Clive Ruggles, 169–77. Proceedings of the 278th Symposium of the International Astronomical Union, Lima, January 5–14, 2011. IAU Symposium Proceedings Series, 278. Cambridge: Cambridge University Press.

Marcone, Giancarlo, and Luis Enrique López-Hurtado. 2002. "Panquilma y Cieneguilla en la discusión arqueológica del horizonte tardío en la costa central." *Boletín de Arqueología PUCP* 6:375–94.

Matsumoto, Go. 2005. "Pachacamac GIS Project: A Practical Application of Geographic Information Systems and Remote Sensing Techniques in Andean Archaeology." Master's thesis, Department of Anthropology, Southern Illinois University at Carbondale, Carbondale.

Menzel, Dorothy. 1964. "Style and Time in the Middle Horizon." *Ñawpa Pacha* 2: 1–105.

Menzel, Dorothy. 1968. "New data on the Huari Empire in Middle Horizon Epoch 2A." *Ñawpa Pacha* 6:47–114.

Menzel, Dorothy. 1977. *The Archaeology of Ancient Peru and the Work of Max Uhle.* Berkeley: R. H. Lowie Museum of Anthropology, University of California.

Paredes, Ponciano. 1988. "Pachacamac—Pirámide con rampa N° 2." *Boletín de Lima* 55:41–58.

Paredes, Ponciano. 1991. "Pachacamac: Murallas y caminos epimurales." *Boletín de Lima* 74:85–95.

Paredes, Ponciano, and Régulo Franco. 1988. "La huaca pintada o el templo de Pachacamac." *Boletín de Lima* 55:70–84.

Patterson, Thomas C. 1966. *Pattern and Process in the Early Intermediate Period Pottery of the Central Coast of Peru.* Berkeley: University of California Press.

Patterson, Thomas C. 1985. "Pachacamac: An Andean Oracle under Inca Rule." In *Recent Studies in Andean Prehistory and Protohistory,* ed. Peter Kvietok and Daniel Sandweiss, 159–75. Ithaca, NY: Cornell University.

Pavel Svendsen, Trine. 2011. "La presencia Inca en las pirámides con rampa de Pachacamac: Una propuesta para su cronología y función desde la perspectiva de la cerámica." Master's thesis, Andean Studies Program, Graduate School, Pontificia Universidad Católica del Perú, Lima.

Polo de Ondegardo, Juan. 1916 [1571]. *Informaciones acerca de la religión y gobierno de los Incas.* Ed. Horacio H. Urteaga. Lima: Imprenta y Librería Sanmartí.

Ramos Giraldo, Jesús A. 2011. *Santuario de Pachacámac: Cien años de arqueología en la costa central.* Lima: Cultura Andina.

Ravines, Rogger. 1996. *Pachacáma: Santuario universal.* Lima: Editorial Los Pinos.

Rostworowski de Diez Canseco, María. 1972. "Breve informe sobre el señorío de Ychma o Ychima." *Arqueología PUCP* 13:37–51.

Rostworowski de Diez Canseco, María. 1999. *El señorío de Pachacamac: El informe de Rodrigo Cantos de Andrade de 1573.* Lima: Instituto de Estudios Peruanos.

Rostworowski de Diez Canseco, María. 2002a. *Pachacamac y el señor de los Milagros: Una trayectoria milenaria. [1992].* Lima: Instituto de Estudios Peruanos.

Rostworowski de Diez Canseco, María. 2002b. *Señoríos indígenas de Lima y Canta. [1978].* Lima: Instituto de Estudios Peruanos.

Rowe, John H. 1979. "An Account of the Shrines of Ancient Cuzco." *Ñawpa Pacha* 17:1–80.

Salomon, Frank. 1995. "'The Beautiful Grandparents': Andean Ancestor Shrines and Mortuary Ritual as Seen through Colonial Records." In *Tombs for the Living: Andean Mortuary Practices,* ed. Tom Dillehay, 315–53. Washington, DC: Dumbarton Oaks Research Library and Collection.

Salomon, Frank, and George L. Urioste. 1991. *The Huarochirí Manuscript: A Testament of Ancient and Colonial Andean Religion.* Austin: University of Texas Press.

Salomon, Frank, Jane Feltham, and Sue Grosboll. 2009. *La revisita de Sisicaya, 1588: Huarochirí veinte años antes de dioses y hombres.* Lima: Fondo Editorial de la Pontificia Universidad Católica del Perú.

Shimada, Izumi. 1991. "Pachacamac Archaeology: Retrospect and Prospect." In *Pachacamac: Report of the William Pepper, M.D., LL.D., Peruvian Expedition of 1896* [reprint of 1903 edition by Max Uhle], ed. Izumi Shimada, 15–56.

Philadelphia: University Museum of Archaeology and Anthropology, University of Pennsylvania.

Shimada, Izumi. 2003. Preliminary Results of the 2003 Fieldwork. http://www .pachacamac.net/papers/PAP_RESULTS2003.pdf.

Shimada, Izumi. 2004. Summary Report of the 2004 Season of the Pachacamac Archaeological Project. http://www.pachacamac.net/papers/PAP_RESULTS2004. pdf.

Shimada, Izumi. 2007. "Las prospecciones y excavaciones en Urpi Kocha y Urpi Wachaq: Estudio preliminar." In *Arqueología de Pachacamac: Excavaciones en Urpi Kocha y Urpi Wachak*, ed. Rafael Vega Centeno, 13–18. Cuadernos de Investigación del Archivo Tello, no. 5. Lima: Museo de Arqueología y Antropología, UNMSM, Lima.

Shimada, Izumi, Rafael Segura Llanos, María Rostworowski de Diez Canseco, and Hirokatsu Watanabe. 2004. "Una nueva evaluación de la plaza de los peregrinos de Pachacamac: Aportes de la primera campaña de 2003 del Proyecto Arqueológico Pachacamac." *Bulletin de l'Institut Français d'Études Andines* 33 (3): 507–38.

Shimada, Izumi, Rafael Segura Llanos, David J. Goldstein, Kelly J. Knudson, Melody J. Shimada, Shinoda Ken-ichi, Mai Takigami, and Ursel Wagner. 2010. "Un siglo después de Uhle: Reflexiones sobre la arqueología de Pachacamac y Perú." In *Max Uhle (1856–1944): Evaluaciones de sus investigaciones y obras*, ed. Peter Kaulicke, Manuela Fischer, Peter Masson, and Gregory Wolff, 109–50. Lima: Fondo Editorial de la Pontificia Universidad Católica del Perú.

Spalding, Karen. 1984. *Huarochirí: An Andean Society under Inca and Spanish Rule*. Palo Alto, CA: Stanford University Press.

Stanish, Charles, and Brian S. Bauer, eds. 2004. *Archaeological Research on the Island of the Sun and Moon, Lake Titicaca, Bolivia: Final Results from the Proyecto Tiksi Kjarka*. Monograph 52. Los Angeles: Cotsen Institute of Archaeology, University of California.

Strong, William Duncan, and John M. Corbett. 1943. "A Ceramic Sequence at Pachacamac." *Columbia Studies in Archaeology and Ethnology* 1 (2): 27–122.

Tello, Julio C. 2009 [1940–41]. *Arqueología de Pachacamac: Excavaciones en el templo de la luna y cuarteles, 1940–1941*. Cuaderno de Investigación del Archivo Tello, no. 6. Lima: Museo de Arqueología y Antropología, Universidad Nacional Mayor de San Marcos.

Uhle, Max. 2003 [1903]. *Pachacamac: Informe de la expedición peruana William Pepper de 1896*. Lima: Universidad Nacional Mayor de San Marcos.

Urbano, Enrique. 1981. *Wiracocha y Ayar: Héroes y funciones en las sociedades andinas*. Cusco: Centro de los Estudios Rurales Andinos "Bartolomé de las Casas."

van de Guchte, Maarten. 1990. "'Carving the World': Inca Monumental Sculpture and Landscape." PhD diss., Department of Anthropology, University of Illinois at Urbana-Champaign. Ann Arbor, MI: University Microfilms.

Villacorta, Luis Felipe. 2004. "Los palacios en la costa central durante los periodos tardíos: De Pachacamac al Inca." *Bulletin de l'Institut Français d'Études Andines* 33 (3): 539–70.

Villacorta, Luis Felipe. 2010. "Palacios yungas y la racionalidad andina en la costa central prehispánica." In *Señores de los imperios del sol*, ed. Krzysztof Makowski, 163–71. Lima: Banco de Crédito del Perú.

Williams León, Carlos. 2001. "Sukankas, quipus y ceques: El tiempo y la sacralización del espacio en el Cusco." *Revista del Museo Nacional (Lima)* 49:123–62.

Ziólkowski, Mariusz, and Robert Sadowski. 1992. *La arqueoastronomía en la investigación de las culturas andinas*. Quito: Banco Central del Ecuador.

Zuidema, R. Tom. 1980. "El ushnu." *Revista de la Universidad Complutense* 28 (117): 317–62.

Zuidema, R. Tom. 1982. "Catachillay: The Role of the Pleiades and of the Southern Cross and Alpha and Beta Centauri in the Calendar of the Incas." In *Ethnoastronomy and Archaeoastronomy in the American Tropics*, ed. Anthony F. Aveni and Gary Urton, 203–29. Annals of the New York Academy of Sciences, vol. 385. New York: New York Academy of Sciences.

Zuidema, R. Tom. 1988. "The Pillars of Cuzco: Which Two Dates of Sunset Did They Define?" In *New Directions in American Archaeoastronomy*, ed. Anthony F. Aveni, 143–69. Proceedings of the 46th International Congress of Americanists. BAR Intenational Series 454. Oxford: BAR.

Zuidema, R. Tom. 2008. "The Astronomical Significance of Ritual Movements in the Calendar of Cuzco." In *Pre-Columbian Landscapes of Creation and Origin*, ed. John E. Staller, 249–67. New York: Springer.

Zuidema, R. Tom. 2010. *El calendario inca: Tiempo y espacio en la organización ritual del Cuzco. La idea del pasado*. Lima: Fondo Editorial del Congreso del Perú, Fondo Editorial de la Pontificia Universidad Católica del Perú.

Zuidema, R. Tom, and Gary Urton. 1976. "La constelación de la llama en los Andes peruanos." *Allpanchis Phuturinqa* 9:59–119.

6

Of Blood and Soil

*Tombs, Wak'as, and the
Naturalization of Social
Difference in the Inka Heartland*

STEVE KOSIBA

According to Inka legend, the world was forever changed when their ancestors ascended the craggy peak of Wanakauri, their gaze falling for the first time on the valley of Cuzco. From atop this summit, the ancestral Inkas first performed the dramatic acts that would later characterize their imperial supremacy. One of them used his sling to level mountains and gouge out valleys in a feat of creative destruction that led his siblings to bury him alive in a nearby cave. Another joined his body to a local wak'a—a personified and hallowed place.[1] By embedding his flesh in these soils, this ancestor became Wanakauri, the principal Inka wak'a. After receiving a signal of divine favor, yet another of the Inka ancestors planted the first maize and then asserted control over the Cuzco Valley and its "barbarous" inhabitants. In making this place and molding its environs, these mythic ancestors claimed Cuzco as their own. They became Inka.[2]

Similar stories cast the Inkas as deific rulers who alone possessed the capacity to create and convert the land and its people. Indeed, although the Inkas did not have a written history, they often boasted to Spanish scribes of how their ancestors introduced the fundamental lineaments of Andean civilization—maize agriculture, weaving, irrigation, and urban life—to the people of Cuzco and beyond (Betanzos 1968 [1551]:13; Cabello Balboa 1951 [1586]:294; Cobo 1964 [1653]:62, 72; Garcilaso 1976 [1609]:48, 59; Molina 1947 [1573]:129; see also Julien 2000:254–68; Kosiba 2010:58–104; Murra

DOI: 10.5876/9781607323181.c006

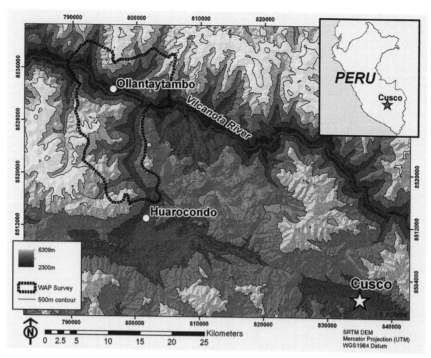

FIGURE 6.1. *Map showing location of Ollantaytambo area. The dashed line corresponds to the Wat'a Archaeological Project (WAP) survey zone (~200 km²).*

1956:24). The Inkas inscribed these boasts into the Cuzco valley's soils and stones. Fields, boulders, and peaks were reborn as sacred wak'a where rituals evoked a history in which the Inkas appeared as both the architects and custodians of the Andean world (cf. Bauer 1996; Dean 2010, this volume).

In both their stories and rituals, then, the Inkas declared that Cuzco was the embodiment of their divine mandate to civilize and order the Andes. But how did this region, which was undoubtedly invested with local and pre-Inka cultural understandings, come to be *naturalized* as inherently Inka? This chapter investigates the social practices and environmental transformations through which the Inkas assembled their imperial capital in Cuzco (Inka Imperial period, ca. 1400–1533 CE). It presents recent archaeological and ethnohistorical data from Ollantaytambo, a monumental Inka city in the Cuzco region, to discuss how the construction of this urban center required the redefinition of lands, places, and people throughout an area that extended far beyond the city's walls (Figure 6.1). In particular, the chapter argues that wak'as manifested the essential social differences of Ollantaytambo's imperial landscape. By attending to the biographies and social roles of Inka wak'as, the chapter examines how state authority is established and an empire is born—not solely through the domination of "natural resources," but through the definition of "nature" itself.

THE STATE OF NATURE AND THE NATURE OF THE STATE

Anthropological archaeologists have long been interested in how state consolidation requires the reorganization and objectification of what might be called "nature." After all, state governance is a process through which particular people, places, and lands are revalued and repositioned as they are molded into a new, unitary environment (Kosiba 2012a). Many archaeological studies, however, define "nature" according to Judeo-Christian ontological premises, which treat the "natural world" as a preanthropogenic terrain, a backdrop for human action, an ecology without humans, or a set of pristine environmental resources for humans to dominate, domesticate, and exploit (see critiques of this point of view in Balée and Erickson 2005; Denevan 1992; Escobar 1999; Glacken 1976; Little 1999; Worster 1994). In employing these premises, archaeological studies often describe the state as a top-down managerial solution to ecological problems such as population pressure, agricultural risk, water distribution, and land allocation (e.g., Algaze 1993, 2001; Balkansky 1998; Johnson and Earle 1987; Sanders and Price 1968; Spencer and Redmond 2004; Wittfogel 1955). No matter whether these solutions are achieved through consensus (Service 1975) or conflict (Fried 1967), what is rendered is a sharply political economic picture of the state as a rational plan, an administrative net designed to capture, dominate, and domesticate natural resources.

Such studies describe how political regimes with regional aspirations *see* the "natural" world (sensu Scott 1998). But they often overlook how both political regimes and local social actors define "nature" when they struggle to establish or maintain their authority. Whether in social contract theory or contemporary discourse, agents of the state describe "nature" as a problem to be solved, a force to be controlled, or a primitive stage of human and environmental development to be surpassed, civilized, and extinguished. For instance, the state project in nineteenth-century Argentina was in part realized by disseminating imaginaries of a "civilized nation" by spreading ideas about the "wild, indigenous" people who dwelled within and beyond its boundaries (Gordillo and Hirsch 2003). Similarly, in the ancient world, the rulers of Urartu declared that they carved their state from a dark and savage wilderness (Smith 2003). In these instances, political regimes cast the state as an unprecedented moment in which a group of inspired leaders triumph over a primordial, chaotic "nature" by instituting a new order that is in accord with a notion of natural law or an idea about the proper structure of the world (see Alonso 1994; Schama 1995).[3] "Nature," then, is not an a priori state of being or a set of resources—it is a political claim.

The uniformity of these claims throughout prehistory and history suggests that state power is not only derived from the domestication and domination of natural resources. Rather, the state itself rests on a proposition about *the nature* of the world—an ontological proposition. Herein, the term "ontology" refers to an understanding of what it means to be, an understanding that is manifested in social practices rather than concepts or representations (Dreyfus 1991, 2000; Merleau-Ponty 1962). A state projects an ontological proposition by building an environment designed to cultivate idealized practices and bodily dispositions that define people, places, things, and lands (Kosiba 2010). For example, the urban spaces and architectural forms (*urbs*) of Europe's early Christian states projected an ontological proposition that humans are creatures who should, in their everyday practices, conform to an ideal of order (*civitas*)—a way of life in which people efficiently exploit natural resources, work competently at their vocation, and avoid pleasures of the flesh (e.g., Cummins 2002a; Rama 1996; Wernke 2013; B. S. Rousse, personal communication, June 25, 2013; see discussion in Lefebvre 1991:41). To understand and perhaps undermine the genesis of a state, then, is to inquire into how (and the circumstances under which) political regimes stake claims about ontology and, moreover, how such claims are rooted in or opposed to antecedent cultural understandings and political practices.

INKA IMPERIAL ORDER

The Inka Imperial period exemplifies how political regimes seek to disseminate and legitimate an ontological understanding of the world, in particular an understanding of what it means to be a person. Similar to other indigenous American societies, the Inkas did not possess a word or concept akin to a Judeo-Christian notion of "nature" (B. Mannheim, personal communication, June 25, 2013; cf. Descola 1994). But the Inkas, in their narratives and practices, certainly projected ontological propositions about *the nature*—that is, the essential characteristics—of persons and their relationships with other persons, places, things, and lands. Above all, Inka rule rested on a claim to absolute social difference between deified Inkas and barbarous non-Inka people and places (Kosiba 2012a; Kosiba and Bauer 2013; Patterson 1992; Silverblatt 1988). Inka elite interviewees repeated that pre-Inka peoples were lazy and lost (*ociosos y perdidos*) and that this was the innate condition (*condición y naturaleza*) of the indigenous Andean people prior to the establishment of the Inka order (e.g., Levillier 1940: 130, 139, 147, 156, 171).

To realize these claims to social difference, the Inkas redefined and grouped non-Inka land and people in a manner akin to an agriculturalist's project to reshape weeds into carefully sown rows of crops. The Inka Empire was a social taxonomy comprising different categories of people, places, things, and land (D'Altroy 2002; Kolata 2013). Particular types of people were rooted in specific places and lands and defined by their innate capabilities and formal characteristics.

The Inkas recognized absolute distinctions between types of non-Inka persons. The Inkas created essential categories of non-Inka subjects that corresponded to different structural positions within the empire (see Zuidema 1990:12), such as ethnicities (e.g., Colla, Chachapoya), qualitative distinctions (e.g., chosen women [*aqllakuna*], retainers [*yanakuna*], specialists [*camayoq*]), and workers (*mitmaqkuna*). These categories reflect two kinds of essentialism. Ethnicities suggest a sortal essentialism, which is a claim that people of a single category, and only that category, bear specific attributes (on essentialism, see Gelman and Mannheim 2007).[4] These people were relegated to specific areas, required to recognize a distinct place of origin, and distinguished by their practices and dress, which conformed to a state-mandated identity (e.g., Cobo 1990 [1653]:196–97, 206; Garcilaso 1976 [1609], bk. I, chap. 22). On the other hand, *yanakuna* and *aqllakuna* suggest an ideal essentialism based on formal characteristics such as "efficiency" or "beauty" (Santillán 1968 [1563]:114, 116; see also Murra 1980:154, 163). In a similar vein, the Inkas also uprooted people from their homelands and settled them in distant lands as *mitmaqkuna*, who were identified strictly by their capacity for generalized labor (Murra 1980, 1982; Patterson 1985; Wachtel 1982). These new types of people—*yanakuna, aqllakuna*, and *mitmaqkuna*—were no longer tied to their communities or their homelands. They were subject only to the Inkas.

These categorical distinctions were rooted in the land. Upon incorporating a region, the Inkas redefined the land by allotting particular fields and pastures to the local community and then allocating select areas to imperial institutions and religious cults (see Cobo 1964 [1653]:120; Murra 1980:31, 57; Polo de Ondegardo 1916 [1571]:154). The Inkas reorganized land and labor in the Cuzco valley, creating an elaborate system of social and spatial divisions made up of individual strips or sections of land (*chapas*) and the ritual lines that divided them (*zeques*) (Betanzos 1968 [1551]:35; see also Bauer 1998; Zuidema 1964, 1990). Situated along these *zeques* were wak'as, which personified places where Andean people engaged in practices that sustained the new Inka landscape. At these places, Andean people poured maize beer to ensure that the wak'as would not cause earthquakes (Calancha 1974–81 [1638], 3: 855; Murúa 1962–64 [1590], bk. I, chaps. 35–36); they made offerings to appease the peaks and ensure safe travels (Cobo 1990 [1653]: 116); and they made sacrifices to guarantee the health of the Inka royalty (e.g., ibid.: 170, 172, 177). The Inkas required subject populations to produce social and spatial divisions that replicated the *zeques* and wak'a of Cuzco (ibid.: 167; Polo de Ondegardo 1916 [1571]:112; Pizarro 1978 [1571]:51; see also Bauer 1998; Bauer and Orosco 1998). By categorizing social groups, marking fields, and naming wak'as, the Inkas shaped new political subjectivities. And, as I will argue, they altered the essential relationships between people, place, and land that structured personhood in the Andes.[5]

But how did the Inkas alter these relationships? To inquire into what constitutes this kind of categorized and compartmentalized landscape is to examine the oft-neglected politics of *naturalization*—the material and symbolic practices that work to embed claims to social difference and social order within the environment (Smith 2004; see also Harvey 1996; Kosiba and Bauer 2013). In this sense, we might think of how Maya elite staged ritual practices in which they positioned themselves atop stone friezes of the Cauac monster (a deity and chthonic force) to signify that only elites were allied with environmental forces (Scarborough 1998: 152). Or we may recall how the rulers of ancient South India constructed reservoirs that imitated the architecture of majestic temples to disseminate among their subjects the belief that elite authority was legitimate and "natural"—that rulers met their moral obligation to improve the environment and provide for their people (Bauer and Morrison 2008; Morrison 1993, 2009, 2010: 188). In these situated practices, political actors attempt to define what it means to be a particular kind of person by building (or razing) spaces and orchestrating (or refuting) practices that naturalize claims about "the way things were/are" and "the way things should have been/ should be" (cf. Bell 1992:176; Geertz 1981:123–24, 130–31; for relevant case studies, see Bray 2013; Smith 2004; Swenson 2003, 2012).

Inka wak'as provide analytical points of entry into how political regimes seek to etch their claims to absolute authority into the ground. Indeed, as the opening tale of Wanakauri suggests, wak'a were essential to practices that created and intermeshed social and ontological boundaries. The tale of Wanakauri—a tale that was regularly performed and ritually reenacted—is not only a story of Inka origins or the Inka domination of "nature" (cf. Bauer 1996; Dean 2010). It is a story about the creation and naturalization of an Inka ontological order, for in this tale we see practices that established categorical differences between types of people (Inka, non-Inka), places (Wanakauri, a preceding wak'a), lands (Inka Cuzco, the non-Inka outside), and times (Inka present, barbarous past). The birth of this wak'a inaugurated a new understanding of what it meant to be a person. But scholars often overlook the political salience of wak'as, treating them as apolitical reflections of an enduring Andean cosmology or passive places that encoded relationships between people and "nature" (e.g., Sherbondy 1982, 1992; Zuidema 1964, 1990). They rarely take into account how the social roles of wak'as and the meanings of their attendant rituals changed as new regimes came to power (for notable exceptions, see Bauer 1998; Moore 2010; van de Guchte 1999). To address such changes requires a shift from accounts about the structure of Inka rule and Andean cosmology to an analysis of the dynamic practices through which Inka social divisions and political ontologies were first put into place. By examining the practices that birthed new wak'a and people at Ollantaytambo, we can begin to explore the roots of the Inka imperial order.

OLLANTAYTAMBO

Ollantaytambo is a massive Inka imperial city situated 42.5 aerial kilometers from the Inka capital of Cuzco.[6] At Ollantaytambo, the Inka built an urban center within a striking environmental setting (Figure 6.2). The city's palatial complexes were situated upon a broad alluvial terrace at the junction of two river valleys, both of which ultimately provide entry to the lower-altitude Andean jungle (*selva*) and access to its valued products like coca leaves, feathers, and hot peppers (*aji*). As Ollantaytambo was built, massive terraces were raised, reshaping the land as they descended from the central plazas of the city to the banks of the Vilcanota, a turbulent and wide river. Springs, streams, and glacial lakes were canalized to carry water to the fields of Ollantaytambo. Storage houses, temples, and walls were affixed to the sheer cliffs that surround the city, creating an environmental aesthetic in which state institutional structures seem to organically emerge from salient geological features.

In building Ollantaytambo, the Inka created an extensive urban landscape. Indeed, the monumental structures that are now frequented and photographed by international tourists were only a small part of a grand design. These structures, terraces, and plazas were the ritual core of a vast complex of settlements, roads, shrines, and fields spread across the valley's slopes. In

FIGURE 6.2. *The monumental Inka city of Ollantaytambo (arrow, left), the canalized Vilcanota River (top right), and an example of the agricultural terrace complexes that constitute Ollantaytambo's environment (bottom right) (photographs by author).*

several early colonial litigation cases, both indigenous elites and Spanish lords declared that the formal juridical boundaries of Ollantaytambo encompassed a broad area that incorporated several adjoining valleys and settlement systems (Archivo Regional de Cusco [ARC] 1555–1729:fol. 7v, fol. 11v–12; ARC 1568–1722). The city's eastern border was marked by the Inka complex at Pachar, situated 5.5 aerial kilometers from the central plaza (ARC 1555–1729:fol. 178). Ollantaytambo also stretched into the nearby Soqma Valley, where the monumental enclosure of Perolniyoq (or Korimarka) prominently marked both the Inka imperial presence and the southern boundary of the city (ibid.:fol. 1, 8, 13, 16–17). Other documents indicate that Ollantaytambo and its associated land claims reached far into lowlands located a considerable distance from the city's core (Kosiba 2012b; see Archivo General de la Nación [AGN] 1576; ARC 1568–1722:fol. 294).

Ollantaytambo's Inka occupation, however, was brief. Recent research indicates that the Inkas built Ollantaytambo during the fifteenth century (Protzen 1983, 1986, 1991; for radiocarbon dates, see Bengtsson 1998; Hollowell 1987; Kendall 1985). Excavations, surface collections, and surveys have not revealed evidence for substantial pre-Inka occupation at Ollantaytambo (Galiano and

Apaza 2004; Gibaja 1982, 1984; Kosiba 2010; Soto and Cabrera 1999; Vera 1986), though it is possible that the Inkas built the city by reusing architectural materials from an earlier and presently unknown site (see Hollowell 1987).[7] Spanish documents indicate that Ollantaytambo was constructed during the imperial period, perhaps as the royal estate of Pachakuti Inka (Protzen 1991; Rostworowski 1962; Rowe 1997) or of Viracocha Inka (ARC 1568–1722:fol. 296v).

By constructing complexes such as Ollantaytambo, Maras, or Machu Picchu, the Inka royalty established inalienable and lineage-based rights over land and people (e.g., Covey 2006; Covey and Amado 2008; D'Altroy 2002; Murra 1980; Niles 1993, 1999; Quave 2012). Similar to the other Cuzco complexes, Ollantaytambo was a mélange of people from Cuzco and farther afield, including elites (Araccama, Chinchaysuyu, and Cuzco ayllus), retainers (*yanakuna*, *aqllakuna*), and laborers (*mitmaqkuna*) (Covey and Amado 2008; Glave and Remy 1983; Malca Olguin 1963; Rowe 1997). These new types of people were defined relative to their practical relationships with the land: the royal ayllus claimed the land and redistributed its products while the *yanakuna* and *mitmaqkuna* worked the city's fields and built its terraces (Biblioteca Nacional del Perú [BNP] 1629:fol. 89–158).[8]

Clearly, the creation of Ollantaytambo initiated new understandings of people, place, and land. In examining the dynamic history through which Ollantaytambo was produced, we see how these understandings were generated in practices of construction that produced particular *types* of persons and places. The archaeological data presented here are from the Wat'a Archaeological Project (WAP), a multiscalar survey and excavation project that was carried out between 2005 and 2007 that focused on the Ollantaytambo region (Kosiba 2010, 2011, 2012a). Ethnohistorical data were obtained through archival research conducted in Cuzco and Lima between 2011 and 2013.

BEFORE OLLANTAYTAMBO

Prior to Inka ascendancy, during the Ollanta phase (ca. 1000–1300 CE), the people of the Ollantaytambo area defined their identity and declared their autonomy by assembling discrete and highly localized communities. These groups organized economic and ritual practices in distinct areas to buttress their claims to specific lands, natural resources, and culturally significant sites. Each community was a tightly woven skein of settlements centered on a particular town (Figure 6.3) (Kosiba 2011). Situated directly between high pastures and low maize lands, these towns were likely the hubs of "compact

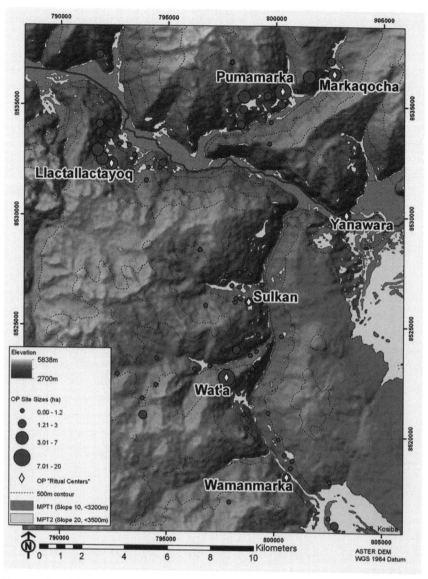

FIGURE 6.3. *Map of pre-Inka (Ollanta phase) settlement clusters and ritual centers throughout the Ollantaytambo area. The map shows the location of sites relative to optimal (MPT1) and potential (MPT2) maize production terrain. Settlements are tightly grouped between maize production and high pastoral lands.*

vertical" economies with farming and pastoral activities occurring in adjoining ecological zones (see Brush 1976; Yamamoto 1985; cf. Hastorf 1993).

Specific architectural features marked these towns as political and ritual centers, making them recognizable to others as the roots of a local community's claim to autonomy and authority. These features, which included tomb sectors, plazas, and platforms, were found at all of the towns but no other sites dating to this period (see Kosiba 2010, 2011). The towns also contained common types of ritual space. Concentric terraces and platforms were built on abruptly rising hilltops, transforming them into stepped, truncated "pyramids" (Figure 6.4). Surface collections on these hilltops produced very high densities of decorated Ollanta phase serving vessel fragments, suggesting that these spaces were used for ritual activity (Kosiba 2011). Moreover, the towns contained exclusive spaces for the veneration of ancestors (e.g., the mummified, physically dead, whether recognized as collective or individual "ancestors" [Salomon 1995]). Ancestor veneration next to visible, open, and aboveground tombs was a new type of political practice that emerged during the twelfth to the fourteenth centuries in the Cuzco and Ollantaytambo areas (Bengtsson 1998; Dean 2005; McEwan et al. 2002). In comparison with other Ollanta phase sites, the towns were the only places that contained architecture and artifacts associated with ancestor veneration practices, including discrete mortuary complexes with multiple aboveground tower-shaped tombs (*chullpas*), platforms and plazas, and very high densities of decorated serving vessels (see data in Kosiba 2011: 132–38; cf. Covey 2006). Within these towns' mortuary complexes, individual tombs adjoined small platforms and terraces, suggesting that people feted, fed, and conversed with specific ancestors in intimate rituals (Figure 6.5).

Before the rise of the Inka, then, Andean people anchored communities in specific localities. People constructed and venerated these places, and in so doing, they became "a people." Over time, such practices reiterated affective ties between "a people" and "a place," thereby marking a local community's claims to authority and autonomy. Each of these localities was likely akin to what we understand as a *llaqta*—a microscale ecology comprising a town, a local environment, associated settlements, and a ritual space (cf. Murra 1980: 29; Ramírez 2005: 53). Conveying an intimate relation between people and locality, Salomon (1991: 23) remarks that the people of a *llaqta*—the *llaqtayoq*—possessed a place and were possessed by it. It appears as though, during the centuries prior to Inka rule in the Cuzco region, place, *llaqta*, and *llaqtayoq* expressed the shared and sharply localized *essence* of people and land, blood and soil. These local communities thus rested on a political and ontological

FIGURE 6.4. *Pre-Inka political and ritual centers near Ollantaytambo that were built around distinct geomorphological prominences and terraced. Clockwise from top left: Wat'a, Sulkan, Markaqocha (Ayapata), and Ankasmarka (photographs by author.)*

claim of affinity and mutuality of being between a particular people and place, a kind of sortal essentialism that simultaneously linked a people's connection to particular soils and marked social differences between localized communities. Prior to the Inkas, these claims were staked during situated social practices, such as ancestor veneration ceremonies staged within ritual centers. As we will see, these local claims and their attendant practices became the basis of a new Inka regional order.

ASSEMBLING OLLANTAYTAMBO

Many of the Ollanta phase towns were reborn during the process of Inka state formation (ca. 1300–1400 CE) (Figure 6.6). At Wat'a and Pumamarka, local towns that had been occupied for over a millennium, elites directed the construction of buildings bearing the insignia of the nascent Inka state—double-jamb doorways, trapezoidal niches, and double-frame windows (Kendall 1984, 1988, 1996; Kendall et al. 1992; Kosiba 2012a; compare with findings in the

FIGURE 6.5. *Ollanta phase tomb structures often adjoin small terraced platforms, suggesting that the tombs were sites of secluded ritual practices. The arrows and lines show the entry and terrace wall of one tomb platform (Tomb A) from above and below (photographs by author).*

Pisaq area [Covey 2006] and the Cuzco valley [Bauer 2004; McEwan 2006; McEwan et al. 2002]). I have argued that, by reconstructing these sites and redesigning their ritual spaces, local elites and local ethnic groups cemented their privileged positions within the nascent Inka state (Kosiba 2012b; see also Bauer 2004; Covey 2006; Niles 1980). They razed various parts of their towns, constructing massive buildings and walls at the entryways to mortuary sectors and terraced hilltops. In so doing, they converted long-used tombs and platforms that once marked a people's intimate connections to their ancestors into exclusive *Inka* spaces that manifested the new regime's claims to exclusivity and absolute social difference (Kosiba 2010, 2012a, 2012b). Spaces for collective ceremony became spaces explicitly linked to Inka power. In consequence, the ancestral places of local communities became Inka. That is, these places were recast as exclusive and elite places within an Inka order of people, places, and things.

Later on, in the early fifteenth century, the Inka elite detached their claims to authority from powerful ancestral places such as Wat'a and Pumamarka. They constructed new urban centers and estates at Ollantaytambo, Pisaq, and Machu Picchu (Covey 2006). These urban centers and estates all emphasized public ceremony in vast plazas. Throughout the Ollantaytambo area, new kinds of elites (*kurakas*) were stationed in imperial complexes (Chusicasa, Markaqocha, Ñawpa Colegio, Pachar, and Perolniyoq) and positioned to maximize surveillance of Inka lands, roads, and settlements (Kosiba and Bauer 2013). The mortuary precincts that had long defined local pre-Inka towns were not included in these complexes, suggesting that the Inkas introduced new ritual places and political practices in the imperial period. Indeed, in the Ollantaytambo area, aboveground, visible tombs and/or mortuary precincts cannot be found at any Inka complex, including the urban core of Ollantaytambo itself.[9] Further indicating a shift in the spaces of social life, new residential settlements and lands were created to house new kinds of subjects such as *mitmaqkuna, aqllakuna,* and *yanakuna* (ARC 1555–1729:fol. 132, 182). In particular, the Inkas implanted an array of differentiated places on the banks of the Vilcanota—they arranged activities, emplaced social memories, and encoded spaces as if they were tying knots on an extensive *khipu* (cf. Urton 2012:494–95).

These changes, and these new social categories, were in part manifested through construction practices. Specifically, the construction of Ollantaytambo entailed the production of land along a 12 km corridor of the Vilcanota River. Initiating one of the Cuzco region's most challenging engineering feats, the Inkas built retaining walls to direct the flow of the Vilcanota River (Farrington 1983; Niles 1999). The walls minimized damage from floods and transformed

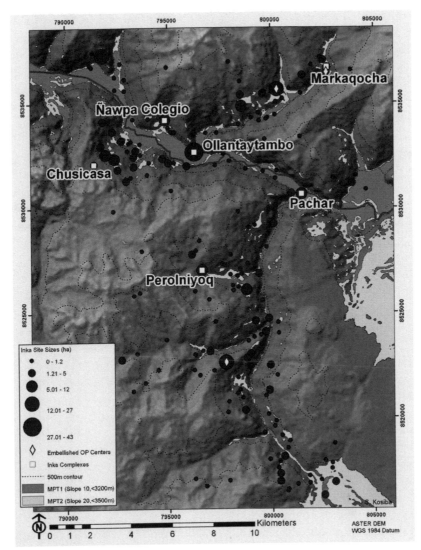

FIGURE 6.6. *Map of Inka Imperial period settlement patterns throughout the Ollantaytambo area. Throughout the transition to Inka rule, select preexisting political and ritual centers were dramatically transformed and embellished with Inka architecture. During the Inka Imperial period, newly constructed monumental administrative complexes (e.g., Chusicasa, Ñawpa Iglesia, Pachar, and Perolniyoq) became the anchors of political authority that defined Ollantaytambo's urban landscape. The Inkas also directed the construction of monumental structures on the plain called Markaqocha, below the pre-Inka town of Markaqocha (Ayapata).*

marshy banks into productive agricultural lands. The Inkas further increased the land area along the Vilcanota River by constructing terraces that controlled colluvium (Kosiba 2012b; see also Farrington 1983; Heffernan 1989, 1996; Niles 1993). My Geographic Information Systems (GIS) analysis of ASTER data indicates that these Inka projects created approximately 134 ha of new lands between Pachar and Ollantaytambo's center and approximately 270 ha of new lands along the 12 km area that borders Ollantaytambo (Kosiba 2012b).

Here the Inkas created not only new lands but also new spaces that grouped people, places, land, and socioeconomic tasks. A royal road traversed these new lands, providing passage from Cuzco to Ollantaytambo's monumental gate. An extensive canal directed water from Kulluspukio (also called Kusillo), a spring situated high above the Huarocondo Valley, to fields and terraces strung along an 11 km stretch of the Vilcanota River. In constructing and maintaining this road and canal, local people became subjects of an Inka notion of social and ecological order. Their labor was linked to the labor of other, distant communities. Indeed, the terraces, roads, and canals would have required synchronized labor and task scheduling among the inhabitants of different communities. A rupture within an 11 km canal or the flooding of a road, for instance, would potentially damage crops within multiple fields and effectively sever the regional connections and economic interdependencies of this system (cf. Hastorf 1993:202; Mitchell 1976; Sherbondy 1982). Thus, the city introduced not only new understandings of people, places, and land but also new understandings of people's obligations to an Inka order.

WAK'AS OF OLLANTAYTAMBO

As mentioned above, Inka urban centers and administrative complexes in the Ollantaytambo area do not contain the conspicuous tomb structures or mortuary precincts that defined localities and communities prior to the Inka. Rather, the borders and entryways of Inka Ollantaytambo are defined by other monumental features: stone wak'as. The construction and veneration of these wak'as appears crucial to the reformulation—indeed, the *Inka*-ization—of the Ollantaytambo area. Many scholars have discussed Cuzco wak'as and the system of ritual pathways and land divisions (*zeques*) that they constituted (Bauer 1998; MacCormack 1993; Niles 1987; Rowe 1985; Sherbondy 1992; Zuidema 1964, 1990). Researchers have argued that the Cuzco wak'as were parts of an unchanging yet politically inflected calendrical structure (e.g., Zuidema 1964) or a dynamic landscape that undergirded different versions of Inka history (e.g., Bauer 1998). Few, however, have considered how systems of Inka wak'as functioned outside of Cuzco itself (for an exception, see Bauer and Orosco 1998). Here I complement the previous research by demonstrating that Inka wak'as were personified places (cf. "place-persons," Mannheim and Salas, this volume) who manifested and maintained an Inka social order throughout Ollantaytambo, from its distant borders to the very heart of the region.

The archaeological documentation of wak'as is no easy task. Any object or place can be a wak'a, and so it is difficult to distinguish wak'as through archaeological methods alone. Cuzco's wak'as were often "natural places"—environmental features that people modified, named, and fed to ensure the well-being of the soils, the water, their community, and the empire.[10] Thus, I concentrate on sites containing distinct forms of ritual architecture, for example, stand-alone carved boulders, platforms, and walled enclosures, which are explicitly associated with notable environmental features such as caves, springs, and canals. These sites were *adoratorios* (places for veneration), a word often used by Spaniards to further clarify the term "wak'a" (Acosta 1954 [1590]: 142, 152; Arriaga 1968 [1621]: 197; Cieza 1946 [1553]: 304). Cuzco's imperial wak'as were largely places where people made offerings and staged feasts. More particularly, they were places sated and feted with "foods" that humans do not eat.[11] Given these insights, I focus on the practices—building and feasting—through which people gave life to, engaged with, and attributed personhood to Inka wak'as and, in so doing, cemented their own social position and sense of personhood within an Inka order.

My analysis concentrates on ten modified boulders or wak'as, eight of which are situated along the royal road from Cuzco to Ollantaytambo and two that mark the southern border of Ollantaytambo in the Soqma Valley (Figure 6.7). Though there are surely other kinds of wak'a in the Ollantaytambo region, these boulders are important to our understanding of an Inka order because of their materiality, visibility, and temporality. Hewn from andesite and located along an Inka road, these particular kinds of wak'a appear as enduring and conspicuous guardians of an Inka world. Though modified andesite boulders are common near Cuzco, they are rare in the Ollantaytambo area (only ten were identified throughout the 200 km² area of the WAP survey), suggesting that these wak'as had a particular function and/or meaning. I conducted total surface collections at each of these shrines (which are small and appropriate for total collections) to determine their occupational history and use. Excavation data from several Peruvian colleagues provide additional insights into practices at the shrines.

The sequence of wak'as begins outside of Ollantaytambo's borders, deep within the sheer walls of the Huarocondo canyon. The Inka road from Cuzco

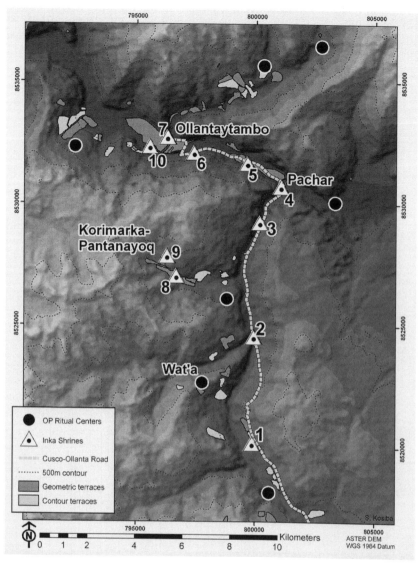

FIGURE 6.7. *Map indicating locations of wak'as discussed in this chapter. The map shows how the wak'as were situated away from preexisting ritual centers, in or near select newly developed agricultural lands with large "geometric" terraces (e.g., between Pachar and Ollantaytambo), along the road from Cuzco to Ollantaytambo, and at the boundaries of Ollantaytambo (e.g., Pachar, Korimarka): (1) Saratuhuallya, (2) Pomatales, (3) Ñawpa Iglesia, (4) Pachar (Hatun Kancha Raqay), (5) Chulluraqay, (6) the dual boulders at Choqana, (7) Sala, (8) Perolniyoq, (9) Korimarka, and (10) Vilcanota.*

to Ollantaytambo meanders through this canyon, passing the pre-Inka town of Wat'a. Boulder shrines are located at places where one gains and loses visibility of Wat'a, at Saratuhuallya and Pomatales. The andesite boulders of Saratuhuaylla are encircled by an immense Inka wall. From inside the wall, one sees the early Inka walls that enclosed Wat'a and its mortuary complex. Two carved andesite boulders also sit at Pomatales, affording a view of the mortuary complex below Wat'a. The larger and more elaborate boulder at Pomatales ("Baño de la Ñusta") contains a central bench motif—a horizontal plane cut into the boulder's surface—above which four niches are carved (Figure 6.8). The boulders at Saratuhuaylla and Pomatales call attention to Wat'a and its mortuary precincts. In so doing, they draw an analogy (sensu Wernke 2007, 2013) between the Inka wak'a and a pre-Inka ancestral place, an analogy that is further emphasized at other shrines in Ollantaytambo through the manipulation of water (for comparison at another Inka estate, see Bray 2013:172–75).

Farther along the road, one encounters the shrine of Ñawpa Iglesia (also called Choqella), a modified cave that contains multiple tombs. This shrine is connected to the spring of Kulluspukio, which courses toward the center of Ollantaytambo and thus links the shrine to Inka fields along the Vilcanota River. At Ñawpa Iglesia, terraces ascend a conical hill (Figure 6.9). An impressive carved andesite boulder stands atop these terraces in front of two finely worked slabs of granite, which form an immense cave. The boulder contains a triple-jamb door design and multiple bench motifs. Monumental walls and buildings are situated on either side of the cave. Tombs can be seen within the cave's interior, intimating that this shrine was explicitly linked to ancestors.

The Inkas constructed Ñawpa Iglesia on unoccupied terrain. Alluvial deposits (fine sand and round cobbles) were uncovered near the base of several excavation units at the site, suggesting that the Huarocondo River regularly flooded this location before the construction of the terraces (Arredondo Dueñas 2009:58, 63, 72). Several canal features were uncovered during the excavations, linking the construction of the shrine to the canalization of the Kulluspukio and the creation of new land along the Vilcanota. Particularly high densities of polychrome Inka pottery and serving vessels suggest that people propitiated this place and its ancestors by feasting with or feeding the wak'a (ibid.:133). Similar to Saratuhuaylla and Pomatales, the shrine was situated in a private space—it was located between massive walls and accessible by only one path. The site's walls and restricted entry suggest that feasting or feeding practices at Ñawpa Iglesia were personal affairs during which people participated in practices that linked powerful environmental forces with Inka ancestors.

Figure 6.8. *The modified boulders of Pomatales (above) and Saratuhuallya (below) (photographs by author).*

FIGURE 6.9. *Ñawpa Iglesia, an intricately carved boulder (above) that sits at the entry to a modified cave (below) (photographs by author).*

A connection between place and Inka ancestors is also foregrounded at the next shrine on the road, which personifies an Inka queen. The royal road steadily descends from Ñawpa Iglesia to Pachar, where travelers from Cuzco turned toward Ollantaytambo's core. An immense boulder towers over the road. The boulder is situated on a hill and surrounded by Inka walls. A document from 1574 sheds light on this place, revealing that near Pachar's bridge there was a wak'a called (at the time) Hatun Kancha Raqay (ARC 1555–1729:fol. 181). The document states:

> . . . in the high part on the left bank of the river when going from Cusco or the town of Maras to Tambo, one league from Tambo. . . here one finds a mound of earth piled high near a rock that appears as though it was a site of sacrifice and wak'a for the indigenous people. . . it is said that this mound of earth and associated buildings in the complex or corral served the Inka; it was a kind of ancient shrine [mochadero]. . . It is said that this is where the Inka sat. (ARC 1555–1729: fol. 181, 181v; my translation)[12]

The shrine was a mochadero, a place that people venerated and personified by making kissing expressions (mochar) (e.g., Arriaga 1968 [1621]:211, 250; Polo de Ondegardo 1916 [1571]:136). The site belonged to Mama Oqllo, the principal wife of the eleventh Inka emperor Wayna Qhapaq (ARC 1555–1729:fol. 181, 181v) (see discussion below). Surface collections and excavations near the wak'a indicate that it was constructed de novo in the Inka Imperial period (Solís and Olazabal 1998).[13] The walls at this site demonstrate that it was a secluded space where ritual practices directed attention toward the shrine. The wak'a's specific association with Mama Oqllo and Pachar suggests, as was the case for many of Cuzco's wak'as, that the rituals enacted here would have manifest a sense of shared ancestry as they invoked the Inka royalty, their biographies, and the land. Many of these wak'as thus directed attention to entities from the past that were key to Inka imperial strategy—entities such as the site of Wat'a, ancestors such as those people who were entombed in the cave at Ñawpa Iglesia, or Inka nobility such as Mama Oqllo.

Other wak'as further accentuate the new Inka land. Several carved boulders are positioned within the fields along the royal road to Ollantaytambo. Near the Inka settlement of Chulluraqay, a large boulder sits in the middle of the Inka canal from Kulluspukio. A channel was carved through the base of the stone, allowing the canal to enter and exit. The boulder is not located near a center of population or an elite complex—it is quite literally part of the canal and the agricultural terraces. A small platform is situated on one side of the boulder, suggesting that offerings were made at this place in private engagements with the wak'a. A short distance ahead, carved andesite stones stand over either side of the road as it passes Choqana, a fortified and monumental Inka site. Each stone bears a bench motif and is attached to a small platform for offerings. In feting or feasting with the stones at Chulluraqay and Choqana, people would have recognized and venerated the newly built Inka agrarian landscape.

The final stone on this route sits at the terminus of the road from Cuzco, below the majestic and intricately sculpted rock outcrop of Ollantaytambo.[14] A carved andesite boulder, now lightheartedly named *la Sala de Operaciones* ("Sala"), is positioned at the edge of the lower Inka plaza. The boulder was situated in an exclusive sector and partially surrounded by a wall (Galiano and Apaza 2004:99), suggesting that the site was built for private ritual activities. Similar to the other worked boulders on the road from Cuzco, the rock's designs include a quadrangular bench motif.

Recent excavations reveal that "Sala" was constructed as part of the terrace system that faces the city's lower plaza (ibid.). The excavations uncovered high densities of Classic Inka decorated serving vessels, suggesting that this place was established in the Inka period and it was feted or fed quite regularly.[15] Indeed, an offering of animal bones was recovered at the boulder, and other offerings of miniature Inka vessels and a llama figurine were uncovered at a nearby fountain, leading the excavators to suggest that the boulder and its environs were places for sacrifices (ibid.:123).

Wak'as situated along the distant borders of Ollantaytambo also required practices that recognized the new Inka land and its structures. The Inkas modified two caves at Korimarka, a ridge situated on the upper slopes of the Soqma Valley that marked the southern boundary of Ollantaytambo (ARC 1555–1729:fol. 1, 8, 13). Korimarka consists of two neighboring caves of almost identical size that overlook the spring of Pantanayoq. Platforms with distinct Inka stonework face the cave. Adjacent to these platforms, a series of immense monumental terraces ascend a narrow ravine, leading to a pass that affords a view of Ollantaytambo.

Water flows from the marshy plains of Korimarka and Pantanayoq to a three-tiered, ~150 m tall waterfall that cascades through the craggy bluff below the Inka complex of Perolniyoq (Figure 6.10). At Perolniyoq, carved stones and monumental Inka spaces draw attention to this striking environmental feature. The buildings of Perolniyoq surround two carved andesite boulders, each exhibiting a bench motif similar to the other rocks on the road to Ollantaytambo. The Inka buildings and ritual spaces of Perolniyoq connect the Korimarka spring to Soqma agricultural lands. Indeed, the site is inseparable

FIGURE 6.10. *The monumental complex of Perolniyoq (upper left), which the Inka built directly above a majestic waterfall (below) (photograph by author).*

from the waterfall that feeds the valley's terraces. In turn, people fed the wak'a at Perolniyoq. As at the other sites, our surface collections recovered unusually high densities of Inka polychrome serving vessels in the sector of Perolniyoq that surrounds the carved stone, suggesting that in this space people feasted with the wak'a.

The shrines at Perolniyoq and Korimarka point to broader themes among the wak'as of Ollantaytambo. First, all of these shrines were exclusively associated with recently created spaces—fields, canalized springs, monumental terraces, and newly constructed settlements. More particularly, all of the shrines were positioned near areas where the Inka built monumental agricultural systems—"geometric" terraces that formed angular shapes and intricate designs as they modeled hillsides and mountain facades (Kosiba 2012b). The shrines were specifically *not* constructed near preexisting political centers, such as Wat'a, Pumamarka, and Llactallactayoq, even though some were sited to view these pre-Inka towns. Nor were the shrines constructed in new Inka political centers or towns.

Most of the shrines were situated along the road and in the fields from Cuzco to Ollantaytambo. On the road, shrines were sited at regular intervals, each of them located approximately two to four kilometers from the preceding one. Their positioning on this road—and their regular spacing—suggests that when approaching or leaving Ollantaytambo, it was important to engage with a sequence of wak'as in a way that replicated Cuzco's *zeque* system. That is, as people approached the sacred city, they would have visited a series of ritual stations that influenced their practices and bodily dispositions while calling to mind Inka actors and Inka history. At present, it is not clear whether Ollantaytambo had a *zeque* system, but a Spanish document explicitly states that the city used *zeque* lines to mark land divisions (ARC 1568–1722:fol. 354, 355). Not all Inka subjects could traverse the royal roads, thus some of these wak'as (e.g., Perolniyoq, Ñawpa Iglesia, Sala) might have been seen and revered only by select persons. However, many wak'as were situated near fields and canals (e.g., Saratuhuaylla, Pomatales, Pachar, Choqana, and Chulluraqay Korimarka), suggesting that they were seen and propitiated by different kinds of person and subject.

DEFINING LAND, PEOPLE, AND PLACE

Colonial documents from Ollantaytambo provide further insights into this landscape, suggesting that these wak'as, and the lands in which they were situated, were essential to Inka ontological claims. Ollantaytambo wak'as resided in the very places where the Inkas established new land claims and new social roles (*yanakuna, kuraka*). For instance, in a series of litigations against the Monasterio de Santa Clara in Cuzco (see also Burns 1999), Don Felipe de Coritopa Inka, the grandson of Pachakuti, stated that he was the *kuraka* of Pachar (ARC 1555–1729:fol. 178). Coritopa confirmed the role of the *kuraka* as the caretaker of a section of the city's environment (ibid.: fols. 1–2). He claimed usufruct rights over land in Korimarka and Pachar, and stated that this privilege was derived from his obligation to care for the land (ibid.: fol. 4v). Such cases suggest that the lands associated with the shrines corresponded to the royal claims of direct Inka ownership and *kuraka* oversight that defined the imperial period. The documents also show that the development of these lands emplaced new kinds of people. Specialized laborers (*yanakuna*) were stationed near Korimarka, Pantanayoq, and Pachar (ibid.:fols. 12, 16–17, 216v–17, 232). Numerous people from the nearby town of Maras testified to the Spanish that "*mamaconas*" from their community resided in the Pachar buildings next to Hatun Kancha Raqay, suggesting that these women maintained the wak'a (ibid.:fol. 182).[16] *Mamaconas* ("mothers") were *aqllakuna* of high rank—older women who often taught younger women or women whom the Inka ruler gifted as bridewealth to become servants (see Acosta 1954 [1590]:155–56; Betanzos 1968 [1551]:53; Zuidema 2007). The documents, then, show that laborers and servants of a special status and class cultivated and cared for the land at Pachar and Soqma. Inka elite administrators like Coritopa would have directly overseen these laborers. A hierarchy of social categories and roles was anchored in particular lands that housed wak'as.

The wak'as lived in land that the Inkas created and managed. Several documents indicate that lands established due to the canalization of the Vilcanota River were the exclusive domain of the imperial religion and the Sun (Burns 1999:52). According to Spanish ontological premises, such land was not "owned" since it was assigned to "pagan" deities. Lands of the Sun, in particular, appear regularly in colonial litigations since they could be acquired by eager representatives of the crown and the church (e.g., AGN 1559–60:fol. 1–16). For instance, in 1557, Francisco de Mayontopa, the powerful kuraka of Ollantaytambo, argued against the Monasterio de Santa Clara in Cuzco for rights over approximately 580 ha of land near Pachar (ARC 1555–1729:fol. 452v).[17] Representing Santa Clara's interests, Jeronimo de Costilla stated that the lands should not remain in Ollantaytambo's jurisdiction since they belonged to the Sun. Recounting his management of the land, Mayontopa answered that the people of Ollantaytambo were the rightful owners since they had created and cultivated these fields (Burns 1999:54). He petitioned his case to the Corregidor of Cuzco, Polo de Ondegardo, who sided with the aging kuraka.

In a case that pitted Mayontopa against the Convento de la Merced in Cuzco, both parties declared that fields along the Vilcanota River were dedicated to the Sun and the divine Inka royalty (AGN 1559–60). The contested land was situated in Colcabamba, a place where maize was grown and stored for Ollantaytambo (ibid.; Burns 1999). These lands were maintained by Colla and Chinchaysuyu mitmaqkuna (AGN 1559–60:fol. 13, 26v, 29). Exemplifying the Spanish perspective on private property, the Mercederians claimed that the lands were "dedicated during the time of the Inka to the Sun and to the Inka, who was the lord of this region, and never in his life did Francisco Mayontopa possess them as his own, nor did his Indians possess them as their own" (ibid.:fol. 5; see also Burns 1999:55).[18]

These cases illustrate how definitions of the environment are at the heart of imperial projects. Indeed, as Burns (1999:57) cogently argues, within the folios of these documents we see a collision of imperial aims—an Inka project to define land use and a Spanish colonial effort to equate land with property. The kurakas claimed rights to Pachar and Soqma because they had dutifully overseen the labor and products of these lands. Spanish ecclesiastical groups argued that labor performed at Pachar and Soqma was specifically dedicated to the imperial cults and thus could not be claimed as private property. Under the Spanish regime, Coritopa makes a counterclaim for these lands as his territory (due to his labor management) and petitions for permission to establish or reconstruct clear territorial markers (*mojones*) (ARC 1555–1729:fol. 2, 4). The documents surely reflect the motivations of Inka kurakas influenced by European ideas of value. But if we read between the competing claims of "rulership" and "ownership," we also see that these arguments are largely about different ontological understandings of people, place, and land.

DISCUSSION: CREATING PLACES, CULTIVATING PERSONS

As the Inkas assembled Ollantaytambo, they attempted to reconfigure relationships between people and the land, repositioning people and places according to their "essential" qualities. Local labor was distributed throughout a system of agricultural and pastoral lands, categorized according to the characteristics of the laborers, and managed by new administrative authorities. Likewise, rituals were detached from earlier ancestral places like Wat'a and redistributed along the border and road that connected the region to Cuzco.

When the Inkas constructed the city's monumental structures, they raised wak'as in new lands assigned to Inka authorities and in terrain tilled by new people. As in the Wanakauri myth, so it was at Ollantaytambo: wak'as, people, and land were co-created.

The wak'as embodied this newly wrought Inka environment. They attached a common suite of signs—carved stones, geometric motifs—to spectacular environmental features. Commonalities in the materiality and style of wak'as suggest that they were meant to be used and perceived in similar ways. Many of them contain boulders that stand out relative to the surrounding architecture and geology. That is, these are all single, detached boulders, unlike the immense outcrops of carved rocks that constitute wak'a sites above the city of Cuzco. All of the Ollantaytambo stones exhibit bench motifs that focus the viewer's attention on a particular facade of the boulder (Figure 6.11). As with many of the new Inka administrative sites, the wak'as were manufactured in previously unoccupied or newly established lands, suggesting a semiotic association between new imperial land claims and new Inka spaces. Situated next to springs and waterfalls, amidst monumental geometric terraces, and along an extensive road, the shrines emphasized Inka transformations of the environment. Conspicuous in their locations along the borders and roads of Ollantaytambo, the wak'as marked new Inka royal claims to land ownership—claims that were inalienable. The similarities in settings suggest that the boulders were positioned to aestheticize and accentuate agrarian lands, creating a landscape in which it appeared as though Inka imperial power sprouted directly from the earth (see also Dean 2010, this volume).

Even so, such a claim to power cannot be grounded in aesthetics and appearances alone. The data suggest that the power and personhood of the wak'as were manifested in situated practices of construction and veneration. These practices likely gained cultural purchase by invoking familiar, pre-Inka understandings about relationships between people and places. Indeed, the architecture and artifacts of the wak'as demonstrate that practices at these sites worked within the same semiotic register as ancestor veneration practices at pre-Inka ritual centers.[19] The excavations and surface collections revealed high densities of decorated serving vessels and faunal remains near multiple wak'as, indicating that these places were feted or fed in ways that called to mind the practices through which pre-Inka people engaged with their ancestors. Similar to earlier aboveground tombs, the wak'as were enclosed within walls and/or adjoined by small platforms, revealing that both wak'a rituals and ancestor veneration practices were secluded affairs during which small parties of people or individuals confronted powerful beings. Finally, like the aboveground tombs of the

FIGURE 6.11. *Common stylistic attributes of many of the carved boulders in the Ollantaytambo region include bench motifs that adorn specific facades of the stones. Clockwise from the top left: Pomatales, Perolniyoq, Ñawpa Iglesia, Choqana Boulder One, Choqana Boulder Two, and Sala (photographs by author).*

preceding epoch, the wak'as were emplaced in lands worked by discrete kinds of people and/or distinct, highly localized communities.

Considering these data, I argue that the Ollantaytambo wak'as operated as if they were Inka ancestors rooted in the land (cf. Salomon 1995:322).[20] During the centuries before Inka ascendancy, the people of the Ollantaytambo area participated in ancestor veneration ceremonies and came to understand that their flesh and blood were of the same substance as the soils and rocks of the places where their ancestors dwelled. In these ceremonies, they marked their possession of, and affinity with, a place. They were *particular people of a particular place.*

Ollantaytambo birthed a regional order of people, places, and lands, all of whom were subject to the Inka royalty. In laboring to shape the city's stones, plant its fields, and serve its elites, Andean people became essential types of persons—e.g., Colla masons, *mitmaqkuna* workers, and *yanakuna* retainers. By performing traditional ancestor rites for the wak'as of these new lands, the new subjects of the state engaged with and attributed personhood to Inka wak'as and, ultimately, signified their connections (as particular types of laborers) to Inka soils. They became *particular types of persons within a universal Inka landscape.* By analogy with older ancestor rites, they reified their roles as socially distinct kinds of persons within an Inka kin network. In ritually forging kin relations with Inka lands and wak'as (personified places and Inka ancestors), they became "new people" in a new Inka world.

A closer look at the architecture of the Ollantaytambo wak'as reveals how people engaged with these wak'as and, consequently, affirmed their roles within the Inka landscape. The sites' spatial layouts suggest that these were private spaces in which individuals confronted wak'as. The only other people present may have been the specialized attendants who could converse with the shrines (e.g., Cobo 1964 [1653]:204; Molina 1947 [1573]:47). All of the shrines were either partially enclosed in perimeter walls or flanked by formal platforms. These architectural elements enhanced the privacy and solemnity of wak'a rites by limiting people's access to the sites, directing their movement, and focusing their attention toward specific features or facades of the place. For instance, in approaching many of these wak'as (e.g., Ñawpa Iglesia, Perolniyoq, Pomatales), one sees only the particular facade of a stone bearing a bench motif. For instance, if presenting an offering at Chulluraqay, one must stand directly above the canal that enters and exits this carved stone. At Korimarka, the caves only come into view once one has reached the platforms on the adjoining ridge.

Such private, personalized and controlled spaces would have manifested a markedly different kind of ritual practice than the public Inka plaza ceremonialism that is typically understood as central to the Inka state religion. In Inka plazas, the royalty hosted lavish feasting ceremonies during which they offered their subjects special foods and plentiful drinks (Bray 2003; Cummins 2002b; Morris 1993; Ogburn 2005; Ramírez 2005). In these performances of state redistribution and largesse, people avowed their subject positions as laborers, while Inka elites confirmed their ascribed roles as the managers of society (Godelier 1977; Kolata 1996). The architecture of Inka plazas suggests that feasts involved generalized, collective subjects. Dressed in their ethnic groups' representative attire, subjects confronted state officials in public spaces designed for massive gatherings (Morris and Thompson 1985; Ramírez 2005). By comparison, the architecture of the Inka wak'as appears to emphasize individual roles and subject positions. In approaching these spaces people moved from open fields and roads to enclosed settings where they met Inka beings and ancestors. In these secluded engagements, people would have become aware of their roles within the broader environment, validating the connection between Inka authority and environmental forces, while verifying their personal obligations to an Inka landscape.

The wak'as were thus agentive inasmuch as they called out or interpellated (sensu Althusser 1971) people as particular kinds of persons and subjects, whether commoner or elite. People would have seen and revered these wak'as in different ways, in accordance with their social station. Ritual practices enacted in the shadows of these boulders would have worked to naturalize social differences as they ascribed "distinctions to realities thought to transcend the powers of human actors" (Bell 1992:74). Elites that made offerings at the wak'as would have confirmed their roles as the caretakers of people, land, and labor. On the other hand, the wak'as likely manifested new social roles and obligations for the new people of Ollantaytambo (see Topic 1998; also Chase, this volume). Severed from their kinship ties and ancestral lands, the new people of Ollantaytambo served only the Inka royalty and worked only Inka lands. In engaging with these wak'as, the new people directed their ritual practices toward the Inka themselves and the Inka land. But, in so doing, they were not passively reacting to state power. At these places, Andean people solidified their positions as the subjects—indeed, the offspring—of the Inka world that they themselves had constructed.

CONCLUSION: NATURALIZING SOCIAL DIFFERENCES

After consolidating their power within the Cuzco region and abroad, Inka rulers began to manifest their authority and declare their divine status by constructing monumental urban complexes, such as Ollantaytambo. They founded vast landscapes—integrated environments of palatial edifices, terrace systems, canal networks, roads, and residential settlements. The construction of these environments inaugurated new definitions of people, places, and land. Usufruct rights and labor practices shifted radically as people were detached from the lands and places of their ancestors and directed to work land and tend animals for seemingly abstract beings—the Inka rulers, the wak'as, and the Sun. Ritual practices conducted at the wak'as personalized the new labor relationships and naturalized the recently imposed social differences of the Inka state. The wak'as were thus essential to the Inka ontological proposition that social differences between Inkas and others were, put simply, "natural."

In attending to these wak'as, we see that the ontological proposition of the Inka state—a proposition that paired types of people and land—was assembled through social practices and perceptions that were, in part, derived from Cusco's pre-Inka cultural landscape. By building these wak'as and reshaping Cusco's lands, then, the Inkas created a perhaps irresolvable contradiction between their state's and local people's definitions of a "natural" mode of being. Such contradictions can be found within the very roots of the Inka state and, by extension, the broader concept of "the State." Indeed, political regimes often seek to liken a state to an unchanging natural order by building personified places, such as the stoic faces of Mount Rushmore, the opulent gardens of Versailles, the ornate reservoirs of ancient India, and the embellished natural places of Cusco's wak'as. These places are designed to be sites of authorization where people, through their political and religious conviction and commitment, are meant to recognize or revere the power of a state. But these places are also potential sites of subversion where people challenge and reject the universal and naturalizing propositions of the state. After all, the "nature" that these places embody is a politically contested and socially manifested claim.

ACKNOWLEDGMENTS

I thank Tamara Bray for inviting me to participate in the Dumbarton Oaks symposium that led to this volume. I am especially grateful to Tammy for her invaluable insights and productive criticisms. I am also indebted to the scholars who helped me to strengthen my argument: John Topic, Bruce Mannheim, Zach Chase, Anna Guengerich, Andrew Roddick, John Powell Warner, John Janusek, B. Scot Rousse, Rebecca Bria, and two anonymous reviewers. I thank Jesús Galiano Blanco for his tireless work in the archives and Vicentina Galiano Blanco for her invaluable help with the documentation of the sites considered in this study. Funding for the research was provided by a Fulbright-Hays Doctoral Dissertation Research Abroad Fellowship; a National Science Foundation Dissertation Improvement Grant; a University of Alabama College Academy of Research, Scholarship, and Creative Activity Grant; and a University of Alabama Research Grants Committee Grant. The

ASTER data used in this study are a product of the National Aeronautics and Space Administration (NASA) and Japan's Ministry of Economy, Trade, and Industry (METI).

NOTES

1. Most Spanish sources state that this ancestral Inka merged with a preexisting wak'a—both a place and the "form of a person" (*bulto de persona*)—near the town of Sano (Cabello Balboa 1951 [1586]:262; Molina 1947 [1573]:23; Murúa 1962–64 [1590], 1:23; Sarmiento 1965 [1572]:215). In contrast, see Betanzos (1968 [1551]:13), who claims that the Sun ordered one of the brothers to become Wanakauri.

2. The Spanish sources disagree on which ancestral Inka brother was entombed in the cave. Some claim it was Ayarcachi: Betanzos 1968 [1551]:12; Cieza 1967 [1553]:17; Sarmiento 1965 [1572]:215. Others state that it was Ayarauca: Cabello Balboa 1951 [1586]:261; Molina 1947 [1573]:21; Murúa 1962–64 [1590], 1:23. Moreover, the sources disagree on which ancestral brother becomes Wanakauri. Some claim Ayarcachi: Cabello Balboa 1951 [1586]:263; Cieza 1967 [1553]:17; Molina 1947 [1573]:137; Murúa 1962–64 [1590], 1:23. And others list Ayaruchu: Betanzos 1968 [1551]:13; Sarmiento 1965 [1572]:215). These variations most likely reflect the divergent historical and political claims of Inka elites during the early colonial period (sensu Urton 1990). In all variations, though, an Inka ancestor reshapes the valleys and mountains of Cuzco; the ancestral Inka see a rainbow; an Inka ancestor attaches or offers himself to a local wak'a and becomes Wanakauri; and finally the Inka stake their claim to both possess and rule Cuzco.

3. Such claims can be easily located in both ancient and contemporary texts. They are central to the Epic of Gilgamesh, Maya inscriptions, the accounts of Julius Caesar's campaign in Gaul, the arguments of Las Casas, the documents of Thomas Jefferson, the speeches of Frederick Jackson Turner, the writings of Lenin, etc.

4. For instance, the Inka recruited the Cañaris as royal guards due to this ethnic group's unrivalled ferocity in battle (e.g., Cabello Balboa 1951 [1586], chaps. 22–23).

5. Some Spanish chroniclers remark that the Inka established wak'a when they first declared their authority over Cuzco (Cobo 1964 [1653]:64, 153; Guaman Poma de Ayala 1980 [1615]:58). Others specifically state that wak'a veneration was instituted by the ninth emperor Pachakuti Inka (Bandera 1968 [1557]:500; Sarmiento 1965 [1572]:242) or the tenth emperor Topa Inka (Santillán 1968 [1563]:111). Sixteen of the Cuzco wak'as were said to have been mandated by order of specific Inka rulers, suggesting that the elite created shrines to embed state narratives of history within the land (e.g., Cobo 1964 [1653]:177).

6. Ollantaytambo has had many names. Early documents call it "Collatambo" or "Tambo" (AGN 1559–60:fol. 23). These names refer to the Tampu pre-Inka ethnic group

that resided in the area and the Colla people that the Inka moved to the city. In the sixteenth century the Spanish called the city "Pueblo de Zarza," then "Santiago de Tambo" (Glave and Remy 1983:2). Soon after, the name "Ollantaytambo" became common (e.g., Sarmiento 1965 [1572]).

7. No excavation unit in Ollantaytambo has uncovered more than a handful of pre-Inka artifacts or any pre-Inka architecture. Some excavations have recovered Killk'e (pre- or early Inka) ceramics, but these samples are always very small and always found in excavation levels bearing high percentages of Classic Inka ceramics (e.g., see Galiano and Apaza 2004).

8. *Yanakuna* cultivated the fields of the royal Inka, including the lands of Pacha-kuti and Topa Inka (Malca Olguin 1963; Rostworowski 1993:141–42). *Mitmaqkuna* likely built the towering edifices of the city and tilled the fields dedicated to the Sun and the wak'a (AGN 1559–60:fol. 26v, 46v). The *mitmaqkuna* were from the distant Collao region (southern Peru) and the Chinchaysuyu region (northwestern Peru, outside of the Cuzco region) (ibid.:fol. 14–16, 26v).

9. There are multiple *chullpa* tombs near Kachiqhata, across the Vilcanota River. Our surface collections reveal that many of these tombs were used during the Inka imperial period. However, these tombs are almost exclusively associated with small residential sites rather than large, central towns.

10. The vast majority of Cuzco wak'as (82.9%; 272/328) were non-built or modified land features (Cobo 1964 [1653]). The most common of these were rocks (26.5%; 87/328), springs (25.6%; 85/328), mountains/peaks (9.1%; 30/328 [excluding "rocks on mountains"]), places (7%; 23/328 ["place where the Inka sat," "place where one loses sight of Cuzco," etc.]), and plains (*llanos*) (6.1%; 20/328). Most of the other wak'as (14.9%; 49/328) were built features, the most common being houses of Inka royalty (4%; 13/328) and tombs of Cuzco's elite (2.7%; 9/328).

11. The best source on Inka wak'as is Bernabé Cobo's 1653 list, which drew from an unknown earlier source to document 328 Cuzco wak'as (Bauer 1998:14, 21). Cobo's list suggests that the vast majority of Cuzco wak'as were places for offerings and sacrifices (Cobo 1964 [1653]). The list contains information on the practices enacted at 151 of Cuzco's wak'as. The most common offerings were seashells (27.2%; 41/151), children (19.9%; 30/151), clothes (11.9%; 18/151), and meat (6.6%; 10/151). Gold, silver, and coca were also proffered. Many wak'as received more than one of these materials, or they were given the generic "ordinary things" (9.9%; 15/151), "everything" (5.3%; 8/151), or "everything except for children" (4%; 6/151). It is notable though that many Andean wak'as did indeed receive tribute in the form of comestibles, particularly corn beer, maize, or sacrificed camelids (e.g. Arriaga 1968 [1621]:209).

12. The original Spanish reads: ". . . en lo alto a mano yzquierda como ymos del Cuzco e del pueblo de Maras a Tambo / lo qual estara una legua del dho pueblo de

Tambo. . . en lo qual halle un monton de tierra alto sobre una peña que paresçio aver sido sacrificadero e guaca de los naturales. . . aquel monton de tierra y edifiçios que está en el dho que servia a los yngas o fuera algun Mochadero antiguo / dixo que a oydo dezir que era donde se sentaba el Ynga." In this passage, the Spanish ask Francisco Manya Ura, the alcalde of Ollantaytambo, about his knowledge of the wak'a at Hatun Kancha Raqay. The alcalde responds that he does not know about the site. However, the Spanish line of questioning suggests that they had already heard about this place and its previous function—their assumptions were confirmed later in the document when the *kuraka* of the nearby town of Maras stated that Hatun Kancha Raqay was a wak'a served by the special women (*mamakona*) of the Inka queen Mama Oqllo (see below).

13. Excavations at Pachar and the nearby settlement of Chulluraqay recovered very few pre-Inka artifacts and no pre-Inka cultural levels (Solís and Olazabal 1998:103, 137–38).

14. One other carved stone sits directly in the Vilcanota River, at the edge of the city's core. Another carved stone is situated in Piscacucho, the western boundary of Ollantaytambo (ARC 1568–1722:fol. 294). These other stones further demonstrate the association between carved boulders and the extension of the city.

15. Although pre-Inka/early Inka (Killk'e-related) pottery was recovered in this area, it was always associated with Classic Inka pottery. Killk'e-related sherds constitute 0–2% of the ceramics recovered from particular levels and 1.15% of the total amount of sherds. In a nearby plaza, only 1.32% of the total recovered sherds were Killk'e-related while 40.53% were Inka. The adjacent fountain sector contained a bit more Killk'e-related pottery (6.4%), but also more Inka pottery (55.4%) (see Galiano and Apaza 2004:110–11).

16. The document reads: ". . . And in order to obtain more information about this [Hatun Kancha Raqay] Don Sancho Usca Paucar, the principal *kuraka* of Maras, was questioned. He promised under oath to tell the truth. He was asked about the walls and structures [*los dhos corrales e paredones*] and what they were called, and he responded that these walls and structures, and the lands and terraces that were adjacent to them, were called Pachar . . . and the walls and structures belonged to [*eran y avian sido de*] Mama Oqllo, the mother of Wayna Qhapaq. He added that he knows this because his ancestors [*pasados*] told him, and because some *mamaconas* from Maras resided in these structures . . ." (my translation). The original Spanish reads: "E para mas ynformacion de lo suso dho tome e rreçebi juramento de Don Sancho Usca Paucar caçique prinçipal del pueblo de Maras el qual prometio de dezir verdad de lo que supiese e le fuese preguntado / al qual pregunte que los dhos corrales e paredones cuyos eran e como se llaman el qual dixo que los dhos corrales e paredones e tierras e andenes que estan junto a ellos se llama todo Pachar/ e que si de otra manera lo llaman algunos yndios que es compuesto / e que los dhos corrales e paredones eran y avian sido de

Mama Oclo madre que fue de Guayna Capa y que esto sabe porque se lo an dho sus pasados e que en los dhos corrales uvo algunos mamaconas que eran del pueblo de Maras . . ." The reference to mamaconas, who were high-rank *aqllakuna* "mothers," suggests that the town of Maras gave women to Ollantaytambo and its associated towns, much like the towns surrounding Cuzco gave women to the Inka nobility (see Zuidema 2007).

17. The litigation concerned 200 *fanegadas* of land situated in Pachar (Burns 1999:50). A *fanegada* was equivalent to the amount of land that one could sow with a *fanegada* of seed, approximately 2.9 ha.

18. The Spanish reads: "son tierras que fueron dedicadas en tiempo de los Yndios Yngas para el Sol e para el dho Ynga señor que fue destos rreynos e que nunca las tuvo ny poseyo en su vida Don Francisco Mayontopa ny sus Yndios por suyas ny como suyas y que son sin perjuizio del dho Mayontopa e de sus Yndios."

19. Arriaga (1968 [1621]:248) claims a similar isomorphism between ancestors and wak'as, stating that the founders of a town (the "Huaris") venerated wak'as, while the second and third generation of newcomers to an area ("the Llacuaces") venerated the mummies of their ancestors. In this example, people performed their attachment to the land by engaging with one of these two kinds of emplaced person.

20. The Inka royalty lived on as the ancestors and the leaders of the empire. Their mummies were essential to political ceremony and action (see general discussions in Bauer 2004; D'Altroy 2002; Dillehay 1995; Kolata 2013; McEwan 2006). But contrary to pre-Inka practice, very few Inka subjects would ever see a mummified Inka or an Inka ancestor. Instead, Inka subjects performed their social roles by venerating wak'as, which personified the Inkas, their actions, and their lands.

REFERENCES CITED

Acosta, José de. 1954 [1590]. "Historia natural y moral de las Indias." In *Biblioteca de Autores Españoles*, no. 73. Madrid: Ediciones Atlas.

Algaze, Guillermo. 1993. "Expansionary Dynamics of Some Early Pristine States." *American Anthropologist* 95 (2): 304–33. http://dx.doi.org/10.1525/aa.1993.95.2 .02a00030.

Algaze, Guillermo. 2001. "Initial Social Complexity in Southwestern Asia: The Mesopotamian Advantage." *Current Anthropology* 42 (2): 199–233. http://dx.doi .org/10.1086/320005.

Alonso, Ana Marie. 1994. "The Politics of Space, Time and Substance: State Formation, Nationalism and Ethnicity." *Annual Review of Anthropology* 23 (1): 379–405. http://dx.doi.org/10.1146/annurev.an.23.100194.002115.

Althusser, Louis. 1971. *Lenin and Philosophy and Other Essays.* New York: Monthly Review Press.

Archivo General de la Nación (AGN). 1559–60. Fondo: Derecho Indígena, legajo 31, cuaderno 614.

Archivo General de la Nación (AGN). 1576. Fondo: Real Audiencia "Causas Civiles," legajo 15, cuaderno 77.

Archivo Regional de Cusco (ARC). 1555–1729. Fondo: Beneficencia Publica, Seccion: Colegio de Ciencias, legajo 46 (previously labeled as 26B),.

Archivo Regional de Cusco (ARC). 1568–1722. Fondo: Educandas, legajo 2.

Arredondo Dueñas, Nicolas. 2009. "Investigación arqueológica Ñaupa Iglesia-Ollantaytambo. Research report (informe)." Manuscript on file, Ministerio de Cultura, Dirección de Investigación y Catastro, Subdirección de Investigación, Lima.

Arriaga, Pablo José de. 1968 [1621]. "Extirpación de la idolatría del Pirú." In *Biblioteca de Autores Españoles*, no. 209. Madrid: Ediciones Atlas.

Balée, William, and Clark L. Erickson. 2005. "Introduction: Time and Complexity in Historical Ecology." In *Time and Complexity in Historical Ecology: Studies from the Neotropical Lowlands*, ed. William Balée and Clark Erickson, 1–12. New York: Columbia University Press.

Balkansky, Andrew K. 1998. "Urbanism and Early State Formation in the Huamelulpan Valley of Southern Mexico." *Latin American Antiquity* 9 (1): 37–67. http://dx.doi.org/10.2307/972127.

Bandera, Damián de la. 1968 [1557]. "Relación del origen e gobierno que los Ingas tuvieron." In *Biblioteca Peruana*, vol. 3, 491–510. Lima: Editores Técnicos Asociados S.A.

Bauer, Andrew M., and Kathleen D. Morrison. 2008. "Water Management and Reservoirs in Southern India and Sri Lanka." In *Encyclopedia of the History of Science, Technology, and Medicine in Non-Western Cultures*, ed. Helaine Selin, 2213–14. New York: Springer. http://dx.doi.org/10.1007/978-1-4020-4425-0_8843.

Bauer, Brian S. 1996. "The Legitimization of the State in Inca Myth and Ritual." *American Anthropologist* 98 (2): 327–37. http://dx.doi.org/10.1525/aa.1996.98.2 .02a00090.

Bauer, Brian S. 1998. *The Sacred Landscape of the Inca: The Cusco Ceque System.* Austin: University of Texas Press.

Bauer, Brian S. 2004. *Ancient Cuzco: Heartland of the Inca.* Austin: University of Texas Press.

Bauer, Brian S., and Wilton Barrionuevo Orosco. 1998. "Reconstructing Andean Shrine Systems: A Test Case from the Xaquixaguana (Anta) Region of Cusco, Peru." *Andean Past* 5:73–87.

Bell, Catherine. 1992. *Ritual Theory, Ritual Practice*. Oxford: Oxford University Press.

Bengtsson, Lisbet. 1998. *Prehistoric Stonework in the Peruvian Andes: A Case Study at Ollantaytambo*. Ethnologiska Studier 44, GOTARC series B, no. 10. Goteborg: Ethnografiska museet.

Betanzos, Juan de. 1968 [1551]. "Suma y narración de los Incas." In *Biblioteca de Autores Españoles*, no. 209. Madrid: Ediciones Atlas.

Biblioteca Nacional del Perú (BNP). 1629. Fondo: Manuscritos, Documento B-1030.

Bray, Tamara L. 2003. "Inka Pottery as Culinary Equipment: Food, Feasting, and Gender in Imperial State Design." *Latin American Antiquity* 14 (1): 3–28. http://dx.doi.org/10.2307/972232.

Bray, Tamara L. 2013. "Water, Ritual, and Power in the Inca Empire." *Latin American Antiquity* 24 (2): 164–90. http://dx.doi.org/10.7183/1045-6635.24.2.164.

Brush, Stephen B. 1976. "Man's Use of an Andean Ecosystem." *Human Ecology* 4 (2): 147–66. http://dx.doi.org/10.1007/BF01531218.

Burns, Kathryn. 1999. *Colonial Habits: Convents and the Spiritual Economy of Cuzco, Peru*. Durham, NC: Duke University Press.

Cabello Balboa, Miguel. 1951 [1586]. *Miscelánea Antártica, una Historia del Perú Antiguo*. Lima: Universidad Nacional Mayor de San Marcos, Instituto de Etnología.

Calancha, Antonio de la. 1974–81 [1638]. *Crónica moralizada del orden de San Agustín en el Perú, con sucesos ejemplares en esta monarquía*. Edición de Ignacio Prado Pastor, 6 vols. Lima: Universidad Nacional Mayor de San Marcos.

Cieza de León, Pedro de. 1946. [1553]. *La Crónica del Perú*. Mexico City: Editorial Nueva España.

Cieza de León, Pedro de. 1967 [1553]. *El Señorío de los Incas*. Lima: Instituto de Estudios Peruanos, Lima.

Cobo, Bernabé. 1964 [1653]. "Historia del nuevo mundo, II." In *Biblioteca del Autores Españoles*, vol. 92, ed. Luis A. Pardo. Madrid: Ediciones Atlas.

Cobo, Bernabé. 1990. [1653]. *Inca Religion and Customs*. Austin: University of Texas Press.

Covey, R. Alan. 2006. *How the Incas Built their Heartland: State Formation and the Innovation of Imperial Strategies in the Sacred Valley, Peru*. Ann Arbor: University of Michigan Press.

Covey, R. Alan, and Donato Amado González. 2008. *Imperial Transformations in Sixteenth-Century Yucay, Peru*. Memoirs of the Museum of Anthropology 44. Ann Arbor: University of Michigan Press.

Cummins, Thomas B.F. 2002a. *Toasts with the Inca: Andean Abstraction and Colonial Images on Quero Vessels*. Ann Arbor: University of Michigan Press.

Cummins, Thomas B.F. 2002b. "Town Planning, Marriage, and Free Will in the Colonial Andes." In *The Archaeology of Colonialism (Issues and Debates)*, ed. Claire L. Lyons and John K. Papadopoulos, 199–240. Los Angeles: Getty Press.

D'Altroy, Terence. 2002. *The Incas*. Malden, MA: Blackwell.

Dean, Emily M. 2005. "Ancestors, Mountains, Shrines, and Settlements: Late Intermediate Period Landscapes of the Southern Vilcanota Valley, Peru." PhD diss., Department of Anthropology, University of California, Berkeley. Ann Arbor, MI: University Microfilms.

Dean, Carolyn. 2010. *A Culture of Stone: Inka Perspectives on Rock*. Durham, NC: Duke University Press. http://dx.doi.org/10.1215/9780822393177.

Denevan, William. 1992. "The Pristine Myth: The Landscapes of the Americas in 1492." *Association of American Geographers* 82 (3): 369–85. http://dx.doi.org/10.1111/j.1467-8306.1992.tb01965.x.

Descola, Phillippe. 1994. *In the Society of Nature: A Native Ecology in Amazonia*. Cambridge: Cambridge University Press.

Dillehay, Tom D., ed. 1995. *Tombs for the Living: Andean Mortuary Practices*. Washington, DC: Dumbarton Oaks Research Library and Collection.

Dreyfus, Hubert L. 1991. *Being-in-the-World: A Commentary on Heidegger's Being and Time Division I*. Cambridge, MA: MIT Press.

Dreyfus, Hubert L. 2000. "A Merleau-Pontyian Critique of Husserl's and Searle's Representionalist Accounts of Action." *Proceedings of the Aristotelian Society* 100 (3): 287–302. http://dx.doi.org/10.1111/1467-9264.00081.

Escobar, Arturo. 1999. "After Nature: Steps to an Antiessentialist Political Ecology." *Current Anthropology* 40 (1): 1–30. http://dx.doi.org/10.1086/515799.

Farrington, Ian S. 1983. "Prehistoric Intensive Agriculture: Preliminary Notes on River Canalization in the Sacred Valley of the Incas." In *Drained Field Agriculture in Central and South America*, ed. Janice P. Darch, 221–35. British Archaeological Reports, International Series 189. Oxford: BAR.

Fried, Morton H. 1967. *The Evolution of Political Society: An Essay in Political Anthropology*. New York: Random House.

Galiano Blanco, Vicentina, and Luz Marina Apaza Bustamente. 2004. "Arqueología de Ollantaytambo-Manyaraki: Una introducción a su estudio." Thesis on file, Facultad de Ciencias Sociales, Universidad Nacional de San Antonio Abad del Cusco, Cusco.

Garcilaso de la Vega, El Inca. 1976 [1609]. *Los comentarios reales de los Incas*. Caracas: Biblioteca Ayacucho.

Geertz, Clifford. 1981. *Negara: The Theatre State in Nineteenth-Century Bali*. Princeton: Princeton University Press.

Gelman, Susan A., and Bruce Mannheim. 2007. "Essentialism." In *International Encyclopedia of the Social Sciences.* 2nd ed., ed. W. A. Darity, 630–31. London: MacMillan Library Reference.

Gibaja Oviedo, Arminda M. 1982. "La ocupación neoinca del valle de Urubamba." In *Arqueología de Cuzco,* ed. Italo Oberti, 81–93. Cusco: Instituto Nacional de Cultura.

Gibaja Oviedo, Arminda M. 1984. "Requencia cultural de Ollantaytambo." In *Current Archaeological Projects in the Central Andes,* ed. Ann E. Kendall, 225–46. British Archaeological Reports, International Series 210. Oxford: BAR.

Glacken, Clarence J. 1976. *Traces on the Rhodian Shore: Nature and Culture in Western Thought from Ancient Times to the End of the Eighteenth Century.* Berkeley: University of California Press.

Glave Testino, Luis Miguel, and María I. Remy. 1983. *Estructura agraria y vida rural en una región andina: Ollantaytambo entre los siglos XVI–XIX.* Cusco: Centro de Estudios Rurales Andinos Bartolomé de las Casas.

Godelier, Maurice. 1977. "The Concept of 'Social and Economic Formation:' The Inca Example." In *Perspectives in Marxist Anthropology,* ed. Maurice Godelier, 63–69. Cambridge: Cambridge University Press.

Gordillo, Gastón, and Silvia Hirsch. 2003. "Indigenous Struggles and Contested Identities in Argentina: Histories of Invisibilization and Reemergence." *Journal of Latin American Anthropology* 8 (3): 4–30. http://dx.doi.org/10.1525/jlat.2003.8.3.4.

Guaman Poma de Ayala, Felipe. 1980 [1615]. *El Primer Nueva Corónica y Buen Gobierno.* Mexico City: Siglo Veintiuno.

Harvey, David. 1996. *Justice, Nature and the Geography of Difference.* Oxford: Blackwell.

Hastorf, Christine. 1993. *Agriculture and the Onset of Political Inequality before the Inka.* Cambridge: Cambridge University Press.

Heffernan, Kenneth J. 1989. "Limatambo in Late Prehistory: Landscape Archaeology and Documentary Images of Inca Presence in the Periphery of Cuzco." PhD diss., Department of Prehistory and Anthropology, Australian National University, Canberra.

Heffernan, Kenneth J. 1996. *Limatambo: Archaeology, History and the Regional Societies of Inca Cusco.* British Archaeological Reports, International Series 644. Oxford: BAR.

Hollowell, J. Lee. 1987. "Precision Cutting and Fitting of Stone in Prehistoric Andean Walls." Research report on file. Washington, DC: National Geographic Society.

Johnson, Allen W., and Timothy K. Earle. 1987. *The Evolution of Human Societies: From Foraging Group to Agrarian State.* Palo Alto, CA: Stanford University Press.

Julien, Catherine. 2000. *Reading Inca History.* Iowa City: University of Iowa Press.

Kendall, Ann E. 1984. "Archaeological Investigations of Late Intermediate Period and Late Horizon Period at Cusichaca, Peru." In *Current Archaeological Projects in the Central Andes*, ed. Ann E. Kendall, 247–90. British Archaeological Reports, International Series 210. Oxford: BAR.

Kendall, Ann E. 1985. *Aspects of Inca Architecture: Description, Function, and Chronology.* Parts 1 and 2. British Archaeological Reports, International Series 242. Oxford: BAR.

Kendall, Ann E. 1988. "Inca Planning North of Cuzco between Anta and Machu Picchu and along the Urubamba Valley." In *Recent Studies in Precolumbian Archaeology*, ed. Nicholas J. Saunders and Olivier de Montmillon, 457–88. British Archaeological Reports, International Series 421. Oxford: BAR.

Kendall, Ann E. 1996. "An Archaeological Perspective for Late Intermediate Period Inca Development." *Journal of the Steward Anthropological Society* 24:121–56.

Kendall, Ann E., Rob Early, and Bill Sillar. 1992. "Report on Archaeological Field Season Investigating Early Inca Architecture at Juchuy Coscco (Q'aqya Qhawana) and Warq'ana, Province of Calca, Department of Cuzco, Peru." In *Ancient America: Contributions to New World Archaeology*, ed. Nicholas J. Saunders, 189–256. Oxford: Oxbow Books.

Kolata, Alan L. 1996. "Principles of Authority in the Native Andean State." In *Structure, Knowledge, and Representation in the Andes*, ed. Gary Urton, 61–84. Special issue of *Journal of the Steward Anthropological Society* 24.

Kolata, Alan L. 2013. *Ancient Inca*. Cambridge: Cambridge University Press.

Kosiba, Steve. 2010. "Becoming Inka: The Transformation of Political Place and Practice during Inka State Formation (Cusco, Perú)." PhD diss., Department of Anthropology, University of Chicago. Ann Arbor, MI: University Microfilms.

Kosiba, Steve. 2011. "The Politics of Locality: Pre-Inka Social Landscapes of the Cusco Region." In *The Archaeology of Politics: The Materiality of Political Practice and Action in the Past*, ed. Peter Johansen and Andrew Bauer, 114–50. Cambridge: Cambridge Scholars Publishing.

Kosiba, Steve. 2012a. "Emplacing Value, Cultivating Order: Places of Conversion and Practices of Subordination throughout Early Inka State Formation (Cusco, Perú)." In *Constructions of Value in the Ancient World*, ed. Gary Urton and John Papadopoulos, 97–127. Los Angeles: Cotsen Institute of Archaeology, University of California, Los Angeles.

Kosiba, Steve. 2012b. "Cultivating the Sacred State: Political Ecology, Environmental Management and the Production of Social Difference in the Early Inka Polity." Paper presented at the 77th Annual Meeting of the Society for American Archaeology, Memphis, TN.

Kosiba, Steve, and Andrew Bauer. 2013. "Mapping the Political Landscape: Toward a GIS Analysis of Social and Environmental Difference." *Journal of*

Archaeological Method and Theory 20:61–101. http://dx.doi.org/10.1007/s10816-011
-9126-z.

Lefebvre, Henri. 1991. *The Production of Space*. Malden, MA: Blackwell Publishing.

Levillier, Roberto. 1940. *Don Francisco de Toledo, supremo organizador del Perú, su vida, su obra (1515–1582). Tomo II: Sus informaciones sobre los incas (1570–1572)*. Buenos Aires: Espasa-Calpe.

Little, Paul E. 1999. "Environments and Environmentalism in Anthropological Research: Facing a New Millennium." *Annual Review of Anthropology* 28 (1): 253–84. http://dx.doi.org/10.1146/annurev.anthro.28.1.253.

MacCormack, Sabine. 1993. *Religion in the Andes: Vision and Imagination in Early Colonial Peru*. Princeton, NJ: Princeton University Press.

Malca Olguin, Oscar. 1963. "Los descendientes del Inca Tupac Yupanqui y las tierras del sol y del inca año 1559." *Revista del Archivo Nacional del Perú* 27:3–26.

McEwan, Gordon F. 2006. *The Incas: New Perspectives*. Santa Barbara, CA: ABC Clio.

McEwan, Gordon F., Melissa Chatfield, and Arminda Gibaja. 2002. "The Archaeology of Inca Origins: Excavations at Chokepukio, Cuzco, Peru." In *Andean Archaeology I: Variations in Sociopolitical Organization*, ed. William Harris Isbell and Helaine Silverman, 287–301. New York: Kluwer Academic. http://dx.doi .org/10.1007/978-1-4615-0639-3_10.

Merleau-Ponty, Maurice. 1962. *The Phenomenology of Perception*. London: Routledge.

Mitchell, William P. 1976. "Irrigation and Community in the Central Peruvian Highlands." *American Anthropologist* 78 (1): 25–44. http://dx.doi.org/10.1525/aa.1976 .78.1.02a00030.

Molina, Cristóbal de (del Cusco). 1947 [1573]. *Ritos y fábulas de los Incas*. Colección Eurindia 14. Buenos Aires: Editorial Futuro.

Moore, Jerry D. 2010. "Making a Huaca: Memory and Praxis in Prehispanic Far Northern Peru." *Journal of Social Archaeology* 10 (3): 398–422. http://dx.doi.org/10 .1177/1469605310381550.

Morris, Craig. 1993. "Value, Investment, and Mobilization in the Inca Economy." In *Configurations of Power: Holistic Anthropology in Theory and Practice*, ed. John Henderson and Patricia Netherly, 36–50. Ithaca, NY: Cornell University Press.

Morris, Craig, and Donald Thompson. 1985. *Huánuco Pampa: An Inca City and its Hinterland*. London: Thames and Hudson.

Morrison, Kathleen D. 1993. "Supplying the City: The Role of Reservoirs in an Indian Urban Landscape." *Asian Perspective* 32:133–51.

Morrison, Kathleen D. 2009. *Daroji Valley: Landscape, Place, and the Making of a Dryland Reservoir System. Vijayanagara Research Project Monographs*. Delhi: Manohar Press.

Morrison, Kathleen D. 2010. "Dharmic Projects, Imperial Reservoirs, and New Temples of India: An Historical Perspective on Dams in India." *Conservation & Society* 8 (3): 182–95. http://dx.doi.org/10.4103/0972-4923.73807.

Murra, John V. 1956. "The Economic Organization of the Inca State." PhD diss., Department of Anthropology, University of Chicago.

Murra, John V. 1980 [1956]. *The Economic Organization of the Inka State*. Greenwich, CT: JAI Press.

Murra, John V. 1982. "The Mit'a Obligations of Ethnic Groups to the Inka State." In *The Inka and Aztec States 1400–1800: Anthropology and History*, ed. George A. Collier, Renato I. Rosaldo, and John D. Wirth, 237–62. New York: Academic Press.

Murúa, Martín de. 1962–64 [1590]. *Historia general del Perú, origen y descendencia de los Incas*. 2 vols. Colección Joyas Bibliográficas, Biblioteca Americana Vetus, 1, 2. Madrid: Instituto Gonzalo Fernández de Oviedo.

Niles, Susan A. 1980. "Pumamarca: A Late Intermediate Site near Ollantaytambo." *Ñawpa Pacha* 18:49–62.

Niles, Susan A. 1987. *Callachaca: Style and Status in an Inca Community*. Iowa City: University of Iowa Press.

Niles, Susan A. 1993. "The Provinces in the Heartland: Stylistic Variation and Architectural Innovation near Inca Cuzco." In *Provincial Inca: Archaeological and Ethnohistorical Assessment of the Impact of the Inca State*, ed. Michael A. Malpass, 145–76. Iowa City: University of Iowa Press.

Niles, Susan A. 1999. *The Shape of Inca History: Narrative and Architecture in an Andean Empire*. Iowa City: University of Iowa Press.

Ogburn, Dennis. 2005. "Dynamic Display, Propaganda, and the Reinforcement of Provincial Power in the Inca Empire." *Archaeological Papers of the American Anthropological Association* 14 (1): 225–39. http://dx.doi.org/10.1525/ap3a.2005.14.225.

Patterson, Thomas. 1985. "Exploitation and Class Formation in the Inca State." *Culture (Canadian Ethnology Society)* 5:35–42.

Patterson, Thomas. 1992. *The Inka Empire: The Formation and Disintegration of a Pre-capitalist State*. Oxford: Berg Publishers.

Pizarro, Pedro. 1978 [1571]. "Relación del descubrimiento y conquista de los reinos del Perú." In *Biblioteca de Autores Españoles*, no. 168. Madrid: Ediciones Atlas.

Polo de Ondegardo, Juan de. 1916 [1571]. "Informaciones acerca de la religión y gobierno de los incas (1a. parte)." In *Colección de libros y documentos referentes a la historia del Perú*, series 1, 3:3–208. Lima: Imprenta y Librería Sanmartí y Ca.

Protzen, Jean-Pierre. 1983. "Inca Quarrying and Stonecutting." *Ñawpa Pacha: Journal of Andean Archaeology* 21:183–214. http://dx.doi.org/10.2307/990027.

Protzen, Jean-Pierre. 1986. "Inca Stonemasonry." *Scientific American* 254 (2): 94–105. http://dx.doi.org/10.1038/scientificamerican0286-94.

Protzen, Jean-Pierre. 1991. *Inca Architecture and Construction at Ollantaytambo.* Oxford: Oxford University Press.

Quave, Kylie E. 2012. "Labor and Domestic Economy on a Royal Estate in the Inca Imperial Heartland (Maras, Cuzco, Peru)." PhD diss., Department of Anthropology, Southern Methodist University, Dallas, TX. Ann Arbor, MI: University Microfilms.

Rama, Angel. 1996. *The Lettered City.* Durham, NC: Duke University Press.

Ramírez, Susan E. 2005. *To Feed and be Fed: The Cosmological Bases of Authority and Identity in the Andes.* Palo Alto, CA: Stanford University Press.

Rostworowski de Diez Canseco, María. 1962. "Nuevos datos sobre tenencia de tierras reales en el incario." *Revista del Museo Nacional* 31:130–59.

Rostworowski de Diez Canseco, María. 1993. *Ensayos de historia andina: Elites, etnias, recursos.* Historia Andina 20. Lima: Instituto de Estudios Peruano.

Rowe, John H. 1985. "La constitución Inca del Cuzco." *Histórica* 9:35–73.

Rowe, John H. 1997. "Las tierras reales de los incas." In *Arqueología, antropología, e historia en los Andes, homenaje a María Rostworowski,* ed. Rafael Varón Gabai and Javier Flores Espinoza, 277–87. Lima: Instituto de Estudios Peruano.

Salomon, Frank. 1991. "Introduction." In *The Huarochirí Manuscript: A Testament of Ancient and Colonial Andean Religion,* ed. Frank Salomon and George Urioste, 1–38. Austin: University of Texas Press.

Salomon, Frank. 1995. "'The Beautiful Grandparents': Andean Ancestor Shrines and Mortuary Ritual as Seen through Colonial Records." In *Tombs for the Living: Andean Mortuary Practices,* ed. Tom D. Dillehay, 315–53. Washington, DC: Dumbarton Oaks Research Library and Collection.

Sanders, William T., and Barbara J. Price. 1968. *Mesoamerica: The Evolution of a Civilization.* New York: Random House.

Santillán, Hernando de. 1968 [1563]. "Relación del origen, descendencia, política y gobierno de los Incas." In *Biblioteca de Autores Espanoles,* no. 209. Madrid: Ediciones Atlas.

Sarmiento de Gamboa, Pedro. 1965 [1572]. "Historia de los Incas." In *Biblioteca de Autores Españoles,* no. 135. Madrid: Ediciones Atlas.

Scarborough, Vernon L. 1998. "Ecology and Ritual: Water Management and the Maya." *Latin American Antiquity* 9 (2): 135–59. http://dx.doi.org/10.2307/971991.

Schama, Simon. 1995. *Landscape and Memory.* New York: Vintage Books.

Scott, James C. 1998. *Seeing like a State: How Certain Schemes to Improve the Human Condition Have Failed.* New Haven, CT: Yale University Press.

Service, Elman R. 1975. *Origins of the State and Civilization.* New York: Morrow.

Sherbondy, Jeannette E. 1982. "The Canal Systems of Hanan Cuzco." PhD diss., Department of Anthropology, University of Illinois, Champaign-Urbana.

Sherbondy, Jeannette E. 1992. "Water Ideology in Inca Ethnogenesis." In *Andean Cosmologies through Time: Persistence and Emergence,* ed. Robert V. H. Dover, Katharine E. Seibold, and John H. McDowell, 46–66. Bloomington: Indiana University Press. Ann Arbor, MI: University Microfilms.

Silverblatt, Irene. 1988. "Imperial Dilemmas, the Politics of Kinship, and the Inca Reconstruction of History." *Comparative Studies in Society and History* 30 (1): 83–102. http://dx.doi.org/10.1017/S001041750001505X.

Smith, Adam T. 2003. *The Political Landscape: Constellations of Authority in Early Complex Polities.* Berkeley: University of California Press.

Smith, Adam T. 2004. "The End of the Essential Archaeological Subject." *Archaeological Dialogues* 11 (1): 1–20. http://dx.doi.org/10.1017/S1380203804211412.

Solís Díaz, Francisco, and Nancy Olazabal. 1998. "Arqueología de Pachar: Una introducción a su pasado." Thesis on file, Facultad de Ciencias Sociales, Universidad Nacional de San Antonio Abad del Cusco, Cusco.

Soto, H. M., and C. D. Cabrera. 1999. "Arquitectura inca en Ollantaytambo: Registro descripción y análisis técnico-morfológico del área urbana de un Tambo Inca." Thesis on file, Facultad de Ciencias Sociales, Universidad Nacional de San Antonio Abad del Cusco, Cusco.

Spencer, Charles S., and Elsa M. Redmond. 2004. "Primary State Formation in Mesoamerica." *Annual Review of Anthropology* 33 (1): 173–99. http://dx.doi.org /10.1146/annurev.anthro.33.070203.143823.

Swenson, Edward R. 2003. "Cities of Violence: Sacrifice, Power, and Urbanization in the Andes." *Journal of Social Archaeology* 3 (2): 256–96. http://dx.doi.org/10.1177/146 9605303003002006.

Swenson, Edward R. 2012. "Moche Ceremonial Architecture as Thirdspace: The Politics of Place-Making in the Ancient Andes." *Journal of Social Archaeology* 12 (1): 3–28. http://dx.doi.org/10.1177/1469605311426548.

Topic, John R. 1998. "Ethnogenesis in Huamachuco." *Andean Past* 5:109–27.

Urton, Gary. 1990. *The History of a Myth: Pacariqtambo and the Origin of the Inkas.* Austin: University of Texas Press.

Urton, Gary. 2012. "Recording Values in the Inka Empire." In *Constructions of Value in the Ancient World,* ed. Gary Urton and John Papadopoulos, 475–96. Los Angeles: Cotsen Institute of Archaeology, Univerity of California, Los Angeles.

van de Guchte, Maarten. 1999. "The Inca Cognition of Landscape: Archaeology, Ethnohistory, and the Aesthetic of Alterity." In *Archaeologies of Landscape:*

Contemporary Perspectives, ed. Wendy Ashmore and A. Bernard Knapp, 149–68. Malden, MA: Blackwell.

Vera, L. 1986. "Informe arqueológico, inkamisana y andén." Research report on file. Ministerio de Cultura, Cusco.

Wachtel, Nathan. 1982. "The Mitimas of the Cochabamba Valley: The Colonization Policy of Huayna Capac." In The Inca and Aztec States 1400–1800: Anthropology and History, ed. George A. Collier, Renato I. Rosaldo, and John D. Wirth, 199–235. New York: Academic Press.

Wernke, Steven A. 2007. "Analogy or Erasure? Dialectics of Religious Transformation in the Early Doctrinas of the Colca Valley, Peru." International Journal of Historical Archaeology 11 (2): 152–82. http://dx.doi.org/10.1007/s10761-007 -0027-5.

Wernke, Steven A. 2013. Negotiated Settlements: Andean Communities and Landscapes under Inka and Spanish Colonialism. Gainesville: University Press of Florida. http:// dx.doi.org/10.5744/florida/9780813042497.001.0001.

Wittfogel, Karl. 1955. "Developmental Aspects of Hydraulic Societies." In Irrigation Civilizations: A Comparative Study, ed. Julian Steward, 43–52. Washington, DC: Pan American Union.

Worster, Donald. 1994. Nature's Economy: A History of Ecological Ideas. Cambridge: Cambridge University Press.

Yamamoto, Norio. 1985. "The Ecological Complementarity of Agro-Pastoralism: Some Comments." In Andean Ecology and Civilization, ed. Shozo Masuda, Izumi Shimada, and Craig Morris, 85–100. Tokyo: University of Tokyo Press.

Zuidema, R. Tom. 1964. The Ceque System of Cuzco: The Social Organization of the Capital of the Inca. Leiden: E. J. Brill.

Zuidema, R. Tom. 1990. Inca Civilization in Cuzco. Austin: University of Texas Press.

Zuidema, R. Tom. 2007. "El Inca y sus Curacas: Poliginia Real y Construcción del Poder." Boletín del Instituto Francés de Estudios Andinos 37:47–55.

7

Men Who Would Be Rocks
The Inka Wank'a

CAROLYN DEAN

Indigenous people of the Andes characterize mountain lords as the owners of all natural resources within their ranges of vision. *Nevados*, or glaciated peaks, are commonly referred to as "great watchers" (Allen 1988:41). The authority of these peaks relates to their ranges of vision; thus, if you can see a mountain—and it can see you—you stand in its realm. Contemporary reverence for mountains and the belief that sentient mountains exercise their authority through vision date from the prehispanic period.[1] Related in ancient times to mountains as "watchful owners," only on a smaller scale, were *wank'a* (also spelled *huanca*).[2] These were rocks that were understood to be the sacred, sentient, and petrified owners of defined places, such as fields, valleys, and villages.

Wank'a can be understood as a particular kind of wak'a specializing in territorial possession and whose ownership was linked to sight. Wank'a, like the larger mountains to which they were conceptually related, could see, feel, think, and act transactionally, if not actually. Some wank'a were said to have once been human, and certain human beings were capable of becoming wank'a. According to lore, the most common means of transformation from human being into wank'a was through petrifaction. In the Inka period, however, sitting on stone and surveying territory from a petrous perch may well have cast the human sitter as a wank'a. After a summary of what is known about wank'a in general, we will turn our attention to Inka sighting

DOI: 10.5876/9781607323181.c007

practices and monuments used by Inka rulers in order to re-create themselves as possessive watchers or, more precisely, as "fleshed wank'a."

Given the wide range of locations in which they have been identified, wank'a surely preceded the rise of the Inka.[3] According to records from 1660, cited by Pierre Duviols (1979:7, 9) in his classic study of wank'a, every village in the high agricultural zone between 2,800 and 4,000 m in altitude of the southern Andes of Peru had at least one wank'a; coastal communities may also have had them. Often, while one wank'a, called the wank'a *markayuq*, was identified as the founder and owner-guardian of a village, agricultural fields had another petrous possessor-protector called the wank'a *chakrayuq*. Juan Polo de Ondegardo, the Spanish magistrate of Cuzco, writing in the sixteenth century, describes the chakrayuq as a *piedra luenga* (long rock) found in the middle of a *chakra* (or *chacra*, meaning field), which it protected.[4] Chakrayuq were identified with the fields they possessed and could be given offerings and supplicated for crop fertility. The Jesuit extirpator of idolatries Pablo Joseph (or José) de Arriaga (1999:37, chap. 2) also identifies rock guardians of irrigation canals, which surely were part of the wank'a complex.[5] We have fuller descriptions of chakrayuq (the field owner) than markayuq (the owner of a village, or *marka*), or any other kind of wank'a. This might be because the practice of supplicating chakrayuq persisted throughout the colonial period, providing ample opportunity for study by those Spaniards who were interested in indigenous religious beliefs.

The art historian George Kubler (1946:402) suggests that chakrayuq, or what he calls "guardian stones in the fields," survived Spanish colonial extirpation campaigns aimed at eliminating indigenous religious practices because they were determined to be "harmless instances of vain observance" not affected by demonic influence. Evangelizers appear to have classified them as folk traditions and, given the enormity of the task of eradicating more pernicious indigenous Andean religious practices, did not take them as seriously as they did other objects of reverence. Although chakrayuq were not altogether disregarded by Spanish authorities such as Polo and Arriaga, who identified them as elements of Andean religious practice, relatively little energy was expended trying to eradicate them.

Markayuq, on the other hand, were more aggressively attacked by evangelizers, probably because these petrous village guardians were more readily comparable to Catholic patron saints. Unlike chakrayuq, which were mostly left unmolested, markayuq tended to be converted into Catholic shrines, whether by extirpating evangelists or fervent Andean Christians, by means of the erection of crosses, the painting of Catholic images, or the building of chapels and shrines, as happened on the eastern slopes of Mount Pachatusan where the image of a tortured Christ tied to a column was painted on the side of a rock outcrop around which a temple was raised (Sallnow 1987:243–58). This shrine is aptly named Señor de Wank'a, embedding a numinous prehispanic rock within the trappings of Catholic tradition. Because of these colonial-period alterations, the original significance and the reverential practices surrounding many wank'a markayuq were obscured and transformed.

What meager information we have about prehispanic wank'a—whether chakrayuq, markayuq, or some other kind whose name has been lost to history—indicates that they were rocks located in the places they owned and protected, and that they were generally large enough to preclude movement, if they were not actually outcroppings and so a part of the bedrock. They were ancestral, connecting the living inhabitants of a place to its past residents all the way back to its origins. Duviols (1978:359) concludes that "the huanca was therefore the tangible and permanent image of the colonizing hero" (le huanca était donc l'image tangible et permanente du héros colonisateur). Although Duviols uses the word "image," a term that tacitly suggests a figural representation and implies some sort of resemblance between petrous wank'a and human being, there is no solid evidence that wank'a were intentionally anthropomorphic or in any way naturalistically representational.[6] Like Polo, Arriaga (1999 [1621]:37, chap. 2) describes wank'a as "una piedra larga" (a long or oblong rock). Apparently they varied in both form and size.[7] Although there was no standardized form, we can say that wank'a were notable rocks in the landscape, just like many other entities considered to be wak'as. Their specific function was to indicate that the place they occupied was possessed and protected; in other words, wank'a marked space as place, and land as territory.

Wank'a were apparently always gendered male. There are no reports of female wank'a, and the actions associated with these tutelary monoliths are those of conquest and control over territory.[8] Wank'a commemorated the masculine activity of conquest, whether actual—the taking of land—or metaphorical, as is the case of tilling agricultural fields; they also commemorated the possession of what was taken and signaled that their location was under supervision and protection. The wank'a, as a visible and immobile part of the landscape, kept an otherwise absent owner alive and present in the material world. The durable quality of rock conveyed the immortality of territorial owners and thus pronounced continually an enduring claim to possession. Wank'a also visibly and physically linked this world—the world of the living—to the world of the ancestors, asserting a sacred dimension to territorial possession. In wank'a, time and place were thus conjoined. This aspect of wank'a is particularly apt given the fact that a single word—*pacha*—refers to both time and land in the dominant languages of the Andes.

Since wank'a owned various places, their locations and positioning were key: the owner of a field occupied and surveyed its field; the owner of a village looked over the village near or in which it was located; and the owner of a valley was located in the valley it possessed. As with the mountain watchers mentioned at the outset, possession was linked to the wank'a's sight, particularly its "oversight"; that is, looking at something from above and being seen by whatever is below.[9] It is certainly not coincidental that human beings in the Andes also exercised oversight by elevated viewing. Indeed, human overseers, by virtue of their acts of public supervision, asserted a conceptual linkage to wank'a, as well as to sacred mountains (see also Meddens, this volume). While it is likely that Inka sighting rituals were derived from prior practices, we have little concrete information concerning early Andean supervisory rites (but see Janusek, this volume).[10] Because we can be relatively certain that Inka rulers performed acts of possession by seeing from above and being seen from below, the remaining discussion will focus specifically on the Inka.

By their imperial period, Inka rulers were likening themselves to wank'a through sighting practices. Juan de Betanzos, writing in the sixteenth century, describes a visit that the eleventh ruler, Wayna Qhapaq, made to towns within 20 leagues of Cuzco; however scant, the information he provides proves instructive with regard to Inka viewing rituals: "They had in the plaza a certain seat which resembled a high platform and in the middle of the platform, a basin full of stones. On reaching the town, the Inca climbed up on the platform and sat there on his chair. From there he could see everyone in the plaza, and they could all see him" (1996 [1557]:168).[11] Betanzos is explicit about the Inka ruler both seeing and being seen. The chronicler Bartolomé de Segovia (as Molina 1943 [1553]:22) supports Betanzos by writing that in each town of the Inka empire was a plaza with an elevated rectilinear platform, accessed by a stairway, from which the Inka ruler could view and speak to the people gathered below.[12] Segovia thus implies that Inka rulers repeated the sighting performance described by Betanzos at numerous locations throughout their empire.

The importance of penetrating vision from an elevated vantage point is emphasized at the Inka's provincial settlement of Huánuco Pampa, where a platform is positioned in the main plaza so that the sightline from its center extends through a series of four well-joined, cut-stone doorways along an east-west axis.[13] Sighting practices likely also occurred at Vilcashuamán, a major settlement on the *qhapaq ñan* (royal road) that served as a collection point for coastal tribute and as a military staging area.[14] A multi-level platform in the manner of a small pyramid with a single stairway dominates the settlement. Here, as on numerous other elevated platforms throughout the realm, the Inka ruler assumed the role of supreme supervisor in the literal sense of seeing from above as well as directing and superintending.[15] Supervision, or oversight, presupposes a line of sight from the one who oversees to those who are overseen. In Inka plazas, which were basically enormous open theaters-in-the-round where many different segments of society could gather, the raised platform provided a formal structure for seeing and being seen.[16] The importance of oversight from an elevated platform is still emphasized in the oral culture in the area near Vilcashuamán. Tom Zuidema (1980:355) reports that modern local tradition in the area holds that one can see both to Cuzco and to Lima. Although such supervision would literally require "super" vision, this popular notion underscores the act of oversight associated with a viewing platform.

In addition to elevated viewing, Betanzos (1987 [1557]:185), in the description cited above, mentions a *silla* (chair) on which the Inka ruler sat to exercise ceremonial oversight. Interestingly, a finely carved stone dual "seat" remains atop the elevated platform at Vilcashuamán, although its precise location in prehispanic times is unknown (Figure 7.1).[17] Writing in the first half of the sixteenth century, Pedro de Cieza de León (1984 [1553]:209, pt. 1, chap. 89) describes Vilcashuamán's double seat as the place where the Inka ruler went to pray. He says it was made of a single block of stone, with two places for sitting, and also reports that he was told that, before the Spaniards arrived in the Andes and demanded a ransom in gold and silver, it had been adorned with gold, jewels, and precious stones. In addition to being a site of prayer, the elevated stone seat also apparently played a critical part in the Inka rite of royal visitation. The indigenous chronicler Felipe Guaman Poma de Ayala (1988 [ca. 1615]:413; f. 445 [447]) identifies the elevated seat at Bilcas Guaman (Vilcashuamán) as a place where the Inka ruler received the principal lords of his realm. Similarly, indigenous author Joan (or Juan) de Santa Cruz Pachacuti (1993 [ca. 1613]:245; f. 32r) refers to a seat in Uillcas (i.e., Vilcashuamán) where subjects paid obeisance to the Inka ruler.

From these records we can surmise that Inka rulers, on specific occasions, occupied elevated seats from which they surveyed whatever was visible from their vantage point: their subjects, of course, but even more so, their land. Indeed, the elevated position at Vilcashuamán sacrifices the view immediately surrounding the pyramid for increasing the distance viewed, placing an emphasis on the extensive territory possessed as much as the immediate settlement. It is unfortunate that we do not have more complete details of sighting

FIGURE 7.1. *Inka carved double "seat" at Vilcashuamán (photograph by author).*

practices from more sites, but the information we do have—from chroniclers as well as the platforms themselves—indicates that rites of sight emphasized elevated viewing. Elevated observation was likely significant because it recalled the oversight of both mountains and wank'a. What's more, stationary viewing—conveyed by sitting—furthers the linkage between human sitter on the one hand and wank'a and mountains on the other, whose immobility and spatial anchoring were key to their territorial claims.

Some stone seats may have been part of what the Inka called an *usnu* (or *ushnu*), a concept much discussed but still poorly understood (see Meddens, this volume). Guaman Poma (1988 [ca. 1615]:236, 239, 357, 370) identifies the seat at Vilcashuamán specifically as an "usno," which he defines as the Inka ruler's *trono* (throne) and a site of sacrifice.[18] Similarly, Santa Cruz Pachacuti (1993 [ca. 1613]:245; f. 32r) indicates that the seat at Vilcashuamán was much like a seat situated in the main plaza of Cuzco, which he calls *capac usno* (royal usnu).[19] He defines usnu as "piedras puestas como estrado" (stones positioned like a dais) (ibid.:200, f. 9v). Gasparini and Margolies (1980:271) identified the usnu at Huánuco Pampa as a place where justice was done. Interestingly, Diego González Holguín (1901 [1608]:386) defines usnu as a rock outcrop or large stone that was firmly set in the earth and used as a place of judgment; likewise, the verb *usnuni* means to hold a tribunal.[20] Given González Holguín's definitions identifying the usnu as, at least sometimes, a place of justice, it is interesting to note that the Spaniards erected their pillory over the site of the usnu in Cuzco's main plaza.[21] It would not be inconsistent with Spanish practices for the conquistadors to have replaced the Inka's symbol of justice with one of their own.

From these various descriptions and definitions, it is possible to identify some lithic seats as important components of usnu, locations erected in part for oversight and the administration of justice. Other early colonial-period authors, however, identify usnu as altars for worship and as sites of propitiation.[22] The author of a sixteenth-century Quechua dictionary, Domingo de Santo Tomás (1951 [1560]:332), defines *ozño* or *osño* as an "ara para sacrificar" (altar or altar slab for sacrifice). Albornoz (1989 [1581–85]:176) ties several of these functions together, indicating that usnu were places for making offerings and seats for lords to sit on; he identifies them as wak'as found on royal roads and in the plazas of settlements.[23] In his memoirs Pedro Pizarro (1986 [1571]:90–91; chap. 15) recalls the use of what must have been the usnu located in Cuzco's main plaza; he describes at length a ceremony involving the mummies of deceased rulers who were fed in the plaza of Cuzco along with a rock that embodied the sun.[24] While the food was burned, chicha was poured over the petrous sun and into a basin that drained into the earth. Pizarro's description matches elements needed to fulfill the various functions associated with the usnu: a basin for burned and liquid offerings and a seat for a dignitary, which, in this case, was a rock embodiment of the sun.[25] When seats were associated with usnu, they became the focal points for both governance and supplication—that is, the exercise of power as well as the acknowledgment and propitiation of higher powers.

FIGURE 7.2. *Inka carved double "seat" at Ollantaytambo (photograph by author).*

While usnu were generally located in the centers of settlements, rites of oversight involving elevated sitting also took place in more peripheral locations where they emphasized territorial ownership rather than political supervision (although the two are clearly related). The prominent seat at Ollantaytambo, for example, perches on a crag on the edge of, and facing away from, the temple area (Figure 7.2). It looks east over the settlement and allows the sitter to survey the Patakancha River valley. A sitter on the outcrop seat companioned by finely carved steps at Saqsaywamán, which is today called the Throne of the Inka, surveys Cuzco and its valley, meeting the gazes of the powerful watcher Mount Ausangate to the viewer's left and, to the right, the sacred hill of Waynakauri, where one of the first four Inka brothers petrified (Figure 7.3).

That these seats, and others like them, do not directly face plazas or oversee parade grounds has puzzled students of the Inka. Heinrich Ubbelohde-Doering (1967:198), one of the first to comment on the fact that the "throne" does not face the so-called parade ground in front of the zigzag walls of Saqsaywamán, has been echoed numerous times by those nonplussed by the direction of the throne, which is roughly east-southeast. Yet, once the position of the throne is understood to convey claims to territorial possession, its "failure" to face the parade ground in favor of a valley vista becomes clear. Likewise the fact that the dual seating at Ollantaytambo turns its back on the temple to gaze over the river valley makes perfect sense once its territorial claims are perceived. Seating in the midst of agricultural terraces, reservoirs, and rivers

Figure 7.3. *"Throne of the Inka" at Saqsaywamán above Cuzco (photograph by author).*

likewise conveys the critical linkage between sitting, seeing, and ownership. Consider, for example, a double seat carved into a boulder that sits in, and looks out over, the flowing waters of the Vilcanota River, which was so important to agricultural activity in what today is called the Sacred Valley of the Inka (Figure 7.4).[26]

Of symbolic importance is the dual seating provided by many of these monuments. Dual seating reflects Andean notions of complementarity. In the same way that Andean communities were commonly divided into *hanan* (upper) and *urin* (lower) sectors, the body politic and political power were conceived of as conjoinings of upper and lower aspects. We may imagine that, at times, the hanan leader of a particular community would have assumed the right-hand seat while to his left sat the urin leader. Another possible pairing might have been the ruler on the right and his designated heir on the left, or the visiting Inka emperor and the chief local administrator, or the leader and his primary wife.[27] We might also imagine that the Inka ruler (or other human dignitary) could have been paired with the lithic wank'a of a particular territory, the mummy of one of his predecessors, or another embodied numina. Regardless of who (or what) sat, dual seating indexes a paramount pair who are stronger as a complementary set than they are individually (see the notion of *yanantin* discussed by Topic, this volume).

FIGURE 7.4. *Inka carved double "seat" in the Vilcanota River, Urubamba Valley (photograph by author).*

The material of which the seat was composed—rock—was critical to the success of oversight ceremonies and the identification of a human being with sacred overseers. That sitting on stone could materially manifest the linkage between living rulers and known petrous possessors—both wank'a and mountains—is made clear in Andean stories about sitting on stone, petrifaction, and ownership. The historian María Rostworowski de Diez Canseco (1988:33) identifies the petrified Ayar Auca, one of the first four Inka brothers who turned to stone while on the Inka's legendary migration to the Cuzco Valley, as a wank'a. According to chronicler Pedro Sarmiento de Gamboa (1942 [1572]:57, chap. 13), Ayar Auca was told by his brother Manco Capac (Manku Qhapaq) to go to a *mojón* (rock marker); by sitting on the rock, he was to take possession of the place. Ayar Auca did as he was instructed and was turned to stone once he sat. Thus, he became a wank'a, the owner of that place. The Inka later built the Qurikancha—their primary temple and most sacred of structures—on the site of Ayar Auca's sitting. In the story petrifaction marks ownership, as the sitter becomes one with the rock on which he sits, which, in turn, is part of a specific topography. The sitter thereby commingled his individual identity with the specified territory, sharing both its essence and its substance (which were likely not distinguishable in Andean thought). His act of sitting simultaneously transformed him into a wank'a and the land he surveyed into territory he owned.

A story from the Andean coast, recorded by Duviols (1979:11–12), also links sitting on stone to territorial possession and suggests that the connection between sitting on stone and territorial ownership was pan-Andean. Featured in the story is a peripatetic wank'a, the ancestral owner of several valleys on Peru's coast, who used to visit the series of valleys of which his domain consisted. In each of the valleys possessed by this wank'a, he sat in a stone seat as a show of his authority. The act of sitting on stone identified the sitter as a wank'a, that is, the owner of whatever was visible from the seat. I suggest that other, future sitters, emulating Ayar Auca and the peripatetic wank'a, became wank'a as well. At least some stones, likely with flattened surfaces prepared for sitting, were located in places where Inka rulers exercised literal oversight, and the petrous seats located there were featured in rites designed to convey the emperor as a fleshed wank'a. The seats were anchored spatially—that is, they remained fixed in specific locations—while the ruler, like the peripatetic wank'a, moved throughout his realm exercising the rites of oversight by sitting on stone and surveying.

It is unclear precisely how the human sitter became a wank'a; the very act of sitting on stone was likely construed as wak'a activity, especially when claims to ownership were being asserted. The Inka, like other Andeans, believed that physical contact with something could result in a transfer of identity. Cristóbal de Albornoz (1989 [1581–85]:171), a priest who worked to extirpate Andean idolatries in the Cuzco region in the late sixteenth century, tells us how indigenous Andeans could both relocate and duplicate their wak'as: if the wak'a was a rock or a hill, they could take an actual piece of the original and, by placing the fragment on a new rock, transform the new rock into an embodiment of the original. They could also take a textile that had touched the original wak'a and, by placing the textile on a stone in some new location, successfully transform the new rock into the revered wak'a. The new wak'a would be addressed by the original wak'a's name and in all ways would be the same without distinction between original and copy. In his instructions for destroying wak'as, Albornoz (ibid.:196) advises would-be extirpators to seize first and then burn all precious textiles (specifically, *bestidos de cumbe*), for if any of the textiles touched wak'as (things he terms relics), devotees could readily re-create their wak'as elsewhere. Rocks, as part of local topography, metonymically shared the identity of particular locations. Rocks on which human beings sat, by means of the principle of transference described by Albornoz, became identified with, and may well have been understood to embody, the sitter. Because the sitter in a stone seat makes direct contact with the local topography, their identities are merged at that place.[28] The sitter thereby became an "overseeing owner" somewhere on the continuum of petrous possessors from sacred mountains to petrified owners of fields; the height of, and view from, the petrous seat indicates the scope of ownership. Thus petrous seats enabled human sitters to merge with the earth, to symbolically petrify for a period of time, and to become themselves watchers.

Rock, in Andean lore, is capable of transubstantiation and animation: rock becomes human; humans become rock; and rocks both speak and move (see Dean 2010). Although some petrous seats, like that of Vilcashuamán, were squared off and apparently decorated, most extant examples of lithic seats retain the natural shape of the boulder or outcrop from which they were hewn. With many, it seems important that the seat look natural, providing a place for the sitter to commingle with the bedrock, to share identities with the natural topography, at a designated location. A surface decorated in jewels and precious metals might well have impressed those who were overseen, but the decoration would have been less significant than the petrous composition of the seat itself. Such seats were locations of transformation, places where sitters became fleshed wank'a and places where rocks embodied rulers and other authorities. When seat and sitter merged, a wank'a, simultaneously stone and flesh, came into being.

Given the function of petrous seats as places of "wank'a-fication"—of merging with territory for the purpose of asserting guardianship—it is not surprising that the seats themselves were considered to be wak'as, as was the act of sitting on the stone itself. As the sitter's identity merged with the place, the place's identity merged with the person, thereby bringing into being a place-person, or wak'a, as discussed by Bruce Mannheim and Guillermo Salas Careño (this volume). The set of carved diorite seats and steps on the rock outcrop known as the Suchuna, or Rodadero, at Saqsaywamán, was clearly an important wak'a. The Jesuit Bernabé Cobo (1956 [1653], 2:172; 1990 [1653]:57), copying from an earlier source, identifies it by the name Sabacurinca and describes it as a "un asiento bien labrado, donde se sentaban los Incas" (a well-carved seat where the Incas sat) (van de Guchte 1990:124). Specifically, Cobo names it as the sixth wak'a on the fifth *siq'i* (*ceque*, or line) of Chinchaysuyu. The Inka venerated the seat itself and made sacrifices to it. In fact, Cobo goes so far as to say that it was "por respecto deste asiento se adoraba toda la fortaleza" (on account of this seat the whole fortress [of Saqsaywamán] was worshiped).[29]

Likewise, several of the seats named by Cobo (1990 [1653]:54, 55, 64, 76, 82) as part of Cuzco's siq'i system of sacred places were said to be places where an Inka ruler or other significant personage rested. The second wak'a on the second siq'i of Chinchaysuyu was a stone called Racramirpay, where a conquering hero who aided Inca Yupanqui in battle had sat.[30] The eighth wak'a on the second siq'i of Chinchaysuyu, called Guayllaurcaja, was a roadside seat, along a pass formed in the middle of a hill, where Viracocha Inca sat to rest. A wak'a called Caynaconga, described as a resting place for the Inka ruler, was the seventh on the second siq'i of Antisuyu. Cunturpata, the first wak'a on the twelfth siq'i of Cuntisuyu, was a seat on which Inka rulers rested during one of their festivals.[31] Tampucancha, the first wak'a on the ninth siq'i of Collasuyu, is described as a seat where the ruler Mayta Capac was known to sit; Cobo writes, "While he was sitting here he arranged to give battle to the Acabicas [Alcabiças]. Because he defeated them in the battle, they regarded the said seat as a place to be venerated."[32]

These seats, which were themselves wak'as, were all linked to famous individuals and apparently were wak'as precisely because of that association. When the sitter vacated the seat, it retained his identity and provided a permanent, material trace of him. The durability of rock underscores the endurance of the fleshed wank'a, and the size, weight, and immobility of the rock upon which territorial sitting (and sighting) was exercised conveyed the sustained presence of the overseeing owner. Thus the seat was henceforth identified with the original sitter, whom it embodied, and remained as a permanent marker of the sitter in the landscape. Such places of sitting brought to mind historic events and people related to the places where they are located, linking any future sitters to the important events that had taken place at or near them. The unoccupied petrous seat did not merely evoke the original sitter, however; it embodied him in a real or literal, rather than a conceptual or figural, manner. That is, while the site of sitting reminded viewers of the absent sitter, it was also perceived to be the sitter himself in lithic form. Such sites might be said to have "presenced" the sitter; in other words, they made him permanently present in the landscape.[33] The Inka case makes it clear that petrous seats were co-identified with the sitter, especially since, at times, individuals were said to have turned to rock in the places they sat. Regardless of whether petrifaction was real or implied, petrous seats recalled the significant actions that took place in a specified location. The sat-upon rock evoked a metaphysical time/space in which past acts of possession persisted into the present and future.

But just what is meant by the term "seat" in the Inka context? This question is highly relevant since Inka elites customarily sat on *tiana*, or stools, with either one or two legs, made of wood, and which bear little formal resemblance to the stone seats that we have been discussing. The vertical, back-supporting element that comes to mind when we think of a seat was mostly absent in the prehispanic Andes, although seats on litters may well have had vertical supports for the back. Thus "seats" is likely not an appropriate appellation for the spaces cut from rock which functioned as seats, at least sometimes, but which from an Inka perspective looked little like the tiana on which they normally sat.

Conceptually, sitting on stone was likely related to the practice of integrating stonemasonry into rock outcrops such that structures appear grafted into bedrock (Figure 7.5). Carved-out "seats" feature a single large, horizontal cut and one to three vertical cuts forming a back with zero, one, or two sides. Such "seats" bear some resemblance to bedding joints—cuts made in outcroppings of rock in preparation for the seating of stone blocks (normally parallelepiped ashlars)—especially those designed to visually integrate the masonry wall with the bedrock. Cuts in bedrock for the purpose of integrating ashlars can best be seen where worked blocks were plundered for reuse following Spanish colonization (Figure 7.6). The places remaining after the removal of ashlars generally have one horizontal cut on which the worked block was set, one vertical cut against which the back of the block was placed, and sometimes one or two side cuts as well.

Outcrop integration—the placement of stone blocks on extrusions of bedrock—united Inka walls with the topography of a specific location in order to visualize the union between the order of Inka civilization and unordered

FIGURE 7.5. *Inka wall integrated with rock outcropping at Ollantaytambo (photograph by author).*

nature, as well as the transformation from disorder to order upon Inka occupation (Dean 2010:81–90, 111–12). Many sites of outcrop integration feature vertical and horizontal cuts like those seen in objects specifically identified as places for sitting, such as the Vilcashuamán seat and the Throne of the Inka at Saqsaywaman (see Figures 7.1 and 7.3). In the case of finely joined, high-status mortarless masonry, bedding joints carved into the outcrop ensure that the wall of worked masonry sits on, and becomes one with, the natural stone, much as the human sitter ensconced in a carved "seat" must have been perceived as one with the topography of a specific location. For integration joints and what we have been calling "seats," the carved-out space was ideal for placing things. The placement, importantly, was a placement into and not just on top of (as a single horizontal plane might be). While the horizontal cut provides a flat place to set something, the vertical cuts provide a housing for that something where it may be embraced by rock.

We might characterize the function of these carved-out spaces as "place holding," and the carved-out spaces themselves as emplacements.[34] Place-holding

FIGURE 7.6. *Muyuqaqa, or Mesa Redonda, in Cuzco (photograph by author).*

refers to Inka efforts to sustain and bolster their claims to particular territories. Obvious placeholders include garrisons, storage facilities, *aqllawasi* (houses for "chosen women" who worked for the state maintaining religious shrines and producing textiles and alcoholic beverages for imperial use), and other signs of Inka presence that contributed to their ability to hold territory. Stone emplacements also served in this capacity, although their function was often more symbolic, or transactional, rather than practical or utilitarian. Once carved with emplacements, boulders and outcrops, which had once been part of undifferentiated nature, were *Inka* boulders and outcrops; they were enculturated, filled with meaning, signifying that the places where they stood were Inka territory and were under the Inka's protection and governance (see also Kosiba, this volume).

Whether occupied or not, they served a propagandistic function as part of a system of place-holding monuments through which the Inka state continually reasserted its presence.[35] Petrous emplacements not only recalled territorial occupation, but they also summoned the specter of oversight by embodying the absent or invisible supervisor and conveying his numinous powers. From the monument known as the Intiwatana at Machu Picchu, for example, the sitter, with the gnomon at his back, joins the great mountain watchers

FIGURE 7.7. *The intiwatana at Machu Picchu (photograph by author).*

of the region (Figure 7.7).³⁶ Directly east of the Intiwatana is Wakay Willka, or Mount Verónica; Huayna Picchu is to the north, the Pumasillo range is to the west, and, although not visible from the Intiwatana, Salcantay is to the south (Reinhard 1992:110–11). Together, these powerful beings oversee the region, with the Intiwatana emplacement marking the land as territory subject to both natural laws, enforced by the mountain deities, and the Inka's cultural order, imposed by the state. What's more, because the Intiwatana emplacement has a doubled identity—is concurrently rock and ruler—it need not be occupied to implicate the presence of the territorial owner.

Petrous emplacements, then, are likely specific instantiations of oversight. They commemorate acts of possession by tracing, in a general way, the 90-degree angle formed by some sitting anthropomorphic overseer. In addition, they permanently embody that now-absent overseer, making the overseer ever present in that place. Just because emplacements appear to have been made for sitting, however, does not mean that all of them were actually sat upon by physical beings. The carving only proclaims the location *as subject to* oversight, whether or not any physical body ever sat there. A petrous emplacement located near a road or a body of water or a series of agricultural terraces thus marks the place as territory under supervision regardless of whether it actually ever functioned as a seat. It should also be noted that some emplacements may well have been locations for the setting of offerings, a possibility suggested by Uhle (1910), Bingham (1979:79), and others.

Regardless of what or who was "set," the emplacements mark the rock as an occupied zone, as a possessed place rather than undifferentiated space. To the Inka, emplacements that could not be sat on or were never sat on by human beings may have referred to the oversight of absent, invisible, or distant numina. When they were occupied by a human supervisor, however, they linked the sitter to the other powerful watchers of the Andean cosmos: mountains, the sun, the moon, planetary bodies, lightning, and rainbows. They enabled Inka rulers and administrators to watch over defined territories just as wank'a did, and, indeed, they made it possible for the sitter to become a fully fleshed wank'a, a part of the local topography whose identity was indelibly merged with the rock. By occupying a stone emplacement, the ruler became a double metonym for the empire; he was both a part of the empire as a member of it and part of the material stuff comprising imperial land, sharing its identity and it sharing his.

NOTES

1. For a consideration of the Andean regard for mountains, both ancient and modern, see Reinhard (1985, 1992). Indigenous Andeans today refer to mountain deities by a variety of names, including *achacila, apu, apusuyu, aposento, awki, awkillo, jurq'u, mamani, urqutaytacha, urqu yaya,* and *wamani* (see Earls and Silverblatt [1978:310]; Gutiérrez Estévez [1979]; Urton [1985:258]). There is some disagreement about whether Andeans recognize that living spirits reside in mountains (and other inert natural objects) or that those objects are themselves alive; for a discussion of this issue, see Kuznar (2001:41–42). Neither the variance in terminology across the Andean region nor the question of whether it is the mountain itself or mountain spirits that affect human affairs is of significant consequence to my present argument.

2. The plural case of Quechua nouns is indicated by the suffix "kuna." Unfortunately, using the Quechua plural proves confusing for many readers. Rather than adding an "s" at the end of a Quechua word, thereby creating an awkward bilingualism, I have elected to maintain Quechua words in their singular form regardless of whether they are singular or plural.

3. The site of Caral on Peru's central coast, the oldest city in the Americas, with pyramidal structures dating to the fifth millennium BCE, features an unhewn elongated monolith centered in the main plaza; today the monolith is referred to in the scholarly literature as a wank'a and it may well have functioned as one (Shady 2004, 2005).

4. Polo (1916 [1571]:191) writes that the Inka used to locate "en medio de las Chacras vna piedra luenga para desde allí inuocar la virtud de la tierra y que para que le guarde la Chacra." Murúa (1986 [ca. 1613]:423, bk. 2, chap. 28), borrowing from Polo, writes that the Inka "ponían en medio de las chácaras una piedra grande, para en ella invocar a la Tierra, y le pedían les guardase las chácaras."

5. Arriaga specifically identifies them as "compa" and "larca villana," the meaning of which is unclear; for discussion, see Henrique Urbano (in Arriaga 1999 [1621]: 37n84).

6. The term *representation* can create confusion since it refers both to the way something looks and to what it means. The former uses representation in the denotative sense, while the latter uses it connotatively. Wank'a were likely not denotatively representational but may have connotatively represented the permanence and durability of founding owners, as will be discussed later.

7. See also Duviols (1978:359). Doyle (1988:64–65) discusses the possibility that some wank'a were carved imagistically, but the evidence is not particularly convincing as it comes from extirpation campaigns conducted by individuals who were looking for "idols."

8. Duviols (1979:21) reports a legend in which two brothers transform into wank'a while their sister became a *puquio* (spring or fountain). This suggests that springs, commonly gendered female, were complements to masculinized rock wank'a. Furthering the identification of wank'a with males is the fact that Wank'a (or its cognates Huanca or Guanca) was used as a name for males among the Inka. See, for example, Betanzos (1996 [1557]:207, pt. 2, chap. 7); Cieza (1998 [ca. 1550]:185, pt. 3, chap. 39); or Cobo (1979 [1653]:167).

9. Kuznar (2001:49–50) discusses the importance of lines of sight with regard to sacred Andean things. See Tuan (1977:37) on the ways elevated viewing is privileged universally.

10. The fact that Moche rulers are pictured sitting on elevated platforms—symbolic mountains—indicates that sighting rituals were well known to Andean societies prior to the rise of the Inka state. The degree to which they influenced Inka practices is unknown, however.

11. "Le tenían hecho cierto asiento a manera de un castillejo alto y en do medio del castillejo una pileta llana de piedras y como llegase el Ynga al pueblo subíase en aquel castillejo y allí se sentaba en su silla y de allí veía a todos los de la plaza y ellos le veían a él" (Betanzos 1987 [1557]:185, pt. 1, chap. 42).

12. Segovia's report was published under the name Cristóbal de Molina; he writes: "[E]n cada pueblo [había una] plaza grande real y en medio de ella un cuadro alto de terraplén, con una escalera muy alta; se subían el Inca y tres señores a hablar al pueblo y ver la gente de guerra cuando hacían sus reseñas y juntas."

13. Photographs and site plans of Huánuco Pampa can be found in Gasparini and Margolies (1980:105–8) and Morris and Thompson (1985). For a discussion of the layout of the Inka's regional capital of El Shincal, in northwestern Argentina, which focused on and was organized around an elevated masonry platform, see Raffino et al. (1997).

14. Vilcashuamán was an Inka center located to the north of the Soras and Lucanas province. The area was repopulated with *mitmaq*, mostly from Lucanas and Aymaraes (Julien 1993:200). For a full description of the viewing platform at Vilcashuamán, see Hyslop (1990:69–101). Imaginative site reconstruction may obscure whatever sighting practices once took place there.

15. For a discussion of the notion of surveying and its implications, see Summers (2003:416).

16. For an insightful comparison of Inka plazas with those of other Andean peoples, see Moore (1996). For a study of platforms (possibly *usnu* or *ushnu*) at the Inka *tampu* of Huánuco Pampa, Taparaku, Chakamarka, and Pumpu, see Pino (2004).

17. The word *seat* is used here only to describe a place where someone likely sat; the problematical nature of this term will be discussed below.

18. See ff. 262 [264], 265 [267], 385 [387], and 398 [400]. Guaman Poma (1988 [ca. 1615]:356, 370; ff. 384 [386] and 398 [400]) also illustrates two usnu: one at Cajamarca and one at Cuzco.

19. There is no solid evidence of an elevated platform associated with Cuzco's usnu. Hyslop (1990:70) suggests that the elevated platform may have been a particular feature of usnu in conquered territories. Zuidema (1968:48) also stresses a close association between usnu and conquered areas, concluding that usnu symbolized the power of the Inka state in conquered communities (see Meddens, this volume).

20. González Holguín (1901 [1608]:386) defines "usnu" as "tribunal del juez, de una piedra incada. Mojón, cuando es de piedra grande hincada"; he defines the verb "usnuni" as "hacer los tribunals: hincar los mojones." "Ushnu" means "pantano" (swamp, marsh, lake), and the verb "ushnuni" means "empantanarse, enterrarse en pantano. Remojar en agua, humedecer metiendo en agua un cuero, un trapo." The word usnu and its cognates are still used in the central highlands of Peru to mean a variety of things, including holes, wells, subterranean places, rock walls, ruins, and places associated with the dead and with the prehispanic past. Usnu also refers to places where water is filtered and places of gravel, or pure rock, as well as platforms on the tops of high mountains. José Luis Pino Matos (2004) proposes that the concept of the usnu was originally developed in the Andes to the north and west of Cuzco (in Chinchaysuyu) as a place where water runs through rocks. The Inka politicized it, retaining its function as a receptacle and drainage for liquid offerings, but adding ceremonial functions as well as astronomical observations to its uses. Under the Inka, the usnu became a sign of authority and centrality and so was used in planning important provincial settlements.

21. Betanzos (1996 [1557]:47, pt. 1, chap. 11) identifies the Spanish gallows as having been built in the middle of Cuzco's main plaza on the site where the Inka displayed a lithic embodiment of the sun. Both Aveni (1981) and Zuidema (1981) identify the site of the gallows as the location of the prior usnu. While some believe that the sugar-loaf-shaped solar stone, described by Betanzos, was itself the usnu, it is likely that the solar stone was placed on the seat atop the usnu where it could "oversee" the people gathered there and receive their libations.

22. See, for example, Albornoz (1989 [1581–85]:176), the Anonymous Jesuit (1953 [1594]:354–55), Cabello Balboa (1945 [1586–1603], 1:343, pt. 3, chap. 21), and Hernández Príncipe (1923 [1622]:63). The anonymous Jesuit describes two kinds of Inka "temples," natural and artificial or constructed. He says that usually nothing was built at natural temples (such as lakes, springs, mountain peaks, rushing rivers, caves, and so on); but sometimes, he writes, "hacían en los tales lugares un altar de piedra, que llamaban *osno* para sus sacrificios." Cabello Balboa refers to the *usnu* of Tomebamba, saying, "Edificó así mismo en la plaza cierto lugar llamado Usno (y por otro nombre Chuquipillaca) donde sacrificaban la chicha al sol, a sus tiempos y coyunturas."

23. Albornoz writes: "Ay otra guaca general en los caminos reales y en las plaças de los pueblos, que llaman uznos," and says that "sentávanse los señores a bever a el sol en el dicho uzno y hazían muchos sacrificios a el sol." He also reports, however, that usnu were shaped like skittles used in bowling games, saying that "eran de figura de un bolo," were "hecho de muchas diferencias de piedras o de oro y de plata," and that all of them had buildings (*edificios*) with "torres de muy hermosa cantería." In another passage Albornoz (1989 [1581–85]:179) describes the usnu of Cuzco as "un pilar de oro donde bevían al Sol en la plaça."

24. Pizarro describes the rock as round and covered with gold. Also associated with the round stone were a basin and a seat, adorned with colorful feathers, where a *bulto* (statue) of the sun was placed. Pizarro reports: "Esta piedra [redonda] tenía una funda de oro que encaxaua en ella y la tapaua toda, y asimismo tenía hecho una manera de buhihuelo [buhío] de esteras texidas, rredondo, con que la cubrían de noche. Asimismo sacauan un bulto pequeño, tapado, que dezían que hera el sol, lleuándolo un yndio que ellos tenían como a çaçerdote. . . . Para donde asentauan este bulto que ellos dezían hera el sol, tenían puesto en la mitad de la plaça un escaño pequeño, todo guarnesçido de mantas de pluma muy pintadas, y aquí ponían este bulto. . . . Pues dauan de comer a este sol por la horden que tengo dicho la dauan a los muertos, y de beuer."

25. The solar stone described by Pizarro is likely the same as that mentioned by Betanzos (1996 [1557]:48, pt. 1, chap. 11). Although some believe that the solar stone might be the usnu itself, it is more likely that the stone was the sun's lithic *wawqi* (brother; also spelled *wawqe*) and that it was sometimes brought into the plaza and placed on the

usnu's seat. Pizarro (1986 [1571]:92, chap. 15) also tells of a stone bench encased in gold inside the Qurikancha on which the "sun" sat when it was not in the plaza.

26. For a thorough discussion of this seat, see van de Guchte (1990:195–96).

27. Silverblatt (1987) has suggested that while the Inka ruler had ultimate authority, power was structured so that the ruler supervised men, while his primary wife, the *quya* (*qoya, coya*) was the leader of all women in the Inka empire.

28. There is some ethnographic evidence to suggest that people who come into contact with a powerful wak'a could thereby (and not necessarily intentionally) share its identity; for anecdotal evidence relating to sacred mountains see Reinhard (1992), who, by climbing powerful and sentient mountains, has been on more than one occasion identified with the sacred power of those mountains.

29. Paternosto (1996:79), with no supporting evidence, suggests that this carved seat prefigured the Inka usnu.

30. According to Cobo (1990 [1653]:54), "In a certain battle which Inca Yupanqui fought against his enemies, an Indian appeared to him in the air and helped him to conquer them." After the victory had been won, he came to Cuzco with the said Inca, sat down in this window (which included a stone "a little way below where the monastery of San Agustín is now"), and petrified.

31. Cobo (ibid.:82) specifically refers to "the festival of the Raymi" here.

32. The original Spanish reads: "y que sentado aquí concertó de dar la batalla a los Acabicas [Allcahuizas]; y porque en ella los venció, tuvieron el dicho asiento por lugar de veneración" (Cobo 1956 [1653], 2:182).

33. Employing the word "presence" as a verb indicates the material embodiment of a living being in an object; see, for example, Clunas (2006).

34. I am grateful to Bruce Mannheim for suggesting this apt term.

35. See Dennis Ogburn (2005:234–36), who explores the propagandistic aspects of Inka stories (sometimes presented as ballads) about military conquests, the suppression of rebellions, and the punishment of rebels or other offenders. Such stories bolstered Inka claims to acquired territory.

36. The Intiwatana has been identified as an usnu by Gasparini and Margolies (1980:267), and Valencia and Gibaja (1992:89), among others.

REFERENCES CITED

Albornoz, Cristóbal de. 1989 [1581–85]. "Instrucción para descubrir todas las guacas del Pirú y sus camayos y haziendas." In *Fábulas y mitos de los Incas*, ed. Henrique Urbano and Pierre Duviols, 161–98. Crónicas de América, 48. Madrid: Historia 16.

Allen, Catherine J. 1988. *The Hold Life Has: Coca and Cultural Identity in an Andean Community*. Washington, DC: Smithsonian Institution Press.

Anonymous Jesuit (aka Luis López; published as Blas Valera). 1953 [1594]. "Relación de las costumbres antiguas de los naturales del Piru." *Revista del Archivo Histórico del Cuzco* 4 (4): 346–415.

Arriaga, Pablo Joseph de. 1999 [1621]. *La extirpación de la idolatría en el Pirú.* Ed. Henrique Urbano. Cuzco: Centro de Estudios Regionales Andinos "Bartolomé de Las Casas."

Aveni, Anthony F. 1981. "Horizon Astronomy in Incaic Cuzco." In *Archaeoastronomy in the Americas*, ed. Ray A. Williamson, 305–18. Los Altos, CA: Ballena Press.

Betanzos, Juan de. 1987 [1557]. *Suma y narración de los Incas.* Ed. Martín Rubio María del Carmen. Madrid: Ediciones Atlas.

Betanzos, Juan de. 1996 [1557]. *Narrative of the Incas.* Ed. and trans. Roland Hamilton and Dana Buchanan. Austin: University of Texas Press.

Bingham, Hiram. 1979. *Machu Picchu: A Citadel of the Incas (Report of the Explorations and Excavations made in 1911, 1912 and 1915 under the auspices of Yale University and the National Geographic Society).* New York: Hacker Art Books.

Cabello Balboa, Miguel. 1945 [1586–1603]. *Obras.* 2 vols. Quito: Editorial Ecuatoriana.

Cieza de León, Pedro de. 1984 [1553]. *La crónica del Perú (primera parte).* Ed. Raúl Porras Barrenechea. Lima: Promoción Editorial Inca S. A.

Cieza de León, Pedro de. 1998 [ca. 1550]. *The Discovery and Conquest of Peru: Chronicles of the New World Encounter.* Ed. and trans. Alexandra Parma Cook and Noble David Cook. Durham, NC: Duke University Press.

Clunas, Craig. 2006. "'Not One Hair Different . . .': Wen Zhengming on Imaging the Dead in Ming Funerary Portraiture." In *Presence: The Inherence of the Prototype within Images and Other Objects*, ed. Robert Maniura and Rupert Shepherd, 31–45. Aldershot, UK: Ashgate.

Cobo, Bernabé. 1956 [1653]. *Obras del P. Bernabé Cobo.* 2 vols. Ed. Francisco Mateos. Biblioteca de Autores Españoles, 91–92. Madrid: Real Academia Española.

Cobo, Bernabé. 1979 [1653]. *History of the Inca Empire: An Account of the Indians' Customs and Their Origins Together with a Treatise on Inca Legends, History, and Social Institutions.* Ed. and trans. Roland Hamilton. Austin: University of Texas Press.

Cobo, Bernabé. 1990 [1653]. *Inca Religion and Customs.* Ed. and trans. Roland Hamilton. Austin: University of Texas Press.

Dean, Carolyn. 2010. *A Culture of Stone: Inka Perspectives on Rock.* Durham, NC: Duke University Press. http://dx.doi.org/10.1215/9780822393177.

Doyle, Mary Ellen. 1988. *Ancestor Cult and Burial Ritual in the Seventeenth and Eighteenth Century, Central Peru.* PhD diss., Department of Anthropology, University of California at Los Angeles. Ann Arbor, MI: University Microfilms.

Duviols, Pierre. 1978. "Un Symbolisme Andin du Double: la Lithomorphose de l'Ancêtre." *Actes du XLIIe Congrès International des Américanistes* (Paris, 2–9 Septembre 1976) 4:359–64.

Duviols, Pierre. 1979. "Un Symbolisme de l'Occupation, de l'Aménagement et de l'Exploitation de l'Espace: Le Monolithe Huanca et sa Fonction dans les Andes Préhispaniques." *L'Homme* 19 (2): 7–31. http://dx.doi.org/10.3406/hom.1979 .367954.

Earls, John, and Irene Silverblatt. 1978. "La realidad física y social en la cosmología Andina." *Actes du XLIIe Congrès International des Américanistes* (Paris, 2–9 September 1976) 4:299–325.

Gasparini, Graziano, and Luise Margolies. 1980. *Inca Architecture.* Trans. Patricia J. Lyon. Bloomington: Indiana University Press.

González Holguín, Diego. 1901 [1608]. *Arte y diccionario quechua-español.* Lima: Imprenta del Estado.

Guaman Poma de Ayala, Felipe. 1988 [ca. 1615]. *El primer nueva corónica y buen gobierno.* 2nd ed. Ed. John V. Murra and Rolena Adorno. Mexico City: Siglo Veintiuno.

Gutiérrez Estévez, Manuel. 1979. "Sobre el origen de algunas creencias populares." *Revista del Instituto Azuayo de Folklore* 6:61–83.

Hernández Príncipe, Rodrigo. 1923. [1622]. "Mitología andina." *Inca* 1:25–68.

Hyslop, John. 1990. *Inca Settlement Planning.* Austin: University of Texas Press.

Julien, Catherine J. 1993. "Finding a Fit: Archaeology and Ethnohistory." In *Provincial Inca: Archaeological and Ethnohistorical Assessment of the Impact of the Inca State,* ed. Michael A. Malpass, 178–233. Iowa City: University of Iowa Press.

Kubler, George. 1946. "The Quechua in the Colonial World." In *Handbook of South American Indians,* vol. 2, ed. Julian H. Steward, 331–410. Washington, DC: United States Government Printing Office.

Kuznar, Lawrence A. 2001. "An Introduction to Andean Religious Ethnoarchaeology: Preliminary Results and Future Directions." In *Ethno-archaeology of Andean South America: Contributions to Archaeological Method and Theory,* ed. Lawrence A. Kuznar, 38–66. Ethnoarchaeological Series, 4. Ann Arbor, MI: International Monographs in Prehistory.

Molina, Cristóbal de [Bartolomé de Segovia]. 1943 [1553]. "Destrucción del Perú." In *Las crónicas de los Molinas,* ed. Francisco A. Loayza, 2–88. Lima: Domingo Miranda.

Moore, Jerry D. 1996. "The Archaeology of Plazas and the Proxemics of Ritual: Three Andean Traditions." *American Anthropologist* 98 (4): 789–802. http://dx.doi.org /10.1525/aa.1996.98.4.02a00090.

Morris, Craig, and Donald Thompson. 1985. *Huánuco Pampa: An Inca City and Its Hinterland*. London: Thames and Hudson.

Murúa, Martín de. 1986 [ca. 1613]. *Historia general del Perú*. Ed. Manuel Ballesteros Gaibrois. Crónicas de América 35. Madrid: Historia 16.

Ogburn, Dennis. 2005. "Dynamic Display, Propaganda, and the Reinforcement of Provincial Power in the Inca Empire." *Archeological Papers of the American Anthropological Association* 14 (1): 225–39. (Special Issue, *Foundations of Power in the Prehispanic Andes*, ed. Kevin Vaughn, Dennis E. Ogburn, and Christina A. Conlee.) http://dx.doi.org/10.1525/ap3a.2005.14.225.

Paternosto, César. 1996. *The Stone and the Thread: Andean Roots of Abstract Art*. Trans. Esther Allen. Austin: University of Texas Press.

Pino Matos, José Luis. 2004. "El *ushnu* Inka y la organización del espacio en los principales *tampus* de los *wamani* de la sierra central del Chinchaysuyu." *Chungara: Revista de Antropología Chilena* 36 (2): 303–11.

Pizarro, Pedro. 1986 [1571]. *Relación del descubrimiento y conquista de los reinos del Perú*. 2nd ed. Ed. Guillermo Lohmann Villena. Lima: Pontificia Universidad Católica del Perú.

Polo de Ondegardo, Juan. 1916 [1571]. "Relación de los fundamentos acerca del notable daño que resulta de no guardar a los indios sus fueros." In *Informaciones acerca de la religión y gobierno de los Incas*, ed. Horacio H. Urteaga, 45–188. Lima: Imprenta y Librería Sanmartí.

Raffino, Rodolfo, Diego Gobbo, Rolando Vázquez, Aylen Capparelli, Victoria G. Montes, Rubén Itturriza, Cecilia Deschamps, and Marcelo Mannasero. 1997. "El ushnu de El Shincal de Quimivil." *Tawantinsuyu* 3:22–39.

Reinhard, Johan. 1985. "Sacred Mountains: An Ethno-Archaeological Study of High Andean Ruins." *Mountain Research and Development* 5 (4): 299–317. http://dx.doi.org/10.2307/3673292.

Reinhard, Johan. 1992. "Sacred Peaks of the Andes." *National Geographic* 181 (3): 84–111.

Rostworowski de Diez Canseco, María. 1988. *Historia del Tahuantinsuyu*. Lima: Instituto de Estudios Peruanos.

Sallnow, Michael J. 1987. *Pilgrims of the Andes: Regional Cults in Cusco*. Washington, DC: Smithsonian Institution Press.

Santa Cruz Pachacuti Yamqui Salcamaygua, Joan de. 1993 [ca. 1613]. *Relación de antigüedades deste reyno del Pirú*. Ed. Pierre Duviols and César Itier. Travaux de l'Institut Français d'Études Andines, vol. 74. Cuzco: Institut Français d'Études Andines; Centro de Estudios Regionales Andinos "Bartolomé de Las Casas."

Santo Tomás, Domingo de. 1951 [1560]. *Lexicon ó vocabulario de la lengua general del Perú.* A facsimile of the first edition with an introduction by Raúl Porras Barrenechea. Lima: Instituto de Historia Grammática.

Sarmiento de Gamboa, Pedro. 1942 [1572]. *Historia de los Incas.* 2nd rev. ed. Ed. Angel Rosenblatt. Buenos Aires: Emecé Editorial.

Shady Solís, Ruth. 2004. *Caral, la ciudad del fuego sagrado / Caral, the City of Sacred Fire.* Lima: Interbank.

Shady Solís, Ruth. 2005. *Caral Supe, Perú: La civilización de Caral-Supe, 5000 años de identidad en el Perú.* Lima: Instituto Nacional de Cultura.

Silverblatt, Irene. 1987. *Moon, Sun, and Witches: Gender Ideologies and Class in Inca and Colonial Peru.* Princeton, NJ: Princeton University Press.

Summers, David. 2003. *Real Spaces: World Art History and the Rise of Western Modernism.* London: Phaidon.

Tuan, Yi-Fu. 1977. *Space and Place: The Perspective of Experience.* Minneapolis: University of Minnesota Press.

Ubbelohde-Doering, Heinrich. 1967. *On the Royal Highway of the Inca.* New York: Praiger.

Uhle, Max. 1910. "Datos para la explicación de los intihuatanas." *Revista Universitaria* 5 (1): 325–32.

Urton, Gary. 1985. "Animal Metaphors and the Life Cycle in an Andean Community." In *Animal Myths and Metaphors in South America,* ed. Gary Urton, 251–84. Salt Lake City: University of Utah Press.

Valencia Zegarra, Alfredo, and Arminda Gibaja Oviedo. 1992. *Machu Picchu: La investigación y conservación del monumento arqueológico después de Hiram Bingham. Municipalidad del Qosqo.* Cuzco: Qosqo.

van de Guchte, Maarten. 1990. "'Carving the World': Inca Monumental Sculpture and Landscape." PhD diss., Department of Anthropology, University of Illinois at Urbana-Champaign. Ann Arbor, MI: University Microfilms.

Zuidema, R. Tom. 1968. "La relación entre el patrón de poblamiento prehispánico y los principios derivados de la estructura social incaica." In *XXXVII Congreso Internacional de Americanistas, República Argentina, 1966, Actas y Memorias* (Buenos Aires) 1:45–55.

Zuidema, R. Tom. 1980. "El ushnu." *Revista de la Universidad Complutense* 28 (117): 317–62.

Zuidema, R. Tom. 1981. "Inka Observations of the Solar and Lunar Passages through Zenith and Anti-Zenith at Cuzco." In *Archaeoastronomy in the Americas,* ed. Ray A. Williamson, 316–42. Los Altos, CA: Ballena Press.

8

*The Importance
of Being Inka*

Ushnu Platforms and Their
Place in the Andean Landscape

FRANK M. MEDDENS

The Inka structures identified as *ushnu* platforms represent one material form of *wak'a*. The role of these
features links to the need of the imperial Inka state
to project power across its territory in a manner that
would have been instantly recognizable to subject
groups. The ushnu complex demonstrated Cuzco's
dominance over regional deities and expressed to non-
Inka peoples their place within the imperially constructed cosmology. This paper seeks to show how the
Inkas took a signature architectural form and charged
it with religious and political meaning. This facilitated
its use in the co-opting and subjugating of local deities,
bringing local liminal space under the control of cen-
tralizing forces and enabling the Inka elite to manage
non-Inka peoples across ethnic and ecological boundaries. The ushnu was not just recognizable by all parties
but was also a critical element in annual and cyclical
state rituals that served to confirm who was and who
was not Inka.

THE USHNU

One of the most important features identified in
recent archaeological investigations in the Ayacucho
region of the central Andean highlands is a composite
feature of Inka affiliation comprising a platform and an
ushnu that I refer to as an "ushnu complex" (see Figure
8.1; Hyslop 1990; Meddens et al. 2008, 2010).[1] A total
of twenty-five such complexes were identified in this

DOI: 10.5876/9781607323181.c008

FIGURE 8.1. *Map of sites mentioned in the text and distribution of ethnic groups and ushnu platforms around the Department of Ayacucho, Peru.*

region. In his original interpretation of the Inka ushnu, Zuidema (1980, 1989) defined it as a basin structure that formed a conceptual axis mundi into which liquids were poured and channeled into the ground, and through which Inka rulers and priests mediated between the sacred realms of *hanan pacha, kay pacha,* and *uku pacha* (the upper world, this present world, and the lower/inner world). In the present chapter the ushnu platform is viewed as an integral part of the ushnu complex, which, like the *apacheta* construct, arguably represents a model mountain (Dean 2010; Meddens 1997). These features can be classified into three principal types: (1) those forming part of Inka administrative sites located in large communal spaces or plazas (such as found at Vilcashuamán, Pumpu, and Huánuco Pampa); (2) those found at major pilgrimage sites; and (3) those comprising isolated units often located on high mountaintops. These three categories of ushnu sites are discussed in detail in the second half of this chapter.

USHNU LOCATIONS: CUZCO VS. THE PROVINCES

In his discussion of the ushnu complex in the seminal work *Inka Settlement Planning,* Hyslop (1990:70–71) noted that no ushnu platforms had been identified in the Cuzco region; rather they are found exclusively in regions conquered by the Inkas or otherwise occupied by non-Inka groups. The reported absence of these features in the Cuzco region can be questioned, however, and indeed evidence of the possible remains of such a platform in the principal plaza of Hawk'aypata in Cuzco proper has recently been flagged and discussed by Farrington (2014:197–207). These remains were uncovered in excavations in the immediate vicinity of the nineteenth-century fountain located in the middle of the Plaza de Armas, where its Colonial and Republican predecessors have stood since 1583 (Viñuales 2004:22). Another ceremonial platform that bears some resemblance to the isolated mountaintop structures identified in Ayacucho (Meddens et al. 2008, 2010) is also known from a mountaintop in the Inka heartland. This is the summit site of Pachatusan (Reinhard and Ceruti 2010:169). In general, however, the observation that ushnu platforms were predominately associated with areas conquered by the Inkas rather than the heartland per se seems to be correct and may in fact be an important clue in explaining their distributional pattern around the empire.

The lack of solid physical evidence for a stepped platform structure in Hawk'aypata, and indeed its general lack of mention in the early documentary sources that treat the plaza, its configuration, and the rituals conducted therein (Betanzos 1987; Pizarro 1978 [1571]), has been previously commented upon by Inka scholars (e.g., Farrington 2014; Zuidema 1989). Only one of the early chroniclers remarks upon a structure in Hawk'aypata plaza that, from its description, could suggest a stepped platform. This was Cieza de León (1985 [1553]:90–93), who states that there was a feature—which he called a "teatro"—consisting of a square stepped platform with a staircase located in the plaza that was used during Capac Laymi. He described Capac Laymi,[2] celebrated at the end of August, as the most important festival of the Inkas, but he is unique among the chroniclers in its naming. The timing given is also slightly anomalous but would not be inconsistent with the Situa festival said to have been celebrated in September. According to Cieza, this "teatro" would have had the idol of Viracocha placed atop it during the Capac Laymi celebrations. The idol was addressed as part of the ceremonies conducted from the base of the structure by the Inkas (ibid.:91; Segovia 1968 [1552]:22).

Farrington (2014:197–207) considers the archaeological evidence for what he believes to represent the remains of the "teatro" discussed by Cieza unearthed in the 1996 excavations conducted by Miguel Cornejo of the National Institute of Culture (INC) of Peru. These excavations revealed a 3.4 m deep sequence of cultural materials extending from ground level to the underlying undisturbed natural alluvial clay loam deposits. The Inka part of the sequence comprised a substantial, finely built wall at least 19.25 m long on an alignment of 341°, an associated floor, polychrome Inka ceramics, metal objects, figurines, and camelid bone (Farrington 2014; Cornejo 1996). Zuidema, however, rejects the possibility that this structure may have constituted the ushnu platform at Hawk'aypata, suggesting rather that these remains may represent an early Inka feature perhaps predating the imperial reorganization of Cuzco (R. Tom Zuidema, personal communication, 2011). He considers a possible alternative location for a prototype of the ushnu platform to have perhaps been at the site of the Cathedral on the east side of the Plaza (ibid.).

The ushnu complex located in Hawk'aypata is described by various early chroniclers (e.g., Betanzos 1987 [1551–57]; Molina 1989 [1576]; Pizarro 1978 [1571])—who make no reference to any associated platform structure—as being a stone fountain or basin lined with a band of gold that had a hole into which libations to the sun were poured and which led to a conduit that drained to the houses of the Sun, Thunder, and the Creator at the Coricancha (Molina 1989 [1576]:79). Regardless of whether the Hawk'aypata ushnu complex included a platform or not, it was crucial to the ceremonial events that served to simultaneously exclude and include "foreigners," or non-Inkas, at the capital of the Inka state and confirm them in their role and place within the state.

There is broad agreement among all specialists who have addressed the subject that the Hawk'aypata was the focal point of Inka public rituals—including those involving the elite, the more general class of non-elite Inka, and "foreign" or non-Inka populations resident in the capital—and that some of these ceremonies involved a structure identified with the term "ushnu." The annual purifying ritual of Situa held in September was one such ceremony. For the initial part of the Situa celebrations all foreigners and people with disabilities were required to remove themselves from Cuzco to a distance of two leagues. Four groups of one hundred warriors each then gathered at Hawk'aypata around the ushnu. Each group took one of the four main roads leading out of Cuzco to the four quarters or suyus of the empire, crying out to banish evil, corrupt, and polluted things as they departed. These cleansing responsibilities were handed over every two leagues to various attendant groups of mitimaes en route from the capital. The different factions carried the cries aimed at expelling the pollution and evil to the main rivers, which then drained the malevolent elements to the sea, thus purifying the state; weapons and clothes were also washed in these waters (ibid.:73–75).

On the next day the ayllus and panacas of the Cuzco Inkas gathered in Hawk'aypata around the ushnu with their ancestral mummies and the mummies of former Inka kings and attendants. The mummies were seated in the plaza according to their genealogical order, status, and moiety divisions. The Cuzqueños danced and sang and ate and drank, and the ancestral mummies were also given food and drink. The Cuzqueños gave thanks to the Creator (Viracocha), the Sun, and the Thunder gods, and the Sapa Inka drank with these entities. The sun deity purportedly had a large, golden drinking vessel placed in front of it that the Inka filled with chicha. The principal priest took this vessel and poured the drink in or on the ushnu, from which it ran via a tube or channel to the houses of the Sun, Creator, and Thunder gods located in the Coricancha. The priest himself consumed the sacrificed food and drink. At the end of this day the deities and people returned to their temples and houses (ibid.:75–79).

In total, the celebration of Situa lasted four days. The first day involved the removal of foreigners and the purification rituals; the second day was for the Creator, Sun, and Thunder gods; and the third day was dedicated to the moon and earth (mother). On the final day, "all the subject nations of the Inca came with their wak'as in their national dress, and they and their priests came to do homage to the Creator, Huanacauri, Sun and Thunder" (ibid.:94). This included not just the "foreigners" resident in and around Cuzco but representatives of the subject populations from across the empire. This ritual served to unite all the Inka groups, ayllus, and subject nations. Thus, in a rigid and synchronized manner, this annual ritual pilgrimage manifested and defined the social political space of the Inka state (Urbano and Duviols 1989:74n48) and indeed confirmed it in its purified unity.

INKA USHNU PLATFORM SITES IN THE AYACUCHO REGION
TYPE 1: CAPAC USHNU PLATFORMS

The main Inka administrative sites outside the Inka heartland with capac ushnu platforms, including Huánuco Pampa (Morris and Thompson 1985:31), Vilcashuamán (Salas 2002: 59–60; González Carré and Pozzi-Escot 2002:19) and possibly Pumpu (Matos 1994), appear to have been predominantly associated with a non-Inka population (Pino Matos 2004: 307), as indeed most or all Inka provincial centers would have been.[3] Of the sites with capac ushnu, one—Vilcashuamán—is located within the area of Ayacucho that has been the focus of recent archaeological investigation (Figure 8.2) (see also Dean, this volume). This site constituted the capital of the Inka province of Vilcashuamán. Cieza de León noted that according to the native people of the region, Vilcas was an important center within Tawantinsuyu and that it was greatly honored by the Inkas, and that llamas and young children were sacrificed here. He likens its significance to that of the capital of an empire and describes a number of features comprising the ushnu complex at the site without naming it as such (Cieza de León 1947 [1553], chap. 89:435). This site was a principal interregional Inka administrative and redistribution center located at the intersection of the main Inka trunk roads running along the Andes mountain chain and down to the coast (González Carré and Pozzi-Escot 2002).

The ushnu platform located here comprises a pyramidal structure of four tiers with a staircase of thirty-six steps located on the eastern side that permits access to the top via a stone portal. The stonework of the structure consists of very finely cut stone ashlars, with the largest stones measuring up to 1.14 × 0.39 × 0.57 m in size. The east-west axis of the structure is oriented on 96°, while the north–south alignment is oriented on 6°. The uppermost tier of the structure has a ramp on its west side that connects to the third tier immediately below. The top tier measures 15.77 × 12.3 m and is equipped with a monolithic carved double seat (see Dean, this volume). From the summit of the structure, the north, south, and west horizon profile views are relatively distant, while the horizon profile on the eastern side is comparatively close and therefore perhaps less important as it does not include the view of any locally important *wamanis* (revered mountain peaks, or apus).

Near the base of the eastern side of the ushnu structure are two approximately square structures and beyond these, the remains of a large *kallanka* (Inka great hall), with a second such possible edifice existing opposite it across a large open space. Located to the west is the present-day town cemetery. To the east and northeast is the main colonial plaza where extensive and elaborate Inka remains interpreted as the footings of the local temples of the sun

FIGURE 8.2. *The ushnu platform at Vilcashuamán, south elevation, Department of Ayacucho (photograph by author).*

and moon have been identified. The entire site overlooks the valley of the Rio Pampas. Though the ushnu platform at Vilcashuamán has been extensively restored—its summit and small eastern plaza covered over with concrete—this ushnu complex remains the example par excellence of the variant of ushnu site associated with administrative centers and plazas.

TYPE 2: USHNU PLATFORM PILGRIMAGE SITES

As noted above, interregional pilgrimage sites were one of the three types of sites containing ushnu complexes that would have been of considerable importance in the management of the Inka cultural landscape and non-Inka populations. In the one example from Ayacucho, the site of Usccunta has two ushnu platforms and is associated with one of the principal interregional wak'as. This wak'a, which was named Auqui Uscuntay, was the focus of seasonal pilgrimages undertaken by various local ethnic groups. It was described as a rock on top of the Usscunta mountain and identified as the principal wak'a of the Soras people; the mountain was also recognized as a major *apu* (lord) of the Rucanas and several other ethnic groups in this part of the southern Ayacucho region (Duviols 1967:28). As there is but a single example of this type of platform site in our regional data set, it merits detailed description.

The site of Usscunta is located in Lucanas Province on the boundary between the districts of Aucara and Cabana Sur at an elevation of approximately 4,500 m a.s.l. It covers approximately 80 ha and contains kallanka, *chullpas* (burial towers), and habitation-type structures as well as two ushnu platforms (Figure 8.3a and b). The site encompasses three mountains which include Usscunta, the largest and tallest of the three, Warmitalle (or Huarmitalle) and Canrarac (Cavero Palomino 2010). The summit of Usscunta consists of a rounded peak delimited by a vertical rock face that rises like a pinnacle from the center, making access to the top difficult. This pinnacle feature is almost certainly the stone described by Cristóbal de Albornoz on the summit of the same mountain, the one he reports as having been the principal wak'a of the Soras (Duviols 1967:28). Warmitalle is located immediately west of Usscunta and consists of a ragged, stepped, and denuded peak that reaches skyward. Canrarac, which also has a rounded summit, is situated on a plain to the south-southeast of Usscunta.

The main archaeological remains at Usscunta are spread across three sectors (Cavero Palomino 2010). Concentrated on the eastern slope of Canrarac are a series of approximately forty circular structures measuring between 3.5 and 4 m in diameter. On the large saddle stretching between the peaks of Usscunta and Canrarac are the two Inka ushnu platforms. In the immediate vicinity of the ushnu platform nearest Usscunta mountain (identified as "Intiwatana 2") are a number of rectangular and circular structures. The rectangular ones make up a patio group (*kancha*), with at least some of the buildings being constructed of finely cut, polygonal ashlars. The circular structures, which are poorly preserved, are built of modified fieldstone and measure from 4 to 5 meters in diameter. The first terrace of the mountain is accessed via a 1.5 m wide and 6 m high staircase built of carefully selected and modified fieldstone that is located immediately northeast of the Intiwatana 2 ushnu platform. This terrace has at least three kallanka and three patio groups containing rectangular buildings as well as a group of circular structures on the south and southwest sides. The rectangular buildings on this terrace include several built of finely cut polygonal stone blocks. To the north of these architectural remains are a series of circular corrals built of stone.

On the east and southeast slopes of Usscunta mountain are a series of chullpa-like features and small buildings. Above these is a natural terrace on the mountainside that is accessed by a staircase. The stairs pass through an opening in a tall encircling wall approximately 2.2 m in height. While this wall may have been defensive in nature, given the religious character of the site,[4] it is also possible that it served to restrict access to select celebrants of ritual

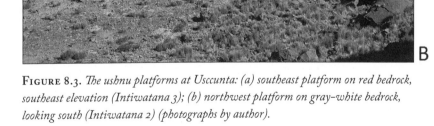

FIGURE 8.3. *The ushnu platforms at Usccunta: (a) southeast platform on red bedrock, southeast elevation (Intiwatana 3); (b) northwest platform on gray–white bedrock, looking south (Intiwatana 2) (photographs by author).*

activities performed here. This uppermost level has a large number (more than 100) of small circular structures of variable diameters, grouped in clusters of three to five units around patio-like spaces. These structures are constructed of modified fieldstone and suggestive of temporary, perhaps seasonal, occupation and use. The top of the pinnacle forming the summit of Usccunta is crowned by a number of *saywas* (stone markers) and also has a number of cup-marked rocks.

The two ushnu platforms found at the site are identified as Intiwatana 2 and Intiwatana 3. They are separated from one another by an open space measuring approximately 520 m N-S. Intiwatana 2, the northern platform, is built upon bedrock that is medium gray in color. It has two tiers with the upper component measuring 15.25 × 9.93 m and the lower basal element 19.67 × 12.59 m. The retaining wall of the upper tier is constructed of finely fitted, cut stone ashlars made of gray andesite, while the lower portion is constructed of modified fieldstone. Abutting the center of the northern wall of the basal component is a 1.6 m wide staircase with three steps. The long axis of the rectangular Intiwatana 2 platform is oriented on 334°.

The southern platform (Intiwatana 3) is situated 19 m lower than the northern one and is built on bedrock that is medium red in color. This platform also has two tiers, the upper one measuring 16.40 × 9.76 m, and the lower measuring 18.09 × 11.53 m. The upper level is similarly constructed of finely fitted, cut stone ashlars made of gray andesite, while the lower platform is again formed of modified fieldstone. The orientation of the long axis of Intiwatana 3 is 341°. These orientations approximate that of the Inka wall excavated in the Hawk'aypata plaza in Cuzco that has been interpreted as a remnant of the capac ushnu of the capital city (Farrington 2014). The positioning of the two ushnu platforms at Usccunta, with one situated slightly higher than the other and built upon on gray bedrock and the other built at a lower elevation on red bedrock, likely expresses the dual social structure of the non-Inka communities involved in the use of the site.

The architectural elements found at the site of Usccunta are characteristic of the Late Intermediate period and the Late Horizon. The artifactual materials collected at the site consist of surface finds only; though two small trenches were excavated in the ushnu platforms, no artifacts were encountered here. Among the types of lithic items found at the site were small stone "balls" that may have been used as either slingstones or gaming pieces. Interestingly, slings and slingstones were sometimes used in rituals associated with Illapa, the entity associated with lightning and hail (Staller 2014). The pottery recovered consisted mostly of styles dating to the Late Intermediate period and Late Horizon. There were some sherds of Chanca, Soras, and Rucanas affiliation as well as a minor amount of Inka material (1.9% of the collection) that comprised mainly fragments of aríbalos and shallow plates. One special find consisted of a small copper or silver spatula with a human figure positioned atop the handle—its left hand pointing up and its right hand pointing down. This object probably dates to the Late Horizon. Similar artifacts identified as being of coastal Chancay origin are found in the collections of the Ethnologisches Museum in Berlin (Baessler 1906:12, fig. 162).

The site of Usccunta is situated immediately southwest of a major intersection of intervalley roads dating to the late prehispanic period. An *apacheta* (stone cairn) is located north of the site, and several saywas are present on various rocky outcrops in the immediate vicinity. Several sizable lakes, including Laguna Turpococha to the northwest, Laguna Huancacocha to the south, and Laguna Lliullisja to the southeast, are all located within about 5 km of the site, with several streams draining away from the mountain to these water catchment basins and beyond. While the cultural material associated with Usccunta predominantly dates to the Late Intermediate and Late Horizon periods, and though there is a clear Inka presence manifest in the site's architecture, the fact that less than 2 percent of the pottery recovered at the site is Inka or provincial Inka in style suggests that the principal ethnic associations of this site was with non-Inka peoples.

Type 3: Isolated Ushnu Platform Sites

The third type of Inka ushnu platform site identified in the Ayacucho area consists of stepped platforms located on isolated mountaintops that are recognized as minor local wamanis. These are predominantly located along pre-Inka ethnic territorial boundaries. Of the twenty-five ushnu platforms in the Ayacucho region for which archaeological field data were collected, twenty pertain to this third category. Of these, fourteen comprise single platform structures and six are found to occur in pairs. Some of these sites have associated architectural remains consisting of chullpas, apachetas, saywas, and huancas (stone markers; see Dean, this volume). Artifactual material is generally scarce, though two sites (Incapirca Waminan [Figure 8.4] and Aquqasa-Mesapata) produced conical stone effigies in excavations that were interpreted as "ancestor" or "sun stone" figures (Meddens et al. 2010). Further examples of this type of artifact have been found on mountaintop shrines linked with Capac Hucha offerings at sites in Argentina, Peru, and Chile (Beorchia Nigris 1986; Reinhard and Ceruti 2010).

The distribution of the type 3 isolated Inka ushnu platforms across the Department of Ayacucho suggests a notable regional clustering, with the Rio Pampas constituting an approximate boundary between two apparently

FIGURE 8.4. *The ushnu platform at Incapirca Waminan, looking north, in the Ayacucho region (photograph by author).*

distinct groups. North of the Rio Pampas the platforms are significantly more varied in construction characteristics and orientation, and notably more rustic in appearance than the ones found to the south of the Rio Pampas. The latter tend to be aligned approximately north-south along their long axis, have a staircase centrally placed on the narrow north side, and have walls constructed in a provincial variant of cut stone masonry. In the southern examples, the platform fill consists exclusively of fine, homogeneous materials, with no suggestion of any layering. On the north side of the Rio Pampas, the platform fills have a distinct layered appearance. The one exception to this tendency on the north side is the site of Altarniyoc (Figure 8.5), where the interior body of the structure appears to have been built of a series of walled cells, each with a distinct fill, which includes some with a very fine humic soil material and one filled with similarly sized small stones (Meddens et al. 2010:178–79). In general, the isolated ushnu complexes appear to be located so as to facilitate views of distant horizons by defining panoramas that often include the more prominent mountaintops and wamanis in the wider region. The distances at which prominent mountains can be observed on the horizon from the isolated

FIGURE 8.5. *The ushnu platform at Altarniyoc, west elevation, in the Ayacucho region (photograph by author).*

ushnu complexes range from a minimum of approximately 500 m to a maximum of 170 km.

GIS analysis of all twenty-five ushnu complexes identified in the region suggests that they can be divided into three groups on the basis of shared viewsheds. Each viewshed group contains from two to nine platforms. The ushnu complexes that comprise each grouping share a horizon view that encompasses the most prominent mountain peaks visible within the territory (Branch et al. 2014:99–117). The wamanis found within the Department of Ayacucho are categorized hierarchically, with the principals being Qarwarasu, Rasuwillka, and Pumawanqa (Ansión 1987:138–39) as well as Usccunta and Sara Sara (Bendezu Neyra 1980:33). Two of the viewshed groups share some degree of overlap in the horizon views they command. Contained within these overlapping segments are several of the principal wamanis in the Ayacucho region. In contrast to the apparent interest in the horizon views, intervisibility among the various platform complexes in the sample does not appear to have been a major concern with respect to their positioning.

The focal points within the horizon views obtaining from the isolated ushnu sites consist of the principal ethnic deities, e.g., the local mountain gods or apus. These sacred features of the local landscape might thus be understood as having been co-opted within the proprietary spectrum of the Inka officials who gazed upon them from the sanctified imperial platform sites (Branch et al. 2014). This aspect of laying claim to and appropriating parts of the landscape by viewing them from imperially created and sanctioned locales is associated with various Inka culture heroes such as Manco Capac, who laid claim to Cuzco by viewing it from the summit of Huanacauri. This idea has also been developed by Besom (2009:132–45) as well as Dean (this volume).

TERRITORIAL BOUNDARIES AND USHNU

The ushnu platform, as an Inka architectural element, appears to also have been sited at locations that formed parts of boundaries. In the case of the examples studied in the Department of Ayacucho, the sites tend to be found along the borders of the ethnic territories that formerly comprised the local landscape. Where the ushnu platforms are found on mountain summits, they may also be perceived as marking the boundary between kay pacha and hanan pacha.[5]

In her discussion of the native Andean understanding of the concept of boundary, Crickmay (2006) has noted that the sixteenth-century Spanish term for boundary marker, *mojon*, is equated or overlaps with the Quechua terms saywa, apacheta, and huanca.[6] González Holguín includes "boundary marker" as one of the translations of the term ushnu in his Quechua dictionary (1952 [1608]). In his discussion of Manco Capac's conquest of the Cuzco area, Sarmiento de Gamboa (1988 [1572]:57–61) relates how the Inka instructed his brother Ayar Auca to fly over to the mojon (which was near where the Inka Temple of the Sun, or the Coricancha, would later be erected). Obeying the command, Ayar Auca flew over, settled on the marker, turned to stone, and became a huanca. Ayar Auca's behavior mimics the common conduct of birds in the central highlands, which can often be observed resting on, surveying from, or roosting upon the tops of standing stones that are in fact frequently huancas and saywas. The early Spanish interpretations of the terms saywa, apacheta, huanca, and ushnu thus include the early post-medieval notion of boundary marker. But it is also clear from the variety of interpretations and contextual references in the early colonial sources that these terms included a range of other functions and meanings as well.

In the Department of Ayacucho, the type 3 Inka stepped platforms found in isolated mountaintop locations are associated with the boundaries of the former territories of the Wancas, the Lucanas Andamarcas, the Aymaraes, the Condes, the Quichuas, and the Soras. These territorial borders comprise both significant geographic features such as mountain chains and rivers as well as less obvious territorial divisions such as culturally recognized boundaries associated with, for instance, grazing lands, as recently discerned in ethnographic work in the Circamarca area of Ayacucho (Meddens 2014). In the latter case, the boundaries seem to be less linear and more fuzzy.[7] The mountains on which the isolated ushnu complexes are located represent lesser mountain deities, or wamanis, in the local hierarchy. The word wamani derives from the term waman, which is the Quechua word for "falcon" (Ansión 1987:129). The semantic intersections among the terms ushnu, apacheta, saywa, and huanca expressed in the Spanish word mojón, and the links of wamani and huanca with the falcon—a prominent bird in Inka mythology directly associated with the appropriation and claiming of territory (as reflected in the Ayar Auca myth[8])—converge to suggest one important characteristic of the Inka ushnu. That is, that Inka dominance encompassed not only the local ethnic populations but also the wak'as, wamanis, and sacred sites that comprised the local landscape.

FOREIGNERS, INKAS, AND INKAS-BY-PRIVILEGE

The Inkas deployed the ushnu complex, in one of its manifestations, as a political tool to manage the non-Inka populations incorporated in the areas under their control (Staller 2008:290–94). The documentary sources available for the Ayacucho area indicate that the Inkas opted to augment the local population by installing various *mitmaq* groups.[9] This strategy was enacted specifically in the Huanta and Angareas territories, the whole of the Rio Pampas, and many of its tributary areas, all of which were reportedly settled with groups of "foreigners" (Galdo 1992; Purizaga 1972; Salas 1979; Stern 1986; Urrutia 1985). Although it is easy to generalize, it is important to assess local regions individually to substantiate the presence of mitmaq communities. In the Rio Pampas drainage, for instance, Huamaní Oré (1978) believes that the majority of the population consisted of mitmaqkuna settled there by the Inkas. However, Earls and Silverblatt (1978) suggest that some groups in this region considered to have been mitmaqs, like the Aymaraes, were not necessarily so. The archaeological evidence from the Rio Pampas area suggests a widespread Wari presence during the Middle Horizon, followed by a Chanca or Chanca-related occupation during the Late Intermediate period, after which there appears to be a late pre- or protohistoric Inka presence (Meddens and Vivanco 2005). Elsewhere in the region, groups in the Rio Qaracha drainage appear likely to have been living there from at least the Late Intermediate period. Of the varied populations present in the Rio Pampas and larger Ayacucho region, however, none appear to have been Inka, or alternatively, Inkas-by-privilege.[10]

As noted above, the Cuzco area generally appears to have been devoid of the platform structures associated with ushnu complexes (Hyslop 1990:101). The limited presence of ushnu platforms likely relates to the composition of the local population, e.g., the Inkas and the Inkas-by-privilege, who would have claimed ancestral rights to the territory. According to Zuidema (2010:3), the groups who were designated Inkas-by-privilege had originally inhabited the Anta, Muyna, and Vilcanota-Urubamba valleys, which together with the Cuzco basin comprised the main part of the Inka heartland. During the Late Intermediate period, the regional inhabitants are generally designated by the name Killk'e. The name refers both to an archaeological culture and a ceramic style with a number of local variants (possibly representing different ethnic units) that is found widely distributed throughout the Department of Cuzco primarily in association with round architectural forms. Whether ethnically distinct or not, the broader Inka heartland was dominated by groups thoroughly integrated into the Inka polity and considered Inkas-by-privilege (Covey 2006). The core area of the imperial Inka state extended 50 to 80 km beyond Cuzco proper and was ritually defined by the events associated with the Situa ceremony, its limits demarcated by the waters of the Apurimac near Limatambo at its confluence with the Cusibamba, the Vilcanota River at Pisac, and the Quiquijana River to the southeast (Covey 2006:208–12).

As part of the maintenance of empire, the Inkas carried out regular state visits and inspections around Tawantinsuyu. Betanzos (1987 [1551–57]:185–86) notes that the Inka Huayna Capac traveled throughout his domain, visiting the various curacazgos, pueblos, and provinces, and that before entering the principal towns, "*he dressed in their ethnic dress and had his hair arranged as theirs*" (emphasis added). In this reference, Betanzos continues his account with a description of the Inka's subsequent ceremonial activities in the principal plaza of the community that was being visited which occurred on and around the local ushnu platform (ibid.): "He entered their principal town where he came to the main plaza where they had a platform with a small rock-filled basin, which he climbed, and where he sat down on his seat and reviewed all the people and they saw him. They brought him many llamas, which they sacrificed and they brought him much chicha [maize beer], which they put as a libation in the basin. He drank with them and they with him. Later he descended, danced, ate and sang with them and granted them many blessings. He got them to bring him all the poor, widows and orphans and he got them to tell him what they possessed and nobody would not tell the truth and he provided for them from the storehouses which there are for this purpose in each village" (my translation).

The assertion that the Inka dressed in the ethnic dress of the people he was visiting and had his hair arranged as theirs—in effect becoming himself a "non-Inka"—is particularly noteworthy as this would have been a punishable offense for any other citizen of the Inka state (Cobo 1892 [1653]:240–41). By appropriating the dress and hairstyles of the subjected groups he visited, the Inka seems to have become one of them, or at least at some level, to have become their kin or ancestor. Clearly this symbolic act was essential to the activities to be engaged in on and around the ushnu platform.

The Spaniards at the time of their conquest of Tawantinsuyu noticed that their native allies often seemed to take a peculiar interest in the clothing of their foes, which they would often ritually kill (Murra 1980:76). Similarly, retreating Inka forces would attempt to keep useful resources from falling into the hands of the Spaniards, and a priority for them appears to have been ensuring that their enemies did not get hold of Inka clothing (ibid.). This emphasis on clothing may be related to the instantiation of power and personhood in wak'as in the Andean world (Bray 2008; Dransart 2000). The wrapping of wak'as in textiles may well have served to transfer the animated essence contained in these fabrics. This is suggested by the fact that the sacred essence perceived as present in idols and deities could be transferred from one place and physical manifestation to another by placing a textile on or over a sacred site or object (Albornoz 1989 [1581–85]:196). Transporting the textile to a new location and draping the cloth over another feature or thing served to render this element the equivalent of its distant match. Albornoz remarks that wak'as had clothes made of the finest textiles, which the people could use to reinstate and rededicate the objects following their destruction by Spanish extirpators (ibid.). This characteristic of native religious practice particularly vexed Spanish priests engaged in the proselytization of Andean peoples. These observations offer support for the idea that when the Inka dressed in the native garb of a subjected, non-Inka people, he was likely viewed as charged with a local sacred essence, his own deified status transformed into that of a local ancestor or wak'a.

DISCUSSION AND CONCLUSIONS

The Inka platform sites discussed in this chapter were located in a region that was not dominated by Inka ancestors or Inka landscape deities. Rather, local ethnic groups and resident or seasonally present non-Inka mitmaqkuna groups made up the majority of the regional population. This would be in contrast to the Inka heartland, where the indigenous or local component of comparable sites would have been formed of or equated with Inkas or Inkas-by-privilege.

In the Ayacucho region, isolated ushnu platform structures located on mountaintops associated with the territorial margins of local ethnic groups, as well as the single, type 2 pilgrimage site of Usccunta, constitute seasonally used places that formed part of a wider landscape and people management system. In their configuration as sacred site and wak'a, each ushnu platform would have been conceived as having its own individual characteristics. The individual traits of the regional ushnu complexes and wak'a may well have been constructed in relation to the ethnic identity of the local people. That such sites were purposefully distinguished is confirmed archaeologically. This is evidenced in the differences observed in the shared structural elements of these complexes, including variation in wall and masonry types, number of tiers, presence and location of access stairs, structural orientations, the nature and composition of platform fills, and the presence or absence of placed deposits. The clustering of ushnu platform sites with similar traits suggests the existence of a localized relatedness among structures. An example of this is seen in the similarities among ushnu platforms in the Rio Pampas region where those located to the south form a recognizable group distinct from those to the north.

Frequently the isolated mountaintop ushnu platforms were also found to be surrounded by additional symbolically significant structures such as apachetas, chullpas, huancas, and saywas, all of which further served to define the cultural landscape. It seems that these interrelated features may have actually been required to strengthen and materialize the social and ethnic boundaries that were being defined at these locations. The ushnu platforms themselves nonetheless seemed to have formed the most important and obvious marker of the cultural landscape, standing out from and affixing the fundamentals of both local and imperial space and place. The discovery of stone effigies at two ushnu sites similar to objects recovered at high altitude shrines elsewhere in southern Peru, Argentina, and Chile suggest additional commonalities over an extensive territory. The construction of significant shrines on mountaintops during the Late Horizon may reflect a new political strategy associated with a desire to co-opt the power of mountain deities.

The ushnu complexes, which are found primarily outside of the Inka imperial heartland, served as a kind of shorthand to signify the nucleus of the Inka state—these features being in a real sense part of the public core of the state as defined by the central plaza of Hawk'aypata in the capital of Cuzco. Their presence in the provinces formalized the public aspect of the concept of ushnu in which it acquired a significant element of public performance where the state could demonstrate its power and formal links with the sun deity to the subject population. The core elements of provincial sites such as Huánuco Pampa and Vilcashuamán can be understood in this light. The dominant population in these sites comprised a local elite and mitmaqkuna, not Inkas or Inkas-by-privilege, or the retainers of households or lineages made up of such peoples. It would have likely been for this reason that it was appropriate for Atahualpa to meet the non-Inka Spaniards at the site of the stepped platform in the principal plaza of Cajamarca. This location focused the power and legitimacy of Atahualpa, materializing his links with the center at Cuzco, the ancestors in the world below and the world above in the form of Inti Pachachachic (Creator Sun), although all this symbolism was ultimately wasted on Pizarro and his men.

Similarly the role of a major regional apu such as Usccunta, which prior to being incorporated into the Inka Empire had already constituted a key interregional pilgrimage site (Cavero Palomino 2010), can also be better appreciated from this perspective. During the Late Intermediate period (LIP), Usccunta was likely a focal point for celebrations linking aspects of the mountain, sun, and lightning deities with the ancestors and the gathered pilgrims. Following the imperial conquest of the region, the Inkas saw fit to construct two ushnus adjacent to the extant LIP component of this site. Not only does it appear to have been important for them to formalize a direct link with and demonstrate the dominance of Cuzco here, but there also seems to have been a need to materialize the *hanan* and *hurin* aspects of the Inka cultural construct through performances enacted on and around the dual ushnu platforms. In similar fashion, it seems likely that the isolated mountaintop platforms were also seasonally accessed for ritual purposes that would have served to confirm Inka supremacy and control over non-Inka territorial boundaries.

ACKNOWLEDGMENTS

I am grateful to the members of the ushnu project team, particularly Nick Branch, Francisco Ferreira, Millena Frouin, Rob Kemp, Colin McEwan, Gabriel Ramón, Cirilo Vivanco Pomacanchari, and Katie Willis. Without their enthusiastic input, discussions, and ideas, this chapter would not have been possible. I thank Tom Zuidema for being the original inspiration of ushnu research and for continuing to contribute to the subject with fresh and innovative ideas. I am also grateful to Tamara Bray for inviting me to the Dumbarton Oaks colloquium at which an earlier version of this chapter was presented and for both her and the other participants' critical input and encouragement, as well as the two independent peer reviewers for their constructive criticism. I thank Mark Roughly for producing the map used in Figure 8.1. Finally, I want to thank Johan Reinhard for his help and for having had the courage and long breath to investigate Inka mountaintop shrines across the Andes for many years and gathering and making available much outstanding data, some of which has been used in the current chapter.

NOTES

1. Much of the architectural, distributional, and spatial data upon which the present study is based was collected over the course of several seasons of fieldwork conducted between 2006 and 2010 in the Department of Ayacucho and sponsored by the British Academy, the British Museum, and the Arts and Humanities Research Council. The focus of this interdisciplinary program of research concerned the environment, landscape archaeology, and Inka architecture.

2. The term *laymi*, or any possible spelling variant thereof, is not present in any of the early Quechua or Aymara Spanish dictionaries. The variant *layme* is a recognized term in the vocabulary pertaining to livestock and agriculture. As such, it can refer to an agricultural plot during the dry season in rest; an agricultural plot pertaining to the community in a rotation system of seven or eight years generally dedicated to potatoes; or a system of community labor on communal lands based on a structure of shifting obligations (Beyersdorff 1984:55).

3. The principal and largest ushnu platforms are associated with sites referred to by the chroniclers as "other Cuzcos" and several of the more important Inka provincial centers. The term "capac ushnu" is used by Pachacuti Yamqui, who employs it to reference the ushnu in Vilcashuamán and Hawk'aypata (Pachacuti Yamqui 1993 [1613], f. 32:245).

4. As noted, this was reportedly the principal *apu* of the Soras, and it continues to be a *wamani* of major importance for the present inhabitants of the region (Bendezu Neyra 1980:33; Duviols 1967:28).

5. I address the boundary aspect of ushnu platforms in more detail in a paper originally presented in a conference held at the British Museum in 2010 (Meddens 2014).

6. *Saywa* refers to a community boundary marker that may relate to a specific subgroup within a larger population that typically consists of a small pile of stones; *apacheta* is a sacred focal point associated with roads often located at the highest point on a mountain pass where small personal offerings, such as stones, coca leaves, or hair may be left by travelers; and *huancas* are standing stones sometimes situated on small

platforms that serve as boundary markers and are thought of as proprietors of places (see also Dean, this volume).

7. Infringement of the boundary is not so much related to the crossing of a defined line but more linked to the intensity of grazing by neighboring groups on boundary lands. This type of boundary becomes contested when one group believes it is being taken advantage of by a neighboring group's excessive use of the boundary resource.

8. Admittedly, the species of bird into which Ayar Auca was transformed is not explicitly stated.

9. *Mitmaq* refers to populations removed from their native homeland to colonize other areas of the empire; mitmaqkuna usually kept their own customs, traditions, and dress; resettlement appears to have been for both economic and political reasons—both to break up existing political alliances and to increase Inka control and security over restive conquered polities (Rowe 1946:269).

10. Originally a member of the ten non-royal or non-noble Inka ayllus, the category appears to have been extended under the rule of Pachacuti Inca Yupanqui to include such Quechua-speaking groups as Quiquijana, Caviña, Quechua, Anta, Tampo, Quehuar, Huaroc, Quilliscache, Lare, Masca, Aco, Chillque, Yanahuara, Mayo, Sanco, Equeco, and probably others (Rowe 1946:261).

REFERENCES CITED

Albornoz, Cristóbal de. 1989 [1581–85]. "Instrucción para descubrir todas las guacas del Pirú y sus camayos y haziendas." In *Fábulas y mitos de los Incas*, ed. Henrique Urbano and Pierre Duviols, 161–98. Madrid: Historia 16.

Ansión, Juan. 1987. *Desde el rincón de los muertos, el pensamiento mítico en Ayacucho.* Lima: GREDES.

Baessler, Arthur. 1906. *Altperuanische Metallgeräte*. Berlin: Verlag von Georg Reimer.

Bendezu Neyra, Roger Albino. 1980. *Puquio y la fiesta del agua.* Lima: Servicio de Impresiones "El Carmen."

Beorchia Nigris, Antonio. 1986. *El enigma de los santuarios indígenas de alta montaña.* Mendoza: C.I.A.D.A.M.

Besom, Thomas. 2009. *Of Summits and Sacrifice: An Ethnohistoric Study of Inka Religious Practices.* Austin: University of Texas Press.

Betanzos, Juan de. 1987 [1551–57]. *Suma y narración de los Incas.* Ed. Martin Rubio María del Carmen. Madrid: Ediciones Atlas.

Beyersdorff, Margot. 1984. *Léxico agropecuario Quechua.* Cusco: Centro de Estudios Rurales Andinos "Bartolomé de las Casas."

Branch, Nicholas, Millena Frouin, Rob Kemp, Nathalie Marini, Frank M. Meddens, Chiwetazulu Onuora, and Barbara Silva. 2014. "The Landscape, Environment and Pedo-Sedimentary Context of Inca Stepped Platforms ('Ushnu'), Ayacucho, Peru." In *Inca Sacred Space: Landscape, Site and Symbol in the Andes*, ed. Frank M. Meddens, Katie Willis, Colin McEwan, and Nicholas Branch, 99–117. London: Archetype Press.

Bray, Tamara L. 2008. "Exploring Inca State Religion through the Use of Conceptual Metaphors: A Cross Media Analysis of Inca Iconography." In *Religion in the Material World*, ed. Lars Fogelin, 118–38. Carbondale: Southern Illinois University Press.

Cavero Palomino, Yuri Igor. 2010. *Inkapamisan: Ushnus y santuario inka en Ayacucho*. Ayacucho: N.p.

Cieza de León, Pedro. 1947 [1553]. La crónica del Perú. In *Historiadores primitivos de indias*, ed. Enrique de Vedia, vol. 2, 349–58. Biblioteca de Autores Españoles, no. 26. Madrid: Ediciones Atlas.

Cieza de León, Pedro. 1985 [1553]. *Crónica del Perú, segunda parte*. Ed. Francesca Cantù. Lima: Fondo Editorial, Pontificia Universidad Católica del Perú.

Cobo, Bernabé. 1892 [1653]. *Historia del nuevo mundo*. Vol. 3. Ed. Marcos Jiménez de la Espada. Seville: Sociedad Bibliófilas Andaluces.

Cornejo Gutiérrez, Miguel. 1996. *Informe preliminar de investigación arqueológica. Plaza de armas.* Cusco: Dirección de Investigación y Catastro, Instituto Nacional de Cultura.

Covey, R. Alan. 2006. *How the Incas Built Their Heartland: State Formation and the Innovation of Imperial Strategies in the Sacred Valley, Peru.* Ann Arbor: University of Michigan Press.

Crickmay, Lindsey. 2006. "Stone: Spanish 'Mojon' as a Translation of Quechua and Aymara Terms for 'Limit.'" In *Kay Pacha: Cultivating Earth and Water in the Andes*, ed. Penelope Dransart, 71–76. BAR International Series 1478. Oxford: BAR.

Dean, Caroline. 2010. *A Culture of Stone*. Austin: University of Texas Press. http://dx.doi.org/10.1215/9780822393177.

Dransart, Penelope. 2000. "Clothed Metal and the Iconography of Human Form among the Incas." In *Precolumbian Gold: Technology, Style and Iconography*, ed. Colin McEwan, 76–91. London: Fitzroy Dearborn Publishers.

Duviols, Pierre. 1967. "Un inédit de Cristóbal de Albornoz: La instrucción para descubrir todas las guacas del Perú y sus camayos y haziendas." *Journal de la Société des Américanistes* 56 (1): 7–39. http://dx.doi.org/10.3406/jsa.1967.2269.

Earls, John, and Irene Silverblatt. 1978. "Ayllus y etnias de la región Pampas-Qaracha: el impacto del imperio Incaico." In *III Congreso Peruano. El hombre y la cultura andina*, ed. Ramiro Matos Mendieta, 157–77. Lima: Universidad Nacional Mayor de San Marcos.

Farrington, Ian. 2014. "The Centre of the World and the Cusco *Ushnu* Complexes." In *Inca Sacred Space: Landscape, Site and Symbol in the Andes*, ed. Frank M. Meddens, Katie Willis, Colin McEwan, and Nicholas Branch, 197–207. London: Archetype Press.

Galdo, Virgilio. 1992. *Ayacucho: Conflictos y pobreza: Historia regional, siglo XIV–XIX*. Ayacucho: Universidad Nacional San Cristóbal de Huamanga.

González Carré, Enrique, and Denise Pozzi-Escot. 2002. "Arqueología y etnohistoria en Vilcashuamán." *Boletín de Arqueología PUCP* 6:79–105.

González Holguín, Diego. 1952 [1608]. *Vocabulario de la lengua general de todo el Perú llamada lengua qquichua o del Inca*. Lima: Universidad Nacional de San Marcos.

Oré, Huamaní. Félix. 1978. "Carapo: De la parcialidad de los Andamarcas a una comunidad rural de Víctor Fajardo." Master's thesis (Tésis de Licenciatura), Universidad Nacional San Cristóbal de Huamanga, Ayacucho.

Hyslop, John. 1990. *Inka Settlement Planning*. Austin: University of Texas Press.

Matos Mendieta, Ramiro. 1994. *Pumpu: Centro Administrativo Inka de la Puna de Junín*. Lima: Editorial Horizonte.

Meddens, Frank M. 2014. "Boundaries at the Roof of the World: The Ushnu at the Confines of Territorial and Religious Space." In *Inca Sacred Space: Landscape, Site and Symbol in the Andes*, ed. Frank Meddens, Katie Willis, Colin McEwan, and Nicholas Branch, 57–70. London: Archetype Press.

Meddens, Frank M. 1997. "An Identification and Analysis of Function and Meaning of the Ushnu in Late Horizon Peru." *Tawantinsuyu* 3:4–14.

Meddens, Frank M., Nicholas P. Branch, Cirilio Vivanco Pomacanchari, Naomi Riddiford, and Rob Kemp. 2008. "High Altitude Ushnu Platforms in the Department of Ayacucho, Peru: Structure, Ancestors and Animating Essence." In *Pre-Columbian Landscapes of Creation and Origin*, ed. John Staller, 315–55. New York: Springer. http://dx.doi.org/10.1007/978-0-387-76910-3_10.

Meddens, Frank M., Colin McEwan, and Cirilo Vivanco Pomacanchari. 2010. "Inca 'Stone Ancestors' in Context at a High Altitude Ushnu Platform." *Latin American Antiquity* 21 (2): 173–94. http://dx.doi.org/10.7183/1045-6635.21.2.173.

Meddens, Frank M., and Cirilo Vivanco Pomacanchari. 2005. "The Chanca Confederation: Political Myth and Archaeological Reality/La confederación chanka: Mito político y realidad arqueológica." *Xama: Publicación de la Unidad de Antropología* (Instituto de Ciencias Humanas, Sociales y Ambientales, Mendoza, Argentina) 15–18:73–99.

Molina, Cristóbal. 1989 [1576]. "Relación de las fábulas i ritos de los ingas hecha por Cristóbal de Molina, cura de la parroquia de nuestra señorada de los remedios de el hospital de los naturales de la cuidad de el Cuzco. In *Fabulas y mitos de los Incas,* ed. Henrique Urbano and Pierre Duviols, 47–134. Crónicas de América 48. Madrid: Historia 16.

Morris, Craig, and Donald E. Thompson. 1985. *Huánuco Pampa: An Inca City and Its Hinterland.* London: Thames and Hudson.

Murra, John Victor. 1980. *The Economic Organization of the Inka State.* Greenwich, CT: JAI Press.

Pachacuti Yamqui, Joan de Santa Cruz. 1993 [1613]. *Relación de antigüedades deste reyno del Pirú.* Ed. Pierre Duviols and César Itier. Lima: Institut Français d'Etudes Andines. Cusco: Centro de Estudios Regionales Andinos "Bartolomé de las Casas."

Pino Matos, José Luis. 2004. "El ushnu Inka y la organización del espacio en los principales tampus de los wamani de la sierra central del Chinchaysuyu." *Chungara* 36 (2): 303–11.

Pizarro, Pedro. 1978 [1571]. *Relación del descubrimiento y conquista de los reinos del Perú.* Lima: Pontificia Universidad Católica del Perú.

Purizaga Vega, Medardo. 1972. *El estado regional en Ayacucho.* Ancash: Editorial Yachaywasi.

Reinhard, Johan, and Maria Constanza Ceruti. 2010. *Inca Rituals and Sacred Mountains: A Study of the World's Highest Archaeological Sites.* Los Angeles: Cotsen Institute of Archaeology, University of California, Los Angeles.

Rowe, John. H. 1946. "Inca Culture at the Time of the Spanish Conquest." In *Handbook of South American Indians,* vol. 2, ed. Julian Steward, 183–330. Bulletin 143. Washington, DC: Smithsonian Institution, Bureau of American Ethnology.

Salas, Mirian. 1979. *De los obrajes de Canaria y Chincheros a las comunidades indígenas de Vilcashuamán.* Lima: XVI.

Salas, Mirian. 2002. "Advenedizos y traspuestos: Los mitmaqkuna o mitimaes de Vilcashuamán en su tránsito de los tiempos del Inka al de los 'señores de los mares.'" *Boletín de Arqueología PUCP* 6:57–78.

Sarmiento de Gamboa, Pedro. 1988 [1572]. *Historia de los Incas.* Madrid: Biblioteca de Viajeros Hispánicos.

Segovia, Bartolomé de (Cristóbal de Molina, "el chileno"). 1968 [1552]. "Relación de muchas cosas acaecidas en el Perú." In *Cronicas Peruanas de Interes Indigena,* 57–95. Biblioteca de Autores Españoles 209. Madrid: Ediciones Atlas.

Staller, John E. 2014. "Lightning (Illapa) and Its Manifestations: Huacas and Ushnus." In *Inca Sacred Space: Landscape, Site and Symbol in the Andes,* ed. Frank M.

Meddens, Katie Willis, Colin McEwan, and Nicholas Branch, 177–86. London: Archetype Press.

Staller, John E. 2008. "Dimensions of Place: The Significance of Centers to the Development of Andean Civilization, an Exploration of the Ushnu Concept." In *Pre-Columbian Landscapes of Creation and Origin*, ed. John E. Staller, 269–313. New York: Springer. http://dx.doi.org/10.1007/978-0-387-76910-3_9.

Stern, Steve. 1986. *Los pueblos indígenas del Perú y el desafío de la conquista española: Huamanga hasta 1670*. Madrid: Alianza Editorial.

Urbano, Henrique, and Pierre Duviols, eds. 1989. *Fábulas y mitos de los Incas*. Crónicas de América 48. Madrid: Historia 16.

Urrutia Cerruti, Jaime. 1985. *Huamanga: Región e historia, 1536–1770*. Ayacucho: Universidad Nacional San Cristóbal de Huamanga.

Viñuales, Graciela María. 2004. *El espacio urbano en el Cusco colonial: Uso y organización de las estructuras simbólicos*. Lima: CEDODAL, Epígrafe Editores.

Zuidema, R. Tom. 1980. "El Ushnu." *La Revista de la Universidad Complutense de Madrid* 28 (117): 317–62.

Zuidema, R. Tom. 1989. "El Ushnu." In *Reyes y guerreros: Ensayos de cultura andina, grandes estudios andinos*, comp. Manuel Burga, 402–54. Lima: Fomciencias.

Zuidema, R. Tom. 2010. El calendario inca: Tiempo y espacio en la organización ritual del Cuzco. La idea del pasado. Lima: Fondo Editorial de la Pontificia Universidad Católica del Perú.

9

*Ordering the Sacred
and Recreating Cuzco*

COLIN MCEWAN

In this chapter I consider the role of two distinct types
of portable objects employed by the Inka state in the
course of projecting its imperial ambitions and affirming control over conquered territories. I will argue that
these kinds of objects assumed great cogency within
the Inka religious universe and constitute a special category of Inka *wak'a*. Each is discussed with reference
to particular archaeological contexts in which tripartite
ordering is apparent in the material assemblages (cf.,
e.g., Lechtman 2007:314–27).

The first type consists of portable objects fashioned
in stone—not the familiar small *conopas* and *illas*
sculpted in a range of lithic material, nor the larger
stone receptacles known as *cochas*, but another newly
recognized class of minimally worked stones of various sizes and forms. The majority of these objects have
been found on, or close to, the snow-capped summits
of major peaks in the central and southern Andes at
elevations ranging up to 6,500 m a.s.l. (Beorchia Nigris
1985; Reinhard and Ceruti 2010) (Figure 9.1) Recently
a suite of such stone objects has been discovered in situ
beneath the fill of a tiered platform atop a lesser mountain called Ingapirca Waminan in the Ayacucho region;
these objects have been characterized as "stone ancestors" (Meddens et al. 2010). Another example of this
type of object in the shape of an egg was recently recovered at a site in the Huarochirí region (Chase, this volume), while a much larger revered stone resides to this
day inside the Cuzco cathedral (see Zecenarro 2007, fig.

DOI: 10.5876/9781607323181.c009

19). For all their unprepossessing appearance, fragmentary accounts in ethnohistoric documents describe how, for the Inka, sculpted stones, including aniconic objects, were often invested with animate qualities and charged with special significance and power (Bray 2009; Dean 2010; Duviols 1979; Trever 2011). While an unknown number of these revered objects have undoubtedly been destroyed since the conquest, it seems likely that many have survived and lain hidden or unrecognized.

The second type of object comprises the miniature figurines that feature among the offerings made at the culmination of the celebrated *capac hucha* rituals (Besom 2009; Bray 2009; Dransart 1995, 2000; Duviols 1976; McEwan and Silva 1989; McEwan and van de Guchte 1992; Reinhard 2005; Zuidema 1981, 1989a, 2008). These items are fashioned in a variety of materials ranging from metal (gold, silver, and copper) to marine shell.[1] The majority of these objects are anthropomorphic (both male and female), although miniature zoomorphic forms—almost invariably camelids—are also found associated in some contexts. Interestingly, there are no known miniature capac hucha figurines sculpted in stone.[2]

The aniconic stone objects pertaining to the first type, as well as representational figurative objects constituting the second, were deployed independently as offerings at select locations across the Andean landscape that have often been identified as wak'as.[3] Occasionally the two types of objects are found together at mountaintop sites where small vertically placed monoliths sometimes marked the presence of buried miniature figurines (Beorchia Nigris 1985) and at Inka *adoratorios* associated with specific coastal sites that had come under Inka control (Heyerdahl et al. 1995).[4]

Finds at several sites have revealed how both types of objects could be organized in ordered sets (McEwan and Silva 1989; Meddens et al. 2010). Tripartite ordering is apparent, for instance, in the stone objects excavated at Ingapirca Waminan and in the suite of figurines recovered from La Plata Island off the coast of Ecuador. These finds invite us to consider the significance of such arrangements and what the relationship between the stone objects and the miniature figurines might be. I will argue that they give material expression to fundamentally related and complementary aspects of ritual behavior that involved remembering and recreating Cuzco and asserting Inka hegemony.

MINIATURIZATION

In her intriguingly titled essay "When Pebbles Move Mountains," Catherine Allen (1997) addresses the role of miniaturized "play" activity in the context

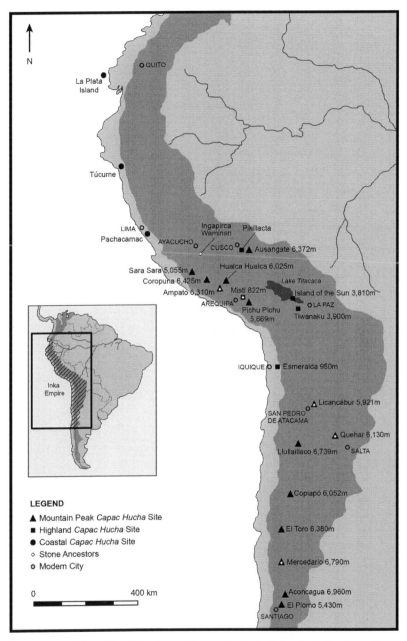

LEGEND

▲ Mountain Peak *Capac Hucha* Site
■ Highland *Capac Hucha* Site
● Coastal *Capac Hucha* Site
◇ Stone Ancestors
○ Modern City

0 _____ 400 km

FIGURE 9.1. *Map of key Inka sites with capac hucha burials, also indicating where revered stone objects have been found.*

of ritual pilgrimages associated with the annual Peruvian festival of Qoyllur Rit'i. The play consists of constructing elaborate miniature houses and corrals using small rocks and populating these scenes with carefully selected stones representing llamas, alpacas, and sheep (see also Meddens 1994; Sillar 1994). The figures are viewed as tiny storehouses of prosperity and well-being and are carefully tended, "fed," and occasionally clothed. They are ritually manipulated to bring their keepers the well-being they represent. These small objects are considered to be animated by superhuman agency—a mountain lord, the earth, or lightning—and thus can serve to effect communication between humans and deities. During pilgrimages, people are temporarily empowered to use the objects to create miniature "texts" as they engage in ritual activities and perform different roles (Allen 1997:81–82).

In considering the underlying motivation for seeking and enacting this kind of communication, Allen points to *ayni*—the fundamental form of reciprocal "give-and-take" that governs the universal circulation of vitality in the Andean world (Allen 2002; for discussion of similar ideas implied in the term *kama* in Aymara, see Duviols 1978; Platt 2014). The flux of vital energy is driven by a system of continuous reciprocal exchanges so that "every category of being, at every level" participates in this cosmic circulation. Thus humans maintain interactive relationships of reciprocity, not only with each other but also with their animals, houses, potato fields, the earth, and other sacred places on the landscape (Allen 1997:76; Allen, this volume).

Here I draw on a combination of archaeological, ethnohistoric, and ethnographic sources to show how these reciprocal relationships were played out on a much larger scale by the Inkas. Revered portable and miniature objects were vital agents in affirming and maintaining a network of dynamic connections between the Inka and extant wak'as in the Cuzco region, as well as new local and regional wak'as encountered or created along the length and breadth of the expanding empire. The state pilgrimages and rituals in which these objects were deployed were instrumental in incorporating the skein of new local and regional wak'as into a larger Inka world order and projecting state power onto a wider stage (McEwan and van de Guchte 1992; Zuidema 2010; also Kosiba, this volume). I will argue that these objects possessed constitutive powers and could serve as activating agents in their own right, functioning essentially as portable wak'as.

I first discuss the stone objects recovered from the mountaintop platform at Ingapirca Waminan situated at the southern edge of the Ayacucho Basin and compare them with similar stone objects reported from high-altitude sites farther afield. I then consider two Inka capac hucha sites, the first found on

Mount Mercedario in Chile and the second on La Plata Island, Ecuador, lying close to the southern and northern extremities of the Inka Empire respectively. Both sites represent the culmination of ritual events that would have taken place at the apogee of state expansion in the years immediately prior to the Spanish conquest. Although found in radically contrasting coastal and mountain settings, they merit comparison because the offerings at each likely originated in Cuzco and would have been carried over long distances by participants in the capac hucha ritual to be interred at the farthest limits of newly conquered Inka territories.

INTERPRETING THE FIND OF STONE ANCESTORS AT INGAPIRCA WAMINAN

The initial phases of the Inka expansion into the territory west of Cuzco demanded the subjugation of pastoralists inhabiting the high *puna* grasslands and the appropriation of the economic wealth represented by their camelid herds. Recent field research has identified some forty Inka tiered platforms faced with polygonal dressed stone masonry on select mountaintops surrounding the Ayacucho Basin (Meddens, this volume; Meddens et al. 2008, 2010; Pomacanchari 2014). Of particular interest here is the site of Ingapirca Waminan, situated at an elevation of 4,430 m a.s.l. (Figure 9.2).

In common with nearly all other mountaintop platforms so far investigated in this area, Ingapirca Waminan commands an uninterrupted, 360-degree panoramic view to the far horizon. It is this commanding visibility, which entailed elements of both seeing and being seen, that seems to have been a compelling criterion for the selection of platform site locations (Branch et al. 2014; McEwan 2014; Meddens, this volume; see also Dean, this volume). Excavations at Ingapirca Waminan revealed the presence of three stones carefully placed in a tripartite configuration in a basin cut into the bedrock below the platform and subsequently overlain by the platform fill (Meddens et al. 2010) (Figure 9.3). This set of objects consisted of a trapezoid-shaped stone made of red andesite, a conical-shaped stone of white andesite, and a crescent-shaped stone of red andesite. These had been placed in the basin sequentially with their "tops" pointing inward and resting against each other. The trapezoidal stone was laid in first on an east-west orientation, then the conical stone was laid oriented west-east, and finally the crescent stone was placed on a north-south axis (Figure 9.4). This is the first time that an undisturbed set of such venerated Inka stone objects has been excavated in situ.[5] While finds of similar individual stones have been recorded at high-altitude capac hucha

FIGURE 9.2. *View of the northeast end of the Inka platform at Ingapirca Waminan in the Ayacucho region (photograph by author).*

sites since the 1970s, their significance has never been well understood (see, for instance, Beorchia Nigris 1985; Reinhard and Ceruti 2010).

A close reading of the ethnohistoric accounts provides new insights into the import of both individual revered stone objects as well as sets of such objects. Betanzos, for example, gives one of the few eyewitness accounts indicating the size and form of a stone object shaped "in the form of a sugarloaf" that stood for the sun and was worshipped by commoners:

> . . . and there [at the temple] they made their sacrifices, their reverences and worship outside [in the plaza] so that the common people could worship there outside as they were not allowed to enter [into the temple]) if they were not lords, and those who were in the plaza arranged to put in the middle of the main square of Cuzco, where at present the judgment post stands, a stone made in the form of a "sugarloaf" with a pointed top and sheathed in a band of gold. This stone was fashioned on the same day that they designated to make the idol bundle of the sun, and this was done so that the commoners could worship

FIGURE 9.3. *Three distinctive stone objects excavated at Ingapirca Waminan: (a) tripartite configuration of the stones, which were found carefully placed in a circular basin carved into the bedrock in fill beneath the platform (photograph by Frank Meddens); (b) profile section of the set of three stones (drawing by Craig Williams).*

it, while the wrapped idol in the House of the Sun was being worshipped by the lords. Not only was this wrapped idol and its servants held in high regard, so were these stones. They were held to be blessed and sacred. (Betanzos 1987 [1551]:52; my translation)[6]

A number of scholars have also discussed how important mountains that featured prominently in the foundation myths for Cuzco, such as Huanacauri, could be represented by individual portable stone objects that were named after them and that could act on their behalf (see Brittenham 2011; Dean 2010; Heffernan 1996; McEwan 2014) (Figure 9.5).

Likewise, beyond the Cuzco Valley, Albornoz (1989 [1584]:182) makes particular note of other revered peaks, such as Sarasara, "a snowcapped mountain on which stood a stone of the same name."[7] Individual stone objects could also serve as the "brother" (huaoque) or double of the Inka king (van de Guchte 1996). In proximity to Sarasara, for example, was a stone wak'a named for Topa Inka Yupanki, which Albornoz (1989 [1584]:182) states was "in the form of the said king, who had won for the Sun the province mentioned," adding that "they paid reverence to this figure, and [it had] many lands."[8]

The portability of these revered objects is emphasized by Albornoz, who notes that "from all the provinces, [the Inka] took [each of] the principal [stones] known to the local people and brought them to Cuzco where they spoke for their months, when the Inkas celebrated their feasts" (ibid.:194; my translation).[9]

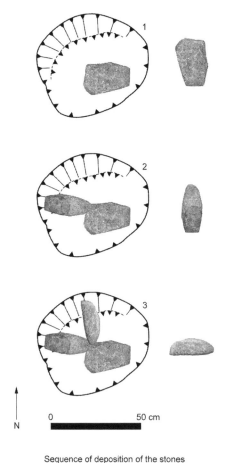

0   50 cm

N

Sequence of deposition of the stones

FIGURE 9.4. *Sequence of deposition of the three stones recovered below the Inka platform at Ingapirca Waminan: (1) red andesite oriented east–west; (2) white andesite placed west–east; (3) red andesite placed on north–south axis (drawing by Craig Williams).*

Elsewhere in the same document, Albornoz further emphasizes how the Inka king could choose to enrich certain wak'as by supplying them with labor, lands, and llamas, presumably as a result of their earnest entreaties in the Inka capital:

> All the above wak'as have labor and lands and herds and [distinctive ethnic] garments and they [each] have their particular prescribed order for their sacrifices and pastures that belong to them where the herds of the said wak'as graze and for all of which they maintain detailed accounts. Among these local wak'as there are many that the Inka rebuilt supplying them with mitimae labor that for this purpose that they transferred from one province to another. He

FIGURE 9.5. *Cuzco people worshipping the mountaintop stone wak'a of Huanacauri in Cuzco (Murúa 2004 [1590]:98v, reprinted with permission).*

(the Inka) gave them many livestock and cups of gold and silver just as they did at all the places that had a view to the sea in all their conquered territories especially to the snow-capped peaks and volcanoes that overlook the sea and from which issue the streams that irrigate the land. (Albornoz 1989 [1584]: 170; my translation)[10]

These observations underline how the movement of portable objects from their wak'as of origin to and from Cuzco was an important aspect of their efficacy and of the partitive nature of wak'as in general (see Bray, this volume).

The excavated find of the set of three stones at Ingapirca Waminan provides empirical evidence in support of the significance of portable stone objects. It corroborates the descriptions of groups of stone objects being associated with wak'as in the *ceque* system of Cuzco and makes it clear that there was a distinction between in situ features such as rock outcrops and portable stone objects that were intentionally placed. Cobo (1964 [1653]), in his account of the ceque lines, records many wak'as as being marked by associated groups of stones. These stones are commonly described as occurring in groups of three, five and ten. Here I will concentrate on the evidence for, and interpretation of, the triadic groupings.

In one case, Cobo states that the last wak'a on the fourth ceque of the Chinchaysuyu quadrant was "a high hill named Chuquiplata, which is next to the fortress, on which were placed three stones in representation of Pachaya-chachic, Inti Illapa, and Punchau [e.g., the Creator, Thunder, and Sun]" (Cobo 1964 [1653]:171, translation in Rowe 1979:21). While no details of their size or form are given, this account seems to suggest that this set of stones may have been deliberately placed.[11] In another account Acosta (1954 [1590]:172) also describes how suites of three statues were made in honor of both the Sun (Inti) and the Thunder god (Illa), and specifies their kin relationships: "The three statues of the sun were called Apu Inti, Churi Inti and Inti Huauque, which means Lord Sun, Son Sun and Sun Brother; and in the same manner they named the three statues of Chuqui Illa, who is the god who presides in the region of the air where it thunders, rains and snows" (translation in van de Guchte 1996:65).

It is apparent from both these accounts that groups of three "stones" or three "statues" could represent key actors in the Inka pantheon—namely the Creator and the Sun and Thunder gods, though we have no precise information on the size or form of these objects. One late sixteenth-century document, which provides a fairly comprehensive list of the main wak'as promoted by the Inkas throughout Tawantinsuyu, indicates that most consisted of individual objects, though there was one grouping of three noted (Albornoz 1989

[1584]:204–15). In general, this list only sketches the distribution of wak'as in the more remote areas of the Inka domain. But for the Jaquijahuana Valley on the western route between Cuzco and Tilka, it describes the types and order of the wak'as in more detail (Table 9.1). The Jaquijahuana Valley list begins by naming the wak'as that were specifically associated with particular local groups resident in the Jaquijahuana hinterlands of Cuzco, which include the Antas, Guarocondos, Mayos, Sancos, Hequeqos, and Conchacalcas. The section concludes with the observation that the Indians brought with them many garments for the wak'as from beyond their lands and dressed the stones with these and made many sacrifices to them (Albornoz 1989 [1584]:204–5).

As can be seen from the descriptions, the stone wak'as found in the Jaquijahuana region clearly manifested different forms—some being unusually shaped natural outcrops that drew attention, while others were individual sculpted figural forms. Descriptions of the latter range from explicit reference to the "figure of a man" to comments about being "finely worked" and "curved." Many were situated either at the foot of a mountain or on its summit and, as in the case of Sarasara, the wak'a Tambocancha in the Jaquijahuana Valley was said to be a house belonging to an Inka king containing his gold statue called Tupa Inka Yupanqui, to which belonged many farms, riches, and attendants. It is clear that both individual stone and gold sculptures could be possessed of agentive power (Bray 2009).

Turning again to groups of stone wak'as, three stones are mentioned together in Albornoz's list that seem to form a related set. These are called Huanacauri, Anaguarque, and Auiraca, and they are described as three stones on a mountain "in memory of those of Cuzco" (Table 9.1). The phrase "in memory of those of Cuzco" raises the question of what role these mountains once played in the ritual geography of the Inka capital. A passage from Sarmiento lends some insight and calls attention to the ritual relationship between Cuzco and two sets of three (e.g., six) of its principal wak'as:

> "In addition to this house [i.e., the Coricancha] there were a number of [other] sacred places encircling the town including Huanacauri and another called Anahuarqui [Anahuarque] and another called Yavira [also known as Yahuira, Sucananca, and Mount Picchu] and another called Cinqa [Senqa] and another Picol and another that was called Pachatopan [Pachatusan]; at many of these they made those cursed sacrifices, that they call capac hucha, which entail burying alive young children of five or six years of age offered to the devil with much ceremony and vessels of gold and silver. (Sarmiento 1988 [1572], chap. 31; my translation)[12]

TABLE 9.1. Albornoz's list of wak'as found in the Jaquijahuana Valley between Cuzco and Tilka

	Name of wak'a	Affiliation	Description
1	Oyñacaca	Guarocondos	an outcrop at the foot of a mountain
2	Rutucayan	Anta	a stone in the form of a man
3	Anta (?)	Anta	a local stone of the Anta Indians
4	Ayaco	—	a stone wak'a of the Indians nearby
5	Achapay	—	a well-worked stone wak'a
6	Timpay	Mayo	a cave in a mountain of the Mayo Indians
7	Panara	Mayo	a wak'a of the said Mayo Indians
8	—	—	a stone on top of a mountain
9	Llimillay	Canco	in the said valley there were different stones
10	Uicacayan	Hequeco	this is a curved stone
11	Mapiguaca	Hequeco	a stone in the form of an Indian
12	Pilco guarda	Conchacalca	a stone placed on a large mountain
13	Guana cauri, Anaguarque, Auiraca,	Cuzcos?	wak'as in the said valley, three stones on a mountain in memory of those of Cuzco
14	Curicancha	Cuzcos?	in memory of that of Cuzco with a stone statue
15	Tambocancha	Cuzcos?	a house that belonged to an Inka (called Topa Inka Yupanki) that has his image in gold in the said house
16	Uilca conga	Cuzcos?	a general wak'a widely acknowledged in all Peru which all worshiped, made offerings, and served
17	Maragoci	Cuzcos?	Guanacauri, a stone where they made many sacrifices in honor of the Guanacauri of Cuzco
18	Guaypon	Cuzcos?	Guanacauri, a stone close to a lake; this is where the Cuzco Indians had their ears pierced
19	Chinchero	Cuzcos?	Guancoari is a stone close to the said wak'a of Guaypon Lake; it has many other related wak'as

continued on next page

TABLE 9.1—*continued*

	Name of wak'a	*Affiliation*	*Description*
20	Pancha	Cuzcos?	Guanacauri, a stone placed on a mountain, next to Pongo Lake
21	Racra	Cuzcos?	Guanacauri is a wak'a placed on another mountain, in front of the one just mentioned

Source: Cristóbal de Albornoz, "Instrucción para descubrir todas las guacas del Pirú y sus camayos y haziendas" (1989 [1584]:204–5).

The first three mountains, Huanacauri, Anahuarque, and Yahuira, feature in the annual initiation rituals for young boys from the Inka nobility. These ceremonies took place in December, a time when all foreigners were ordered to leave the city, and entailed a sequence of ritual movements to prominent mountains around Cuzco that served as points of reference in defining Inka ancestral geography. The sequence began with the novitiates engaging in a footrace to Mount Huanacauri, which stands to the southeast at the threshold of the inner valley. This is where the Inka ancestor and first king, Manco Capac, originally surveyed the Cuzco Valley and claimed possession of the lands within his purview (see Kosiba, this volume).[13] Next, they had to race to Mount Anahuarque, which lies south of and closer to Cuzco. Anahuarque was considered to be the ancestor of local pre-Inka people and also featured in the annual planting feasts celebrated in Cuzco. Later the young male nobles went to Mount Yahuira where they were given their first earspools, after which they assembled on the plaza in Cuzco to watch the sun rise. Finally, six days later, their ears were pierced at places near sources of water.

Zuidema analyzes these movements in terms of the Inka calendar (1983:50, 93–94; see also 1989b:263) and shows how the sequence of movements from the periphery to the center effects a ritual differentiation in space of the distinction between non-Inka (Cayao), pre-Inka (Payan), and Inka (Collana) social groups. Urton (1990:120–21 and fig. 5) also suggests that a concentric configuration of three spatial zones is implicit in the movement of the ancestors recounted in the Cuzco foundation myth and reflects the progressive differentiation and exclusivity of the social categories of non-Inka, pre-Inka, and Inka. These ritual movements were carefully choreographed performances designed to link originary places and their associated mythic events. The set of three named stone wak'as on the mountain in the Jaquijahuana Valley seem intended to reference the sacred places and events of Cuzco in the course of local and regional ceremonies. Parenthetically, we might note that if sets of stones could be placed at regional wak'as to call to mind nonlocal, sacred mountains, then an alternate interpretation for such a set might, for example, establish a connection with a different group of three mountains that figure in the ancestral geography of the Inka capital. One such example could be Sawasiray, Pitusiray, and Urcosiray, which form the backdrop to the myth of Mama Huaco and the ancestral origins of agriculture (Figure 9.6).

INKA CAPAC HUCHA ON CERRO MERCEDARIO

A succinct and potentially related representation of the same kind of three-fold, concentric division of space described for the Cuzco area is materialized near the summit of Cerro Mercedario far to the south in Chile. This imposing mountain lies close to what in the early sixteenth century was the frontier of Inka control and beyond which lay unconquered territory. On the approach to the highest reaches of the peak, the way stations recorded between 5,000 and 6,000 m a.s.l. would have offered shelter for the capac hucha party as it made its way on the exhausting trek toward the summit (Beorchia Nigris 1985). The Inkas went to extraordinary lengths (and heights) to leave an enduring record of their presence. At an elevation of 6,200 m, Beorchia Nigris and his companions discovered an arrangement of three concentric circles of stones, the outermost of which measured approximately 2 m in diameter. At the center of this arrangement stood a small vertical monolith marking a basin excavated into the frozen subsoil containing a single capac hucha figurine (Figure 9.7). This find, along with those reported from Cerro Ampato, Peru (Reinhard 2005; Reinhard and Ceruti 2010), are the best archaeologically documented associations recorded to date between the two categories of portable wak'as discussed in this chapter.

In the account referred to earlier pertaining to Cuzco's six sacred mountains (wak'a), Sarmiento emphasized that these were also the sites of capac hucha burials. This observation establishes a chain of association between stones representing mountains, suites of stones placed in the landscape "in memory of" sacred mountains, and the capac hucha sacrifices made at some of these mountain locations. I next consider another capac hucha site at the extreme northern margins of the expanding empire, which in terms of the chronology of major state capac hucha events is likely to have been roughly contemporaneous with the event at Cerro Mercedario.

Figure 9.6. *Three revered mountains in the Inka myths about Mama Huaco and the origins of agriculture: Sawasiray, Pitusiray, and Urcosiray (Murúa 2004 [1590]:94v, reprinted with permission).*

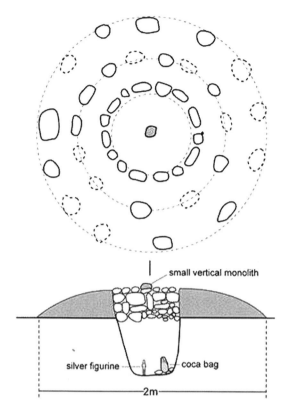

FIGURE 9.7. *Drawing of small tumulus with three concentric stone rings, a vertical monolith in center, and a carved basin with offerings immediately below, found on Cerro Mercedario at 6,200 m a.s.l. (redrawn from Beorchia Nigris 1985, Seccion Documental, Zona "E").*

small vertical monolith

silver figurine — coca bag

2m

INKA CAPAC HUCHA ON LA PLATA ISLAND

The Inka burial excavated by George Dorsey nearly 120 years ago on La Plata Island off the coast of Ecuador originally contained two individuals accompanied by a suite of anthropomorphic figurines made of various materials together with paired miniature ceramic vessels and tupu pins (Bray et al. 2005; Bray 2009, 2012; Dorsey 1901; McEwan and Silva 1989; McEwan and van de Guchte 1992) (Figure 9.8). The burial appears to represent a complete set of objects interred in one event and therefore hints at the sense of order informing the assemblage of capac hucha offerings:

> It was originally comprised of three gold figurines of different sizes, two of which have survived, together with three other female figurines in matching sizes but made of silver, copper and shell. All were most likely dressed in miniature textiles when interred. Along with these were found five pairs of small ceramic vessels: two *urpus* (vessels used for storing and carrying liquids), two

FIGURE 9.8. *View of Drake's Bay on east side of La Plata Island; the Inka capacocha burial documented by Dorsey was discovered in the V-cut quebrada above the sandy beach (photograph by author).*

pedestal vessels, two dishes, two saucers with modeled handles, and two minia-ture plates, the whole making up a set of domestic serving ware. (McEwan and van de Guchte 1992:363)

This assemblage likely accurately reflects the suites of objects presented to the capac hucha participants who were assembled and ritually married in the main plaza of Cuzco prior to being dispatched to the outer reaches of the empire (ibid.:360–61; Betanzos 1987 [1551]:84). The number and types of objects recovered in the La Plata burial appear to represent ordering principles that seem to inform other capac hucha burials in which examples of paired and triadic groupings of objects are also reported (see Beorchia Nigris 1985; Heyerdahl et al. 1995; Reinhard and Ceruti 2010; Schobinger 2001).[14]

If the La Plata figurines are arranged by size and material type, they can be mapped onto what Zuidema (1964) proposed as the "first principle" of tripartite organization underpinning social order in Cuzco, which is based on a distinction between the three ranked social categories of Collana, Payan, and Cayao referred to earlier (Figure 9.9a). The first of these is the endogamous group Collana, whose members were recognized as Inkas-by-birth; the second group, Payan, comprised the progeny of exogamous marriages who were described as Inkas-by-privilege; the third group, Cayao, encompassed the entire non-Inka, unrelated population of the outside world. This tripartite ranking informs the organization of the ceque system in horizontal space and is also played out in the ranked ordering of the ceques and social groupings of Collana, Payan, and Cayao from high to low status (Zuidema 1964, 1989a; see also Lechtman 2007:314–27).

In addition to this tripartite organization, Zuidema identified a concomitant social division into four *ayllu* (extended kin groups), each of which controlled specific lands. The Collana and Payan formed one moiety (hanan), while Cayao and a fourth (unnamed) ayllu formed another, lower moiety (hurin), thus both creating and reflecting the principle of duality (Zuidema 1989b). The principles of dual, triadic, and quadric partition, in combination, are thus seen as underlying the social organization of the Inka capital.[15] An alternative perspective on the way that the ranked order embedded within the tripartite division of Inka society might be played out in social practice can be imagined by rotating the diagram in Figure 9.9a by 90 degrees such that it may be read hypothetically as a template for a ritual procession in which the participants are divided by moiety and appear in rank order (Figure 9.9b).

The idea that sets of figurines such as those found on La Plata may encapsulate fundamental aspects of Inka social organization in Cuzco finds support in ethnohistoric accounts. According to Betanzos, for instance, the Inkas "buried small images of gold as long as a finger of their ancestors organized in small squadrons, as many as there were lineages [of families in Cuzco] around the ushnu" (1987 [1551]:53). Excavations both in and around the Haucaypata plaza

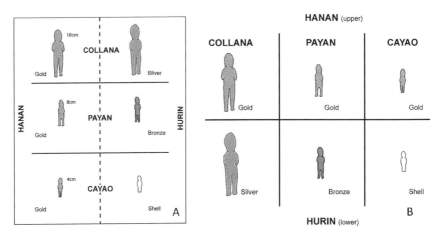

FIGURE 9.9. *Diagram of La Plata capac hucha figurines organized by social groups: (a) the figurines mapped onto the "first principle" of organization; (b) an alternate way of reading the tripartite model of Inka social organization (after Zuidema 1989a:224, fig. 32).*

in Cuzco have revealed miniature gold and silver figurines that help corroborate these accounts; the finds include a line of miniature llamas that also hint at ordered arrangements (Farrington 2013:313–24, table 11.3, 2014; Vargas 2007, fig. 5.1).

PROJECTING INKA POWER

Here I have addressed two distinct types of portable Inka objects—first, the minimally worked aniconic stone objects like those found at Ingapirca Waminan and, second, the ordered sets of miniature capac hucha figurines fashioned in different materials found at La Plata Island and various other capac hucha sites around the Empire. I have described some of the ways in which both types of objects fulfilled vital roles in formalizing transactional relationships that were played out in state ritual practices on a grand scale across the Andean landscape.

I first considered how individual stone objects could act on behalf of and form the focus for the veneration of important mountains, the person of the Inka king, and the sun, respectively. I next noted the way in which groups or sets of stone objects are frequently mentioned as marking the location of wak'as along the ceque lines radiating out from Cuzco. I then explored the implications of a set of three stone objects described by Albornoz at a regional wak'a in newly conquered territory and the way these made direct reference to the ancestral geography of the Cuzco Valley. In this discussion, I proposed that the link between center and periphery was materialized in the form of suites of stone objects selectively placed to mark ethnic boundaries, assert territorial ownership and control, and evoke a remembrance and recreation of originary places and events in the Cuzco Valley. The ritual performances that enacted these new relationships at once cemented the connection between the ancestral past and its re-creation in a continuously unfolding present (see also Chase, this volume).

The generally "unformed" nature of the aniconic stone objects underlines their essentially originary character. From an Andean perspective, the compact hardness of stone (as well as bone) is visible evidence of an earlier prefigurative stage of creation recounted in myths, the material evidence for which is "carried forward" in the kinds of amorphous objects that have been characterized as "stone ancestors."[16] The almost complete dearth of Inka figurative sculpture in stone is remarkable and stands in marked contrast to the iconic character of the suites of miniature figurines in the capac hucha offerings. In broad terms this contrast seems to be predicated on belief in a prehuman era of cosmic creation from which emerged a fully human ordered social universe.

I began this chapter by reprising Allen's insightful analysis of the communicative power of miniature objects. In her study Allen cites Levi-Strauss's observations that "miniaturization facilitates instant apprehension of the whole" and that "miniatures make us reverse the normal process of understanding," concluding that this is because knowledge of the whole precedes knowledge of the parts (Levi-Strauss 1966:23, cited in Allen 1997:81). She also suggests, however, that this falls short of explaining the power of Andean miniatures to change the lived-in world and asserts that the pebble texts of the Qoyllur Rit'i ritual "inscribed on a ground of potentiality and transformation, serve a communicative and even coercive purpose" (ibid.).

I have previously suggested that "the assemblages of figurines accompanying the capac hucha burials can be seen as replicas in miniature of the social universe presided over by the Inka king" (McEwan and van de Guchte 1992:366). The sense of order invested in both the aniconic objects and the miniature capac hucha figurines seems intended to project a potent, materialized expression of the new Inka social order into conquered territories as a means of assuring their effective incorporation into the imperial domain. The burial of both types of offerings instantiates the Inka presence in the landscape and is made to secure, in return, the allegiance and beneficent powers of local and regional wak'as along with the productive capacity they control. In this chapter I hope to have provided a glimpse into how both types of objects, as well as the ritual actions that give meaning to them, relate to each other and intersect in ways that we are still striving to understand.

NOTES

1. This is usually the highly valued, red-rimmed thorny oyster (*Spondylus princeps*).

2. It is interesting to note that miniature anthropomorphic figurines were produced in stone during the Middle Horizon. A set of Wari figurines from Pikillacta is described and analyzed by Cook (1992), who coined the term "stone ancestors."

3. I should note here that while I have used the term "aniconic" to describe the stones that have no obvious figurative characteristics, these conventional western classificatory categories may simply not be applicable in Andean contexts. For example Allen observes that "young couples searched for [natural] stones *shaped like* alpacas, llamas, sheep and cows" (Allen 1997:74; emphasis added). Thus even minimally worked aniconic stones may be imbued with allusive significance.

4. Individual revered stone wak'as with associated capac hucha figurines in Late Horizon Inka contexts are known from coastal sites, such as Túcume, with a long history of prior occupation (Heyerdahl et al. 1995). The vertically placed stone at the Inka "adoratorio" has also been described as a huanca (Bray 2009, fig. 2).

5. We now have good evidence to suggest that after the stones were buried, the site was revisited to make what we presume would have been liquid offerings to feed them by means of a vertical ushnu conduit (McEwan and Meddens, n.d.).

6. ". . . y allí hacían ellos fuera sus sacrificios y sus mochas y adoramientos y para en que la gente común adorasen allá fuera porque no habían de entrar allí si no fuesen señores y éstos en el patio hizo poner en medio de la plaza del Cuzco donde ahora es el royo una piedra de la hechura de un pan de azucar puntiaguda para arriba y enforrada de una faja de oro la cual piedra hizo ansi mismo labrar el día que mandó hacer el bulto del sol y ésta para en que el comun adorase y el bulto en las casas del sol los señores la cual casa era reverenciada y tenida en gran reverencia no solamente el bulto más las piedras della y los sirvientes yanaconas della eran tenidos por cosa bendita e consagrada" (Betanzos 1987 [1551]:52).

7. "Sarasara es un cerro nevado y en él una piedra del dicho nombre" (Albornoz 1989 [1584]:182).

8. "Era una piedra en figura del dicho ynga [Topa Ynga Tupanqui], que fue el que ganó al Sol la dicha provincia, como está referido. Tenían en mucha veneración este bulto, y con muchas haziendas" (Albornoz 1989 [1584]: 182).

9. "...y de todas las provincias tomaron la más prencipal [i.e., wak'a] e de quien tenían los naturales noticia, que las traían al Cuzco e que hablavan por sus meses, cuando hazían sus fiestas los yngas, como está dicho" (Albornoz 1989 [1584]: 194).

10. "Todas las más guacas dichas tienen servicios y chácaras e ganados, y bestidos y tienen sus órenes particulares de sus sacrificios y moyas que son dehesas donde apacientan los ganados de las dichas guacas y tienen gran cuenta con todo. Ay entre estas guacas pacariscas muy muchas que reedificaron los yngas, dándoles muchos mitimas servicios que para este fin los mudava[n] de unas provincias a otras. Dioles [el ynga] muchos ganados y basos de oro y plata como fue en toda la cordillera que mira al mar, en todo lo que conquistó, en especial a cerros de nieves y bolcanes que miran a el mar y que salen de los ríos que riegan tierras" (Albornoz 1989 [1584]: 170).

11. Zuidema (personal communication) identifies the stones mentioned in this account with three large boulders found on flat ground at Chuquiplata.

12. "Había además de esta casa, a redonda del pueblo, algunas huacas, que eran la de Huanacauri y otra llamada Anahuarqui y otra llamada Yavira y, otra dicha Cinqa y otra Picol y otra que se llamaba Pachotopan, en muchas de las cuales se hacia los malditos sacrificios, que ellos llaman capac hocha, que es enterrar vivos unos ninos de cinco o seis anos ofrecidos al diablo con mucho servicio y vasijas de oro y plata" (Sarmiento de Gamboa 1988 [1572], chap. 31).

13. Mount Huanacauri also figures in the harvest when non-Inka people visited the mountain to pay homage to the first ruler.

14. As the suites of objects were carried far afield over long distances, some may have been divided up and dispersed at diverse regional and local wak'as before final interment. Also the various archaeological investigations undertaken at high-altitude capac hucha sites over the years may, for different reasons, have only succeeded in the partial recovery of any original order.

15. In his theoretical reassessment of the social organization of Cuzco, Zuidema (1964) proposed that three different elemental principles of organization involving the simultaneous division of Inka society into three (tripartition), four (cuadripartition), and five (quinquepartition) parts find expression in various aspects of Inka social life and material culture. The tripartite division appears to be reflected in the size range of figurines found across the whole corpus of capac hucha burials, which reveal three modal peaks of figurine heights clustering around 18–19 cm, 8–9 cm, and 4–5 cm, thus defining the size categories of "large," "medium," and "small," respectively.

16. Hard, unusual stones (such as *illas* and *istrillas*) as well as bare bones (like the skull kept for *khuyay* [protection]) are held to be potent sources of energy. They are intimately connected with lightning and sunlight, whose power they absorb and condense (Allen 2002:63).

REFERENCES CITED

Acosta, Jose de. 1954. [1590]. "Historia natural y moral de las indias." In *Obras de P. Jose de Acosta*, preliminary study and edition by Francisco Mateos, 1–247. Biblioteca de Autores Espanoles, no. 73. Madrid: Ediciones Atlas.

Albornoz, Cristóbal de. 1989. [1584]. "Instrucción para descubrir todas las guacas del Pirú y sus camayos y haziendas." *Revista Andina* 2:169–222.

Allen, Catherine. J. 1997. "When Pebbles Move Mountains: Iconicity and Symbolism in Quechua Ritual." In *Creating Context in Andean Cultures*, ed. Rosaleen Howard-Malverde, 73–84. Oxford University Press, Oxford.

Allen, Catherine. J. 2002. *The Hold Life Has: Coca and Cultural Identity in an Andean Community*. 2nd. ed. Washington, DC: Smithsonian Institution Press.

Beorchia Nigris, Antonio. 1985. *El enigma de los santuarios indígenas de alta montaña*. San Juan, Argentina: Centro de Investigaciones Arqueológicas de Alta Montaña.

Besom, Thomas. 2009. *Of Summits and Sacrifice: An Ethnohistoric Study of Inca Religious Practices*. Austin: University of Texas Press.

Betanzos, Juan de. 1987. [1551]. *Suma y Narración de los Incas*. Ed. Martin Rubio Maria del Carmen. Madrid: Ediciones Atlas.

Branch, Nicolas, Millena Frouin, Rob Kemp, Nathalie Marini, Frank Meddens, Chiwetazulu Onuora, and Barbara Silva. 2014. "The Landscape, Environment and Pedo-Sedimentary Context of Inca Stepped Platforms ('Ushnu'), Ayacucho, Peru." In *Inca Sacred Space: Landscape, Site and Symbol in the Andes*, ed. Frank M. Meddens, Katie Willis, Colin McEwan, and Nicholas Branch, 99–117. London: Archetype Press.

Bray, Tamara L. 2009. "An Archaeological Perspective on the Andean Concept of *Camaquen*: Thinking Through Late Pre-Columbian *Ofrendas* and *Huacas*." *Cambridge Archaeological Journal* 19 (3): 357–66. http://dx.doi.org/10.1017/S095977 4309000547.

Bray, Tamara L. 2012. "From Rational to Relational: Reconfiguring Value in the Inca Empire." In *The Construction of Value in the Ancient World*, ed. John Papadopoulos and Gary Urton, 344–57. Los Angeles: Cotsen Institute of Archaeology, University of California, Los Angeles.

Bray, Tamara L., Leah D. Minc, María Constanza Ceruti, José Antonio Chávez, Ruddy Perea, and Johan Reinhard. 2005. "A Compositional Analysis of Pottery Vessels Associated with the Inca Ritual of Capacocha." *Journal of Anthropological Archaeology* 24 (1): 82–100. http://dx.doi.org/10.1016/j.jaa.2004.11.001.

Brittenham, Claudia. 2011. "Imágenes en un paisaje sagrado: *huacas* de piedra de los Incas." In *La imagen sagrada y sacralizada: Memoria del XXVIII coloquio internacional de historia del arte*, ed. Peter Krieger, 1:85–98. Mexico City: Instituto de Investigaciones Estéticas, Universidad Nacional Autónoma de México.

Cobo, Bernabé. 1964. [1653]. *Historia del Nuevo Mundo*. Ed. Francisco Mateos. Madrid: Ediciones Atlas.

Cook, Anita. 1992. "The Stone Ancestors: Idioms of Imperial Attire and Rank among Huari Figurines." *Latin American Antiquity* 3 (4): 341–64. http://dx.doi.org/10.2307/971953.

Dean, Carolyn. 2010. *A Culture of Stone: Inca Perspectives on Rock*. Durham, NC: Duke University Press. http://dx.doi.org/10.1215/9780822393177.

Dorsey, George A. 1901. *Archaeological Investigations on the Island of La Plata, Ecuador*. Field Columbian Museum Publication 56, Archaeological Series 2, no. 5. Chicago. http://dx.doi.org/10.5962/bhl.title.7160.

Dransart, Penny. 1995. *Elemental Meanings: Symbolic Expression in Inka Miniature Figurines*. London: University of London, Institute of Latin American Studies.

Dransart, Penny. 2000. "Clothed Metal and the Iconography of Human Form Among the Incas." In *Precolumbian Gold: Technology, Style and Iconography*, ed. Colin McEwan, 76–91. London: British Museum Press.

Duviols, Pierre. 1976. "La capacocha: Mecanismo y función del sacrificio humano, su proyección geométrica, su papel en la política integracionista y en la economía redistributiva del Tawantinsuyu." *Allpanchis Phuturinga* 9:11–57.

Duviols, Pierre. 1978. "*Camaquen, upani*': un concept animiste des anciens Peruviens." In *Amerikanistische Studien. Festschrift für Hermann Trimborn anlässlich seines 75. Geburtstages*, vol. 1, ed. Roswith Hartman and Udo Oberem, 132–44. Collectanea Instituti Anthropos 20. St. Augustin, Germany: Anthropos Institut.

Duviols, Pierre. 1979. "Un Symbolisme de l'Occupation. de l'Aménagement et de l'Exploitation de l'Espace: Le Monolithe 'Huanca' et sa Fonction dans les Andes Préhispaniques." *L'Homme* 19 (2): 7–31. http://dx.doi.org/10.3406/hom.1979.367954.

Farrington, Ian. 2013. *Cusco: Urbanism and Archaeology in the Urban World*. Gainesville: University of Florida Press. http://dx.doi.org/10.5744/florida/9780813044330.001.0001.

Farrington, Ian. 2014. "The Centre of the World and the Cusco Ushnu Complexes." In *Inca Sacred Space: Landscape, Site and Symbol in the Andes*, ed. Frank Meddens, Katie Willis, Colin McEwan, and Nicholas Branch, 197–207. London: Archetype Press.

Heffernan, Ken J. 1996. "The Mitimaes of Tilka and the Inka Incorporation of Chinchaysuyu." *Tawantinsuyu* 2:23–36.

Heyerdahl, Thor, Dan Sandweiss, and Alfredo Narváez. 1995. *Pyramids of Tucume*. London: Thames and Hudson.

Levi-Strauss. 1966. *From Honey to Ashes: Introduction to a Science of Mythology*. Vol. 2. New York: Harper and Row.

Lechtman, Heather. 2007. "The Inka and Andean Metallurgical Tradition." In *Variations in the Expression of Inka Power*, ed. Richard L. Burger, Craig Morris, and Ramiro Matos Mendieta, 313–43. Washington, DC: Dumbarton Oaks Research Library and Collection.

McEwan, Colin. 2014. "Cognising and Marking the Andean Landscape: Radial, Concentric and Hierarchical Perspectives." In *Inca Sacred Space: Landscape, Site and Symbol in the Andes*, ed. Frank M. Meddens, Katie Willis, Colin McEwan, and Nicholas Branch, 29–47. London: Archetype Press.

McEwan, Colin, and Frank Meddens. n.d. The Platform and Ushnu at Ingapirca Waminan. Unpublished manuscript in possession of authors.

McEwan, Colin, and Maria Isabel Silva I. 1989. "¿Qué fueron a hacer los Incas en la costa central del Ecuador?" In *Proceedings of the 46th International Congress of Americanists*, 163–85. British Archaeological Reports, International Series, no. 503. Oxford: BAR.

McEwan, Colin, and Maarten van de Guchte. 1992. "Ancestral Time and Sacred Space in Inca State Ritual." In *The Ancient Americas: Art from Sacred Landscapes*, ed. Richard F. Townsend, 359–71. Chicago: Art Institute of Chicago.

Meddens, Frank M. 1994. "Mountains, Miniatures, Ancestors and Fertility: The Meaning of a Late Horizon Offering in a Middle Horizon Structure in Peru." *Bulletin of the Institute of Archaeology* 31: 127–50.

Meddens, Frank, Colin McEwan, and Cirilo Vivanco Pomacanchari. 2010. "Inca 'Stone Ancestors' in Context at a High Altitude Ushnu Platform." *Latin American Antiquity* 21 (2): 173–94. http://dx.doi.org/10.7183/1045-6635.21.2.173.

Meddens, Frank M., Nicholas P. Branch, Cirilo Vivanco Pomacanchari, Naomi Riddiford, and Rob Kemp. 2008. "High Altitude Ushnu Platforms in the Department of Ayacuho Peru: Structure, Ancestors and Animating Essence." In *Pre-Columbian Landscapes of Creation and Origin*, ed. John E. Staller, 315–55. New York: Springer. http://dx.doi.org/10.1007/978-0-387-76910-3_10.

Murúa, Martin de. 2004 [1590]. *Historia de los Incas. Historia y genealogía de los reyes Incas del Perú. Códice Galvin*. Ed. Juan Ossio. Madrid: Testimonio Compañía Editorial.

Platt, Tristan. 2014. "Power and Propitiation in the Andes." In *Inca Sacred Space: Landscape, Site and Symbol in the Andes*, ed. Frank M. Meddens, Katie Willis, Colin McEwan, and Nicholas Branch, 269–76. London: Archetype Press.

Pomacanchari, Cirilo Vivanco. 2014. "The Incas in the Territory of the Chankas: Usnukuna Platforms and their Antecedents." In *Inca Sacred Space: Landscape, Site and Symbol in the Andes*, ed. Frank M. Meddens, Katie Willis, Colin McEwan, and Nicholas Branch, 157–64. London: Archetype Press.

Reinhard, Johan. 2005. *The Ice Maiden: Inca Mummies, Mountain Gods, and Sacred Sites in the Andes.* Washington, DC: National Geographic Society.

Reinhard, Johan, and Maria Constanza Ceruti. 2010. *Inca Rituals and Sacred Mountains: A Study of the World's Highest Archaeological Sites.* Los Angeles: Cotsen Institute of Archaeology, University of California, Los Angeles.

Rowe, John H. 1979. "An Account of the Shrines of Ancient Cuzco." *Ñawpa Pacha* 17: 1–80.

Sarmiento de Gamboa, Pedro. 1988 [1572]. *Historia de los Incas.* Madrid: Biblioteca de Viajeros Hispánicos.

Schobinger, Juan. 2001. *El santuario incaico del cerro Aconcagua.* Mendoza, Argentina: Universidad Nacional de Cuyo.

Sillar, Bill. 1994. "Playing with God? Children, Play, and the Ritual Use of Miniatures in the Andes." *Archaeological Review from Cambridge* 13 (2): 47–63.

Trever, Lisa. 2011. "Idols, Mountains, and Metaphysics in Guaman Poma's Pictures of Huacas." *RES* 59/60: 39–59.

Urton, Gary. 1990. *The History of a Myth: Pacariqtambo and the Origin of the Inkas.* Austin: University of Texas Press.

van de Guchte, Maarten J.D. 1996. "Sculpture and the Concept of the Double among the Inca Kings." *RES* 29/30:256–68.

Vargas Paliza, Ernesto. 2007. *Kusikancha, morada de los momias reales de los Inkas.* Cuzco: Casa de la Cultura.

Zecenarro Benavente, Germán. 2007. "Petroglifos y relieves en templos, conventos y casonas del Cusco." *Arqueología y Sociedad (Revista del Museo de Arqueología y Antropología de la Universidad Nacional Mayor de San Marcos)* 18:179–210.

Zuidema, R. Tom. 1964. "The Ceque System of Cuzco: The Social Organization of the Capital of the Inca." PhD diss., Universiteit van Leiden.

Zuidema, R. Tom. 1981. "Inca Observations of the Solar and Lunar Passages through Zenith and Anti-Zenith at Cuzco." In *Archaeoastronomy in the Americas*, ed. Ray A. Williamson, 319–42. College Park, MD: Ballena Press.

Zuidema, R. Tom. 1983. "The Lion in the City: Royal Symbols of Transition in Cuzco." *Journal of Latin American Lore* 9: 39–100.

Zuidema, R. Tom. 1989a. "Mito e historia en el antiguo Peru." In *Reyes y guerreros: Ensayos de cultura andina, grandes estudios andinos*, comp. Manuel Burga, 219–55. Lima: Fomciencias.

Zuidema, R. Tom. 1989b. "The Moieties of Cuzco." In *The Attraction of Opposites: Thought and Society in the Dualistic Mode*, ed. David Maybury-Lewis and Uri Almagor, 255–75. Ann Arbor: University of Michigan Press.

Zuidema, R. Tom. 2008. "The Astronomical Significance of Ritual Movements in the Calendar of Cuzco." In *Pre-Columbian Landscapes of Creation and Origin*, ed. John E. Staller, 249–67. New York: Springer. http://dx.doi.org/10.1007/978-0-387-76910-3_8.

Zuidema, R. Tom. 2010. "Het wereldbeeld van de Inca's. *Hucha, Capac Hucha en Ceques*." In *Inca's Capac Hucha*, ed. Edward K. de Bock, 47–79. Rotterdam: Mercatorfonds, Brussel en Wereldmuseum.

Part IV

*Deeper Histories
of Wak'as in the
Andean Past*

10

The Shape of Things to Come

The Genesis of Wari Wak'as

Anita G. Cook

> Too often texts alone have been and are
> regarded as reliable sources for the study
> of religion, while nonliterary, "alternative
> vehicles of intelligibility"—preeminently art
> and architecture—are consigned to a lower
> evidential tier as supplementary, weaker, less
> reliable evidences. (Jones 2000, 2:3)

Lindsay Jones studies the comparative history of religions and how the sacred is expressed in architecture. He is also a Mesoamericanist, so he shares concerns that preoccupy Americanists in general, not least of which are the obstacles we face in the analysis of a material world that was created and perceived within largely nonliterary contexts and from perspectives that fundamentally differ from those of the West. In the Andes we have a wealth of architectural remains and a remarkably rich archaeological record despite the fact that we lack precolonial written documents. While different perspectives on the Andes are provided by postcontact descriptions and later ethnographic observations, the recovery of meaning and an understanding of the sacred dimensions of these material remains present numerous challenges. As a case in point, the Spanish crown insisted that their mission was to convert Andean people to Christianity. This meant struggling to understand Inka religion and *wak'as*, the meanings and elements of which constantly eluded them. Today wak'as are still recognized as places, things,

DOI: 10.5876/9781607323181.c010

and buildings with special qualities. But how far back in time might we posit the existence of Inka-like wak'as?

The notion of wak'a has rarely been considered for pre-Inkaic contexts. In this chapter I compare two types of Inka architectural wak'as described in early colonial sources with similar archaeological examples found some six hundred years earlier. There are at least two forms of architecture identified as wak'as during Inka times: tombs and temples. In the following pages, I briefly review the colonial sources that discuss Inka architectural wak'as. I then relate these to their potential predecessors from the first Andean empire of Wari (AD 540–1000) by suggesting that there was a degree of architectural conformity that defined these sacred spaces across time. This is not exclusively an exercise in documenting continuity and longevity, nor am I proposing that Inka descriptions will ultimately be directly applicable to the interpretation of Wari wak'as. I do, however, provide some highly suggestive analogues that should open the topic to further study and discussion.

In devising a working definition of wak'as as religious and sacred entities, both for the Inka and earlier times, I make the assumption that different religions can share the same causal explanations for life, death, and everyday events while relying upon distinctly different ritual practices (as in the Jewish, Christian, and Muslim faiths) (Cook 2012; Topic and Topic 2009) We might also expect that imperial heartlands and centers, in adhering to state mandates, might share greater affinities, architectural forms, and ritual practices than would sacred or ritual places and practices in distant hinterlands. More distant sacred places might still display some similarity in architectural form, suggesting that they adhered (at least nominally) to the state politico-religious model while potentially employing distinct folk religious practices; or they might depart from the architectural program altogether, sharing more local traditions. While these differences have not received the attention they deserve and cannot be fully addressed here, an initial glimpse is offered that should shed light on and hopefully motivate further examination into the pre-Inka architectural remains of wak'as in archaeological contexts.

As discussed in the introduction to this volume, Inka wak'as often comprised sacred structures, objects, and things with unusual characteristics. They constituted essential parts of the ritual and religious landscape of the Inka. They were known to have longevity, recognizable morphologies, and specific associated ritual practices. A wide variety of things qualified as wak'as in the colonial literature, but I have selected architecture because it provides the kind of evidence that can be more easily compared with earlier time periods, especially given the paucity of studies dealing with their ancestral forms. Furthermore, standing architecture provides more durable evidence than the portable and perishable remains of ritual activities that may have been conducted inside these spaces.

Numerous references to wak'as are found in colonial documents (e.g., Betanzos 1996 [1557]; Cobo 1990 [1653], chaps. 11, 13; Garcilaso de la Vega 1966 [1609]:73), and almost all make reference to certain sacred architectural structures (see Moore 2010). Agustín de Zarate mentions that native peoples adored both the sun and moon, but in the place of the sun their temples housed stones, called *guacas*, which they venerated (Zarate 1995 [1555], chap. 11:52).[1] Garcilaso de la Vega gives a detailed account of wak'as and notes: "*Huaca* is applied to any temple, large or small, to the sepulchers set up in the fields, and to the corners of their houses where the Devil spoke to their priests and to others. . . . These corners were held sacred and regarded as oratories or sanctuaries . . ." (1966 [1609]:66–67). These observations, which were made between 1555 and 1653, and others like those of Juan de Betanzos (1996 [1557]), who described the desecration of the wak'a at Huamachuco, illustrate how sacred architectural structures that usually accommodated religious idols and ritual activities were venerated and identified as wak'as.

Over time, more information on central Andean practices was collected by early writers indicating that wak'as could also include objects, places, springs, caves, and so on, in the vicinity of a settlement and the generative landscape surrounding it. As described by Sabine MacCormack (1991:146), ". . . the plains, and the mountains, the sky and the waters were both the theatre and the dramatis personae of divine action." The challenge for early Christian missionaries is clearly revealed in the following observation made by Arriaga, one of the better-known extirpators of idolatry: "Some of the huacas are hills and high places which time cannot consume" (Arriaga 1968 [1621]:115). Wak'as can therefore be understood to include shrines, tombs, and even houses that were set within a sacred geography.

The early descriptions of two types of Inka wak'a architecture—temple and tomb—provide the basis for a comparison between the Inka archaeological evidence and possible Wari antecedents. Beyond the recognition that a variety of both Inka temples and tombs were considered wak'as, was there more to this relationship? Descriptions of both temple and tomb wak'as often allude to above- and below-ground sacred places, which suggests that indeed there may have existed a more significant relationship between them. A concern with both vertical and horizontal as well as above- and below-ground sacred space in Andean ceremonial architecture has been noted since preceramic times; similar features are also found to characterize religious architecture in many different parts of the world.

Inka funerary monuments that are described as Inka wak'as by the chroniclers exhibit a wide assortment of shapes (Cobo 1990 [1653], chap. 18). In
part, this may relate to differences in coastal and highland burial practices and
local traditions regarding treatment of the deceased. Elites, however, may have
adopted imperial interment practices to differentiate themselves. As Cobo
noted with respect to Inka tomb architecture on the coast, these structures
sometimes had the same square plan as the houses of local *caciques* (ibid.:247).
So the house plan apparently provided a prototype for funerary wak'a, a
reminder that the life-death continuum so widely recognized in the Andes
may have been materialized in tomb architecture.

CONCEPTUALIZING WAK'A ARCHITECTURE

In this chapter I suggest that Wari wak'as and their Early Intermediate
period (EIP) predecessors, much like their later Inka counterparts, were not
static entities. Rather, they could appear in architectural form, be associated
with different ritual practices over time, and potentially shift shapes in ways
that suggest metamorphosis. In considering the genesis of Wari wak'as, I propose that the predecessors of Wari houses of worship share their circular form
with the domestic structures found on the coast and in the highlands during
the EIP (AD 1–650) and that these constitute the template for the Wari wak'a.
Both Wari and Inka temple architecture included circular walls (e.g., for Wari,
the D-shaped temples, and for the Inka, the Coricancha, special observatories,
and some storage facilities). The circular building form constituted a special-
function structure throughout the central Andes up to the time of the Spanish
conquest.

Over the past two decades, there has been a proliferation of writings on
practice theory and the hermeneutics of place that correlates with an intensified interest in sacred sites and structures (Jones 2000; Moore 2005, 2010; Soja
1996; Swenson 2012). Jones (2000) contributed early on to these debates and
emphasized that the study of structures should focus on occasions rather than
objects. Many of his interests intersect with practice theory and its applica-
tions in the social sciences.

These various approaches involve the idea that meanings are created and
derived from an array of different relational social positions or perspectives
(Bourdieu 1977; Gell 1998; Gillespie 2010; Ortner 2006; Viveiros de Castro
1998; 2004).[2] They share the view that contextual meaning is created externally
between people and places within social relations. Gell (1998) reminds us that
these relations also have an interior dimension:

Whoever imagines that the idol is conscious, thinking, intentional, etc. is attributing "mental states" to the idol which have implications, not just for the external relations between the idol and the devotee (and the form of life in which they co-participate), but for the "inner structure" of the idol, that is, that it has something *inside* it "which thinks" or "with which it thinks." The idol may not be biologically a "living thing" but, if it has "intentional psychology" attributed to it, then it has something like a spirit, a soul, an ego, lodged within it. (Gell 1998:129, emphasis in original)

This notion of interiority relates to the ongoing discussion in the Andes and Amazonia regarding animism (Descola 1992) and perspectivism (Viveiros de Castro 1998:469; see also Allen, this volume). In the South American context, these closely related concepts, which encompass ideas about shifting perspectives and alternative ontologies, are built upon years of ethnographic field research. These and more recent data raise interesting questions regarding how we might identify and interpret possible wak'as in the material remains of ancient Andean cultures.

The Amazonian literature, while varied, offers relevant case studies with potential application in the Andes. The central highland region of Ayacucho has a long history of economic engagement with the eastern lowlands. This is documented in current movements of goods and in recovered archaeological remains such as implements of *chonta* (a tropical hardwood), bows and arrows, coca leaves and other curing paraphernalia, feathers, and tropical plant and animal iconography, to name but a few examples (Bergh 2013; Isbell and Cook 2002). So interactions with lowland peoples occurred in the past and can serve as additional sources of information regarding how neighboring groups view and materialize the sacred.

A growing number of recent ethnographic studies from rain forest, tundra, and Andean contexts (Brightman et al. 2012) suggest that humans exist in the world by engaging in different often nuanced views of the body. Vilaça has suggested that in Amazonia "what are objectified are specific human bodies" (Vilaça 2005:452). A more expanded view implies that "humanity is not restricted to what we conceive as human beings: animal and spirits may also be human, which means that humanity is above all a position to be continually defined (ibid.:448)." Furthermore, in Amazonia it is widely accepted that one cannot speak of the body without speaking, for lack of a better term, of the soul (Conklin 1996:375) and that there are distinct ways of expressing this relationship, e.g., between body and soul (Vilaça 2005:452–53).

Views of the world are closely related to context, to activities engaged in, and to the types of relations humans have with other humans and nonhumans at particular moments in time. Among the Wari of Amazonia, with whom Vilaça works, the understanding "... seems to be not that the soul gives [the] body feelings, thoughts and consciousness, but that it gives it *instability*" (ibid.:453, emphasis in original). The body is thus not the same everywhere. Pollock (1996:320) and others have critiqued the universalizing tendency that underlies much of the embodiment literature, which takes the body as "the locus of authentic experience whose 'embodied' reality is supposedly hidden or distorted by such cultural practices as mind/body dualism" (quoted in Vilaça 2005:447). As Vilaça notes,

> ... a rock only becomes an object of interest when it is perceived by someone as a spirit or as a tool, bench, or other object associated with a human.... one myth tells how the baskets made by women in the past walked by themselves, carrying the heavy loads of maize by hopping along forest trails. One day two women were walking in front of a group of these animated baskets when one of the women turned around and, startled by the comical way the baskets walked, burst out laughing. Deeply offended, the baskets resolved never again to act in such an extraordinary way. (Vilaça 2005:456)

For the Amazonian Wari, the baskets had lost their soul. In brief, it is the observer's way of perceiving an activity that identifies the appearance of a body or soul: "... when its activity is ordinary, it is said to be a body; when extraordinary [involving what appears from his/her point of view as a transformation], it is called soul" (Vilaça 2005:454).

A metamorphosis, or what Praet (2009) refers to as "shape-shifting," can occur then when humans and spirits cease to be seen as distinct categories and instead are seen as equivalents—hence the idea that they can assume different shapes. Ritual practitioners have the capacity to move between different ways of "being." As Urton (1985:270–72) has suggested, Bear Dancers in the Andes dress up as spectacled bears not to represent or symbolize them but rather to become them. In addition, as Erikson (2003:130) observes, "indigenous Amazonia appears to be characterized by its refusal to envisage both individual and collective identities as fixed entities. Boundaries between ethnic groups and even between different biological species are particularly unstable." Vilaça (2005:458) discusses the volatility and relational aspects of what she calls the "split character of the body," which has recently received increasing attention (see also Taylor 1998). Although some of these comments concern contemporary Amazonian peoples, there are interesting parallels that can be drawn with the Andes both present and past (see also Allen, this volume).

The concept of metamorphosis may help explain the perceived mutability of people, things, and figures in pre-Columbian Andean art, and even the frequency with which objects and, in our case, buildings were ritually killed, resurfaced, or rebuilt (see also Alberti and Marshall 2009; Descola 2005:300; MacCormack 1991:289; Viveiros de Castro 2002:72–88). How might these types of perceptions be materially expressed (Harris and Robb 2012:670)? We have seen that many different things can be wak'as, hence wak'as can have different bodies. In this vein, I consider ancient temples, tombs, and architectural models as examples of concrete and materialized wak'as. Like idols and other nonhuman beings, buildings can also be considered to possess personhood and have subjectivity.

Can an object in the shape of a building and decorated with human features, such as eyes and mouth, have agency? We may not know if the religious built forms discussed in the following pages have agentive potential because today only shamans and ritual specialists have the ability to see souls in specific nonhuman objects (Vilaça 2005:456). Yet, as simple as this reasoning may be, the observable differences that distinguish a building that is just a building from one with human-like subjectivity may provide at least one possible avenue worth exploring.[3]

These concerns guide the suggestion that the Wari of the Middle Horizon materialized the sacred in a number of observable ways. One was to attribute human characteristics to temples, tombs, and certain objects. Shrines and tombs, especially collective tombs, provide for emplacement, while portable objects (e.g., idols) may have served in a variety of other ways (see McEwan, this volume). These were sacred places and things with agency; as wak'as, they may have been associated with the performance of a variety of ritual activities and continued to be so well after the fall of the Wari Empire.

Architects have long recognized how monumental architecture can serve as a vehicle for transforming human experience (see Jones 2000; Moore 2005). The kind of transformation and metamorphosis that I wish to focus attention on here is of a specific, far less tangible sort. Take the facade of a miniature replica of a building, for instance, with two windows and a door positioned to resemble a human face. A western mind set would perceive the miniature as standing for something else, e.g., its full-sized counterpart. Another example might be painted figures or anthropomorphic figurines that exhibit otherworldly features or combine attributes of several species. In the West we typically seek to identify and classify these objects and images. We give them names and search for their meaning in myth or folklore. But the miniature house and the anthropomorphic figurine, if examined from the point of view expressed in Amerindian ethnographies, might be better understood as active expressions of transformation or metamorphosis—as transitions from one state of being, or body, to another.

While miniatures, as opposed to full-scale architecture, are more frequently discussed as containing life-engendering qualities in the Andes, it may be fruitful to entertain the concept that large-scale structures such as temples, tombs, and even houses also contained transformative and possibly generative characteristics. We might therefore suggest the idea that wak'as could have provided settings for the transformation of human experience, in addition to (potentially) being viewed as animate, nonhuman participants. While it is admittedly difficult to identify such functions or attributes in the archaeological record, it offers an alternative perspective that may widen our understanding of these ancient monuments.

A good example of such treatment in the Andes is again found in the miniature objects that are frequently reported upon ethnographically and described as possessing a generative principle (e. g., Flores Ochoa 1977:218). Such objects are sometime referred to as *inqa,* which, according to Arguedas (1956:74), means "emperor," and elsewhere have been referred to as "the original model[s] of every being" (Allen 1997:78). So miniatures, models, icons, and images are not just archetypes but may also actually embody and engender the origins of well-being, fecundity, vitality, and life (ibid.:77–79). Revered ancestors and their places of rest were also considered to have generative qualities, so these different domains appear to be intimately linked.

In what follows, the ideas presented above are used as a backdrop to discuss several examples of ancient portable objects and their full-scale counterparts from the Middle Horizon as wak'as.

At Conchopata, an important Wari site located within the urban limits of the modern city of Ayacucho (Ochatoma and Cabrera 2010), fragments of an unusual architectural model were recovered within a disturbed tomb at the rear of a residence in what is now recognized as a common house burial pattern (Figure 10.1). This piece may represent a shrine, a mortuary tower that housed the ancestors (e.g., *chullpa*), or a dwelling surrounded by a wall. At present there are no known Wari buildings in the form exhibited by this miniature model. The front and back facades of the miniature are strongly reminiscent of the familiar aboveground chullpas that dominated northern and southern highland landscapes from the early first millennium AD to Inka times.

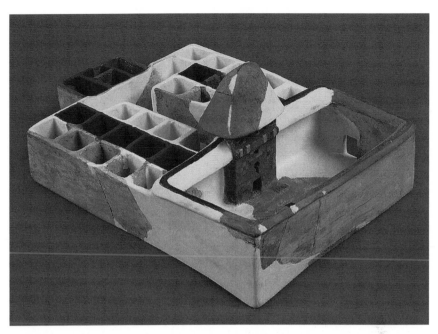

FIGURE 10.1. *Wari ceramic model excavated in a looted cylindrical cist tomb that had originally been capped at the site of Conchopata in Ayacucho, Peru (photograph courtesy of Daniel Giannoni).*

When we compare this object with an earlier Warpa effigy vessel (Figure 10.2) from the EIP, we see that the architectural models share many features in common including a doorway and two windows or niches arranged to form a human face. On the foreground at the base of the tower facing the courtyard, one notices a foot was delicately modeled and incised giving the structure even more of a human-like character (the other foot was missing and is not part of the reconstruction). Humanizing a stone or adobe building in this manner is an ancient tradition in the Andes. Although chullpas are not common in the central highlands during the Wari Middle Horizon, they are more frequent in the north-central region of the Andes (Herrera 2007:169–71). The architectural model from Conchopata shares features in common with these ancestor houses that become popular again during post-Wari times in the southern altiplano.

Curiously, the human facial features visible on the Wari period architectural model excavated at Conchopata can also seen on an extraordinary tunic dating to the early Tiwanaku period (ca. AD 200–400) (Young-Sánchez 2004; Figure

FIGURE 10.2. *Warpa effigy vessel with various figures and two well-preserved towers similar to the Wari model in Figure 10.1. Note that the door, windows, and paint on the towers have human-like facial features (photograph by author).*

10.3a and b). At the top center of the tunic on either side of the neck slit are two buildings symmetrically positioned as mirror images of one another. Each structure is rotated on its axis horizontally so that only half of the building is visible from the front. The symmetry was potentially interrupted when the garment was worn and a person's head would have emerged between the two buildings, thus emphasizing both duality and tripartition with the individual wearing the tunic appearing dominant over the two halves.

A detailed image of one of the multi-storied structures depicted on the tunic (Figure 10.3b) reveals two flanking profile figures with staffs running toward the building. Both structures exhibit human-like facial features (e.g., the windows as eyes, the door as mouth) that closely resemble those seen on the much later architectural model mentioned above. The band with multi-colored,

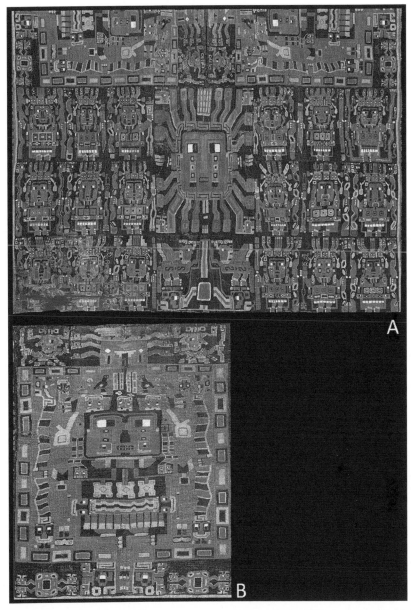

FIGURE 10.3. *Early Tiwanaku woven tunic displaying the Staff Deity iconography: (a) eighteen different front-facing, staff-bearing figures flank either side of a large, elevated rayed head; (b) two similar shoulder panels mirror one another on the tunic shoulder (photographs courtesy of the Denver Art Museum).*

nested rectangles forms a perimeter, perhaps a wall, within which appears a full-bodied Staff Deity. This perimeter band or wall terminates in an opening at the bottom where three small feet can be seen as though signaling motion through a passageway. The opening is flanked by two profile heads that face outward toward the sides of the tunic. Such symbols may have conferred a plurality of meanings that enhanced the agentive potential of these objects as embodied personalities—whether human or nonhuman—in the world. I go on to propose that these artifacts represent fertile ground for the interpretation of pre-Inka wak'as both in miniature and in their larger-scale architectural equivalents.

Full-scale wak'as in architectural form can be recognized as sacred places because they are actualized through ritual practice. Built religious forms, which centralize experience, may reveal the remains of ritual activity in below-floor caches, in niches, as burnt substances, and so on. This is how we most often materially discern the sacred archaeologically. In the Wari context, I propose that circular buildings that contained the sacred remains of ritual offerings, sacred stones, human sacrifice, and other nondomestic remains functioned as wak'as. While they may not share the human features associated with the aforementioned portable items, their architectural history and contents reveal various ritual properties that link the living with the dead and regeneration. These structures faced open plazas where onlookers could view staged ritual performances. Thus I argue that these specific agentive objects and structures exhibit the properties of ancient wak'as. Such structures may also have served to bring folk religion into contexts where ritual protocol and practice could be more easily appropriated by a centralized political apparatus, perhaps ushering in the use of such buildings as a standard Wari wak'a throughout the empire.

FROM INKA TO WARI WAK'AS

When political landscapes change and expansive states or empires arise, as in the case of the Inka and the Wari, they leave behind monuments and material remains that bear their signature. Under these circumstances, although folk religious practices may continue (if somewhat disguised or altered), we often see the state sanctioning particular religious practices through the construction of large temples and mortuary monuments. It is often the case, too, that certain existing sacred places come to be favored over others. While definitions of wak'a are discussed elsewhere in this volume, it is worth including a few additional observations and examples here in an attempt to reflect upon Wari practices in light of Inkaic concepts of the sacred.

Can we trace any commonalities between early colonial descriptions of Inka wak'as and the archaeological evidence of much earlier shrines that date to the Middle Horizon? Colonial descriptions provide a kaleidoscopic view of the contact period through a Christian and Iberian lens. While most of the ethnohistoric accounts are Cuzco-centric, a few relate specifically to the extirpation of idolatries and provide glimpses into late pre-Columbian religious practices in areas beyond the Inka capital. This is especially true for the countryside and areas that were formerly under earlier state governments such as the central highland valley of Ayacucho where the remains of the Middle Horizon capital of Wari are located. In addition to the filtering of Inkaic politics, economics, and religion through a European lens, the 400-year gap between the Wari and Inka empires also poses significant challenges. If we do not consider ethnographic and colonial sources, then the understanding of Wari sacred architecture and objects is confined to direct archaeological associations. But I suggest, as have others, that many Andean literary sources and ethnographies, if studied with care, allow us to piece together a richer understanding of Andean views that in turn have a direct bearing on our insights into the more distant past.

Juan de Santa Cruz Pachacutic Yamqui (1950 [1613]:41) drew the Temple of the Sun in Cuzco as a house/structure within which he sketched a map of the universe. The simple roofed structure depicted in this drawing could describe any number of Andean architectural entities, from a humble dwelling to the highest temple of the land. There are many modern examples from the Andes and Amazonia indicating that the house is viewed as a microcosm of the cosmos and in many instances has clearly demarcated and gendered spaces with specific cosmological associations (e.g., Allen 1997:79; Reichel-Dolmatoff 1971:105; Gose 1991; Guss 1989:22–47; Hugh-Jones 1978; W. Isbell 1978; Palacios 1982). In most instances, we interpret the remains of a temple as a structure that encloses sacred space. Yet as suggested by Santa Cruz Pachacutic Yamqui, the house as a domestic everyday reality serves as the archetype for the temple, which for the Inka was a wak'a (e.g., Allen 1997:79; Carsten and Hugh-Jones 1995:42; Moore 2010), materially collapsing the sacred/profane divide that structures so much of western thinking.

The house archetype is found in numerous contexts in the Andes; here I mention just a few examples to illustrate my point. Architectural models are rarely found in excavated contexts. The Conchopata miniature, however, was found in association with a Wari cist tomb. The subterranean cist, covered with a capstone at ground level, with a structure erected on top, was a common intermediate elite and royal Wari mortuary feature.[4] There are several forms of

FIGURE 10.4. *D-shaped wak'a in the Cheqo Wasi sector at the capital city of Wari; the fine cut stone masonry houses of the dead were built on top of capped cist tombs (photograph by author).*

the aboveground mortuary houses associated with such stone-capped cists at Wari sites (Cook 2001; Tung and Cook 2006). The best known are the monumental structures of fine-cut stone masonry that are built atop the cist tombs. In one known instance, such an ancestor house was found inside a D-shaped structure at the capital of Wari (Cook 2001, fig. 7.5; Figure 10.4). In many cases the cist tombs are better preserved than their superstructures, which often consist only of remnant walls encircling the cist, as seen, for instance, at Batan Urqo south of Cuzco. Other aboveground structures appear as miniature mortuary houses in the corners of residences, which abut the wall in such a way as to create small enclosed chambers with doorways that sheltered the capped cists inside (Isbell and Cook 2002, fig. 9.23).[5]

There are also other types of markers indicating the presence of graves within residences where surface features like capstones are absent. Such tombs may simply be indicated by a slightly elevated portion of the plaster floor in the corners of interior rooms; such areas will also often have a small bench, low platform, or low perimeter wall associated as well. Some of the densest groupings of Wari stone-capped, cylindrical cists have been found inside the dwellings excavated at Conchopata. With few exceptions (see Isbell and Cook 2002), the capstones of these cist tombs were removable to allow for reentry, and the repeated addition of human remains and offerings was evident in many. Some of the underground mortuary areas at Conchopata were found to comprise complex beehive catacombs not unlike their elite counterparts in the city of Wari. My main point here is that people were often either buried at home in residential structures, or within chullpa-style structures that were nonetheless also house-like, suggesting that such dwellings were considered the appropriate place of repose for both the living and the dead.

As discussed above, the early Tiwanaku period textile in Figure 10.3 also displays a multi-storied, chullpa-like structure. In front of this structure and inside of what appears to be a patio with perimeter walls is one of several images of the Staff Deity represented on this tunic. Figures with staffs are traditionally identified in the literature as deities (e.g., Isbell and Cook 1987; Menzel 1964). These so-called "deities," which I suggest may actually represent personified versions of wak'as (Cook 2012), continue as one of the principal Middle Horizon icons into later Wari times. The association between the walled patio, the multi-storied structure, and images of the Staff God strongly suggests the representation of a sacred place in woven format. Hundreds of kilometers and just as many years likely separate this textile and the Conchopata miniature architectural model discussed earlier. But their close resemblance is a reminder that an image like the Staff Deity and the chullpa-like resting places of the deceased share a permanence that seems to resurface time and again until they become historically documented as wak'as.

The preceding discussion should aid in the identification and interpretation of pre-Inkaic, Middle Horizon wak'as. Below I propose a trajectory of architectural modifications from round shrines that predate the Wari to the well-known Wari D-shaped structures. These special-function buildings appear to have been places where a variety of ritual practices occurred. The interior spaces of these structures are too confined to have accommodated more than a small number of people. In addition, it seems that the D-shaped structures may well have been open arenas that lacked roofs and had low walls (80 to 120 cm high in extant examples). Thus it is conceivable that the activities that took place inside these enclosures may have been viewed by audiences assembled in the large plazas outside and in front of these buildings. While it is not possible to fully explain why this presumably sacred architecture underwent such morphological changes, it is notable that these changes coincide with the emergence of the Wari Empire.

There are two types of civic-ceremonial buildings that are widely recognized as imperial Wari signature architecture: the orthogonal patio and gallery complex, and the D-shaped structure (Cook 2001; Isbell and McEwan 1991). A site is often identified as Wari if one or both of these types of architecture are found. Both architectural forms are suggestive of state intervention because they are known at the capital of Wari (where they are often monumental in size). The D-shaped structures never have domestic refuse associated and are, as I argue below, the pre-Inka temple wak'a exemplars.

There is strong evidence that these forms developed in the northern highlands during the EIP (Herrera 2007; Shady and Rosas 1976; Topic and Topic 1984). Herrera (2007:180) suggests that during this period, the location of "collective ceremonial architecture and tombs vis-à-vis specific rocks and mountains and other significant landscape features provides one means [of approaching] how people materialize memory, [and] generate and negotiate social identity. . . ." Shortly thereafter, during the Middle Horizon, I note a similar pattern for the Ayacucho region. Temple wak'as, houses of the living and dead, and the landscape are even more entangled pointing to an increasing concern with ritual emplacement, and the transformation of these loci into places where folk ritual practices undergo more centralized control and perhaps institutionalization.

PRE-INKA WAK'AS

The sacred architectural tradition of the Middle Horizon that culminated in the D-shaped shrines known from the capital of Wari and many other Middle Horizon sites (see Cook 2001) was not a sudden local invention of the residents of the Ayacucho Valley. Rather the ceremonial structures that make up this tradition, including their elaborate offerings, formed part of a long history of sacred architecture in the central highlands and south coast that lends support to the notion that these structures may have functioned as wak'as.[6]

EIP residential architecture is reported far less often than better-known civic-ceremonial structures of this era. While there is variation in both form and construction materials dictated by location (e.g., valley floor versus hill slopes) and available resources, EIP structures on the coast often incorporated circular floor plans for both houses and temples that sometimes involved the use of concentric walls (Paulsen 1983; Schreiber 1989:70–72; Vaughn 2009:70). Such circular floor plans are also known from the central highlands near

Ayacucho during this period (Cook 2001; Isbell 1987; Isbell and Cook 2002; Schreiber 1989). The circular temple and house plan appears to continue from the EIP through the beginning of the Wari Middle Horizon. Changes in the architectural footprint, building orientation, floor plan, associated iconography, and ritual practices seem to have occurred as the D-shaped sacred architecture replaces the circular form at some point during the eighth century AD, just as Wari begins to expand its political, economic, and ideological reach. No longer round or concentric, the later Wari D-shaped buildings emerge as modified versions of their predecessors.

Another important change during the Middle Horizon concerns the number of sacred structures found at any given site. With respect to the early circular shrines, there is usually only one per site, and it typically defines the ceremonial center of the site, as seen at the sites of Huaca del Loro, Tres Palos II, and Pacheco (Strong 1957:40) on the south coast, and in the Warpa component of the highland site of Ñawinpukyo (Leoni 2004:124–26, 633). In contrast, Middle Horizon sites typically contain two or more D-shaped structures that are the key component of the civic-ceremonial sector, as seen, for instance, at the capital of Wari, the later occupation of Ñawinpukyo, and Honco Pampa in the highlands, as well as at Cerro Baul on the far south coast (Cook 2001).

The EIP examples of ceremonial architecture with concentric walls contain a central circular structure with low walls (Leoni 2004:124–26). The later D-shaped structures also have low walls but include a flat side that often contains a doorway near the center facing onto an open area where people may have gathered to view performances taking place within. Multiple floors have been recorded within several D-shaped structures at Wari and Conchopata, testifying to their longevity and the care involved in their use and preservation (Isbell and Cook 2002; Ochatoma 2007). Excavations at the site of Conchopata suggest a change through time with respect to the kinds of materials deposited in the temples. The floor of the earliest dated temple contained modified human remains (e.g., perforated occipital bones, phalanges, and trophy heads) as well as camelid and deer offerings. Later temples evidenced multiple layers and distinct concentrations of purposefully smashed ceramic vessels consisting of large, decorated feasting urns and jars as well as miniature gold foil felines, camelid remains, and other offerings.

Various examples of multi-story ancestor houses made of cut stone are known from different sectors of the Wari capital, with one such structure literally found inside a D-shaped edifice, as seen in Figure 10.4, reinforcing the idea that the latter form may have lacked a roof (Benavides 1991, figs. 2, 3; Gonzalez Carré et al. 1999). Another clue as to the ceremonial significance of the D-shaped structures is that many appear to have been formally closed via a termination ritual involving offerings of various kinds, after which they were permanently sealed. The lack of domestic household refuse and the presence of offerings inside and around these structures further confirm their special function.

In sum, the transition from the EIP to early Wari times involved a modest yet significant change in the principal form of sacred architecture from a circular shape based on EIP domestic structures to a new and innovative D-shaped form.

CIRCULAR WAK'AS IN THE NASCA VALLEY

Poorly preserved circular ceremonial structures dating to the Middle Horizon were first reported by Strong (1957:36) on the south coast of Peru at the sites of Huaca del Loro on the north bank of the Tunga (Trancas) River and at Tres Palos II on the Rio Grande in Nasca. At these sites, and several others nearby, his excavations produced Late Nasca and Middle Horizon Loro-style pottery (ibid., table 1; Paulsen 1965, 1983; Schreiber 1989). Allison Paulsen (1965:53; 1983, fig. 1b) had access to Strong's unpublished 1952 excavation field notes from the site of Huaca del Loro, and she included a detailed discussion of the circular structure that he described as built of stone with adobe mortar. Paulsen apparently also found an important reference to another circular structure of stone and adobe construction described in the unpublished field notes of Ron Olson's excavations at the site of Pacheco that were deposited at the American Museum of Natural History in New York (Menzel 1964:24 and n. 112). This suggests that "special function" circular structures on the south coast may have been more common than previously thought (Paulsen 1965:53).

Paulsen (1965, 1983) studied the pottery and architecture at the site of Huaca del Loro and concluded that the ceramics dating to Nasca phases 6, 7, and 8 corresponded to the late Warpa and early Wari phases in the highlands. The similarities in architectural form and stone construction techniques between the coastal and highland Warpa communities were cited as further support for this interpretation. Paulsen concluded that Huaca del Loro was a coastal Warpa colony. Schreiber (1989) later challenged this interpretation on the basis of her settlement pattern survey data, which revealed a long history of round dwellings both in the Nasca Valley and the adjacent highlands that significantly predated the construction of Huaca del Loro. These data obviated the need to posit that an intrusive highland population had migrated to the coast.

Nonetheless, the highland construction style of the Huaca del Loro circular temple and its unique form in the midst of rectilinear architecture is best known in the highlands. Tres Palos II and Pacheco, where circular structures had been previously detected, were either never excavated or are now destroyed, and it remains to be seen if such temples occur at other south coast sites. All this argues in favor of highland influence, but the ceramic styles leave some unanswered questions (Leoni 2004; Nishizawa 2011). While there are few radiocarbon dates for sites with Huaca del Loro–style ceramics (Strong [1957, table 4] published dates of AD 755 ± 80 to 1055 ± 70), the most recent C14 determinations indicate a range of AD 470–620 for Nasca phases 6 and 7 (equivalent to the Warpa phase in Ayacucho) and AD 660–790 for Loro Middle Horizon–style materials (Unkel et al. 2012:2299).

At Huaca del Loro, there was one circular temple with an east-facing doorway. It had a plastered, red-painted floor and several small rooms with ramps that angled off the main structure (Paulsen 1965, 1983, fig. 4, from Rose Solecki's 1952 field notes; Schreiber 1989, fig. 4). Offerings that were recovered within the temple included mummified macaws, llamas, guinea pigs, exotic bird feathers, unworked monoliths, and pregnant female figurines (Strong 1957:36–39). The innovative circular temple found at Huaca del Loro is not known at earlier Nasca sites in the region, and I suggest that its shape echoes the common round house form of the EIP.

The three principal sites reported on by Strong and Olson provide important points of comparison because there has since been disagreement regarding whether the circular so-called temples uncovered here were natural local outgrowths of the post-Nasca era, or whether these structures were associated with highland Warpa colonies that immigrated to the coast. Recent excavations in the Ayacucho Valley show that the form and construction of the circular ceremonial structures found at the coastal sites bear close resemblance to the circular ceremonial structures in the highlands. It is unlikely, however, that the debate regarding the direction of influence will be resolved without additional radiocarbon dates and ceramic analysis. Nonetheless, it seems reasonable to assume that there was ongoing interaction between the central highlands and the south coast region throughout the period of interest.

CIRCULAR WAK'AS IN THE AYACUCHO VALLEY

In the capital city of Wari, only two circular structures have been reported to date (Isbell et al. 1991), and excavators indicate that they were used for the processing and storage of semiprecious greenstone artifacts. Circular and

D-shaped structures have also been documented at the sites of Ñawinpukyo (Leoni 2000, 2004) and Conchopata in the Ayacucho Valley (Isbell and Cook 2002; Ochatoma 2007). As indicated above, excavations at these sites reveal temporal changes in the form and contents of these ceremonial buildings.

The hilltop site of Ñawinpukyo, which commands a breathtaking view of the valley below, contains one of the earliest circular ceremonial buildings in the Ayacucho basin (late fifth to early sixth centuries AD). While seemingly a prototype of things to come, this ceremonial structure lacks a perimeter wall and in this respect differs from later forms. Excavations produced evidence of suprahousehold feasting but no basic domestic refuse. The general design of the Ñawinpukyo ceremonial structure bears close resemblance to the coastal shrines as well as to structures found at the site of Conchopata located 5 km away.

Ñawinpukyo's ceremonial space, dating to the late Warpa period, AD 425–537 (1σ, calibrated) or AD 408–560 (2σ, calibrated) (Leoni 2004:124–26, 153–65, 633), is the earliest candidate for a wak'a in the Ayacucho Valley. The interior of the circular ceremonial structure found here contains two low concentric walls. These do not display the same amount of care evidenced in the construction of the building's outer wall, which may have been added at a later date because the masonry style employed (double-faced stone walls with rubble fill) is a Wari construction technique also seen in later D-shaped structures. The interior walls are thinner and composed of either a single row of stones set in mortar or two parallel horizontal rows of stones (Leoni 2004:154). The exterior circular wall has one doorway, a small opening 30 cm in width that faces north toward Rasuwilka, which is considered the most sacred snow-capped peak in the valley (Anders 1986; B. J. Isbell 1978). On the slopes below Ñawinpukyo's main ceremonial space, two D-shaped structures pertaining to the later Wari occupation have been identified, though only one has been excavated (see Cook 2001).

Below Ñawinpukyo is the site of Conchopata, which is situated on a large flat expanse. Occupation of this site spans the period from Early Intermediate Warpa times to the decline of the Wari Empire, ca. AD 1000 (Isbell and Cook 2002). Given the length of occupation, it is possible to trace the transition from Warpa to Wari civic-ceremonial architecture at the site. Two circular buildings (Figure 10.5) constitute the earliest ceremonial architecture at the site. These appear to be superseded later in time by architectural modifications that culminate in the final D-shaped ceremonial structures that are found here and at sites throughout the Wari Empire, as discussed below.

At Conchopata the larger and better preserved of the two earlier circular temples is quite extraordinary. It has a formal entrance facing northwest

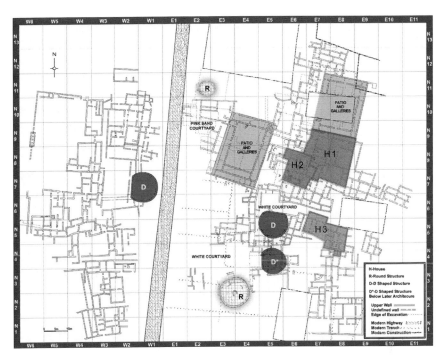

Figure 10.5. *Map of Conchopata indicating early circular temples ("R") and later D-shaped structures ("D") (drawing by Patricia Wolff).*

(Figure 10.6) and a white plastered floor made of diatomaceous earth that was laid prior to the construction of most of the other architecture found at the site. At the entrance to the structure are several steps that descend into a sunken interior court with smaller rooms walled off on either side of the entrance. Excavations in the southeastern quadrant of the floor revealed discrete piles of human cranial and phalange fragments, while the southwestern quadrant contained three parallel rows of small pits, some of which contained llama offerings. The structure was eventually filled and sealed, and no later architecture was constructed atop this location.

At the center of this building in the middle of the interior sunken court is a low circular stone wall (40 cm high) enclosing a central cylindrical pit or cist (1.5 m in diameter) that was excavated into bedrock. The pit contained some stratified human bone fragments. Also within the pit, situated in a bed of sand, were eight carefully placed modified boulders and small stones, four of which were standing upright in much the same fashion as later Inka huancas (Figure 10.7) (see also Chase, McEwan, Meddens, this volume; Meddens et al. 2010;

FIGURE 10.6. *Three-dimensional site reconstruction at Conchopata with circular wak'a (EA-143) in the foreground showing entrance and central cylindrical cist containing sacred stones (produced and rendered by Amirali Abadi, School of Architecture, Catholic University of America).*

Pérez and Amorín 2011:174–76). Recall here Zarate's comment, cited above, in which he observes that the Inka venerated stones housed in temples called *guacas*. While the central cist feature in this structure is the only known one of its kind, it does appear later in time at the site when family members are buried inside their dwellings, a topic I return to below.

D-SHAPED WAK'AS IN THE AYACUCHO VALLEY

The next temple or wak'a to be built at Conchopata was situated 10m northeast of the circular structure just discussed. It marks a departure from the circular morphology and introduces the innovative D-shaped building design. However, unlike later manifestations, this structure had a sunken interior court like its immediate predecessor. The semicircular structure with one flat side was to be maintained as the principal ceremonial architectural form for centuries to come. The early D-shaped building at Conchopata may have been in use at least partially contemporaneously with the circular temples at

FIGURE 10.7. *Carefully laid sacred stones at the base of the central cylindrical cist in the circular wak'a EA-143 (photograph by author).*

the site (Ketteman 2002). In lieu of a cylindrical cist, however, this structure had two fire pits in its center. These were filled with stacked pieces of wood arranged in a lattice pattern that had been burned. Eventually this building was intentionally closed and filled. The circumstances that prompted its abandonment remain unresolved. Shortly after it was decommissioned, however, at least two new D-shaped edifices were built that continued in use until the site of Conchopata ceased to be occupied.

The new D-shaped structures conform closely to one another in terms of size and general characteristics. The interiors of these structures mostly contained smashed votive ceramics with elaborate iconography and llama sacrifices. One structure had a single subfloor cache containing human trophy heads (Tung 2008). In the center of the floor of this structure (Figure 10.5: D structure with flat side facing north), an upright cone-shaped artifact was recovered that excavators interpreted as a gnomon (Ochatoma 2007; Ochatoma and Cabrera 2001a, 2001b; see also Meddens et al. 2010).

I interpret the circular and D-shaped Middle Horizon ceremonial structures found at Conchopata, both of which are enclosed within perimeter walls, as Wari wak'as. Like a (near) circle in a square, the surrounding perimeter wall frames the D-shaped building and sets it apart from other structures. Small rectangular rooms are often found in the space between the perimeter wall and the D-shaped building. These rooms contained vessels with food remains and possibly other ritual items. Subfloor canals have also been identified in some rooms, perhaps related to the circulation of ritual fluids into and out of the interior ceremonial spaces. The D-shaped wak'as can thus be understood as enclosed places. The structures also generally exhibit plastered masonry walls that often retain traces of paint. The thickness of the walls, which ranges from 0.7 to 1.7 m, significantly exceeds that of other buildings. Some of the ceremonial circular and D-shaped structures are more ornate than others and may contain large interior wall niches; the best examples of these are found at the sites of Wari and Cerro Baul.

The D-shaped structures at Wari proper are exceptional on many levels: they are fairly numerous, found in many different sectors of the site, are very finely constructed, and exhibit a considerable degree of variation in internal morphology (González Carré et al. 1999). More than nine different D-shaped structures have been recorded at this site, most of which have large niches in the interior walls. Recent excavations at Wari have revealed a stone gnomon found near the center of the largest D-shaped temple in the Vegachayoq sector of the capital city (Ochatoma and Cabrera 2012). This compares to the find made in Conchopata noted above (Figure 10.7; Ochatoma and Cabrera 2002, fig. 8.3b). So offerings and shadow-casting objects like gnomons appear to take center stage in the Wari D-shaped wak'as.

The unusual practice of constructing cist tombs of cut stone masonry inside the D-shaped structures only occurs at Wari in the Cheqo Wasi sector—the elite mortuary zone at the site. This area contains one D-shaped edifice with five multi-storied elite ancestor funerary houses inside the structure.[7] These elaborate houses of the dead at Wari, especially those contained within D-shaped structures, bear close resemblance to the architectural model recovered at Conchopata (Figure 10.1).

D-shaped structures appear both at the capital and many other major Wari sites, suggesting there was a statewide design for Wari sacred/mortuary architecture. Important features of this architecture include: (1) monumentality; (2) restricted access; (3) association with highly decorative devotional objects bearing figural iconography; (4) use of unroofed spaces (suggesting possible observatory functions); (5) interior niches and mural painting; (6) evidence of animal and human sacrifice; (7) evidence of offerings, including semiprecious stone figurines and shell ornaments; and (8) a complete lack of domestic debris.

Wari wak'as may have taken many forms, but the EIP round dwellings that the coastal shrines emulated seemed to resonate most in the highlands. As the earliest examples of their kind, the circular coastal temples may have influenced the new Wari state temple design. The rituals associated with the Wari D-shaped temples involved specific types of offerings that were distinct from the sacrifices associated with the earlier circular shrines. The form underscores the continuous use of round and later D-shaped temple architecture, though changes in contents and offerings signal possible changes in ritual practices relating to the rise of Wari Empire.

WAK'A ARCHITECTURE: D-SHAPED
STRUCTURES AND ANCESTOR HOUSES

In the Wari heartland at the site of Conchopata, the use of a central cylindrical cist in a wak'a interior is only known to occur in the earliest wak'a structures; it reappears, however, in the context of elite Wari burials at the capital and elsewhere (Isbell and Cook 2002; Tung and Cook 2006). What follows is a brief description of the innovative use of the capped cylindrical cist as an elite tomb type found inside certain multi-generational residences—many of which appear to have pertained to expert Wari potters—at the site of Conchopata. The new practice of burying deceased kin inside the home likely held multiple meanings, but some of the significance no doubt related to the potential agency of the ancestors as contributors to fecundity, as transmitters of technical knowledge, and as containers of vitality. Keeping dead kin in one's house assures that they remain a part of and continue to contribute to the well-being of the living. Perhaps this new mortuary pattern was intended to maintain a memory of the significance of the early circular temple. Even if specific knowledge about the old temple eventually faded, the values associated with the original cylindrical cist may have been continued inside individual residences at the site.

The domestic unit at Conchopata consisted of a patio around which were organized a series of rooms for sleeping, cooking, and craft production (Blacker and Cook 2006; Figures 10.8a and 10.8b). Room interiors often had benches of varying sizes that projected from walls. These created work areas and possible seating. The domestic unit often contained a votive room with devotional objects and offerings located next to or near the multiple cylindrical cist burials. This area of the residential unit has been referred to as the mausoleum. Multiple remodeling events were detected in the mausoleum areas of many residences in plaster layering and wall additions where burials would generally have been located.

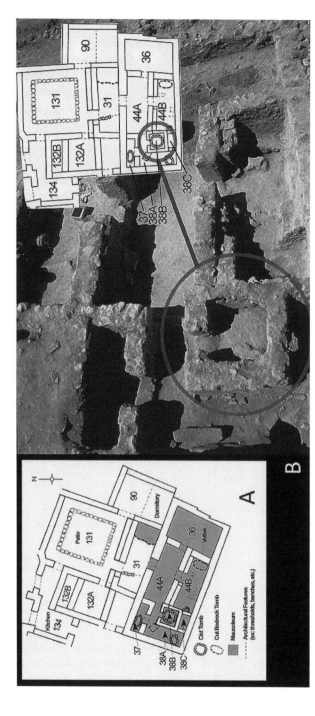

FIGURE 10.8. *Conchopata multi-generational house: (a) plan view of structures and features (drawing by Patricia Wolff); (b) mortuary room (mausoleum) and cylindrical capped cist burials at the back of the house; parts of the architectural model seen in Figure 10.1 were recovered in Room 38B (photograph by William H. Isbell, drawing by Patricia Wolff).*

As burials were intended to be reentered, the cylindrical cists were provided with a removable capstone that sealed the contents. Cists were found to contain human remains, ceramics, *Spondylus*, miniature carved greenstone objects, and, in one case, the architectural model discussed above. Offerings could also be made through a hole carved into the edge of the capping stone, a common feature observed in various Wari mortuary contexts.

Outside of the mausoleum area, simpler subfloor burials were also found in the corners of rooms inside domestic units. Such graves mainly contained women and children. Although many of the corner burials had been previously looted, their location was clearly marked by the slightly elevated molded floors. Some of these corner burial vaults had been prepared but apparently never used, suggesting that they were created late in the history of the site.

The site of Conchopata was characterized by dense, agglutinated architecture that was modified over time, making it difficult to define individual households. The multi-generational houses described above were identified based on both use and circulation patterns. These structures exhibited various additions, sealed doorways, and subdivisions and reworkings of interior spaces. Nonetheless, the use of space and the connections between rooms revealed that we were dealing with self-contained house compounds that had been used and remodeled over many generations.

In these multi-generational residences, many of the reenterable tombs had been looted but still contained identifiable remains of young adult men, women, and, in one case, a child (Tiffiny Tung, personal communication, 2013). Many of the simpler corner burials as well as the larger subfloor group burials contained a mix of individuals who varied in terms of age, sex, apparent vocation, and cause of death (Tung 2008, 2012; Tung and Cook 2006; Tung and Knudson 2008). In general, females were found to outnumber men by a ratio of 2:1. Children, newborns, and fetuses were also present in significant numbers, providing ample evidence of family life at the site. In sum, the traces of material practices associated with the houses at Conchopata in the form of various tomb types and spatial configurations provide insight into how closely related household members used place to materialize memory and emphasize solidarity across generations.

CONCLUDING THOUGHTS

As discussed earlier, like idols and other nonhuman beings, buildings can also be considered to possess personhood and have subjectivity. The structures with human features depicted on the Wari architectural model and the Tiwanaku tunic allude to the idea that these may have been perceived as extraordinary transformations involving the "ensoulment" of nonhuman entities (after Vilaça 2005:454). The Wari circular and D-shaped wak'as served as containers for activities that seem similar to those described for later Inka wak'as, but they lack the human characteristics featured on the portable wak'as described above. Both the circular and D-shaped building may have had additional features that are not preserved. They may also have lost their agentive qualities and been replaced by new structures over time.

Unlike the sequential construction of ritual platforms on the north coast associated with the Moche, and the many other examples of monumental architecture dating as far back as the Pre-ceramic and Initial periods, the special-function Wari structures were not continuously rebuilt in the same exact location. Although there is some evidence of long-term use (e.g., multiple floors), whatever purposes these structures served apparently required their periodic closure and the construction of new buildings in their own separate space and with their own orientation. Perhaps these structures were associated with other spatially segregated activities in which specific social groups, possibly gender- or age-based, constructed and maintained their own sacred sites or wak'as.

The first D-shaped temple at Conchopata with its sunken court and central fire pits is the only structure that was intentionally filled and rebuilt upon by later generations who constructed residences and ceramic workshops on the spot. No other ceremonial structure was treated in this manner. This structure is associated with two fire pits that are reminiscent of similar burning features known from elsewhere in the Wari Empire. It may represent a first attempt at establishing a new form of wak'a that met with local challenges it could not overcome. After all, Conchopata and Ñawinpukyo are just two of many sites with earlier Warpa occupations that had distinctive forms of ceremonial architecture (or wak'as), and the incipient new D-shaped tradition may have at first encountered resistance. The particular building in question represents a significant change in shape and ritual use from its predecessor, the circular ceremonial structure, and it was the prototype for the standard D-shaped ground plan that later became so common.

Unlike the earlier round buildings, the D-shaped structures have one flat side that could face any direction, the specific alignments possibly relating to astronomical phenomena. On rare occasions, as seen at Wari proper, multi-storied ancestor houses with capped and stone-lined mortuary cists were found inside D-shaped structures. There is, therefore, a relationship between aboveground multi-storied buildings, like the house model found at Conchopata, and the subterranean chambers within which the deceased were interred and provisioned with offerings.

We do not know whether the buildings modeled on the Warpa effigy vessel (Figure 10.2) actually represent Warpa architecture, as no such buildings have ever been identified and the piece is of unknown provenience. But the Wari period architectural model from Conchopata bears strong resemblance in form and design to the tower-like structures on the Warpa vessel, suggesting some degree of architectural continuity. The Conchopata piece was originally deposited in the family sepulcher of a multi-generational house in a capped cylindrical cist together with other offerings. The house model was therefore either part of the burial or an offering. While we have no evidence that this effigy vessel was actually intended to represent the type of multi-storied buildings erected atop the capped mortuary cists at Wari, it is similar to the above-ground chullpas known throughout the Andes in later periods.

In summary, my suggestion is that shrine forms from the Early Intermediate Period appear to imitate the circular residential structures found both on the coast and in the highlands during this period. As the Wari state coalesced during the Middle Horizon, protocols for sacred architecture did as well, as seen in the transition from round to D-shaped wak'as. The communities in all likelihood initially built and maintained both types of wak'as. Inside the D-shaped buildings a new kind of standardized votive behavior appears to have become the norm under the empire. Interference by the state in the ritual behaviors associated with D-shaped wak'as seems likely, given the changes observed in the composition of the associated assemblages (Ochatoma and Cabrera 2001a, 2001b). At the capital of Wari, the D-shaped wak'as were found to contain fancy burial chambers or ancestor houses with foundations containing one or more capped cylindrical cists that may have connected this world to that of the ancestors, much like the family sepulchers found at the back of Conchopata houses.

The following ethnohistoric description of a coastal wak'a bears some resemblance to Wari D-shaped structures and offers further support for my interpretation that these features can be construed as wak'as. Felipe de Medina's *Relación* describes the activities he witnessed at an Andean sanctuary located near Huacho on the coast to the north of Lima:

> . . . it was made in a curved manner that they called a horseshoe because it was formed in that way, and the temple lay on a small hill just to the right side of the royal road. One began the approach by walking up the hill and [before] entering the temple itself one passed through a passageway about a block

long with walls on either side made of stone and mud, well and very carefully formed. The temple also was composed of the same kind of construction as the walls of the entrance passageway. One entered the temple through different compartments and divisions. Some [entrances] served only the people from the highlands and others served only the people from the lowlands. And there are also different entrances for women [and men] . . .

. . . the idol was [made] of an extraordinary stone, and not like any from this area, rather it was brought from far away; I noted that it stood three and half varas tall and three varas wide. It has very small eyes carved into the surface and done appropriately; it also has carved into it two very large horns that twist downward in the form of canals, with a depth of about two inches, ending in the snout itself, by which they pour the blood and chicha that they offer to it in sacrifice and there they study (interpret) its [the idol's] signs. (Felipe de Medina 1904 [1650], quoted in Cummins and Mannheim 2011:16–17)[8]

The horseshoe-shaped structure referred to in this colonial description calls to mind a D-shaped form, and although many of the Wari D-shaped structures appear to have only single entranceways, some do have more than one. Medina notes that there was a quadripartite division of entrances into the Huacho shrine. Different groups that came from specific regions of the country, as well as men and women, accessed this wak'a via separate entries. Instead of one structure, the Wari apparently emphasized the presence of dual or multiple structures in close proximity to one another, possibly accommodating the kinds of ethnic, regional, or social divisions associated with the use of multiple doorways noted with respect to the Colonial period wak'a.

Remains recovered from the floor of the early circular wak'as at Conchopata, as noted above, appear to have been subdivided into distinct activity areas suggested by deposits of individual clusters of modified human occipital bone and phalanges, floor depressions or pits to accommodate camelid and related offerings, and walled areas on either side of the entrance. The Huacho sanctuary also had two carved stone canals made from nonlocal material and ending in what Medina refers to as "a snout" from which spilled offerings of blood and chicha. Last but certainly not least is the fact that there was a perimeter wall surrounding the horseshoe-shaped wak'a, a phenomenon also noted for the D-shaped structures of the Middle Horizon.

Despite the continuation of similar ritual practices concerned with the cult of the dead, the offering rituals changed over time from the EIP to the Middle Horizon as the wak'a form evolved. From its genesis as a circular building that echoed earlier residential forms, Wari ceremonial architecture progressed through a series of architectural plans that incorporated sunken courts and finally culminated in the D-shaped form. The central, cylindrical, subterranean cist bears a close resemblance to, and in many respects reaffirms Zuidema's (1980, 1982) interpretation of, the Inka *suntor uaci* in the central plaza of Cuzco as an axis mundi, e.g., a link between a *pacarina* where the founding ancestors of a community emerged into this world and the ancestral world within where humans eventually returned. It is interesting to note that the *suntor uaci* depicted by Guaman Poma (1936 [1615]: 329 [331]) is also similar in shape to the multi-storied house model from Conchopata.

The form and ritual content of the stone-capped cylindrical cists inside the multi-generational houses at Conchopata may be associated with how those occupying these dwellings renewed their connection to their ancestral origins—activities that had formerly been conducted inside the community-based, circular wak'a. Stone-capped cists were also found under monumental, multi-storied structures that have been interpreted as mortuary houses at Wari proper in nondomestic contexts.

Recent archaeological research has identified Inka platforms interpreted as *ushnus* in the department of Ayacucho (Meddens et al. 2008; Meddens, this volume; Pinos Matos 2004). At least one of these features was found to contain a deep pit, at the bottom of which investigators uncovered three carefully buried stones placed on bedrock (Meddens et al. 2008, 2010; see also McEwan, this volume). Although the Inka were well-known proponents of their own state religion, they were tolerant of local practices and required only that state deities be included in local worship. Important local idols were at times brought to the Inka capital and added to those honored by the state. But despite Inka sun worship and divine rulership, concern for the living ancestors on the part of other Andean peoples—as well as subterranean access to them—clearly remained central and ran parallel to imperial state religion. It appears then that the use of cylindrical cists continued unfettered through both the Wari and Inka empires and on into the colonial period.

ACKNOWLEDGMENTS

Many more than I can mention have contributed their thoughts and editorial comments as this piece has evolved. First, I am indebted to two great scholars who are often on my mind, Sabine MacCormack and Franklin Pease, for encouraging my initial forays into ethnohistory. Every time I search the rich array of digitized historical documents, I think of Franklin, who commenced these efforts in the early 1990s, and am saddened that he did not live to experience using them today. Thanks to all the members of the Conchopata Archaeological Project (too many to individually acknowledge here) for all these years of collaboration. Also special thanks to Margaret Young-Sánchez, of the Denver Museum of Art, for facilitating the permission to publish the early Tiwanaku textile under considerable time constraints. A number of graduate students from the School of Architecture at Catholic University helped produce the reconstruction of the archaeological site of Conchopata as part of our seminar on sacred cities. Amirali Abadi is ultimately responsible for the final product and complete rendering of the figure illustrating the circular wak'a. An unpublished earlier version of this chapter received close scrutiny and extensive feedback from Yorke Rowan, whose continued support I deeply appreciate. Patricia Wolff produced the accompanying line drawings. The gift of mindful awareness teachings that Dan Brown, my meditation teacher, shares have made writing a far less painful process. Finally, many thanks to Tammy Bray, who with great patience, attention to detail, and editorial skill made this piece what it is.

NOTES

1. "Tienen y adoran por dios a la Luna y al Sol, y quando juran, es por él y por la tierra, que ellos tienen por madre: y en lugar del sol tienen en los templos vnas piedras a quien veneran y adoran que llaman *guacas*, que es nombre de llorar, y así lloran quando en aquellos templos entran, y a estas guacas o ídolos no llegan sino los sacerdotes dellos" (Zarate 1995 [1555], chap. 11:52).

2. These concerns can also be seen in an array of disciplines beyond anthropology. For instance, social psychologist Alex Gillespie (2010:31) sees symbols as "intersubjective in the sense that they bind together meanings originating from different social positions within the field of action." By intersubjective association, he is referring to associations that entail an explicit switching of perspective.

3. Here I return to Lindsay Jones's work on the hermeneutics of sacred architecture, a detailed study meant to guide analysis of how religious built forms are designed, created, and experienced using sets of what he refers to as "ritual-architectural priorities." One of these, *architecture as orientation*, consists of three intersecting concerns to help orient our material being in the world. One involves the notion of homology (as seen in such things as miniaturized replicas). Another is the continuance of historically conventional patterns (conforming to specific rules or mytho-historic events as seen in the construction of similar structures through time and across space). The third relates to astral orientation involving the observation of celestial phenomena and time reckoning, or naked-eye astronomy.

4. The recently discovered burial of a royal Wari elite personage at Espiritu Pampa, for instance, was found interred in a stone-capped cist.

5. The one known example of this latter variety (Type 5a) was excavated at Conchopata; the surrounding architecture was not sufficiently defined to permit determination as to whether the room was actually within the residence or not.

6. Alexander Herrera (2005) discusses some interesting parallels for the north highlands.

7. Other nearby long rectangular rooms also contain possible multi-story ancestor houses.

8. "[E]l adoratorio cae en una media loma, a mano derecha del camino real; empiezase a caminar y entrar a este adoratorio por un callejón de paredes, por una y otra banda, hecho a mano de piedra y barro, bien formado y muy curioso; tiene más de una cuadra largo y se entra al adoratorio (que también está cercado y hecho de la misma pared que el callejón) por diferentes compartimientos y divisiones, unas que servía para los serranos y otros para las yunga, y para las mujeres destos hacían también diferentes entradas . . . .

"[E]l idolo era de piedra extraordinaria, y no como las de por allí sino traído de muy lejos; noté que tenia de largo tres varas media y de ancho tres, los ojos tenía muy pequeño, grabados y hecho al propósito; tenia grabados también dos cuernos muy grandes que desde arriba venían retorcidos y en forma de canales, de hondo como cuatro dedos, a rematar en el mismo hocico, por donde derramaban al sangre y chicha que le ofrecían en sacrificio y allí se dieron las señales dél. Hallé más adelante un carnerito de la tierra que llaman mamallama, por el aumento dellos . . . que juzgo de oro bajo, halló con toda esa vajilla de madera y barro y otras más que acá quedan con sus keros en que se dicen bebían y coman sus difuntos . . ." (Medina 1904 [1650]:215–16).

REFERENCES CITED

Alberti, Benjamin, and Yvonne Marshall. 2009. "Animating Archaeology: Local Theories and Conceptually Open-Ended Methodologies." *Cambridge Archaeological Journal* 19 (3): 344–56. http://dx.doi.org/10.1017/S0959774309000535.

Allen, Catherine. 1997. "When Pebbles Move Mountains." In *Creating Context in Andean Cultures*, ed. Rosaleen Howard-Malverde, 73–84. Oxford: Oxford University Press.

Anders, Martha B. 1986. "Dual Organization and Calendars Inferred from the Planned Site of Azángaro—Wari Administrative Strategies." PhD diss., Department of Anthropology, Cornell University. Ann Arbor, MI: University Microfilms.

Arguedas, José Maria. 1956. "Puquio: Una cultura en proceso de cambio." *Revista del Museo Nacional* (Lima) 25:184–232.

Arriaga, Pablo José de. 1968 [1621]. *La extirpación de la idolatría en el Pirú*. Colección de libros y documentos referentes a la historia del Perú, series 1, vol 1. Lima.

Benavides, Mario. 1991. "Cheqo Wasi, Wari." In *Huari Administrative Structure: Prehistoric Monumental Architecture and State Government*, ed. William H. Isbell and Gordon McEwan, 55–69. Washington, DC: Dumbarton Oaks.

Bergh, Susan, ed. 2013. *Wari: Lords of the Ancient Andes*. London, New York: Thames and Hudson.

Betanzos, Juan de. 1996 [1557]. *Narrative of the Incas*. Ed. and trans. Roland Hamilton and Dana Buchanan. Austin: University of Texas Press.

Blacker, Juan Carlos, and Anita G. Cook. 2006. "Wari Wasi: Defining Conchopata Houses." Paper presented at the 72nd Annual Meeting of the Society for American Archaeology, San Juan, Puerto Rico.

Bourdieu, Pierre. 1977. *Outline of a Theory of Practice*. Cambridge: Cambridge University Press. http://dx.doi.org/10.1017/CBO9780511812507.

Brightman, Marc, Vanessa Elisa Grotti, and Olga Ulturgasheva, eds. 2012. *Animism in Rainforest and Tundra: Personhood, Animals, Plants and Things in Contemporary Amazonia and Siberia*. New York: Berghahn Books.

Carsten, Janet, and Stephen Hugh-Jones. 1995. "Introduction." In *About the House: Levi-Strauss and Beyond*, ed. Janet Carsten and Stephen Hugh-Jones, 1–46. Cambridge: Cambridge University Press. http://dx.doi.org/10.1017/CBO9780511607653.001.

Cobo, Bernabé. 1990 [1653]. *Inca Religion and Customs*. Ed. and trans. Roland Hamilton. Austin: University of Texas Press.

Conklin, Beth. 1996. "Reflections on Amazonian Anthropologies of the Body." *Medical Anthropology Quarterly* 10 (3): 373–75. http://dx.doi.org/10.1525/maq.1996.10.3.02a00040.

Cook, Anita G. 2001. "Huari D-Shaped Structures, Sacrificial Offerings, and Divine Kingship." In *Ritual Sacrifice in Ancient Peru*, ed. Elizabeth Benson and Anita G. Cook, 127–63. Austin: University of Texas Press.

Cook, Anita G. 2012. "The Coming of the Staff Deity." In *Wari: Lords of the Ancient Andes*, ed. Susan Bergh, 103–22. New York: Thames and Hudson.

Cummins, Tom, and Bruce Mannheim. 2011. "The River around Us, the Stream within Us, the Traces of the Sun and Inka Kinetics." *RES* 59/60:5–19.

Descola, Philippe. 1992. "Societies of Nature and the Nature of Society." In *Conceptualizing Society*, ed. Adam Kuper, 107–26. London: Routledge.

Descola, Philippe. 2005. *Par-delà Nature et Culture*. Paris: Éditions Gallimard.

Erikson, Philippe. 2003. "Comme à toi jadis on l'a fait, fais-le moi à présent: Cycle de vie et ornamentation corporelle chez le Matis (Amazonas, Brésil)." *L'Homme* 167–68 (8): 129–52. http://dx.doi.org/10.4000/lhomme.237.

Flores Ochoa, Jorge. 1977. "Enqa, enqaychu, illa y khuya rumi." In *Pastores de la puna: Uywamichiq punarunakuna*, ed. Jorge Flores Ochoa, 211–37. Lima: Instituto de Estudios Peruanos.

Garcilaso de la Vega, "El Inca." 1966 [1609]. *Royal Commentaries of the Incas and General History of Peru. Part 1.* Trans. Harold V. Livermore. Austin: University of Texas Press.

Gell, Alfred. 1998. *Art and Agency: An Anthropological Theory.* Oxford: Oxford University Press.

Gillespie, Alex. 2010. "The Intersubjective Nature of Symbols." In *Symbolic Transformation: The Mind in Movement Through Culture and Society*, ed. Brady Wagoner, 23–37. London: Routledge.

González Carré, Enrique, Enrique Bragayrac Davila, Cirilio Vivanco Pomacanchari, Vera Tiesler Blos, and Máximo López Quispe. 1999. *El templo mayor en la ciudad de Wari: Estudios arqueológicos en Vegachyoq Moqo-Ayacucho* Ayacucho: Oficina de Investigaciónes, Laboratorio de Arqueología, Facultad de Ciencias Sociales, Universidad Nacional de San Cristóbal de Huamanga.

Gose, Peter. 1991. "House Re-thatching in an Andean Annual Cycle: Practice, Meaning and Contradiction." *American Ethnologist* 18 (1): 39–66. http://dx.doi.org/10.1525/ae .1991.18.1.02a00020.

Guamán Poma de Ayala, Felipe. 1936 [1615]. *Nueva corónica y buen gobierno. Codex péruvien illustré.* Travaux et memoires de l'Institut d'Ethnologie 23. Paris: Institut d'Ethnologie, Université de Paris.

Guss, David M. 1989. *To Weave and Sing: Art, Symbol, and Narrative in the South American Rain Forest.* Berkeley: University of California Press.

Harris, Oliver, and John Robb. 2012. "Multiple Ontologies and the Problem of the Body in History." *American Anthropologist* 114 (4): 668–79. http://dx.doi.org/10.1111 /j.1548-1433.2012.01513.x.

Herrera, Alexander. 2005. "Las kanchas circulares: Espacios de interacción social en la sierra norte del Perú." *Boletín de Arqueología PUCP* 9:233–55.

Herrera, Alexander. 2007. "Social Landscapes and Community Identity: The Social Organization of Space in the North-Central Andes." In *Defining Social Complexity: Approaches to Power and Interaction in the Archaeological Record*, ed. Sheila Kohring and Stephanie Wynne-Jones, 161–85. Oxford: Oxbow Books.

Hugh-Jones, Christine. 1978. *From the Milk River: Spatial and Temporal Processes in Northwest Amazonia.* Cambridge: Cambridge University Press.

Isbell, Billie Jean. 1978. *To Defend Ourselves: Ecology and Ritual in an Andean Village.* Prospect Heights, NY: Waveland Press.

Isbell, William H. 1978. "Cosmological Order Expressed in Prehistoric Ceremonial Centers." In *Actes du XLIIe Congrès International des Américanistes: Congrès du Centenaire* (Paris, 2–9 Septembre 1976), vol. 4, 269–97. Paris: Société des Américanistes.

Isbell, William H. 1987. "State Origins in the Ayacucho Valley, Central Highlands, Peru." In *The Origins and Development of the Andean State*, ed. Jonathan Haas, Sheila Pozorski, and Thomas Pozorski, 83–90. Cambridge: University of Cambridge Press.

Isbell, William H., Christina Brewster-Wray, and Lynda Spickard. 1991. "Architecture and Spatial Organzation at Huari." In *Huari Administrative Structure: Prehistoric Monumental Architecture and State Government*, ed. William H. Isbell and Gordon McEwan, 19–53. Washington, DC: Dumbarton Oaks.

Isbell, William H., and Anita G. Cook. 1987. "Ideological Origins of an Andean Conquest State." *Archaeology* 40 (4): 26–33.

Isbell, William H., and Anita G. Cook. 2002. "A New Perspective on Conchopata and the Andean Middle Horizon." In *Andean Archaeology II: Art, Landscape and Society*, ed. Helaine Silverman and William H. Isbell, 249–305. New York: Kluwer Academic/Plenum Publishers. http://dx.doi.org/10.1007/978-1-4615-0597-6_11.

Isbell, William H., and Gordon McEwan, eds. 1991. *Huari Administrative Structure: Prehistoric Monumental Architecture and State Government.* Washington, DC: Dumbarton Oaks.

Jones, Lindsay. 2000. *The Hermeneutics of Sacred Architecture: Experience, Interpretation, Comparison.* 2 vols. Cambridge, MA: Harvard University Press.

Ketteman, William G. 2002. "New Dates from the Huari Empire: Chronometric Dating of the Prehistoric Occupation of Conchopata, Ayacucho, Peru." Master's thesis, Department of Anthropology, State University of Binghamton, New York.

Leoni, Juan Bautista. 2000. "Reinvestigando Ñawinpukio: Nuevos aportes al estudio de la cultura Huarpa y del Periodo Intermedio Temprano en el valle de Ayacucho." *Boletín de Arqueología PUCP* 4:631–40.

Leoni, Juan Bautista. 2004. "Ritual, Place and Memory in the Construction of Community Identity: A Diachronic View from Ñawinpukyo (Ayacucho, Peru)." PhD diss., Department of Anthropology, State University of New York. Ann Arbor, MI: University Microfilms.

MacCormack, Sabine. 1991. *Religion in the Andes.* Princeton, NJ: Princeton University Press.

Meddens, Frank M., Nicholas P. Branch, Cirilio Vivanco Pomacanchari, Naomi Riddiford, and Rob Kemp. 2008. "High Altitude *Ushnu* Platforms in the

Department of Ayacucho, Peru: Structure, Ancestors and Animating Essence." In *Pre-Columbian Landscapes of Creation and Origin*, ed. John E. Staller, 315–55. New York: Springer Press. http://dx.doi.org/10.1007/978-0-387-76910-3_10.

Meddens, Frank M., Colin McEwan, and Cirilo Vivanco Pomacanchari. 2010. "Inca 'Stone Ancestors' in Context at a High Altitude Ushnu Platform." *Latin American Antiquity* 21 (2): 173–94. http://dx.doi.org/10.7183/1045-6635.21.2.173.

Medina, Felipe de. 1904 [1650]. "Relación del licenciado Felipe de Medina visitador general de los idolatrías de arzobispado de Lima, inviada al ilustrisimo y reverendismo senor arzobispo della en que en le da cuenta de las que se han descubierto en el pueblo de Huacho, donde ha comenzado a visitar desde 9 de febrero hasta 23 de marzo de 1650." In *La imprenta en Lima (1584–1824)*, vol. 1., 215–21. Santiago: Casa del Autor.

Menzel, Dorothy. 1964. "Style and Time in the Middle Horizon." *Ñawpa Pacha* 2:1–106.

Moore, Jerry D. 2005. *Cultural Landscapes in the Prehispanic Andes: Archaeologies of Place*. Gainesville: University of Florida Press.

Moore, Jerry D. 2010. "Making a Huaca: Memory and Praxis in Prehispanic Far Northern Peru." *Journal of Social Archaeology* 10 (3): 398–422. http://dx.doi.org/10.1177/1469605310381550.

Nishizawa, Hide. 2011. "Shifting Power and Prestige in the Ayacucho Valley of Peru's South Central Highlands: Materiality of Huarpa and Wari Ceramics." PhD diss., Department of Anthropology, American University, Washington, DC. Ann Arbor, MI: University Microfilms.

Ochatoma, José. 2007. *Alfareros del imperio Huari: Vida cotidiana y áreas de actividad en Conchopata*. Lima: Universidad Nacional de San Cristóbal de Huamanga Facultad de Ciencias Sociales and Gráficos de Corporación VASPA sac/CANO.

Ochatoma, José, and Martha Cabrera. 2001a. "Arquitectura y áreas de actividad en Conchopata." *Boletín de Arqueología PUCP* 4:449–88.

Ochatoma, José, and Martha Cabrera. 2001b. "Ideología religiosa y organización militar en la iconografía del área ceremonial de Conchopata." In *Wari: Arte precolombino peruano*, ed. Luis Millones, 173–211. Seville: Fundación El Monte.

Ochatoma, José, and Martha Cabrera. 2002. "Religious Ideology and Military Organization in the Iconography of a D-shaped Ceremonial Precinct at Conchopata." In *Andean Archaeology II: Art, Landscape and Society*, ed. Helaine Silverman and William H. Isbell, 225–47. New York: Kluwer Academic/Plenum Publishers.

Ochatoma, José, and Martha Cabrera. 2010. "Los espacios del poder y el culto a los ancestros en el imperio Huari." In *Señores de los imperios del sol*, ed. Krzysztof Makowski, 129–51. Lima: Banco del Credito.

Ochatoma, José, and Martha Cabrera. 2012. "Wari: Una joya en bruto. Excavaciones arqueológicas revelan nuevos secretos del primer imperio andino." *Revista El Tejuelo* 2 (4): 24–26.

Ortner, Sherry. 2006. *Anthropology and Social Theory: Culture, Power and the Acting Subject.* Durham, NC: Duke University Press. http://dx.doi.org/10.1215/97808 22388456.

Palacios Rios, Felix. 1982. "El simbolismo de la casa." *Boletín del Instituto de Estudios Aymaras* 2 (2): 37–57.

Paulsen, Allison C. 1965. "Pottery from Huaca del Loro, South Coast of Peru." Manuscript in author's possession.

Paulsen, Allison C. 1983. "Huaca del Loro Revisited: The Nasca-Huarpa Connection." In *Investigations of the Andean Past, Papers from the First Annual Northeast Conference on Andean Archaeology and Ethnohistory,* ed. Dan Sandweiss, 98–121. Ithaca, NY: Latin American Studies Program, Cornell University.

Pérez, Ismael, and José Amorín Garibay. 2011. "Nuevas evidencias sobre la planificación urbana y elementos culturales asociados en Conchopata." *Conchopata: Revista de Arqueología* 3:167–227.

Pinos Matos, José Luis. 2004. "El ushnu inka y la organización del espacio en los principales tampus de los wamani de la sierra central del Chinchaysuyu." *Chungará* 36 (2): 303–11.

Pollock, Donald. 1996. "Personhood and Illness among the Kulina." *Medical Anthropology Quarterly* 10 (3): 319–41. http://dx.doi.org/10.1525/maq.1996.10.3 .02a00010.

Praet, Istvan. 2009. "Shamanism and Ritual in South America: An Inquiry into Amerindian Shape-shifting." *Journal of the Royal Anthropological Institute* 15 (4): 737–54. http://dx.doi.org/10.1111/j.1467-9655.2009.01582.x.

Reichel-Dolmatoff, Gerardo. 1971. *Amazonian Cosmos: The Sexual and Religious Symbolism of the Tukano Indians.* Chicago: University of Chicago Press.

Santa Cruz Pachacutic Yamqui, Joan de. 1950 [1613]. "Relación de antigüdades deste reyno del Pirú." In *Tres relaciones de antigüdades peruanas,* ed. Marcos Jiménez de la Espada, 207–81. Madrid: Impresas y Fundición de M. Tello.

Schreiber, Katharina. 1989. "On Revisiting Huaca del Loro: A Cautionary Note." *Andean Past* 2:69–79.

Shady, Ruth, and Hermilio Rosas. 1976. *Enterramientos en chullpas de Chota (Cajamarca).* Investigaciónes de Campo, no. 1. Lima: Museo de Anthropología y Arqueología.

Soja, Edward W. 1996. *Thirdspace: Journeys to Los Angeles and Other Real-and-Imagined Places.* Malden, MA: Wiley-Blackwell.

Strong, William Duncan. 1957. *Paracas, Nazca and the Tiahuanacoid Cultural Relationships in South Coastal Peru.* Memoirs of the Society for American Archaeology, no. 13; American Antiquity 22, no. 4, pt. 2. Salt Lake City, UT: Society for American Archaeology.

Swenson, Edward. 2012. "Moche Ceremonial Architecture as Thirdspace: The Politics of Place-making in the Ancient Andes." *Journal of Social Archaeology* 12 (1): 3–28. http://dx.doi.org/10.1177/1469605311426548.

Taylor, Anne-Christine. 1998. "Corps immortel, devois d'oublie: Forms humaines et trajectoires de vie chez les Achuar." In *La production du corps: Approches antropologique et historiques*, ed. Maurice Godelier and Michel Panoff, 317–38. Amsterdam: Édition des Archives Contemporaines.

Topic, Theresa Lange, and John R. Topic. 1984. *Huamachuco Archaeological Project: Preliminary Report on the Third Season June–August 1983.* Trent University Occasional Papers in Anthropology, no. 1. Peterborough, Ontario: Department of Anthropology, Trent University.

Topic, Theresa Lange, and John R. Topic. 2009. "Variation in the Practice of Prehispanic Warfare on the North Coast of Peru." In *Warfare in Cultural Context: Practice, Agency and the Archaeology of Violence*, ed. Axel Nielsen and William H. Walker, 17–55. Tucson: University of Arizona Press.

Tung, Tiffiny. 2008. "Dismembering Bodies for Display: A Bioarchaeological Study of Trophy Heads from the Wari Site of Conchopata, Peru." *American Journal of Physical Anthropology* 136 (3): 294–308. http://dx.doi.org/10.1002/ajpa.20812.

Tung, Tiffiny. 2012. *Violence, Ritual and the Wari Empire: A Social Bioarchaeology of Imperialism in the Ancient Andes.* Gainesville: University Press of Florida. http://dx.doi.org/10.5744/florida/9780813037677.001.0001.

Tung, Tiffiny, and Anita G. Cook. 2006. "Intermediate Elite Agency in the Wari Empire: The Bioarchaeological and Mortuary Evidence." In *Intermediate Elites in Pre-Columbian States and Empires*, ed. Christina Elson and Alan Covey, 68–93. Tucson: University of Arizona Press.

Tung, Tiffiny, and Kelly J. Knudson. 2008. "Social Identities and Geographical Origins of Wari Trophy Heads from Conchopata, Peru." *Current Anthropology* 49 (5): 915–25. http://dx.doi.org/10.1086/591318.

Unkel, Ingmar, Marcus Reindel, Hermann Gorbahn, Johny Isla Cuadrado, Bernd Kromer, and Volker Sossna. 2012. "A Comprehensive Numerical Chronology for the Pre-Columbian Cultures of the Palpa Valleys, South Coast of Peru." *Journal of Archaeological Science* 39 (7): 2294–303. http://dx.doi.org/10.1016/j.jas.2012.02.021.

Urton, Gary, ed. 1985. *Animal Myths and Metaphors in South America.* Salt Lake City: University of Utah Press.

Vaughn, Kevin. 2009. *The Ancient Andean Village*. Tucson: University of Arizona Press.

Vilaça, Aparecida. 2005. "Chronically Unstable Bodies: Reflections on Amazonian Corporalities." *Journal of the Royal Anthropological Institute* 11 (3): 445–64. http://dx.doi.org/10.1111/j.1467-9655.2005.00245.x.

Viveiros de Castro, Eduardo. 1998. "Cosmological Deixis and Amerindian Perspectivism." *Journal of the Royal Anthropological Institute* 4 (3): 469–88. http://dx.doi.org/10.2307/3034157.

Viveiros de Castro, Eduardo. 2002. *A Inconstância da Alma Selvagem*. São Paulo: Cosac & Naify.

Viveiros de Castro, Eduardo. 2004. "Exchanging Perspectives: The Transformation of Objects into Subjects in Amerindian Ontologies." *Common Knowledge* 10 (3): 463–84. http://dx.doi.org/10.1215/0961754X-10-3-463.

Young-Sánchez, Margaret. 2004. "Tapestry Tunic." In *Tiwanaku: Ancestors of the Inca*, ed. Margaret Young-Sánchez, 46–49. Lincoln: University of Nebraska Press.

Zarate, Agustín de. 1995 [1955]. *Historia del descubrimiento y conquista del Perú*. Lima: Pontificia Universidad Católica del Perú, Fondo Editorial.

Zuidema, R. Tom. 1980. "El ushnu." *Revista de la Universidad Complutense* 28 (117): 317–62.

Zuidema, R. Tom. 1982. "Bureaucracy and Systematic Knowledge in Andean Civilization." In *The Inca and Aztec States, 1400–1800: Anthropology and History*, ed. George A. Collier, Renato I. Rosaldo, and John D. Wirth, 419–58. New York: Academic Press.

11

Of Monoliths and Men

*Human-Lithic Encounters and
the Production of an Animistic
Ecology at Khonkho Wankane*

John W. Janusek

As enchanted as our [western] universe may
still be, it is also still ordered by a distinction of
culture and nature that is evident to virtually
no one else but ourselves.
(Sahlins 2008:88)

In 2002 I participated in an austral winter solstice ritual
at Qhunqhu Liqiliqi, a community in Jesus de Machaca
that is home to the archaeological site of Khonkho
Wankane, where I was directing archaeological research.
This solstice ritual is a relatively recent event that was
first held at the nearby site of Tiwanaku at the end of
the 1980s (Sammels 2012) and is now enacted at multiple altiplano locales considered to have a preemi-
nent precolonial past. Each local event is unique, but
Qhunqhu community members are clear that theirs is
"authentic"—the true "Aymara New Year" or Machac
Mara (Figure 11.1). Members of each of Machaca's
constituent communities, and especially political leaders and aspiring politicians, are required to attend. June
of 2002 was dead center of a national maelstrom that
ultimately brought Evo Morales, Bolivia's first self-
identified Aymara president, to power. The communities of Jesus de Machaca had positioned themselves at
the forefront of this political movement. Heated, anti-
neoliberal political discourse saturated speeches and
events at Qhunqhu's Machac Mara.

At one point, while arguing that the Aymara have
suffered centuries of subjugation at the hands of

DOI: 10.5876/9781607323181.c011

FigURE 11.1. *The opening ritual of the June solstice, or Machac Mara, at Khonkho Wankane involves a llama blood sacrifice. In these images, a llama has just been sacrificed. The animal's blood stains the ground and the stone on the right—Khonkho's Late Formative period Tata Kala monolith (photographs by author).*

outsiders, one local claimant to leadership, in the midst of a loud and heated diatribe, reached down and repeatedly slapped one of the ancient stone mono-liths that lies on the site, saying, "We are this stone, this stone is us" ("Somos esta piedra, esta piedra es nosotros"). What he said resonated and drew grand applause.

People in Qhunqhu and related communities understand stone—especially manifested in skyscraping peaks, dramatic outcrops, and carved prehispanic objects—as ancestral progenitors of their communities (Abercrombie 1998; Arnold 1992). This cosmology inscribes a political ideology of primordial ori-gins that anchors Andean communities to places such as the site of Khonkho Wankane. At the 2002 Machac Mara event, an aspiring politician applied this cosmology to a novel political context to great effect. Stone was rendered vital to native human identification and political action. While discursively addressing "outsiders," an intimate human-lithic relation was astutely con-structed and rendered politically polarizing. Similar arguments were being made in communities across the Bolivian altiplano, and less than four years later, "Evo" was inaugurated as Bolivia's first indigenous president.

This ethnographic instance demonstrates just how central stone can be to political action and ritual practice in the Andes. Several other chapters in this volume demonstrate as much (see particularly Dean, McEwan, this volume).

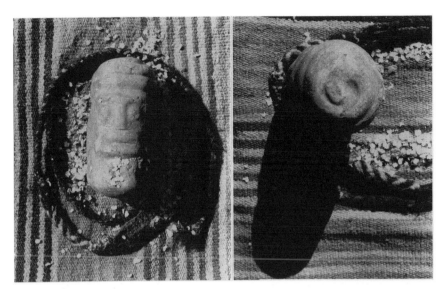

Figure 11.2. *The diminutive Turiturini monolith from Sullkatiti (photographs courtesy of Astvaldur Astvaldsson).*

Yet its power resides not just in the representational efficacy of lithic objects—whether as mediational icons or in regard to their surficial aesthetic qualities. It is rooted in the full materiality of a given stone—its hardness, texture, color, composition, mineralogy, and place of origin, among other potential qualities. The social power and value of stone is frequently afforded in specific acts of corporeal engagement during ritually charged contexts.

Ethnographic research in Sullkatiti, a community adjacent to Qhunqhu Liqiliqi, demonstrates the power of lithic materiality and the significance of human engagement with stone. According to Astvaldsson (1998), a small (15 cm tall) anthropomorphic stone head known as Turiturini is the most powerful ancient wak'a (*wak'a achachila*) in the community (Figure 11.2). Critiquing Eliade's epistemology of the sacred, Astvaldsson notes that community members defined the monolith's significance not in regard to some transcendent sacrality but by reference to the material qualities that it manifested: e.g., color, hardness, elegantly carved features, nonlocal origins, and current ritual location (hidden in a cairn on a boundary stream). One of Astvaldsson's (ibid.:209) informants beautifully inverted traditional western notions of transcendent sacrality when he stated that Turiturini must be powerful, "since it is [made of] such fine and extremely hard stone."

Turiturini invited human engagement. Its headdress creates a spiral form that informants identified as *muyumuyu*, a root for Aymara verbs that refer to coiled movement or encompassment (Bertonio 2006 [1612]:616; de Lucca 1983:316–17). Vigorous coiled movements are common to many highland Andean dances (Stobart 2006), while assembling offerings (*muxa misas*) in the altiplano typically involves adding objects by way of continuous, inwardly coiling, clockwise movements of the arm. This clockwise, coiling motion concentrates power and attracts the invoked wak'a (Astvaldsson 1998:20), while the act of undoing witchcraft frequently requires the "uncoiling" of a curse.[1] As one of Astvaldsson's informants pondered the significance of Turiturini's spiral headdress, he simultaneously made a clockwise movement with his hand. He enacted *muyumuyu* as a corporeal movement just as groups of native Andean musicians coil and uncoil as they perform community dances.

These instances cast light on the enduring telluric potency of stone and introduce my discussion of carved monoliths at the Late Formative site of Khonkho Wankane in the southern Lake Titicaca Basin of Bolivia (Figure 11.3) (Janusek et al. 2003; Janusek 2012; Smith 2009). In this chapter I focus on a few key points for understanding Khonkho Wankane as an influential center and the centrality of its monoliths in generating a particular political ecology. First, I argue that materiality was essential to the "sacrality" of Khonkho's monoliths, from their quarrying in distant mountain outcrops through their ritualized destruction and burial. Monoliths embodied the mountainous landscapes from which they were quarried and that they continued to index. Second, I argue that Khonkho's monoliths required human engagement. Recurring rituals and gatherings drew people into the intimate spaces that monoliths inhabited. In these staged spaces monoliths educated the attention (Gibson 1986) of ritual participants to key "natural" processes, celestial cycles, and landscape features. They fostered not an epiphenomenal "religious ideology," but a pragmatic ecology—if "pragmatic" via an authorized logic alternative to western "naturalism" (Descola 1996; Sahlins 2008)—that privileged the animacy of mountain peaks, stone outcrops, and their critical roles in human lives.

I implicate monoliths in the ongoing production of an ontological modality that authorized the animacy of stone and mountains and, crucially, their relational purchase on the well-being of humans, their houses, their herds, and their crops (see Allen, this volume). I term this a "modality" because at any given time, other ontological registers likely thrived in specific social contexts, even if they were not dominant in the overall scheme of the project under construction at Khonkho Wankane. And like the vision that drove Heidegger's

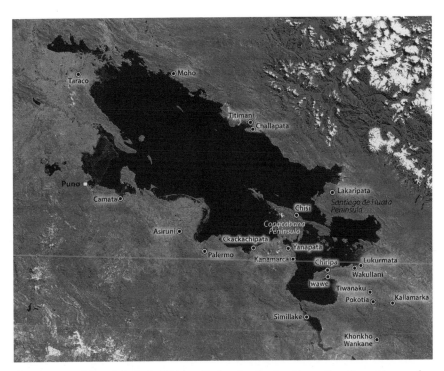

FIGURE 11.3. *Map of the Lake Titicaca Basin, showing key Formative sites with carved stone monoliths (produced by author).*

quest for the "being of Being," made manifest in his idiosyncratic "politics of the word" (Steiner 1979:15), Khonkho's animistic ecology was a political project through and through. Ongoing productions of ontological registers are everywhere steeped in worldly projects, as Weber famously demonstrates in *The Protestant Ethic.* Monoliths were dynamic agents of landscape transformation, political centralization, and urban intensification in the south-central Andes.

This chapter explicates how the fame of Khonkho's monoliths intensified over generations via cyclical gatherings at Khonkho Wankane. These recurring encounters encouraged *animating practices* that affirmed a relational ontological modality that reciprocally rendered both mountains and stones, on the one hand, and persons and communities, on the other, efficacious subjects in the world. Human attention was educated to apprehend monoliths as powerful, animate beings that condensed generative landscape features and cycles, just as these apprehending persons were simultaneously constituted as subjects in the eyes of Khonkho's monolithic beings. A mutual subjectivity of stone and flesh cast monoliths and their generative peaks as central to emergent political authority in the south-central Andes (see Dean, this volume, for similar discussion pertaining to the Inka period). These practices ultimately produced the Tiwanaku city and polity.

WAK'AS AND LATE FORMATIVE MONOLITHS
IN THE TITICACA BASIN

I first address how early prehispanic monoliths can be considered wak'as. Unlike most chapters in this volume, this one treats objects and landscapes created in a past beyond the reach of colonial documents and ethnographic narratives. I address the question by examining wak'as as we have come to understand them from late prehispanic times through the present, in comparison with the total archaeological context surrounding monoliths at Khonkho Wankane. A wak'a, Frank Salomon notes (1991:17), was "any material thing that manifested the superhuman." If no single definition completely captures the complexity of wak'as at any given historical moment (van de Guchte 1990), Salomon's succeeds in excerpting three fundamental elements: wak'as are (1) *material things* that (2) *manifest* (3) the *superhuman*. First, they are material things and not immaterial abstractions. Second, they embody; they do not "materialize" or transcribe nonmaterial abstraction into material form, as if rendering some prior transcendent Platonic essence perceptual. Third, they embody the *superhuman*, not the deified or an Eliadeian sacred. They are *superhuman* but not *supernatural*. Wak'as were not "deities" in the Judeo-Christian sense of an omnipotent but ultimately otiose being that transcends the day-to-day world; nor were they "sacred" in Durkheim's sense of religious power as transcendent collective consciousness. For Eliade, the sacred was "wholly other," a truer reality opposed to profane day-to-day experience. For Durkheim and Eliade, sacred and profane define ontologically distinct realms of being and action, the first more "real" and "real-ly existing" (Eliade 1959:20) than the realm of human life.

Andean wak'as were fully in the world. They were living material denizens of the world in which humans lived and with whom they regularly engaged. If capable of superhuman actions, wak'as were altogether person-like in their gendered personalities and hapless fallibilities, constituting dynamic agents in ever-shifting and often volatile human-landscape relations. As Salomon puts it (1991:19), "huacas are made of energized matter, like everything else, and they act within nature, not over and outside of it." In the Andes, humans routinely engage with wak'as in a relational ecology that, even today, stubbornly refuses to endorse an impermeable rift between "nature" and "culture" (Burman 2011; Cuelenaere 2009). Humans here tend to act according to an ecology that privileges an animistic ontological modality and its epistemological premises. In the world of wak'as, humans are not the only ones alive and kicking.

Yet the power of wak'as transcended the powers afforded humans and nonhuman objects in predominant western ontologies. A particular wak'a might be inordinately powerful, and its power might work toward the benefit or detriment of a person or collectivity. Wak'as were neither essentially "good," as supposedly is the singular Judeo-Christian deity, nor essentially "evil," as is its antagonistic counterpoint, Satan. The doings of wak'as had little to do with such moral essentializing. Rather wak'as were variably powerful depending on their current situations (van de Guchte 1999:155) and the political standing of the communities that identified with them and regularly provided them with offerings (Salomon 1995). The efficacy of particular wak'as was directly proportional to the intensity of the encounters in which they were engaged by the persons and communities who considered them powerful, animate beings. The relation between stone and flesh was reciprocal, but as Mauss (1967) observed, and as the Andean concept of *ayni* instructs (Mannheim 2006), balanced reciprocity hinges on ongoing chains of mutual obligations that, if unrequited or violently broken, beg vengeance. If not essentially good or evil, wak'as can bring "heaven" or "hell" upon their constituents. Via ritual offerings and blood sacrifices, Andean people seek to establish beneficial relationships with wak'as or, better yet, to place wak'as in their debt. Either way, human-wak'a encounters are intrinsically political in theory and practice.

I submit that Khonkho's monoliths were powerful material objects analogous to later Andean wak'as. I do not mean to suggest that monoliths were treated as wak'as in the same way that, for example, the Inka treated many of the powerful places and objects that constituted the *zeq'e* network of Cuzco (Bauer 1998; Zuidema 1964). I do suggest that Khonkho's monoliths and documented aspects of later wak'as shared elements in common. Commonalities include their animate materiality, their status as superhuman persons who regularly interacted with humans, and their collective precipitation of an ontology—always under construction, always at risk, and *always* a situated and potentially fleeting modality—that outlined the rules of human-nonhuman transactions and the contours of monolithic efficacy in the world. I therefore refer to Khonkho's monoliths as proto-wak'as and consider the ontology under construction at Khonkho, the ritual-political project enacted in its ceremonial spaces and surrounding landscape, an animistic political ecology (Janusek 2012).

FORMATIVE MONOLITHS IN THE LAKE TITICACA BASIN

Monolithic stelae are some of the most dramatic denizens of early monumental centers in the Lake Titicaca Basin. The practice of quarrying and carving such stelae dates to the Middle Formative period (800–200 BC) and continued up until the disintegration of the Tiwanaku polity at the end of the Middle Horizon (ca. AD 1000–1100). The peak of monolithic carving, at least as a spatially distributed practice, was the Late Formative (200 BC–AD 500). I focus on this phase here. Monolithic carving and veneration continued to thrive after Tiwanaku emerged as the primary center in the Lake Titicaca Basin after AD 500. In fact, carved monolithic beings were central to Tiwanaku's rise and infectious pan-regional influence. Monolithic carving and veneration were compelling practices that helped produce and shape the Tiwanaku phenomenon. Yet Tiwanaku's emergence corresponded with a dramatic shift in the production, materiality, and ritual significance of monoliths (Janusek 2006). This shift correlated with the hegemonic incorporation of Late Formative centers such as Khonkho and the restriction of monolithic carving to the center of Tiwanaku itself (Janusek 2008, 2012).

Given the visibility and elaboration of monolithic stelae across the Titicaca Basin, it is surprising that so little substantive work to date has focused on them. Most analyses have done the important groundwork of elaborating stylistic seriations. Most fundamentally, pre-Tiwanaku-era monoliths (and related objects, such as plaques and certain ceramic wares) have been categorized as Yayamama (Chávez and Mohr Chávez 1975) or Pajano (Browman 1972) in style. Browman has defined a series of substyles within this broad type. Arik Ohnstad and I (in press) have further refined the chronology of pre-Tiwanaku-era monolithic carving in the basin, and argue that most of it, at least in the southern sector, was conducted during the Late Formative.

Yet very few studies have focused on the *significance* of monolithic carving in the history of the basin or of the ritual roles of carved monoliths in the centers they inhabited. To an extent, this is due to a lack of robust contextual information regarding the precise spatial and temporal contexts of monoliths within early centers. I offer an interpretation of monolithic stelae at one particularly well-excavated center in the southern basin, the site of Khonkho Wankane, where I directed research from 2001 to 2010. I draw on the relatively tight temporal and spatial control we have at that site to build an argument for the centrality of monolithic stelae to ritual and political practices in the region. I suggest that they were critical for emergent urbanism and the creation of inclusive communities in the Titicaca Basin during a dynamic span of prehispanic history.

THE MONOLITHIC PRODUCTION OF AN ANIMISTIC ECOLOGY AT KHONKHO WANKANE

Khonkho Wankane is located at the southern edge of the Lake Titicaca Basin and dates to the Late Formative period. It was established as part of a major transformation in the region that by all accounts began as a relatively long dry spell accompanied by substantial sociopolitical transformations (Abbott et al. 1997; Bandy 2001). Prior Middle Formative (or Chiripa) settlements had focused on lacustrine and riverine environments. The Late Formative witnessed a major settlement shift in which many new centers focused on water sources fed by perennial mountain springs. This shift points to environmental volatility and a desire for secure access to permanent water sources. Khonkho Wankane was one of a network of new centers that, I suggest, were founded as part of an emerging regional political ecology.

The following sections summarize changing configurations of built monumental spaces at Khonkho Wankane and detail three of the four carved monoliths that occupied those spaces.[2]

KHONKHO AS EPISODIC CEREMONIAL CENTER

Khonkho Wankane comprised a cluster of natural terraces in the foothills of the Corocoro range (Figure 11.4). The monumental component of Khonkho consists of two terraces aggrandized as adjacent platforms: Wankane, the main platform, which was built first, and Putuni, built later just to its north. Both platforms were constructed during the early Late Formative (AD 50–250). Seven other terrace mounds surrounded the two main platforms, and all of them revealed surface evidence for human occupation (Lémuz 2006). Yet excavations in four of them revealed no evidence for buried human occupation (Marsh 2007). Their occupations appeared surficial and chimeric. Initial evidence thus suggested that Khonkho Wankane was a classic "empty" ceremonial center.

Deep excavations in the Wankane and Putuni platforms provided additional evidence that, I believe, explains the conundrum. Excavations in the Wankane platform indicate that its construction in 50 BC–AD 50 established Khonkho as a major center (Ohnstad 2007). They exposed an original surface beneath more than 6 m of construction fill. Excavation in the smaller and later Putuni exposed 2 m of construction fill. In this case, fill covered an early occupation zone 30–50 cm thick that was rife with evidence for human occupation (Figure 11.5). Specifically, it consisted of multiple superimposed ephemeral occupation surfaces, each laden with cultural material (small

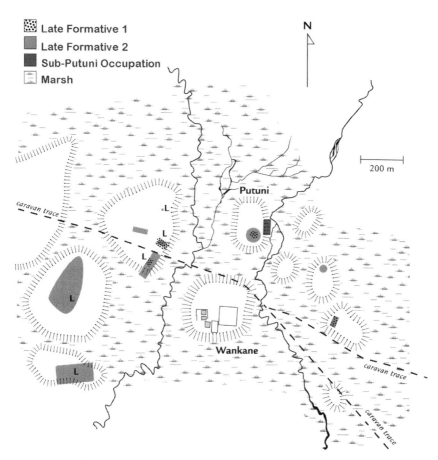

Late Formative 1
Late Formative 2
Sub-Putuni Occupation
Marsh

N

200 m

caravan trace

Putuni

L

L

L

L

Wankane

L

caravan trace

caravan trace

FIGURE 11.4. *The site of Khonkho Wankane and its marshy surrounds; the adjacent platforms Wankane and Putuni comprise Khonkho's core area (drawing by Arik Ohnstad).*

ceramic sherds, fragmented faunal remains, lithic debitage) and several with short-term hearths. Thin layers of sedimentation covered the surfaces, indicating they were periodically left to the elements. At some point after AD 100, the Putuni terrace was then converted into a monumental platform. Much like Wankane's deep fill, Putuni's platform fill covered and preserved its prior, pre-monumental, ephemeral but recurring occupations.

Seven other mounds surrounded the double-platform monumental core. While their surfaces revealed dense evidence for human activities, excavations revealed no subsurface occupations. But, then, none had been aggrandized as a constructed platform, as had Wankane and Putuni. Rather their occupation

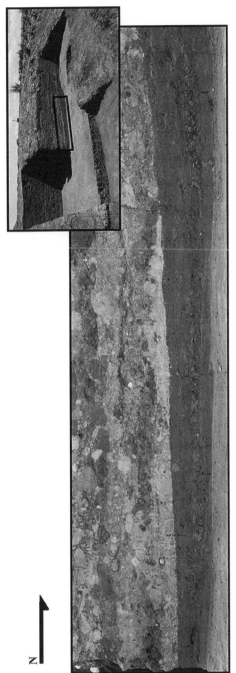

FIGURE 11.5. *View of a stratigraphic profile of the Putuni platform and detail (inset) of superimposed occupation surfaces (photographs by author).*

surfaces have been eroded for centuries by wind- and water-related erosional activities; they have been deflated. Thus they revealed no intact occupations of the sort preserved under the dense clay fill platforms of the Wankane and Putuni mounds. Their chimeric "occupations," like the ephemeral Wankane and Putuni subplatform occupations, are best construed as episodic, temporarily occupied encampments.

Khonkho Wankane was an episodic center. It was not an empty ceremonial center. It incorporated communal spaces and monumental constructions, but it also included adjacent compounds with permanently occupied residential occupations (Janusek et al. 2005; Marsh 2007, 2012; Ohnstad 2008). These occupations were limited in extent. Most permanent inhabitants likely maintained the communal and monumental components of Khonkho Wankane, conducted specialized tasks incumbent on its gatherings, and orchestrated the ritual events that were conducted at the center. Meanwhile, nonlocal residents converged on the center for periodic events, setting up camp on the mounds that surrounded the new platforms.

KHONKHO WANKANE AS BUILT PRODUCTIVE MICROENVIRONMENT

Khonkho was built to enhance the productivity of the landscape it occupied and the efficacy of the perennial water sources that fed it. As noted above, the onset of the Late Formative corresponded with shifting environmental conditions and an intensified desire for reliable fresh-water sources. Building Khonkho Wankane reciprocally produced a productive local environment fed by mountain springs (Figure 11.6). The two earthen platforms required massive quantities of soil drawn from large soil quarry pits (or "borrow pits") excavated from the surrounding landscape. These soil quarry pits simultaneously produced a low marshy landscape that remained critical to the increasing importance of the center and the events that drew regional populations to its built platforms.

Khonkho's builders developed an expertise in moving earth and creating durable constructions (Janusek and Ohnstad, in press). The Wankane and Putuni platforms were constructed of soil that had been finely selected and mixed, and then carefully laid as evenly distributed strata of fill. Soil analysis revealed that fill soils derived from the area immediately surrounding the platforms. Builders created an extensive channel that encircled the site (probably first around Wankane alone, and later around both the Wankane and Putuni mounds). This channel captured water that descended from two local springs located in the nearby Corocoro foothills, periodically creating a marshy

FIGURE 11.6. *View of Khonkho in relation to its immediate landscape. Khonkho consists of the dark shallow rises toward the middle of the photo; the lighter areas surrounding mark the anthropogenic marshy areas associated. The line leading from the place where the photograph was taken (the community water tank) to the site is a new overflow canal. Mount Sajama is in the distance (photograph by author).*

landscape immediately adjacent to the platforms. There is no indication that this landscape was created for intensive farming, for there is no evidence for raised fields, sunken basins, or agricultural terraces. To be sure, most forms of intensive farming would have been difficult in this particular environment. A more likely reciprocal product of monumental construction was a local landscape favorable to maintaining substantial camelid herds, in particular the multiple herds that likely gathered during recurring major events.

A BRIEF HISTORY OF KHONKHO WANKANE'S
CEREMONIAL-RESIDENTIAL COMPLEX

Constructing the two platforms created a monumental center in a place that already had been important for periodic social gathering. Was it located at an early nexus of llama caravan trade routes? Near a place that had been routinely sacralized? Both scenarios are likely and neither excludes the other. Either way, the Wankane platform was a locus of monumental construction and social gathering by the first century AD.

For the purposes of this chapter, we can consider Khonkho Wankane's ongoing ceremonial construction in terms of two successive phases: Early-Middle

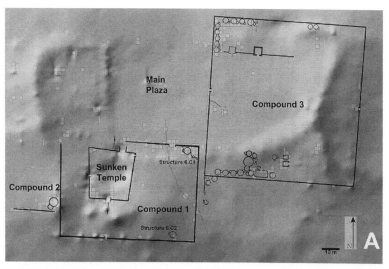

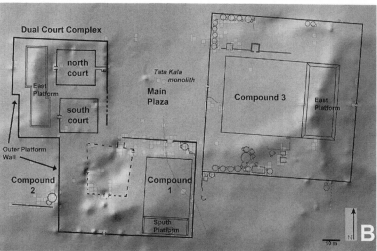

FIGURE 11.7. *Constructions on the Wankane platform in Khonkho's monumental core showing (a) Early-Middle and (b) Late Khonkho architecture (image by author).*

(50 BC–AD 300) and Late Khonkho (AD 300–450) (Figure 11.7). Core elements of its spatial order were established early on. A central plaza occupied the center of the rectangular Wankane platform. The plaza housed large-scale ceremonial and sociopolitical gatherings, and by all indications it maintained this role throughout the Late Formative. A trapezoidal Sunken Temple with

multiple entrances occupied the area southwest of the plaza. Its court served relatively intimate—and perhaps at times exclusive—gatherings that entailed ritualized consumption. Early-Middle Khonkho also witnessed the construction of several large, bounded residential-ritual compounds, most notably Compound 1, built flush with the east side of the Sunken Temple, and Compound 3, located to the northeast. Both compounds enclosed numerous circular domestic structures as well as structures dedicated to ritual activities. For example, the southwest sector of Compound 3 was dedicated to a series of activities that produced human bone reliquaries (Janusek 2009; Smith 2009).

Late Khonkho (AD 300–500) witnessed increasing intricacy and spatial interconnection. The Sunken Temple was abandoned and left to decay at the south edge of the plaza. A new platform and sunken-court complex was constructed on the west edge of the plaza, opposite Compound 3. This "Dual Court Complex" manifested new monumental practices. First, in addition to its dual architectural form, it was oriented according to a (roughly) east-west axis, just as were contemporaneous new structures at Tiwanaku across the Corocoro range (Janusek 2006, 2012). Second, the Dual Court Complex incorporated minor instances of precisely articulated stonework, manifesting early attempts in the fitted architectural masonry style that characterized later Tiwanaku construction. Finally, a massive single revetment, featuring a veneer of sandstone blocks, bounded the west and southwest portions of the platform, effectively encompassing and joining the old Sunken Temple with the new Dual Court Complex.

Khonkho's Carved Monoliths

By Late Khonkho, the Wankane platform incorporated four primary ceremonial spaces: the Main Plaza, the Sunken Temple, and the two sunken courtyards of the Dual Court Complex. It also featured four stone stelae with sculpted iconography (Figure 11.8). Three of the stelae were found ex situ. The fourth, Tata Kala, lies slumped on its back in the center of the Main Plaza, where it originally stood until Khonkho's decline. The numeric correspondence of spaces and stelae may indicate that each stela occupied a particular ceremonial space. Correlating a stylistic lithic seriation with the site chronology (Smith 2009), Arik Ohnstad and I (Janusek and Ohnstad, in press; see also Ohnstad 2005) suggest the following: the earliest monolith, Portugal, occupied the Sunken Temple; the twin Wila Kala and Jinch'un Kala each occupied one court in the Dual Court Complex; and, as we already know, the latest monolith, Tata Kala, occupied the Main Plaza.

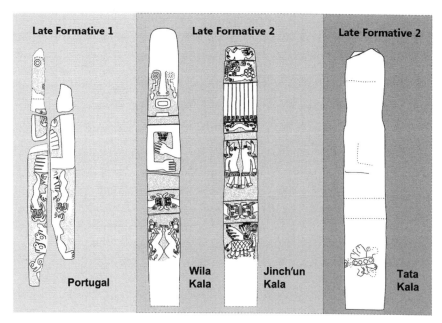

Late Formative 1	Late Formative 2	Late Formative 2
Portugal	Wila Kala Jinch'un Kala	Tata Kala

FIGURE 11.8. *Khonkho Wankane's four carved monoliths (drawing by Arik Ohnstad).*

The monoliths date to the Late Formative period (Janusek and Ohnstad, in press; after Browman 1972 and Portugal 1998). Stylistic seriation in conjunction with recent monolithic iconographic analysis in the Lake Titicaca Basin (Chávez and Mohr Chávez 1975; Portugal 1998) allowed us to designate the Portugal Stela the earliest and Tata Kala the latest carved monolith. The Wila Kala and Jinchu'un Kala, by all indications "twin" monoliths, stylistically fall between these two. We argue that Portugal dated to Early Khonkho (AD 1–150), the twin monoliths to Middle Khonkho (AD 150–300), and Tata Kala to Late Khonkho (AD 300–500).

Khonkho's monolithic stelae were carved of sandstone, and each presented a single anthropomorphic personage decorated with zoomorphic imagery (Ohnstad 2005, 2013; Ohnstad and Janusek 2007).[3] Each personage stands erect with hands positioned over the torso in a gesture unique to the Lake Titicaca Late Formative, with one arm bent at a 90-degree angle over the belly and the second bent at a more acute angle over the chest. Serpent-like creatures with angular, arrow-like heads weave up and down along the sides and across horizontal clothing features (sashes, belts) of the monoliths (Browman 1972, 1997). Our study of local fauna indicates that they referenced a neonatal stage of the catfish (*Trichtomycterus*) that is native to Lake Titicaca and local

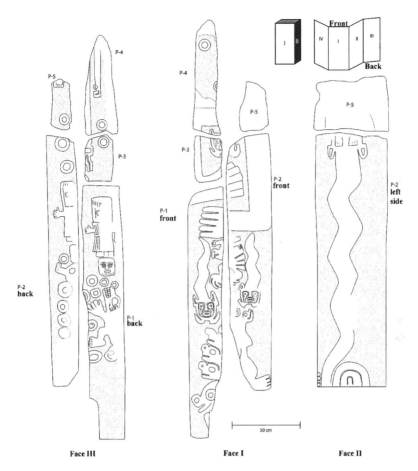

Face III   **Face I**   **Face II**

FIGURE 11.9. *Khonkho's Portugal monolith (drawing by Arik Ohnstad).*

rivers and streams. Unlike those of adults, the face, fins, and barbels of neonate catfish look strikingly like the serpentine images carved on Khonkho's monoliths. Such highly stylized iconography likely invoked mythic narratives, and the depiction of neonate rather than adult fish directs attention to the generative capacities of these aquatic life forms.

PORTUGAL MONOLITH

The Portugal monolith consists of five fragments of a shattered stela crafted of soft, yellowish red sandstone (Figure 11.9). Stylistically earliest, it is also the smallest of Khonkho's monoliths, measuring approximately 3 m high. The Portugal embodies a single anthropomorphic personage with an impassive face and arms crossed over the chest, its left arm lying slightly above the right. A neonate catfish with a long, tightly coiled tail ascends along the remnant left side panel, while two more diminutive catfish descend from the main figure's arms toward a mythical zoomorphic creature. The back side of the stela depicts small human-like figures wearing gathered, pleated tunics and, below them, two ascending zoomorphic figures, one of them a feline. Circular icons surround the figures, and one forms the nose of the feline. I suspect that the icons depict stars, and the bodies of the zoomorphs nightly constellations. Visual paths in the Sunken Temple, which the Portugal likely inhabited, may have, in fact, featured the rise of stellar constellations at critical times of the annual agropastoral cycle (Benítez 2007).

WILA KALA AND JINCH'UN KALA MONOLITHS

Wila Kala and Jinch'un Kala were crafted of more durable red sandstone (Figure 11.10). We are fortunate that the twin monoliths preserved as well as they did. Wila Kala was left facing downward in the southeast portion of the Wankane platform, preserving its front side. Jinch'un Kala was left facing upward at the foot of the Wankane platform, preserving its backside. The sides of each monolith are still fairly intact and virtually identical. Each presents a single human-like personage decorated with carved zoomorphic and anthropomorphic imagery. Unlike the Portugal, these stelae are rigidly quadrangular in plan, and vertical carved panels distinguish clear pictorial zones. The panels form vertically aligned elements of the body and wardrobe: head, headdress, neck, torso, sash, and lower tunic. The monolithic twins manifest a new interest in geometric monolithic form, discrete iconographic zoning, and worn, woven clothing.

I call them "twins," but the monoliths are not perfectly identical. Wila Kala stands 5.3 m and Jinch'un Kala 4.6 m high. They formed an asymmetrical pair. Yet they appear to have embodied paired personages and mythical narratives. Wila Kala presents the front and Jinch'un Kala the back of an anthropomorphic personage. The (front) head portion of Wila Kala presents an impassive face with a large nose and stepped "lightning-bolt" imagery descending from wide-open eyes. The (back) head portion of Jinch'un Kala depicts tresses descending from a headdress depicting surrealistic imagery (Figure 11.11). The top panel of the headdress depicts a thick trunk that "sprouts" coherent living forms, including a human surrounded by feline and camelid heads. The bottom

Wila Kala

right side   front

back   left side

(b)

Jinch'un Kala

1 m

FIGURE 11.10. *Khonkho's "twin" monoliths: Wila Kala and Jinch'un Kala (adapted by author from Arik Ohnstad's original).*

panel of the headdress depicts a floating or flying being with a head supporting a four-bean pod and its back evidencing an animate wing comprised of wave-like volutes and an open hand for a "tail." I interpret the iconography broadly as generative. Unlike other iconographic zones on the monoliths—and unlike the iconography of most known monoliths in the Lake Titicaca Basin—the upper back head portion of Jinch'un Kala depicts hybrid beings and the primordial generation of identifiable living organisms.

Neonate catfish, now highly symmetrical in form and movement, slither up and down the sides and horizontally across the sashes of the two monolithic personages. They define clear paths of movement across the vertical and horizontal axes of the two monoliths, while their serpentine tails make iconic reference to rivers and streams. Indeed, the young catfish guide narrative interpretations of the monoliths. They emerge from the sash of each

FIGURE 11.11. *Generative imagery depicted on the back of the head of the Jinch'un Kala monolith (photograph by author; drawing adapted by author from Arik Ohnstad's original).*

monolithic personage and disseminate in four directions; up and down along both sides, and front-to-back / back-to-front across the sash, the last forming horizontally rendered, double-headed beings. Many earlier monoliths in the Lake Titicaca Basin depicted a stylized "navel" on the belly or "sash" of the primary personage (Browman 1972, 1997; Portugal 1998). On each of Khonkho's twin monoliths, the "navel" was constituted as a face-to-face confrontation of developing catfish that was mirrored on the back side of the monolithic personage.

Each of Khonkho's twin monoliths embodied complex three-dimensional iconography that narrated the life cycle of each primary personage (Ohnstad 2005). Young catfish, themselves becoming adults, helped direct specific elements of this cyclical narrative. They surged upward along the sides of the monolithic personages from the central sash, the metaphorical umbilicus of each personage, and toward its head. They surged down along the sides of the personages from the central sash, toward the place where each monolith would have been entrenched in the earth.

Neither of the monoliths—nor any of the other monolithic personages known from the Lake Titicaca Basin Formative—was depicted with legs and feet (Ohnstad 2005). Monoliths were emplaced such that lithic personages appeared to emerge from the ground of each courtyard. It is likely significant that the bottom front register of Wila Kala depicts a mirrored pair of ascending felines and the bottom back register of Jinch'un Kala a "llama impersonator." Respectively wild and domesticated, felines and llamas are both earthly, mountain-loving creatures. Downward-facing neonate catfish descend into the earth to co-produce the monolithic personages they decorated. The monoliths appear to make a strong didactic point: the aquatic-ichthian cycle produces key elements of the terrestrial realm that is critical for humans, including its wild and domesticated creatures.

This ichthian narrative crosscuts another carved into vertical sequences of panels on the twin monoliths. Ascending paired felines adorn the bottom front portion of Wila Kala, and ascending human-like figures the back torso portion of Jinch'un Kala. Both sides of the lower head portion of each monolith, nevertheless, depict a descending human-like figure with trailing headdress and exposed ribs. Combined, ichthian and descending human imagery "twin" the two monoliths. As they do on the two seated stone personages from Late Formative Pokotia (Portugal 1998; Posnansky 1945), a site en route to Tiwanaku from Khonkho, exposed ribs at Khonkho mark the status of the descending human-like beings as deceased, and possibly mummified persons. Yet like the generative serpentine figures, these figures are in motion, and they move downward within some eco-mythical realm, whether from the sky to the earth, from the top of a mountain to the *pampa*, or from the earth to an underworld. If young catfish and other generative imagery evoke creation and generation, descending human figures evoke the complementary transformation of death. Together, and rendered in zoned imagery across the bodies of monolithic personages, they evoked cyclical narratives. I suggest that they narrated life, death, and regeneration as ancestors of the monumental personage embodied in stone.

Khonkho's Monoliths as Living Great Ancestors

Drawing on ethnographic, historical, and archaeological Andean analogies, I propose that Khonkho's monoliths and their kinetic material imagery evoked a transcendent life history for the eco-mythical figures they embodied. As Abercrombie (1998) and Salomon (1995) point out, death was not necessarily the end of one's career in communities of the prehispanic or historic Andes. It was certainly not necessarily the end of one's political career, especially if it involved becoming a "great ancestor" for one's progeny and macrocommunity. Becoming a great ancestor meant becoming a mythical figure for the multiple living communities that claimed affiliation to that personage. The status of one's great ancestor reflected the political status of those communities

(Salomon 1995). Because the status of any political community was always in flux, so potentially was the status of great ancestors it celebrated.

Becoming a great ancestor, like becoming an influential political community, was no mean feat. Interpreting the ubiquitous floating/flying anthropomorphic figures on Paracas textiles, Frame (2001; see also Ohnstad and Janusek 2007) suggests that, as a master narrative transcending any individual mantle or tunic, Paracas iconography depicted the competitive "becoming" of great ancestors. Like aspirants during their "living" political careers, ancestors began in low-status positions, and perhaps like new political figures they were considered *wawa mallki*, or baby ancestors. Many Paracas mantles depict human-like figures consuming others, which Frame (2001) interprets as the consumption of "newbie" ancestors by more seasoned, or powerful, greater ancestors. This scenario resonates with Salomon's historical and Abercrombie's ethnographic data. Great ancestors embodied the eco-mythical histories of political communities. Thus, successfully becoming a great ancestor was competitive. It was a function of becoming a powerful political community. Becoming a powerful community, in turn, depended on successfully claiming ancestral precedence over many other communities. Those who tended Khonkho Wankane and affiliated with its cult sought to render its resident ancestral monoliths powerful political personages.

The materiality of Khonkho Wankane's monoliths was central to the continued success of this political project. Critical in this regard were their places of telluric "birth." Monoliths were carved from sandstone outcrops located near the summit of the local Corocoro range, located some 12 km and over 600 m above Khonkho Wankane (Ohnstad 2005). In contemporary and historically documented communities of the south-central Andes, mountain peaks and the springs they generate are mythical origin places for humans and the camelid herds that sustain them. Furthermore, mountains and human bodies are mutual metaphors, and both mountain summits and human heads embody generative forces. I believe this explains why the back of the head of Jinch'un Kala's monolithic personage presents such evocative generative imagery. Like the Portugal and Wila Kala, it embodied the mountain peak of which it constituted an authentic portion, and the head portion was the generative "summit" of its monolithic personage.

Monolithic iconography on the stone bodies of these ancestral beings indexed feral and domesticated animals native to mountainous landscapes and the flows of mountain streams and/or bodily fluids. They indexed the "natural processes" that characterized their mountainous places of origin. The Corocoro summits from where the monoliths originate, like other powerful peaks in the region, simultaneously differentiate and mediate landscape and skyscape—the two major interlocking dimensions of the Andean cosmos. The Portugal monolith may feature celestial imagery in the form of a constellation in which one "star" forms the tip of the nose of an upward-facing feline, a mountain-roaming wild creature. Icons on the twin monoliths formed narratives dictated by neonate catfish—young beings in the process of becoming full-fledged catfish, metonymic referents of the ancestral personages they decorated and whose narratives they told—indeed, whose beings they animated. Generative imagery depicting "beings in the process of becoming" also decorates the back of the head of Jinch'un Kala—the metaphorical mountain peak from which the monolith materially derived. I propose that these monoliths depicted narratives of deceased ancestors in the process of becoming great ancestors of the emergent communities that congregated at, and thus identified with, Khonkho Wankane. This was Khonkho's enduring proposition and its bid for fame and ritual-political centrality.

The destruction of the early Portugal monolith dramatically demonstrates the animate power that Khonkho's monoliths embodied. The monolith was violently split in half along its vertical axis, and each half was then split again along its horizontal axis. Remnant pieces were then buried in a single locale just off of Wankane's main platform (Ohnstad 2013). The destruction of the Portugal was a dramatic ritual act, and its burial akin to human interment. Precisely when the Portugal was destroyed remains unclear. Yet the stylistic properties of the monolith correspond temporally with the early Sunken Temple, which was left to collapse sometime during Late Khonkho, in the early fourth century AD. This was just after the Dual Court Complex was constructed, and as I've proposed, the twin monoliths were likely carved to inhabit this new structure. I suggest that the Portugal was destroyed in order to "uncoil" the animate power that its montane, lithic materiality embodied.[4] The particular manner of its destruction, by "quartering," was likely important to its destruction and interment.

KHONKHO WANKANE AS CENTER FOR PROTO-
WAK'A PRODUCTION AND VENERATION

During the Lake Titicaca Basin Late Formative, Khonkho Wankane emerged as a center for the veneration of powerful carved monoliths. Khonkho's monoliths were not wak'as in the strict sense of the Quechua and Aymara terms for late prehispanic "sacred" places and objects. The significance and efficacy of ritually powerful objects changed throughout the long prehispanic era, perhaps especially during the tumultuous Late Intermediate period (AD 1000–1450) when monolithic production and many other entrenched ritual and sociopolitical practices ceased in the Lake Titicaca Basin. Yet Khonkho's monoliths shared certain fundamental elements in common with later wak'as. They were (1) material things (2) that embodied (3) the superhuman. Khonkho Wankane both provided the contexts and produced the subjects that rendered those carved monoliths animate, superhuman agents.

Khonkho's prestige waxed over the course of four hundred years or sixteen to twenty generations. Early occupation under the Wankane platform indicates that Khonkho was a place of regional gathering before its monumental transformation. It may have been a strategic hub for early llama caravan routes and a key locale for ritual encounters. Pre-monumental Khonkho Wankane did not house or directly support the persons required to construct the massive Wankane platform. This ambitious construction project attests Khonkho's precocious regional fame. Most of the people who excavated and carried load after load of soil to build the Wankane platform hailed from elsewhere. They came periodically to the center as participants in cyclical ritual encounters. Whatever Khonkho's early significance, the new platform fixed and aggrandized the locale as a monumental place with which multiple communities identified.

Monumental construction simultaneously produced both a new center and a surrounding productive landscape. Khonkho's anthropogenic microenvironment constituted a watery landscape amenable to intensive pastoralism, an ancient primary productive emphasis that contemporary inhabitants pursue to this day. Camelid pastoralism grounded Khonkho Wankane's emergent political ecology. Located in an environment that precluded most forms of intensive farming, Khonkho Wankane constituted a monumental bid for pastoral intensification. Two of its monoliths depict camelid imagery: Jinch'un Kala portrays a four-legged llama impersonator with a fifth appendage holding a scepter, while Tata Kala exhibits a dancing, two-legged camelid (Janusek and Ohnstad 2013; Ohnstad 2005). Khonkho's monoliths—the only known monoliths in the basin to feature camelid iconography (aside from Middle Wankarani camelid-head effigies)—were unique in ritually celebrating camelid pastoralism.

Recurring ritual encounter at Khonkho Wankane produced an ontological modality that, over generations, fostered an appreciation of carved monoliths as animate proto-wak'as. Corporeal engagement was critical to the animacy of carved stone monoliths. Monoliths inhabited relatively small sunken spaces that facilitated intimate interaction. Artifacts found on the floors of the temples indicate that communal consumption and ritual purification via incense burners took place in their presence.[5] Such activities enhanced the intensity of engagement with monolithic personages. In sum, monoliths were the focus of ritual encounter and political practice at Khonkho. Their lithic materiality embodied the mythicized history and productive capacity that supported community well-being and reproduction.

CONCLUSIONS

Late Formative Khonkho Wankane featured carved stone monoliths analogous to documented wak'as. They constitute what I term proto-wak'as. Monolithic power resided in lithic materiality. Of significance was the indexical relation of Khonkho's monoliths to their quarries of origin near the summit of the nearby Corocoro range. The monoliths presented iconographic themes that captured a vast mythical history and animistic ecology. Existentially, they were humanly crafted portions of nearby mountain peaks. Over the course of cyclical human-lithic engagements at Khonkho Wankane, they were made to *embody* those mountains. Recurring ritual engagements at Khonkho afforded monoliths their animate potency.

This study seeks to demonstrate that ontologies are not essential or static modes of being. They are constructed via human engagement with particular materials and landscapes. If indeed Heidegger problematized this point, it is obscured in his torturous, subversive, poetic stylistic acrobatics—as engaging as they may be (Steiner 1979).[6] The Khonkho case resonates with Descola's (1996) argument that, whether predominantly "animistic" or "naturalistic," any society incorporates differing fundamental experiences of the world, and the relative animacy and power of its constituent beings can vary by sociospatial context. As a case study, Khonkho demonstrates that predominant ontologies are actively constructed through ritual practice—in this case, animating practices focused at an emerging center—and that they crystallize and shift over generations. Coherent understandings of the world, and of one's relations to the things and persons around him/her—including an understanding of what counts as a "person" versus a "thing—are always contingent. Such understandings are constructed in *praxis*, through practical engagements informed by traditional understandings. Recurring practical engagements can produce predominant and relatively coherent ontological modes, as they did at Khonkho Wankane and, indeed, across the Late Formative Titicaca Basin.

Yet the world frequently fails to respond in ways that habitual practices and traditional understandings may lead us to expect. From a perspective that treats ontology as a relatively static phenomenon, such as the one Marshall

Sahlins promotes in *Islands of History* (1985), humans consistently submit their culturally prescribed intentions to the dangerous, unpredictable vagaries of daily life. Considered in the *longue durée*, Khonkho Wankane reminds us that historical shift was always already the name of the game. Predominant notions of "being" shifted over generations. Furthermore, different ontologies likely coexisted in the same society (see Harris and Robb 2012). The question is: how does one come to predominate over others? Here Khonkho Wankane is instructive.

Khonkho's emergence as a major center during the Late Formative corresponded with the emergence of a transformed understanding of being in the south-central Andes. I suggest that it is more accurate to speak of ontological modalities than to essentialize modes of being as static "ontologies." Ontological modalities are constructed and fortified—often tactically so—in specific, often strategically arranged, sociospatial contexts (also Alberti et al. 2011). I argue here that Khonkho Wankane provided just such a sociospatial context. Its ceremonial complex and the indexical iconicity of the monoliths it featured were always under construction, testament to the shifting experiences of the communities that produced them. The same space was susceptible to changing sociospatial relations and interpretations over time. Ontological modalities were potentially in flux, and Khonkho Wankane's sequence of monoliths, as well as the changing configuration of ceremonial spaces that focused attention on them, embodied the shifting practices and understandings of Khonkho's constituent communities.

Khonkho Wankane and its monolithic inhabitants created a predominant ontological modality—an animistic political ecology—through recurring, cyclical ritual encounters at the center. This was a relational ontology that emphasized the animate power of carved monolithic personages, the mountains they physically embodied, and the montane stone outcrops that produced them. This experiential modality favored human-stone engagements and posited stone generally, and the Corocoro range more specifically, as loci for the origins of being. Just as Astvaldsson's informant in Sullkatiti interpreted Turiturini's significance by mimicking the spiral motif atop its head, so the generative power of Khonkho's monoliths and the production of human identities at the Late Formative center were cyclically fortified through recurring visits to Khonkho Wankane and intimate corporeal engagement with its resident monolithic beings.

The current importance of Khonkho Wankane as a ritual space for the annual construction of a novel pan-Aymara identity resonates uncannily with its importance during the Late Formative past. Now as then, the resurgence of Khonkho Wankane and its impressive stone monoliths requires the strategic reshuffling of ontological modalities—now thoroughly steeped in over five centuries of western practices—and their attendant understandings of human-landscape relations. As was theatrically enacted at the Machac Mara event in 2002, Khonkho Wankane's centrality is an ongoing, ever-shifting, long-term political enterprise.

NOTES

1. The importance of "uncoiling" a curse came home to me during the 2006 field season at Khonkho Wankane, when project members recovered evidence for witchcraft at the site. While ritual specialists were never able to pinpoint precisely who perpetrated the witchcraft, nor against whom it was directed, the ensuing "cleansing" ceremony was conducted as a ritual "uncoiling" of the original act.

2. I do not discuss Khonkho's latest monolith, the Tatakala, in part because it is so poorly preserved and in part because it is not critical to the core themes of this chapter.

3. The ensuing discussion of monolithic iconography draws heavily on the iconographic and stylistic research that Arik Ohnstad conducted on the monoliths between 2002 and 2007.

4. As Mauss (1967:102) noted of the destructive expenditure that characterized the potlatch ceremonies of Northwest North American polities: "If property can be 'killed' this means it must be 'alive.'"

5. Although currently unpublished, evidence for the presence of broken ritual burners and abundant ritualized consumption has been presented by Randi Gladwell (2010).

6. As Heidegger expert George Steiner (1979:4) puts it, "his writings are a thicket of impenetrable verbiage."

REFERENCES CITED

Abercrombie, Thomas. 1998. *Pathways of Memory and Power: Ethnography and History among an Andean People.* Madison: University of Wisconsin.

Abbott, Mark B., Michael W. Binford, Mark Brenner, and Kerry Kelts. 1997. "A 3500 ^{14}C Yr High-Resolution Record of Water-Level Changes in Lake Titicaca, Bolivia-Peru." *Quaternary Research* 47 (2): 169–80. http://dx.doi.org/10.1006/qres.1997.1881.

Alberti, Benjamin, Severin Fowles, Martin Holbraad, Yvonne Marshall, and Christopher Witmore. 2011. "'Worlds Otherwise': Archaeology, Anthropology,

and Ontological Difference." *Current Anthropology* 52 (6): 896–912. http://dx.doi
.org/10.1086/662027.

Arnold, Denise. 1992. "La casa de adobes y piedras del Inka: Género, memoria, y
cosmos en Qaqachaka." In *Hacia un orden andino de las cosas*, ed. Denise Arnold,
Domingo Jiménez Aruquipa, and Yapita Juan de Dios, 31–108. La Paz: Hisbol/
ILCA.

Astvaldsson, Astvaldur. 1998. "The Powers of Hard Rock: Meaning, Transformation
and Continuity in Cultural Symbols in the Andes." *Journal of Latin American
Cultural Studies* 7 (2): 203–23. http://dx.doi.org/10.1080/13569329809361935.

Bandy, Matthew S. 2001. Population and History in the Ancient Titicaca Basin. PhD
diss., University of California, Berkeley. Ann Arbor, MI: University Microfilms.

Bauer, Brian. 1998. *The Sacred Landscape of the Inca: The Cuzco Ceque System*. Austin:
University of Texas Press.

Benítez, Leonardo. 2007. "Montañas, plazas semi-subterráneas y la constelaciones de
la llama obscura: Arqueoastronomía en el Khonkho Wankane y en Tiwanaku." In
Khonkho e iruhito: Tercer informe preliminar del proyecto arqueológico Jach'a Machaca,
ed. John W. Janusek and Victor Plaza, 192–201. Research report submitted to the
Bolivian Viceministry of Culture and the Unidad Nacional de Arqueología, La
Paz.

Bertonio, Padre Ludovico. 2006 [1612]. *Vocabulario de la lengua aymara*. Arequipa:
Ediciones El Lector.

Browman, David. 1972. "Asiruni, Pucara-Pokotia and Pajano: Pre-Tiahuanaco South
Andean Monolithic Stone Styles." Paper presented at the 34th Annual Conference
of the Society for American Archaeology, Miami.

Browman, David. 1997. "Pajano: Nexus of Formative Cultures in the Titicaca Basin."
Paper presented at the 49th International Conference of Americanists, Quito.

Burman, Anders. 2011. *Descolonización Aymara: Ritualidad y política (2006–2010)*. La
Paz: Plural.

Chávez, Sergio, and Karen L. Mohr Chávez. 1975. "A Carved Stela from Taraco, Puno,
Peru and the Definition of an Early Style of Stone Sculpture from the Altiplano
of Peru and Bolivia." *Ñawpa Pacha* 13:45–83.

Cuelenaere, Laurence Janin. 2009. "Words Spoken with Insistence: Wak'as and the
Limits of the Bolivian Multi-Institutional Democracy." PhD diss., University of
California, Berkeley. Ann Arbor, MI: University Microfilms.

de Lucca D., Manuel. 1983. *Diccionario aymara-castellano, castellano-aymara*. La Paz:
Comisión de Alfabetización y Literatura en Aymara Villamil de Rada.

Descola, Philippe. 1996. "Constructing Natures: Symbolic Ecology and Social
Practice." In *Nature and Society: Anthropological Perspectives*, ed. Philippe Descola

and Gisli Palsson, 82–102. London: Routledge. http://dx.doi.org/10.4324 /9780203451069_chapter_5.

Eliade, Mircea. 1959. *The Sacred and the Profane: The Nature of Religion*. New York: Harcourt, Brace and World.

Frame, Mary. 2001. "Blood, Fertility, and Transformation: Interwoven Themes in the Paracas Necropolis Embroideries." In *Ritual Sacrifice in Ancient Peru*, ed. Elizabeth P. Benson and Anita Gwynn Cook, 55–92. Austin: University of Texas Press.

Gibson, James J. 1986. *The Ecology of Perception*. London: Lawrence Erlbaum Associates.

Gladwell, Randi R. 2010. "The Role of Camelids in Ritual Contexts at Khonkho Wankane (Bolivia) during the Formative Period." Paper presented at the 75th Annual Meeting of the Society for American Archaeology, St. Louis, MO.

Harris, Oliver J.T., and John Robb. 2012. "Multiple Ontologies and the Problem of the Body in History." *American Anthropologist* 114 (4): 668–79. http://dx.doi.org /10.1111/j.1548-1433.2012.01513.x.

Janusek, John Wayne. 2006. "The Changing 'Nature' of Tiwanaku Religion and the Rise of an Andean State." *World Archaeology* 38 (3): 469–92. http://dx.doi.org/10 .1080/00438240600813541.

Janusek, John Wayne. 2008. "Khonkho Wankane and Alternative Trajectories of State Formation in the South-Central Andes." Paper presented at the 48th Annual Meeting of the Institute of Andean Studies, Berkeley, CA.

Janusek, John Wayne. 2009. "Centralidad regional, ecología religiosa y complejidad emergente durante el periodo formativo en la cuenca del lago Titicaca." *Boletín de Arqueología PUCP* 11:23–52.

Janusek, John Wayne. 2012. "Understanding Tiwanaku Origins: Animistic Ecology in the Andean Altiplano." In *The Past Ahead: Language, Culture, and Identity in the Neotropics*, ed. Christian Isendahl, 111–38. Uppsala: Uppsala University.

Janusek, John W., and Arik T. Ohnstad. In press. "Stone Stelae of the Southern Basin: A Stylistic Chronology of Ancestral Personages." In *The South American Iconographic Series*, ed. William H. Isbell. Los Angeles: Cotsen Institute of Archaeology, University of California, Los Angeles.

Janusek, John W., Andrew P. Roddick, and Maribel Perez Arias. 2005. "El compuesto K1 y su vecindad." In *Khonkho Wankane: Primer informe preliminar del proyecto Jach'a Machaca*, ed. John W. Janusek, 123–40. Research report submitted to the Bolivian Viceministry of Culture and the Unidad Nacional de Arqueología, La Paz.

Janusek, John W., Arik T. Ohnstad, and Andrew P. Roddick. 2003. "Khonkho Wankane and the Rise of Tiwanaku." *Antiquity* 77 (296). http://antiquity.ac.uk /ProjGall/janusek/janusek.html.

Lémuz Aguirre, Carlos. 2006. "Patrones de asentamiento arqueológico en el área de influencia del sitio de Khonkho Wankane." In *Khonkho Wankane: Segundo informe preliminar del proyecto arqueológico Jach'a Machaca*, ed. John W. Janusek and Victor Plaza, 5–44. Research report presented to the Bolivian Viceministry of Culture and the Unidad Nacional de Arqueología, La Paz.

Mannheim, Bruce. 2006. "Ayni." Paper presented at the 34th Annual Meeting of the Midwest Conference on Andean and Amazonian Archaeology and Ethnohistory, Nashville, TN.

Marsh, Eric. 2007. "Pozos de prueba para los montículos cerca de Khonkho Wankane." In *Khonkho y iruhito: Tercer informe preliminar del proyecto arqueológico Jach'a Machaca*, ed. John W. Janusek and Victor Plaza, 187–90. Research report presented to the Bolivian Viceministry of Culture and the Unidad Nacional de Arqueología, La Paz.

Marsh, Eric. 2012. "The Emergence of Tiwanaku: Domestic Practices and Regional Traditions at Khonkho Wankane and Kk'a raña." PhD diss., University of California, Santa Barbara. Ann Arbor, MI: University Microfilms.

Mauss, Marcel. 1967. *The Gift: Forms and Functions of Exchange in Archaic Societies*. New York: W. W. Norton & Co.

Ohnstad, Arik T. 2005. "La escultura de piedra de Khonkho Wankane." In *Khonkho Wankane: Primer informe preliminar del proyecto arqueológico Jach'a Machaca*, ed. John W. Janusek, 52–68. Research report submitted to the Bolivian Viceministry of Culture and the Unidad Nacional de Arqueología, La Paz.

Ohnstad, Arik T. 2007. "Excavaciones en áreas periféricas de los montículos de Wankane y Putuni." In *Khonkho y iruhito: Tercer informe preliminar del proyecto arqueológico Jach'a Machaca*, ed. John W. Janusek and Victor Plaza, 141–86. Research report presented to the Bolivian Viceministry of Culture and the Unidad Nacional de Arqueología, La Paz.

Ohnstad, Arik T. 2008. "Excavaciones en la plaza y el templo hundido." In *Khonkho Wankane y Pukara de Khonkho: Cuarto informe preliminar del proyecto Jach'a Machaca (investigaciones en 2007)*, ed. John W. Janusek and Victor Plaza, 39–63. Research report submitted to the Bolivian Viceministry of Culture and the Unidad Nacional de Arqueología, La Paz.

Ohnstad, Arik T. 2013. "The Stone Stelae of Khonkho Waknane: Inventory, Brief Description, and Seriation." In *Advance in Titicaca Basin Archaeology 2*, ed. Alexei Vranich and Abigail R. Levine, 53–66. Los Angeles: Cotsen Institute of Archaeology, University of California, Los Angeles.

Ohnstad, Arik T., and John W. Janusek. 2007. "The Development of Tiwanaku Style out of the Ideological and Political-Economic Landscapes of the Formative

Period Titicaca Basin." Paper presented at the Southern Andean Iconographic Series: A Colloquium in Pre-Columbian Art and Archaeology, Santiago, Chile.

Portugal Ortiz, Max. 1998. *Escultura prehispanic boliviana*. La Paz: UMSA.

Posnansky, Arthur. 1945. *Tihuanacu: The Cradle of American Man*. Vols. 1 and 2. New York: J. J. Augustin.

Sahlins, Marshall. 1985. *Islands of History*. Chicago: University of Chicago Press.

Sahlins, Marshall. 2008. *The Western Illusion of Human Nature*. Chicago: Prickly Paradigm Press.

Salomon, Frank. 1991. "Introductory Essay." In *The Huarochirí Manuscript: A Testament of Ancient and Colonial Andean Religion*, ed. and trans. Frank Salomon and George Urioste, 1–38. Austin: University of Texas Press.

Salomon, Frank. 1995. "'The Beautiful Grandparents': Andean Ancestor Shrines and Mortuary Ritual as Seen through Colonial Records." In *Tombs for the Living: Andean Mortuary Practices*, ed. Tom D. Dillehay, 315–54. Washington, DC: Dumbarton Oaks.

Sammels, Clare A. 2012. "Calendars and Bolivian Modernity: Tiwanaku's Gateway of the Sun, Arthur Posnansky, and the World Calendar Movement of the 1930s." *Journal of Latin American and Caribbean Anthropology* 17 (2): 299–319. http://dx.doi.org/10.1111/j.1935-4940.2012.01221.x.

Smith, Scott Cameron. 2009. "Venerable Geographies: Spatial Dynamics, Religion, and Political Economy in the Prehistoric Lake Titicaca Basin, Bolivia." PhD diss., University of California, Riverside. Ann Arbor, MI: University Microfilms.

Steiner, George. 1979. *Martin Heidegger*. New York: Viking Press.

Stobart, Henry. 2006. *Music and the Poetics of Production in the Bolivian Andes*. Burlington, VT: Ashgate Press.

van de Guchte, Maarten. 1990. "Carving the World: Inca Monumental Sculpture and Landscape." PhD diss., University of Illinois, Urbana-Champaign. Ann Arbor, MI: University Microfilms.

van de Guchte, Maarten. 1999. "The Inca Cognition of Landscape: Archaeology, Ethnohistory, and the Aesthetic of Alterity." In *Archaeologies of Landscape: Contemporary Perspectives*, ed. Wendy Ashmore and A. Bernard Knapp, 149–68. Oxford: Blackwell Publishers.

Zuidema, R. Tom. 1964. *The Ceque System of Cuzco: The Social Organization of the Capital of the Inca*. Leiden: E. J. Brill.

Part V

*Concluding
Thoughts*

12

Final Reflections

*Catequil as One Wak'a
among Many*

JOHN R. TOPIC

The chapters in this volume all focus on *wak'a*—a concept that is hard to define but crucial to understanding Andean ideas of relationality and causality. Although part of our understanding of wak'a comes from colonial attempts to extirpate Andean "religion" and "idolatry," these words do not allow a precise understanding of the nature of wak'a. Even the Spanish extirpators frequently resorted to the indigenous term *guaca* or *huaca* to describe what they were trying to eradicate. The words "god" or "deity" imply a western dichotomization between the sacred and secular that also obscures the nature of wak'a (see Janusek, this volume).

In trying to understand wak'a, some Quechua concepts are quite helpful, and Bruce Mannheim and Guillermo Salas (this volume) provide a sophisticated linguistic treatment of the term. Here I want to offer some additional signposts to guide the reader through these comments. As Catherine Allen's chapter points out, the Andean world is animated (see also Allen 1997; Bray 2009, and this volume). The essence that animates the world is *callpa* (Taylor 1987:24–27; van de Guchte 1990:257–58). Callpa is a force or energy that references both the power of the body (to perform work) and the "powers of the soul" (i.e., memory, judgment, and will) (González Holguín 1989 [1608]:44–45; Santo Tomas 1951 [1560]:245 [114]). It is important to recognize that callpa also has the sense of running or flowing, even to move quickly (*correr* and *aguijar* in Spanish) (Santo Tomas 2006 [1560]:206–8; Taylor 1987:26). Taylor

DOI: 10.5876/9781607323181.c012

(1987:26) identifies callpa as shamanic power and the power possessed by wak'a. *Camay* is the ongoing process of creation, where the creator (*camac*) constantly renews the creation (*camasca*) (Bray 2009:358; Salomon 1991:16). Taylor (1987:24) considers the process of creation to involve the transfer of a vital force (callpa) from the creator to the object of creation (camasca). Renewal requires that energy (callpa) is always in flux, and those who control the flow of energy have power. Wak'as and shamans possess callpa and can use it to effect change (ibid.:26); hence the flow of callpa is integral to Andean perceptions of causality.

There is continuity between death and life in the Andean world that is reflected in the Bolivian tin miners' phrase "We eat the mines and the mines eat us" (Nash 1979; see also Allen 1997:76; McEwan, this volume). This perspective is widely shared among indigenous peoples of the New World, as seen, for instance, in the Mixtec saying "We eat the earth and the earth eats us" (Monaghan 1990:562–63). The flow of energy, however, is not just a transfer from the dead to the living, but is also a transfer of energy between different elements within the world. As Carolyn Dean notes (this volume), the division between stone and human beings is not "rock solid." Similarly, Anita Cook (this volume) discusses transformation and metamorphosis—for example, when people dress as bears, they become bears. The transformational potential of callpa allows for renewal, as when the mountain *apus* (lords) release llamas out onto the surface of the land through *pukios* (springs) (Flores Ochoa 1979:84–85).[1] The cycling of energy is also neatly captured by the observation that the earth nourishes potatoes, people eat the potatoes and then give food offerings back to Mother Earth (Mannheim and Salas, this volume).

Indeed, in the Andes, the world is conceived as a multi-level universe, an idea shared with many Amazonian groups, with a flow of energy connecting the different levels.[2] Springs, caves, and other points of connection between the levels are *paqarinas*, e.g., places of birth or origin. Both the Mixtec and the Bolivian miners implicitly recognized the reciprocal nature of the flow of energy, this being conceptualized as a cyclical phenomenon rather than as unidirectional.[3] Within this organizing framework, wak'as are agents possessing the potential (e.g., callpa) to transform the world and essential elements for the understanding of Andean cosmology (i.e., the understanding of the universe as an orderly system) (Webster's New Collegiate Dictionary 1960; Topic 2008; Topic and Topic 2009).

The chapters included in this volume explore diverse aspects of wak'as using archaeological, ethnographic, and linguistic data. Three of the main themes explored by the contributors to this volume include: (1) what is wak'a, (2) what is the relationship of wak'a to materiality, and (3) what is the nature of wak'a agency. Within these broad themes, the authors focus on a number of more specific issues that involve the discussion of animism, energy flow, the relationships between wak'as and humans, the partitive nature of wak'as, the relationships of wak'as to landscapes, wak'as as natural versus built features, the personhood of wak'as, their dynamic nature, and their efficacy as agents.

In this chapter, I will explore these themes further by drawing on the information provided in the chapters and comparing it with data from the Huamachuco region of the northern highlands of Peru. The chapters in the volume focus largely on central and southern Peru, so comparison with an example from the north will serve to further broaden our perspective on wak'as. Moreover, we have good archaeological and historical information from the Huamachuco region pertaining to the issues at hand. Indeed, one of the earliest sources to deal with wak'as in any detail is the account of the Augustinian priests who worked in Huamachuco (San Pedro 1992 [1560]). This early Augustinian account discusses a number of different wak'as; some obviously predate the Inka conquest of the area while others are clearly related to Inka domination. The principal wak'a of this region was Catequil, who was also an oracle. Catequil has been the subject of archaeological and historical study for a number of years (Topic 1992; Topic 2008; Topic and Topic n.d.; Topic et al. 2002) and provides an interesting comparison with wak'as from more southern Andean regions.

CATEQUIL

The wak'a known as Catequil was identified with a large cliff at the top of a high mountain (Betanzos 1987 [1551]; San Pedro 1992 [1560]) that is now called Cerro Icchal (Figure 12.1). Flanking this cliff were two smaller outcrops that were identified with Catequil's brother, Piguerao, and his mother, Cautaguan or Mama Catequil (Topic 2008; Topic et al. 2002) (Figure 12.2). Many of the chapters in this volume (e.g., Allen, Cook, Dean, Janusek, Kosiba, Makowski, Mannheim and Salas, McEwan, and Meddens) have related wak'as to landscape features and sightlines. From the top of Cerro Icchal, one can see the snow-capped peaks of the Cordillera Blanca some 150 km to the south as well as Marcahuamachuco, the largest archaeological site in the region, located 25 km to the northeast. Cerro Icchal itself is situated on the continental divide.

In addition to Cerro Icchal, there is a sanctuary, the site of Namanchugo, for the worship of Catequil, which is located below the cliff (Topic 2008; Topic et al. 2002). During the early occupation at Namanchugo (ca. AD 300–1200), the

FIGURE 12.1. *Cerro Icchal from the northeast; the cliff representing Catequil is located part way down the left side of the mountain, below the jagged summit, appearing as a small bump from this view and distance (photograph by author).*

primary activity seems to have been the preparation and consumption of large quantities of food, including the maize based foodstuffs called *sanco* and *chicha* (Topic 2008; Topic et al. 2002; Vásquez Sánchez and Rosales Tham 2006). The sanco contained grease as well as maize and may have been prepared using llama heads and feet for a stock since cranial and foot elements were much more common at Namanchugo than at the other excavated sites in the area (ibid.). In addition, the quantity of serving vessels and large, well-worn grinding stones recovered at the site (Topic et al. 2006) calls to mind the idea of forced feeding as ritual activity discussed by Allen (1997, and this volume).

The Augustinian account (San Pedro 1992 [1560]:171, 177) mentions that Catequil had servants, stewards, priests, herders, and many *haciendas*. Indeed, it seems likely that what later became the Hacienda San José de Porcón was originally the property of Catequil in the prehispanic period, only later to become the property of the Augustinian order for much of the Colonial and Republican periods (Topic 2013). The Hacienda San José de Porcón extends

FIGURE 12.2. *Cerro Icchal from the southeast; the photograph was taken from the platform mound at Namanchugo, which is also the sanctuary of Catequil. The central cliff is Catequil, the small peak on the left is Piguerao, and the curvilinear cliff on the right is Cautaguan or Mama Catequil. There are a large number of springs on the flanks of the mountain below the cliffs. In this view, the central cliff appears to dominate the mountain (photograph by author).*

over more than 150 km² encompassing lands suitable for herding and agriculture—including the cultivation of maize (Figure 12.3). These lands were undoubtedly originally used to support the worship of Catequil, including the feasting activities that Mannheim and Salas (this volume; also Bray 2012) note were crucial to the establishment of relationships between wak'as and people.

Catequil's "estate" is comparable in many respects to the Inka royal estates, one of which is described by Kosiba (this volume). It is also known that the other major wak'as had land for their support. Perhaps the best-known example is Pachacamac, another important oracle (see Chase, Makowski, this volume). Pachacamac also had a number of branch oracles dedicated to his wife and sons, which Rostworowski (1992b:51–52) argues served to provide access to distant resources. As with the royal estates, Catequil also had *yanakona* (i.e., the servants and stewards) dedicated to his service (San Pedro 1992 [1560]:177).[4]

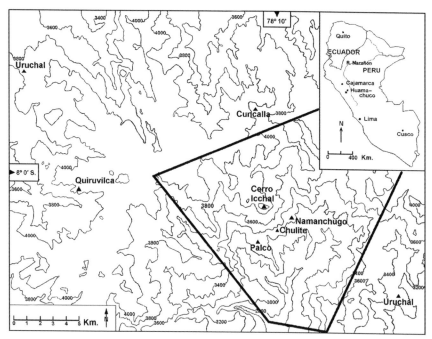

FIGURE 12.3. *Map showing location of Cerro Icchal and Namanchugo. The approximate extent of the Hacienda San José de Porcón is indicated by the polygon around Cerro Icchal. The location of Chulite is also indicated. Chuquicanra is located at Palco (map by Dennis Davies and author).*

Within Catequil's estate, there are a number of archaeological sites, but only three have been excavated in addition to Namanchugo (Downey 2009; Jofré Poblete 2007; Nesbitt 2003; Topic et al. 2006). One of these sites, Chulite, may have housed pilgrims while they were visiting Namanchugo. Another, Chuquicanra, has monumental buildings, storage facilities, and carved stone tenon heads; this site may have housed the stewards and servants of Catequil. The residents of this site seem to have consumed the meatier parts of the camelids, while the feet and heads of the animals were apparently used to prepare sanco at Namanchugo (Vásquez Sánchez and Rosales Tham 2006). While the Inka royal estates were a late innovation (Kosiba, this volume), the occupation of Chuquicanra dates from the middle of the Early Intermediate period through at least the Late Intermediate period. The evidence for feasting at Namanchugo also begins during the middle of the Early Intermediate period, so the provision of lands and yanakona for the service of wak'as probably was a pre-Inkaic practice.[5]

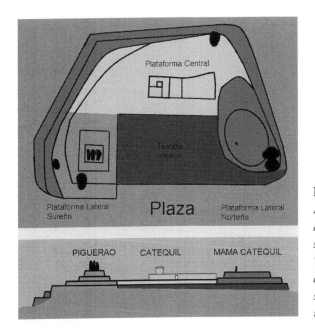

FIGURE 12.4.
Reconstruction of the plan and facade of the late sanctuary at Catequil. The late sanctuary was constructed to imitate the shape of the mountain and its cliffs (cf. Figure 12.2).

Sometime during the Late Intermediate period, possibly about AD 1200, Namanchugo was remodeled. Earlier buildings were filled in and retaining walls constructed in order to create an artificial mound (Figure 12.4). The mound was roughly U- or C-shaped and was purposefully built to imitate the shape of Cerro Icchal with its three cliffs (Topic 2008). Access to the mound was much more restricted than it had been to the earlier buildings, which had been sites of communal feasting. Indeed I think that the term "temple" could be applied to the later sanctuary. The innermost building of the temple complex, which may have housed a sculpture of Catequil (see below), could accommodate only one person at a time; the adjacent inner patio, where prognostications were announced, could accommodate less than a dozen people, probably elite pilgrims to the sanctuary (Topic et al. 2002).

Because of the restricted access, people appear to have begun to make pilgrimages to the top of Cerro Icchal about the same time that the Namanchugo sanctuary was remodeled. The archaeological remains on top of Cerro Icchal are the most extensive in the area, and excavations indicate that the occupation started about AD 1200 (Nesbitt 2003; Pérez Calderón 1988, 1994). The elevation, which is over 4,000 m, and the location on top of the mountain identified with Catequil, make it likely that the architecture found here was intended as temporary housing for pilgrims. The ceramics and other material remains associated with the site are consistent with pilgrims who likely lived within perhaps a 20 km radius, rather than having traveled from more distant regions (Nesbitt 2003). Frank Meddens (this volume) discusses a similar pattern of pilgrimage to the site of Usccunta that also seems to predate Inka conquest of the area.

The built sanctuary of Namanchugo not only imitated the mountain in its shape; it incorporated references to the mythical actions of Catequil, his brother (Piguerao), and his mother (Mama Catequil or Cautaguan) (Topic 2008). The part of the mound that imitated the cliff representing his mother was faced with a retaining wall made of river-rolled boulders. We believe that these egg-shaped stones are a reference to the belief that Catequil and Piguerao were born from eggs laid by Cautaguan, who died giving birth. On this part of the mound there was a statue of Mama Catequil fashioned from a stone with a natural hollow in the abdominal area that looked as though an egg-shaped piece of stone could have been removed from it (Figure 12.5). The concavity in the stone statue references a similar concavity in a natural outcrop on the cliff representing Catequil's mother.

The part of the mound imitating the cliff that represented Piguerao, on the other hand, was faced with angular stones and has huge blocks of stone taken from the mountain that are set upright to mimic the cliff. Janusek (this volume; also Allen 1997:81; McEwan, this volume) also notes the incorporation of stone quarried from sacred mountains in the platforms at Khonko Wankane. The central part of the mound representing Catequil himself was occupied by three stone walled enclosures, the southernmost of which housed the sanctuary itself (Topic et al. 2002) (Figure 12.4). The southern enclosure was paved with river-rolled cobbles the size of slingstones, a reference to Catequil as a lightning deity who makes the thunder with the crack of his sling.

In the southernmost enclosure, there were also three stone-lined receptacles for libations, each filled with river-rolled stones. Libations poured into these receptacles flowed through the small rounded stones and out through conduits under the pavement. These receptacles are one form of *ushnu*, a complex of platforms, stones, and basins that, in Inka practice, were related to rituals often overseen by royalty (see also Dean, Meddens, this volume; Pino Matos 2004). Two of these basins were located in the inner patio of the southern enclosure, which was also provided with a bench where a few people could have sat to observe the prognostications of the oracle as they were announced by the flow of liquid in a special canal (Topic 2008; Topic et al. 2002). The third basin was located in a small but massively built room that might have

Figure 12.5. *The statue of Cautaguan or Mama Catequil: (a) front and side; the part of the statue shown is about 185 cm tall; another 15 cm of the base of the statue was buried in the ground when this drawing was made (drawing by Daniel Castillo Benitez); (b) detail of the abdominal area; the concavity is a natural feature (photograph by author).*

housed a sculptural depiction of Catequil; this room comprised the innermost building of the temple complex and was accessible only from the inner patio just described. This small inner sanctum had a "socket" in the masonry just behind the libation receptacle where a sculpture of Catequil might have been placed.

CATEQUIL AS WAK'A

There are several material manifestations in our study area that could be considered to be the wak'a Catequil. The cliff on the top of Cerro Icchal was certainly one manifestation of the wak'a, and there may also have been a stone sculpture of Catequil located on top of the cliff (Betanzos 1987 [1551], pt. 2, chaps. 16–17; San Pedro 1992 [1560]:177). Atahualpa, the ruling Inka at the time of the Spanish incursion, was angered by a prophecy of the oracle and spent three months with an army in Porcón engaged in the destruction of Catequil (Betanzos 1987 [1551]). He ordered his soldiers to bring firewood to surround the hill and burn it. Then he ordered the soldiers to extinguish the fire with water, to bring more wood, and burn the hill again. This episode took place as Atahualpa's troops captured his rival, Huascar, and as notices of Pizarro's arrival reached him. Atahualpa clearly identified the power of the wak'a with the hill and the cliff, and the attention he devoted to their destruction signals Catequil's importance as well as Atahualpa's anger.

The Augustinians noted that the evidence of Atahualpa's fires were still visible in the 1550s (San Pedro 1992 [1560]:177–78), but they seem to have been more concerned with destroying the built sanctuary. Fathers Antonio Loçano and Juan Ramírez are credited with the destruction of this sanctuary. Archaeological evidence suggests that they pulled down the walls of the structure, mutilated the genital area of the statue of Mama Catequil, toppled the huge boulders that represented Piguerao, and pecked a cross in a boulder in the plaza. They also destroyed pieces of a sculptural representation of Catequil, which had been found in a cave in the mountains rather than in the sanctuary itself. It is quite possible that, influenced by the Christian preoccupation with idols and idolatry (see Mannheim and Salas, this volume), the Augustinians misunderstood the significance of the mountain and focused instead on the built sanctuary and its "idol." On the other hand, the archaeological evidence indicates that the oracle issued its pronouncements from within the sanctuary (Topic et al. 2002), so the Augustinian concern with the sanctuary was not entirely misplaced.

As will be discussed further below, the construction of buildings to house cult objects has a long history in the Andes (Cook, this volume) and may reflect a desire to "domesticate" a landscape (Allen, this volume; Dean, this volume), or, in contrast, create a new state of "nature" (Kosiba, this volume), or establish a co-residence with the wak'a (Dean, this volume; Mannheim and Salas, this volume). Here I consider, as well, whether the imitation of the mountain seen at the sanctuary of Namanchugo may have, in some sense, been intended to represent the creation of a *wawqe,* or brother, of the wak'a that was the mountain. The wawqe would have been revered to the same degree as the mountain itself (van de Guchte 1990:272–94; Allen, McEwan, this volume). Although wawqe are usually considered to be portable objects, in this case the sanctuary seems to have doubled for the mountain and was where the oracular pronouncements were made, as noted above.

There were also portable or sculpted images of Catequil. It is clear that there was at least one sculptural representation that Betanzos and the Augustinians identified with Catequil, and there may have been others as well. Assuming that there was more than one representation of Catequil, one may have originally been associated with the top of the cliff but was apparently destroyed by Atahualpa; it may have been the source of the fragments discovered by the Augustinians (Betanzos 1987 [1551]; San Pedro 1992 [1560]:178). Another representation may have been located within the sanctuary itself. A third may have traveled with Huayna Capac to Ecuador (Sarmiento de Gamboa 1907 [1572]:165–66). Still another was discovered by Father Francisco Cano in Cahuana (modern Cabana) and Tauca, in Conchucos south of Huamachuco (Arriaga 1968 [1621]:203).

Some 300 "sons" of Catequil were discovered by the Augustinians after the destruction of the sanctuary (San Pedro 1992 [1560]:179–80). The first of these was found by a woman who took it to a shaman (hechizero); the shaman asked the stone who he was and the stone responded that he was Tantaguayanay, son of Catequil (ibid.:179). These sons of Catequil are described as small stones and may have been what are now referred to as *piedras del rayo* or "lightning stones." Piedras del rayo are said to be found where bolts of lightning touch ground.[6] They are still used today for curing purposes. Two such stones that I have examined were in fact meteorite fragments. They were heavy and about the shape and size of eggs. Cieza (1984 [1553]:237) mentions that the people of Huamachuco worshiped stones about the size of eggs. Zachary Chase (this volume) also presents interesting data pertaining to egg-shaped stones for the Huarochirí region, where Pariacaca was recognized as the principal wak'a. There are many similarities in the myths of Catequil and Pariacaca, one of which is that they were both born from eggs (Topic et al. 2002). The variety of material manifestations of Catequil is a good illustration of the partitive nature, or distributed personhood, of wak'a, as discussed by Catherine Allen, Tamara Bray, and Colin McEwan in the present volume.

While wak'as were materialized in stones and in landscapes, they also had an animistic aspect (Allen, Bray, Cook, and McEwan, this volume; Bray 2009). Cristóbal de Albornoz (1984 [1583–84]:210) described Catequil as "some tall rocks in a plain and as in the air above these" (unas piedras altas en un llano, y como en el ayre encima destas). The plain might describe the location of the sanctuary at the base of the cliffs, while the allusion to the wak'a being in the air above the rocks is vague. Usually, Albornoz specifies that a wak'a is a rock, lake, mountain, or other physical object (see McEwan, this volume, Table 9.1). His lack of precision in this case may reflect a view that the whole landscape, including the sanctuary and the mountain, was imbued with potency, or callpa. As Taylor (1987:26) points out, people passing near these powerful places associated with the great wak'a could acquire part of that potency or force.

As noted above, both the mountain and the sanctuary have the form of an asymmetrical "U." Donald Lathrap (1985) previously pointed out that this shape is a common form for early platform mounds. He argues that the form was a way to focus power by creating an *axis mundi* (see also chapters by Cook, Janusek, and Meddens, this volume). An excellent example is the "Old Temple" at Chavín de Huántar, where the Lanzón in a cruciform chamber at the center of the U-shaped platform formed an axis mundi. I have argued that both the sanctuary of Catequil and Cerro Icchal also formed axes mundi (Topic 2008). As such, they would be places where the flow of callpa was facilitated.[7] Catequil was, in fact, also an *apu* or major mountain who promised to provide his devotees with food, llamas, and children (San Pedro 1992 [1560]:176). The concept of axis mundi however, is not limited to U-shaped platforms. Ushnus in the sense of stone basins filled with small rocks acted as axes mundi by serving as conduits for libations to penetrate into the earth (Dean, Meddens, this volume). Cook (this volume) describes how below-ground burial crypts were surmounted by multi-storied structures that also formed an axis. The springs and pacarinas, mentioned earlier, might also be viewed as axes mundi through which energy can flow between the different levels of the world. The navel can be considered an axis mundi in the context of the body.[8] John Janusek's description (this volume) of sculptural imagery from Khonko Wankane illustrates this point. There, two anthropomorphic stelae are carved with neonate catfish, representing forces of generation, and a human figure with exposed ribs, representing death. The navel is defined by two face-to-face catfish on the preserved front of one stela, and the same motif is on the preserved back of the other stela. If the two stelae were symmetrical, as Janusek suggests, the navel becomes an axis mundi passing right through the body. Janusek also notes that the location of Khonko Wankane was already a significant nexus of trade routes before the larger platform mounds were constructed.

In all of these cases, places are recognized where the potential for the flow of energy, and therefore the potential for transformation and renewal, is heightened. Some, like Cerro Icchal, the location of Khonko Wankane, and springs, are natural places. Others, like ushnus, platforms, and burial structures, are constructed features that demarcate ritually important spaces.

CATEQUIL AS AGENT

The complex narrative in which Catequil was embedded reveals him as a dynamic agent of transformation and renewal (San Pedro 1992 [1560]; Topic 2008; Topic et al. 2002). He has power over death, which he demonstrates by resuscitating his mother, who had died giving him birth. He establishes a new world order, a *pachacuti*, by destroying the former inhabitants of the province of Huamachuco and repopulating the region with new people. In the process, he and his brother used slings to kill the former inhabitants and gold and silver digging implements to release the new people from their paqarina. It is interesting that both Catequil and his brother, working together, carry out these activities because it references the concept of wawqe mentioned earlier.

In the myth of Catequil the concept of *yanantin* is also present. Yanantin refers to a complementary pair in which both parts are necessary to the proper functioning of the whole (González Holguín 1989 [1608]:181, 364). In Andean thought, the complementary pair par excellence is the male and female couple. As Dean (this volume) points out, the complementary pair working together is stronger than the individual. The mention of the detail that Catequil and his brother use golden and silver digging tools may be an allusion to that sexual division, since gold and silver were often considered to symbolize male and female respectively. Rostworowski (1983:22–23) has commented on the sexual ambiguity represented by pairs of masculine wak'as in the context of the concept of yanantin, specifically citing Catequil and Piguerao as an example.[9]

Zachary Chase (this volume) emphasizes that wak'as exist in time. As Allen (this volume) notes, however, time is not linear but relational, defining different worlds or "suns" where things are perceived in different ways. The pachacuti leading to the replacement of population is depicted by the Augustinians as taking place in the remote past. Catequil's actions, however, in killing and expelling the previous inhabitants also lead to the definition of the boundaries of the Inkaic province of Huamachuco: that is, something that happened in the relatively recent past, less than 100 years before the time that San Pedro was writing (Topic 1998). The places where the previous inhabitants were chased out of the province are still marked by toponyms bearing their name, e.g., *guachemin*. These place-names, and the location of the contemporary paqarina, are in fact situated along the borders of the Inkaic province.

Andean political loyalties were closely related to social relations between the *kuraka* and his subjects, and those subjects could be interspersed with the subjects of other kurakas in discontinuous territories (Rostworowski 1992a). Still, the concern with boundaries and boundary markers that is highlighted by the Huamachuco creation myth demonstrates that a strong sense of territoriality pervaded indigenous communities and polities. A number of the papers in this volume discuss territoriality in terms of sightlines, horizons, and boundary markers (see chapters by Allen, Dean, Makowski, and Meddens). The description of the reorganization and repopulation of Ollantaytambo (Kosiba, this volume) is a striking parallel to the mythical repopulation of Huamachuco by Catequil. Both Inka rulers and powerful wak'as could bring about new world orders.

In a more strictly historical sense, the Inka conquest resulted in a reorganization of the political landscape that placed Catequil, his mountain, and his sanctuary in the center of the province of Huamachuco (i.e., the Late Horizon administrative region) (Topic 1998). It also, by implication, led to the rewriting of the creation myth. Surprisingly, however, the Inkas did not make any obvious changes to the sanctuary or estate of Catequil; this is in contrast to the Inka intervention at Pachacamac, another oracle, where the site of the sanctuary was very heavily impacted (Makowski, this volume).

All of the actions on the part of Catequil referred to above involve movement across the landscape: from the center, where he probably resuscitated his mother, to the northern, eastern, and western extremes of the province, where he chased the *guachemines* down into the yungas, to the southern edge of the province, where he freed the people from their paqarina; then back to the center again, where he commanded that he be worshiped together with his brother and mother as cliffs on Cerro Icchal. Although wak'as are often related to fixed features of the landscape, they can also move through space and, indeed, shape the landscape through their actions (Chase, Dean, Kosiba, McEwan, this volume).

Another interesting aspect of Catequil's agency was his power to make other wak'as speak, as recounted in a story from Huarochirí (Salomon and Urioste 1991:101–2). Chase (this volume) relates how Catequil persuaded Llocllay Huancupa to reveal his identity to humans. The ability to make other wak'as speak may be related to Catequil's aspect of lightning god, since being struck by lightning is one way to become a shaman (e.g., the kamasqa priests mentioned by Allen, this volume). It is interesting also that Llocllay Huancupa was related to water (Salomon and Urioste 1991:101–2, n.472). Catequil as a lightning deity was also the source of abundant rainfall, and Cerro Icchal is still believed to be linked to rainfall; residents in a 20 km radius around the peak keep a close eye on it for signs of rain. Again, a number of chapters in this volume (e.g. Allen, Dean, Makowski, McEwan, and Meddens) highlight the act of watching: mountains watching people, people watching people, and people watching mountains.

The Inkas spread the cult of Catequil to Ecuador where there are seven places that bear the name Catequillay (Topic and Topic n.d.; Topic et al.

2002). These are springs that are still important in healing rites and in rituals of initiation for shamans (Costales et al. 1996). In Ecuador the initiates are immersed in the springs overnight as a test of their strength and will; the Augustinians mention that the principal way that the devil selected his priests in Huamachuco was to lure them into lakes and half-drown them (San Pedro 1992 [1560]:166). Thus, Catequil was not only materialized as a mountain and as stones, but was also closely associated with water.

The transfer of wak'as from one region to another by the Inkas was not uncommon. Makowski (this volume; also Chase, this volume) discusses the mitmaqkuna at Pueblo Viejo, who established their own wak'a in their new town. Dean and Meddens (this volume) note that a wak'a could be transferred from one place to another just by moving a stone or textile that had been in contact with the original. In Huamachuco, mitmaqkuna from Canco in the Cuzco area brought with them a wak'a that was called Llimillay in Canco and Topa llimillay in Huamachuco. Topa llimillay was one of the several stones that had been part of the wak'a in their home territory of Xaquixaguana (Albornoz 1984 [1583–84]; San Pedro 1992 [1560]:186; Topic 1992; McEwan, this volume, Table 9.1).

Although Catequil was materialized primarily as a mountain, he moved about like a person. Like a person, he also had family—a mother, father, brother, aunt, and sons are mentioned (San Pedro 1992 [1560]; also Arriaga 1968 [1621]:202). While no wife is mentioned for Catequil, Pachacamac, another famous oracle, had a wife, sons, and daughters (Rostworowski 1992b; Salomon and Urioste 1991:49). Pat Lyon (1978) drew archaeologists' attention to female supernaturals decades ago, but more research needs to be focused on gender in the study of wak'as. It is not clear to me, for example, if Andean people thought of wak'as as always gendered. It is also unclear if, when the gender of wak'as is mentioned, males outnumber females; Lyon's original article identified relatively few female supernaturals. If there is a male bias in the colonial literature on extirpation, it may, in part, be due to Spanish prudery and general focus on men. The Augustinians, for example, record at least one female wak'a, Guagalmojon, who scandalized them with her exposed genitalia (San Pedro 1992 [1560]:193), and Lyon (1978:118) notes that there was a female oracle at Apurimac.

Not only were wak'a gendered but they were also sexual beings, as depicted lustily in the Huarochirí manuscript (Salomon 1991:18–19; Chase this volume). In Huamachuco, Guagalmojon did not hesitate to remind her devotees that they had their origin in her *"vergüenças mujeriles."* There are also two very odd descriptions of wak'as that may have been shaped as phalluses: (1) Casiapoma:

"...era de palmo y medio de largo era muy mal hecha y fea y tenya vna garganta desgarada y en ella vn agujero y dado por encima un betum (*sic*) q. pareçia cuerpo humano mas q. palo ..." (it was one and a half palms [about 12 inches] in length, it was very badly made and ugly and had a licentious neck and in the neck a hole and a wax or pitch on top that seemed more a human body than a pole); (2) Tantaçoro (who has the same name as a son of Catequil): "...hazia entender a los yndios q. creçia como creçen los h.es [hombres] y no pudo creçer mas de hasta palmo y medio q. tenya de grandeza y altura ..." (he made the Indians understand that he grew as men grow and he could not grow more than up to a palm and a half [about 12 inches] that he had of size and height) (San Pedro 1992 [1560]:183, 191–92). Lyon (1978:111) notes that copulation between male and female supernaturals is shown on Middle Horizon pots from the north and north-central coast; she also mentions the creation of camelids by a married pair of supernaturals, who sent the animals out onto the surface of the earth from their abode in a lake (ibid.:117–18). Sexual reproduction among wak'a was a natural part of the renewal of the world.[10]

As noted above, such activities may also be indicated by paired male and female representations in the archaeological record (Lyon 1978:100–111). Paired figures occur on the Tello Obelisk at Chavín, Yayamama-style stelae in the Titicaca basin, large Wari-style urns, a wooden staff from Pachacamac, etc. It would be interesting to know whether the twin stelae from Khonko Wankane (Janusek, this volume) were a male/female pair. A cotton textile excavated by Junius Bird from the preceramic site of Huaca Prieta may be the earliest representation of a male/female pair (Bird 1963, fig. 3). It is not just reproduction in the sense of duplicating or copying, however, that is being represented. Transformation of material form is also taking place. The union of male and female caimans on the Tello Obelisk, for example, is associated with the emergence of various types of plants (Lathrap 1973).

The Mehinaku from the Xingu region of Amazonia have an interesting myth about the origin of one of their staple crops, the pequí fruit, that bears some relation to the Tello Obelisk insofar as it refers to the caiman as the origin of domesticated plants. According to the myth, a caiman took the form of a handsome man and seduced two sisters from the group. When the men in the tribe found out what was going on, they killed the caiman. In grief, the sisters planted the caiman's genitalia, and the pequí grew from his testicles (Pasini and Wallace 1981).

A similar event is the central theme of a myth from the central coast of Peru. The Sun impregnated an impoverished woman who gave birth to a son. Pachacamac, however, was jealous of the Sun and in anger tore the child apart. So that in the future no one would worship the Sun for lack of food, Pachacamac planted the body parts of the dead infant. From the teeth grew maize and from the ribs and long bones came manioc. The flesh yielded the other fruits (Calancha 1974–82 [1638], 3:931–32). Archaeologically, this may be best represented by plants sprouting from human trophy heads in Nasca art (Carmichael 1994) or the images of death and regeneration on the stelae from Khonko Wankane (Janusek, this volume).[11]

A recurring theme in Andean mythology is the recognition that life requires death (Allen 1997:76). In a myth collected in Huarochirí, humans were originally immortal (Salomon and Urioste 1991:43–44). Humans did die but came back to life after only five days. Huallallo Caruincha, who was the principal wak'a at that time, allowed human couples to have only two children, and he would eat one of these. Even with a slow rate of population increase, the world became overpopulated and people were poor and miserable. Balance was restored when people stopped coming back to life after five days.

Death established a reciprocal relationship with life by allowing the life force to be transformed into another material manifestation. Sometimes, as just discussed, the transformation involves the transfer of energy (callpa) from humans to plants; in the example provided by Dean (this volume), humans are transformed into rocks.[12] At other times, the relationship entails a flow of life from death through the paqarina. Cook, for example (this volume), points out that the paqarina can be the portal from which people both emerge at birth and return at death. Cieza (1984 [1553]:268) describes the paqarina referred to by Cook as a lake where peoples' souls go when they die so that they can be transferred to another body and reborn as humans. Allen (1997:81) notes that "all beings are intrinsically interconnected through their sharing a matrix of animated substance."

It is noteworthy that the reciprocal relationship established between life and death is an intimate one, shaping interaction among closely related individuals. Catequil resuscitates his own mother, though, in order to repopulate Huamachuco, he kills his uncles. In the case discussed by Cook (this volume) and in the myth from Huarochirí, people accept death so that they can have more children. The reciprocal relationship of life and death, however, also establishes intimate relationships between humans and the nonhuman world: Pachacamac kills his half-brother in order to provide food plants for the dead child's mother; the Mehinaku rely on the fruit generated from the body of their brother-in-law; the Tukano hunt their own (or, preferably, other human) ancestors. This is the meaning of "We eat the mines/earth and the mines/earth eat us."

CAMAY, RELATIONSHIP, AND RECIPROCITY

The chapters in this volume emphasize the centrality of social relationships, not only between people but also between people and wak'as, and between and among wak'as. Social relationships are based on reciprocal exchanges of food, drink, labor, and energy, as various authors explain (Allen, Mannheim and Salas, this volume), and the goal of these reciprocal exchanges is the ongoing reproduction of society and the renewal of the world.

González Holguín's Quechua dictionary (1989 [1608]:46, 48) defines *camay* in one place as "the task within a larger work" (*la tarea en el trauajo*) and later as "my obligation" (*mi obligación*). There is an implication that camay as an ongoing process of renewal does require various players to contribute to the larger endeavor, to fulfill their obligation and to perform their duty. As Allen notes in her chapter, the weaver works with the "Weaving Mother" to produce a piece of cloth. In the same way, Catequil "promises" food, children, and camelids to his devotees, but they must work with him to transform earth, seed, and water into food. Feasting and prayer establishes the relationship, but creation is a joint effort of humans and wak'as. Janusek (this volume) provides an example of how wak'a worship can result in a new ecosystem, but the creation of this new productive resource requires hard work (also Kosiba, this volume).

As noted above, the building of structures to house cult objects has a long history in the Andes and may have multiple explanations: the creation of a site for cohabitation with the wak'a, or a means of domesticating a wak'a, or the creation of a new state of nature. Similarly, statues may be viewed as wawqes or brothers of the wak'a; carved stone seats may be places where important humans can meld with stone; and platforms and ushnus can create axes mundi to facilitate the flow of energy. All of these actions are forms of interaction between humans and wak'as, and all relate to camay as a shared and mutual process of creation that is dynamic and ongoing. The phrase *la tarea en el trauajo* suggests an analogy to the mit'a, or work by turns, where larger jobs are divided into smaller tasks that are performed in turns by members of different social groups; as John Murra often phrased it, "each one relieving the other" (personal communication). We might recognize this reciprocal obligation to create in many different ways in the archaeological record.

For example, it was common to build walls around important rock outcrops. The natural outcrop was probably considered wak'a, but what was the purpose of the wall? Kosiba (this volume) points out that such a wall might define a space for private worship that would not be visible to people outside. In contrast, Cook (this volume) considers circular and D-shaped Wari walls to be part of the wak'a itself, built low enough so that rituals performed inside the wall were visible to observers outside. In either case, the act of constructing the wall, as part of a process of working with the wak'a, may have been as important as any other consideration.

The Augustinians noted that people constructed baskets to hold small wak'as and then dressed these baskets in elaborately woven cloth (San Pedro 1992 [1560]:169–70). Larger statues and even sanctuary walls were often ornamented with cloth. Wak'as were also provided by devotees with the accoutrements for their worship such as trumpets, plates, lances, and other necessary objects. The artisans who made all these types of artifacts had the title camayoc—whether the artifacts produced were associated with domestic activities or the worship of wak'as.

People in the Andean region still create small models of desired objects, such as houses, corrals, animals, and vehicles. These are constructed at propitious places. For instance, I have seen these at the archaeological site of Cerro Baul, and they are also made on the pilgrimage to Qoyllur Rit'i (Allen 1988:196–97; 1997). The act of constructing the model is a way of asking the wak'a to grant the "wish" that the model represents. As Cook, Chase, and McEwan (this volume) point out in their discussions of *inqas* and *illas*, the models, in this case small figurines, are considered to have generative properties.

In the Andes it is common practice to carry small stones a short distance along the road in order to deposit them in *apachetas*. Meddens (this volume), for instance, discusses this practice and its relationship to the ushnu complex. The carving of stone seats is another common Inkaic practice and a central theme of Dean's paper (this volume). In both cases, the work performed often defines a place from which a person can view another place that has ritual importance; in both cases, these features also function, at least in part, to establish a spatial relationship between the viewer and the object viewed.

These ritual activities can be considered offerings of material or labor and in that sense they can be viewed as petitions and prayers *to* the wak'a. These activities can also be taken as material evidence of people working *with* the wak'as. In this sense, both people and wak'as are camac, or creators, working together as yanantin, complementary pairs, to produce order in the world by maintaining a right, or correct, relationship.

Another aspect of relationship and reciprocity between humans and wak'as is efficacy. The term efficacy when applied to a wak'a can be understood to reference the wak'a's ability to "effect," e.g., to make some kind of difference in the world—in other words, it refers to its agency (Bray 2009:362). "Efficacy" can also measure the extent to which it is a successful agent, beneficial to its devotees. Bray (this volume) cites Garcilaso's statement that wak'as were not worshiped for their own sake but rather for the advantage that they provided to the community. Wak'as, as well as political leaders, had to demonstrate success if they were to maintain their authority (Topic 2008). Taylor (1987:26; also van de Guchte 1990:257–58) notes that those wak'as that were not successful lost influence. The famous drawing in Guamán Poma (1980 [1615]:261 [263]) of Topa Inka questioning the wak'as about a drought illustrates the point (Figure 12.6). The Inka threatens to stop making offerings (i.e., stop reciprocating) to the wak'a that is not behaving beneficially. A modern parallel is illustrated by the use of human skulls found in the ruins around Huamachuco. Residents of the area tell me that when they find a skull in the ruins, they might take it home and offer it cigarettes and coca in the hope of receiving benefit; if they have bad luck, however, they return it to the place where they found it.

The necessity for humans and wak'as to maintain reciprocal relationships results in a form of complementary or shared agency. For example, a wak'a cannot be "worshiped" until people recognize it as a wak'a. Not every stone, mountain, or spring was a wak'a. The account, mentioned earlier, of the woman finding a "son of Catequil" is an example (San Pedro 1992 [1560]:179; also Arriaga 1968 [1621]:204). Although the woman recognized the small stone as an interesting and unusual object, until she took it to the priest, its true identity was not recognized. Similarly, in the central highland area of Huarochirí, Cuni Raya Vira Cocha was not recognized as a major wak'a because he went around poorly dressed (Salomon and Urioste 1991:46–47). Llocllay Huancupa was not recognized as a wak'a until Catequil coaxed him to reveal his identity. While the term yanantin usually refers to complementary agency between men and women or other paired elements, the term can also describe the complementary interactions between humans and wak'as that are necessary for both to be effective.

Wak'as were sources of fertility and renewal. Humans sought them out and established reciprocal relationships with them. These relationships were necessary to facilitate the flow of energy, callpa, among the different agents within the universe. This was an ongoing process of camay, of renewal, in which all parts of the universe, including humans and wak'a, were involved.

CONCLUSION

Tamara Bray set out an interesting, stimulating, and challenging agenda in asking us to consider wak'a as a point of intersection of materiality, agency, and personhood. The chapters collected in this volume maintain a focus on these key themes while engaging with a rich diversity of issues, times, and spaces.

261

CAPITVLO DELOS IDOLOS
VACA·BILLCA·INCAP

FIGURE 12.6. *Guamán Poma's depiction of Topa Inka talking to the wak'as (Guamán Poma 1980 [1615]:261 [263]).*

I have not attempted to summarize the chapters or to analyze the key concepts and interpretations raised. Instead, I have used the oracle, apu, and wak'a known as Catequil as a means of identifying some of the common ground in Andeanists' thinking about wak'as, as well as topics that are currently contested and invite further exploration. Perhaps these comments will provide a stimulus to readers to return to chapters they have already read with new questions in mind.

Ironically, the major source for understanding late prehispanic wak'as is the literature produced by those who were trying to destroy them. The extirpators clearly believed in the power of wak'as and considered them to be animated by the devil. They employed a methodical approach to extirpation based on the discovery of wak'as, the classification of objects associated with wak'a worship, and the destruction of those objects. While they realized that power could be transferred from one object to another, they attempted to cope with this problem by continued campaigns of physical destruction.

This collection, by focusing on themes such as practice, relationship, reciprocity, agency, and personhood, will stimulate new thinking about the "theology" of wak'as not only within their Andean context but also within the larger context of indigenous cosmology in the New World.

ACKNOWLEDGMENTS

I thank Theresa Lange Topic for encouragement and many helpful comments. Tamara Bray's questions and comments have helped me to clarify my thoughts and language.

NOTES

1. As a further illustration of how concepts are shared with non-Andean peoples, I will use Geraldo Reichel-Dolmatoff's monograph on the Tukano to highlight a number of parallels between Andean and Amazonian thought (Reichel-Dolmatoff 1971). The Tukano Master of Animals, like the Andean Apus, or Mountain Lords, is identified with isolated rocky hills on the otherwise flat plain of the Amazon. The Master of Animals keeps large herds inside these hills, but will release some as a result of negotiations with the Tukano shaman (ibid.:80–86).

2. The basic cosmological view of the Tukano is that the world consists of three levels, with distinctions within the levels, some of which are identified with male principles and some with female principles (ibid.:43–47).

3. The Tukano also view the cyclical circulation of energy between the levels of the universe as resulting in procreation (ibid.:53–55): "The larger circuit of fertilization-fecundity, of the attraction of two fundamental complementary elements, embraces all the biosphere, all the Cosmos, in a grand synthesis of the structure of the Universe" (ibid.:55).

4. The use of the term *yanakona* in this context may need further explanation. In the Inka Empire, yanakona were people who worked full time for the state or for elite nobles. Thus they were exempt from the general labor tax, the *mit'a*. In early colonial Spanish, the yanakona were glossed as *criados*, or members of the household or retainers of the household or people who were brought up within the house of a noble. San Pedro (1992 [1560]:176–77) states that Catequil had "vn gran pueblo para su serbiçio...y como digo todo El pueblo Estava para serbiçio de la guaca y avia grandes Casas de serui.o y tenya munchas (*sic*) haziendas y çinco sacerdotes dos mayordomos y otra muncha (*sic*) gente y criados . . ." ([Catequil had] a large town/people for his service . . . and as I say the whole town/people was for the service of the wak'a and there were great houses for service and he had many estates and five priests and two stewards and many other people and members of his household).

5. In another article (Topic 2009), I have shown that Rowe's (1948) perceptive suggestion that the Chimu had instititutionalized yanakona before the Inka was,

indeed, correct. In the context of Catequil, San Pedro's very explicit description of the personnel and estates dedicated to the service of the cult is a clear parallel to the Inka royal estates worked by yanakona that supported the Inka emperors and their descendants. Note also that Catequil's estates were confiscated by the *encomendero* Juan de Sandoval and that this would only have been possible if the lands were recognized by the Spanish as the property of a pagan cult (Topic 2013).

6. Where lightning touches ground, the Tukano shaman hopes to find crystals, which become an essential part of his tool kit. The "lightning crystals" are thought to cause sickness (Reichel-Dolmatoff 1971:49). The Quechua also view crystals as relating to lightning strikes (Allen 1997:77).

7. This can be seen as somewhat similar to the way the Tukano view the levels of the universe as penetrated by a hollow bone, a phallic element, which unites the levels in perpetual copulation and allows for the circulation of energy between the levels (Reichel-Dolmatoff 1971:49).

8. The Tukano understand the embryo to receive energy through the umbilicus (ibid.:51).

9. The Tukano also recognize masculine and feminine principles that go beyond the physical nature of the body. For example, forest is masculine, while river is feminine, a distinction that parallels the Andean characterization of mountains as masculine (Apu) and flatter fertile earth as feminine (Pachamama). More generally, they recognize two different forms of creative energy: a receptive, feminine form and a forceful, masculine form. The two energies together result in fertilization and fecundity. The Tukano view a leader or shaman as possessing masculine energy (ibid.:54–55). Callpa corresponds to the Tukano concept of masculine energy; González Holguín (1989 [1608]:44) lists *callparuna*, *callpayoc*, and *sinchi* as synonyms, meaning strong (man).

10. The complementarity between the sexes is the basis for the Tukano understanding of the universe and the model of sexual reproduction is how they account for renewal (Reichel-Dolmatoff 1971:243)

11. The Tukano ascribe the origin of the coca plant as well as the hallucinogenic plant, *Banisteriopsis caapi,* to the planting of fingers torn off the bodies of daughters of the Master of Animals during childbirth (ibid.:36–37).

12. Among the Tukano, this is best demonstrated by the relationship between hunter and prey. They consider the amount of energy in the universe to be fixed and therefore recycling the energy is necessary for renewal (ibid.:50, 218–19). Men hunt animals for nourishment, but in exchange the shaman must promise to deliver a certain number of human souls to the Master of Animals in order to replenish the herds (ibid.:82). The hunt itself is viewed in sexual terms as a courtship, where the hunter tries to seduce the game into allowing itself to be killed (ibid.:220).

REFERENCES CITED

Albornoz, Cristóbal de. 1984 [1583–84]. "Instrucción para descubrir todas las guacas del piru y sus camayos y haciendas." In *Albornoz y el espacio ritual andino prehispánico*, ed. Pierre Duviols. *Revista Andina* 2:194–222.

Allen, Catherine J. 1988. *The Hold Life Has: Coca and Cultural Identity in an Andean Community*. Washington, DC: Smithsonian Institution Press.

Allen, Catherine J. 1997. "When Pebbles Move Mountains: Iconicity and Symbolism in Quechua Ritual." In *Creating Context in Andean Cultures*, ed. Rosaleen Howard-Malverde, 73–84. Oxford: Oxford University Press.

Arriaga, Pablo José de. 1968 [1621]. "Extirpación de la idolatría del Pirú." In *Crónicas peruanas de interés indígena*, 192–277. Biblioteca de Autores Españoles, vol. 209. Madrid: Real Academia Española.

Betanzos, Juan de. 1987 [1551]. *Suma y narración de los Incas*. Ed. María del Carmen Martín Rubio. Madrid: Ediciones Atlas.

Bird, Junius B. 1963. "Pre-Ceramic Art from Huaca Prieta, Chicama Valley." *Ñawpa Pacha* 1:29–34.

Bray, Tamara L. 2009. "An Archaeological Perspective on the Andean Concept of *Camaquen*: Thinking Through Late Pre-Columbian *Ofrendas* and *Huacas*." *Cambridge Archaeological Journal* 19 (3): 357–66. http://dx.doi.org/10.1017/S0959774309000547.

Bray, Tamara L. 2012. "Ritual Commensality between Human and Non-Human Persons: Investigating Native Ontologies in the Late Pre-Columbian Andean World." In *Between Feasts and Daily Meals: Towards an Archaeology of Commensal Spaces*, ed. Susan Pollock. *eTopoi. Journal of Ancient Studies* (special volume) 2:197–212.

Calancha, Antonio de la. 1974–82 [1638]. *Corónica moralizada del orden de San Augustín en el Perú*. 6 vols. Ed. Ignacio Prado Pastor. Lima: Imprenta de la Universidad Nacional Mayor de San Marcos.

Carmichael, Patrick. 1994. "The Life from Death Continuum in Nasca Imagery." *Andean Past* 4:81–90.

Cieza de León, Pedro de. 1984 [1553]. *Crónica del Perú: Primera Parte*. 2nd ed. Colección Clásicos Peruanos. Lima: Pontificia Universidad Católica del Perú y Academia Nacional de la Historia.

Costales, Piedad Peñaherrera de, Alfredo Costales Samaniego, and Jaime A. Costales Peñaherrera. 1996. *Mitos Quitu-Cara*. Quito: ABYA-YALA.

Downey, Jordan Thomas. 2009. "*Catequil's Lithics: Stone Tools from an Andean Complex Society*." Master's thesis. Trent University, Peterborough, Ontario.

Flores Ochoa, Jorge A. 1979. *Pastoralists of the Andes*. Trans. Ralph Bolton. Philadelphia: Institute for the Study of Human Issues.

González Holguín, Diego. 1989 [1608]. *Vocabulario de la lengua general de todo el Perú llamada lengua Qquichua o del Inca*. Lima: Universidad Nacional Mayor de San Marcos.

Guamán Poma de Ayala, Felipe. 1980 [1615]. *El primer nueva corónica y buen gobierno*. Ed. John V. Murra and Rolena Adorno. Mexico City: Siglo Veintiuno.

Jofré Poblete, Daniella. 2007. "Namanchugo: Ritual Practices, Changes and Continuities in an Andean Shrine." Master's thesis, Trent University, Peterborough, Ontario.

Lathrap, Donald W. 1973. "Gifts of the Cayman: Some Thoughts on the Subsistence Basis of Chavín." In *Variation in Anthropology: Essays in Honor of John C. McGregor*, ed. Donald W. Lathrap and Jody Douglas, 91–105. Urbana: Illinois Archaeological Survey.

Lathrap, Donald W. 1985. "Jaws: The Control of Power in the Early Nuclear American Ceremonial Center." In *Early Ceremonial Architecture in the Andes*, ed. Christopher B. Donnan, 241–67. Washington, DC: Dumbarton Oaks Research Library and Collection.

Lyon, Patricia Jean. 1978. "Female Supernaturals in Ancient Peru." *Ñawpa Pacha* 16:95–140.

Monaghan, John. 1990. "Sacrifice, Death, and the Origins of Agriculture in the Codex Vienna." *American Antiquity* 55 (3): 559–69. http://dx.doi.org/10.2307/281286.

Nash, June C. 1979. *We Eat the Mines and the Mines Eat Us: Dependency and Exploitation in Bolivian Tin Mines*. New York: Columbia University Press.

Nesbitt, Jason. 2003. *"Cerro Icchal: An Andean Place of Ritual."* Master's thesis, Trent University, Peterborough, Ontario.

Pasini, Carlos, and Melanie Wallace. 1981. *We Are Mehinaku*. 59 min. Carlos Pasini and Melanie Wallace, producers. Odyssey. New York: Grenada Television International.

Pérez Calderón, Ismael. 1988. "Monumentos arqueológicos de Santiago de Chuco, La Libertad." *Boletín de Lima* 60:33–44.

Pérez Calderón, Ismael. 1994. "Monumentos arqueológicos de Santiago de Chuco, La Libertad." *Boletín de Lima* 16:225–74.

Pino Matos, José Luis. 2004. "El ushnu Inka y la organización del espacio en los principales *tampus* de los *wamani* de la sierra central del Chinchaysuyu." *Chungara* 36 (2): 303–11.

Reichel-Dolmatoff, Gerardo. 1971. *Amazonian Cosmos: The Sexual and Religious Symbolism of the Tukano Indians*. Chicago: University of Chicago Press.

Rostworowski de Díez Canseco, María. 1983. *Estructuras andinas del poder: Ideología religiosa y política*. Lima: Instituto de Estudios Peruanos.

Rostworowski de Díez Canseco, María. 1992a. "Etnias forasteros en la visita Toledana a Cajamarca." In *Las visitas a Cajamarca 1571–72/1578,* ed. Maria Rostworowski and Pilar Remy, 1:9–36. Fuentes e Investigaciones para la Historia del Perú, no. 9. Lima: Instituto de Estudios Peruanos.

Rostworowski de Díez Canseco, María. 1992b. *Pachacamac y el señor de los milagros: Una trayectoría milenaria.* Lima: Instituto de Estudios Peruanos.

Rowe, John H. 1948. "The Kingdom of Chimor." *Acta Americana* 6 (1–2): 26–59.

Salomon, Frank. 1991. "Introductory Essay." In *The Huarochirí Manuscript: Testament of Ancient and Colonial Religion,* ed. Frank Salomon and George L. Urioste, 1–38. Austin: University of Texas Press.

Salomon, Frank, and George L. Urioste, eds. 1991. *The Huarochirí Manuscript: A Testament of Ancient and Colonial Andean Religion.* Austin: University of Texas Press.

San Pedro, Juan de. 1992 [1560]. *La persecución del demonio: Crónica de los primeros agustinos en el norte del Perú (1560), manuscrito del Archivo de Indias.* Transcribed by Eric E. Deeds. Malaga, Spain / Mexico City: Algazara / Centro Andino y Mesoamericano de Estudios Interdisciplinarios.

Santo Tomas, Domingo de. 1951. [1560]. *Lexicón o vocabulario de la lengua general del Perú.* Lima: Instituto de Historia.

Santo Tomas, Domingo de. 2006. [1560]. *Lexicón, o vocabulario de la lengua general del Perú, compuesto por el Maestro F. Domingo de. S. Thomas de la orden de. S. Domingo.* Ed. Jan Szemiñski. Lima: Ediciones el Santo Oficio-Códice Ediciones S.A.C.

Sarmiento de Gamboa, Pedro. 1907 [1572]. *The History of the Incas.* Trans. and ed. Clements Markham. Haklyut Society, 2nd ser., no. 22. London: Hakluyt Society.

Taylor, Gerald, ed. 1987. *Ritos y tradiciones de Huarochirí del siglo XVII.* Lima: Instituto de Estudios Peruanos.

Topic, John R. 1992. "Las huacas de Huamachuco: Precisiones en torno a una imagen indígena de un paisaje andino." In *La persecución del demonio: Crónica de los primeros agustinos en el norte del Perú,* by Fray Juan de San Pedro, ed. Teresa Ronzelen, Luis Millones, John R. Topic, José L. González, and Eric E. Deeds, 41–99. Malaga, Spain / Mexico City: Algazara / Centro Andino y Mesoamericano de Estudios Interdisciplinarios.

Topic, John R. 1998. "Ethnogenesis in Huamachuco." *Andean Past* 5:109–27.

Topic, John R. 2008. "El santuario de Catequil: Estructura y agencia. Hacia una comprensión de los oráculos andinos." In *Adivinación y oráculos en el mundo andino antiguo,* ed. Marco Curatola Petrocchi and Mariusz S. Ziółkowski, 71–95. Lima: Fondo Editorial de la Pontificia Universidad Católica del Perú and Instituto Francés de Estudios Peruanos.

Topic, John R. 2009. "Domestic Economy as Political Economy at Chan Chan, Peru." In *Domestic Life in Prehispanic Capitals: A Study of Specialization, Hierarchy, and Ethnicity*, ed. Linda Manzanilla and Claude Chapdelaine, 221–42. Ann Arbor: Museum of Anthropology, University of Michigan.

Topic, John R. 2013. "De 'audiencias' a archivos: Hacia una comprensión del cambio en los sistemas de registro de la información en los Andes." In *El quipu colonial: Estudios y materiales*, ed. Marco Curatola Petrocchi and José Carlos de la Puente Luna, 33–63. Colección Estudios Andinos 12. Lima: Fondo Editorial de la Pontificia Universidad Católica del Perú.

Topic, John R., and Theresa Lange Topic. n.d. "The Inca Diffusion of the Catequil Cult to Ecuador." Paper prepared for the Symposium "Recent Advances Regarding Ancient Advances of the Incas in Northernmost Chinchaysuyu" at the 76th Annual Meeting of the Society for American Archaeology, March 31–April 3, 2011, Sacramento, CA. Rev. January 2012. Manuscript in possession of authors, Peterborough, Ontario.

Topic, John R., Theresa Lange Topic, and Alfredo Melly Cava. 2002. "Catequil: The Archaeology, Ethnohistory, and Ethnography of a Major Provincial Huaca." In *Andean Archaeology I: Variations in Sociopolitical Organization*, ed. William H. Isbell and Helaine Silverman, 303–36. New York: Kluwer Academic/ Plenum Publishers. http://dx.doi.org/10.1007/978-1-4615-0639-3_11.

Topic, John R., Alfredo Melly Cava, Kory Avila Vereau, and Theresa Lange Topic. 2006. *Informe final del proyecto arqueológico Catequil: Namanchugo y Chuquicanra. San José de Porcón, Santiago de Chuco, La Libertad. Junio–Agosto 2005*. Lima: Instituto Nacional de Cultura.

Topic, Theresa Lange, and John R. Topic. 2009. "Variation in the Practice of Prehispanic Warfare on the North Coast of Peru." In *Warfare in Cultural Context: Practice, Agency, and the Archaeology of Violence*, ed. Axel E. Nielsen and William H. Walker, 17–56. Tucson: University of Arizona Press.

van de Guchte, Maarten J.D. 1990. "'Carving the Inca World': Inca Monumental Sculpture and Landscape." PhD diss., University of Illinois at Champaign-Urbana. Ann Arbor, MI: University Microfilms.

Vásquez Sánchez, Víctor F., and Teresa E. Rosales Tham. 2006. *Análisis de restos de fauna y granos de almidón procedentes de Namanchugo y Palco, San José de Porcón, Huamachuco.* Trujillo: Centro de Investigaciones Arqueobiológicas y Paleoecológicas Andinas "Arqueobios."

Webster's New Collegiate Dictionary. 1960. *Webster's New Collegiate Dictionary.* 2nd ed. Springfield, MA: G. & C. Merriam.

CATHERINE J. ALLEN, Department of Anthropology, George Washington University, Washington, DC

TAMARA L. BRAY, Department of Anthropology, Wayne State University, Detroit, MI

ZACHARY J. CHASE, Departments of Anthropology and History, University of Chicago, Chicago, IL

ANITA G. COOK, Department of Anthropology, Catholic University of America, Washington, DC

CAROLYN DEAN, Department of Art History and Visual Culture, University of California, Santa Cruz, Santa Cruz, CA

JOHN W. JANUSEK, Department of Anthropology, Vanderbilt University, Nashville, TN

STEVE KOSIBA, Department of Anthropology, University of Alabama, Tuscaloosa, AL

KRZYSZTOF MAKOWSKI, Department of Social Sciences, Pontificia Universidad Católica del Perú, Lima, Peru

BRUCE MANNHEIM, Department of Anthropology, University of Michigan, Ann Arbor, MI

COLIN McEWAN, Director of Pre-Columbian Studies, Dumbarton Oaks, Washington, DC

FRANK M. MEDDENS, Honorary Research Fellow Royal Holloway, University of London, London, UK, and Director of Pre-Construct Archaeology Ltd.

GUILLERMO SALAS CARREÑO, Department of Social Sciences, Pontificia Universidad Católica del Perú, Lima, Peru

JOHN R. TOPIC, Department of Anthropology, Trent University, Peterborough, Ontario, Canada

Illapa. *See* Lightning
Illas, 105–6, 265, 286n16, 387
Inka: canals, 139–**41**, 173, 180, 182–83, 185, 188, 196, 376; modification of landscape, 109, 127–28, 132, 147, 156–59, 167–68, 173, 180–82, 194–97; origin stories, 154, 167–68, 172–73, 252, 271, 277; social organization, 148, 156, 282–83, 286n15; stonemasonry, 226–27, 246–48; terraces, 93, 99, 148, 173–**74**, 177, 180–85, 188–89, 191, 194, 197. *See also Capac ñan*
Intiwatana, 228–**29**, 234n36, 246–48

Kallanka, 244–46
Kamay. See *Camay*
Kamayuq. See *Camayoq*
Khonkho Wankane, 335–40, 342–49, 356–59
Kin relations, Andean, 9, 60–62, 104, 196

La Plata Island, 269, 280–83
Late Intermediate period: architecture, 92–93, 97–98, **100**, 146, 157, 248; sites, 97–99, 257, 375. *See also* Pottery, Late Intermediate period
Lightning (Illapa), 7, 32, 35, 58, 81, 230, 248, 257, 268, 286n16, 352, 376, 382
Lightning stones, 379
Llacsatambo, 92–102
Llacta (*llaqta*), 86, 92, 97, 102–3, 109, 111n6, 148, 156, 177

Machu Picchu, 175, 180, 228–29
Mamakuna. See *Aqllakuna*
Mama Oqllo (Ocllo), 188, 201n12, 201n16
Manco Capac, 9, 252, 277
Mayontopa, 192–93
Mercedario, Mount, 269, 278, **280**
Metamorphosis, 298, 300–302, 322
Meteorites, 379
Mimesis, 26, 40n4
Miniatures, 7, 189, 265–68, 280–84, 285n2, 301–5, 307, 311, 321, 387
Mitmaqkuna, 85, 148–49, 156–57, 171, 175, 180, 193, 196, 200n8, 232n14, 253–57, 259n9, 383
Models, architectural, 301–3, 307, 318, 321–23, 325, 387
Mojon. See Boundary markers
Monoliths. *See* Stelae
Mullu, 58, 112

Mummies: ancestral: 7, 9, 23, 34, 36–37, 82, 97, 177, 202n19, 221; Inka, 34, 37, 202n20, 219, 221, 243

Naturalization of political order, 84, 168–72, 197–98
Namanchugo, 371–78
Ñawinpukyo, 311–12, 314, 322

Offerings: in buildings, 306, 310–13, 315, 317, 318–19, 324; in burials, 309, 321, 323; of food, 61–64, 67n4, 183, 185, 194; of metal, 150–51, 311; to places, 61, 172, 230, 266; of shell, 150–**51**, 154, 200n3, 318; as transactions, 10, 12, 31, 60–62, 370, 387–88; to wak'as, 23, 58, 83, 87, 150–52, 154, 172, 183, 188–89, 197, 200n11, 214, 219, 230, 244, 249, 258n6, 266, 275–76, 280, 284, 336, 341, 387–88
Ollantaytambo: Inka occupation, 168–69, 173–175, 178–191, 220, 227; during Late Intermediate period, 175–78; wak'as of, 178–93
Ontological perspectivism, 12, 25–26, 35, 39n3, 299–300
Ontology: Amerindian, 12, 25, 299; Andean, 4–8, 10, 47–48, 76, 338–39, 341; Christian, 47, 58, 169–70; as contingent, 359–61; linguistically expressed, 48–52; Western, 5, 8, 76, 169, 341
Oracles: Apurimac, 383; Catequil, 371, 376–78; female, 383; in general, 9, 23, 36–37, 40n14, 83, 383; Pachacamac, 145, 156, 373, 382

Pacarinas, 7, 36, 112n12, 152–54, 156, 325, 356, 370, 381, 382, 385
Pacha, 27, 40n7, 216
Pachacamac: deity, 83, 85, 87, 109, 112n8, 146–47, 157–58, 384–85; oracle, 145, 156, 373, 382–83; site of, 97, 128–47, 382
Pachacuti, 32, 33, 175, 192, 199n5, 200n8, 381
Pachamama, 39n9, 61, 68n16, 39n9
Pariacaca, 27, 87, 92, 102–4, 107–9, 112n8, 379
Personhood: distributed, 10, 12, 31–38, 379; markers of in Andes, 9–10, 12–13; of places, 24, 28, 34–35, 60–64, 172, 183, 225; of things, 24, 29, 31–35, 59–60, 301, 321; of wak'as, 183, 194, 196, 255, 301, 379
Pilgrimage: Andean, 53, 95–**96**, 109, 158, 241, 243, 245, 256–57, 268, 374–76, 387

Place-persons, 24, 26–27, 34–35, 52, 60–64, 225

Plazas: feasting in, 37, 158, 197, 219, 243, 254; Inka, 37, 53, 93, 128–30, 147, 150, 152, 158, 173–74, 180, 189, 196–97, 201n15, 216–17, 219–20, 232n16, 241–45, 254, 256–57, 270, 277, 282, 325; Late Intermediate period, 177; Titicaca basin, 348–49; Wari, 306, 309

Pottery: Early Intermediate period, 137, 303, 312; Inca, **93**, 95, 108, 112n9, 135, **136**–37, **139**, 140, 148, 157, 185, 189, 191, 194, 200n7, 201n15, 242, 248–49, 280–82; Inca-Lurín, 134; Killk'e, 200n7, 201n15, 254; Late Intermediate period, 177, 248–49; Middle Horizon, 312–13; Nasca, 312; Warpa, 303–4, 312

Presencing, 226–29, 234n33

Pueblo Viejo-Pucará: site of, 85–87, 95, 102, 128–30, 147–58; wak'as at, 102, 150–54

Pumpu, 232n16, 241, 244

Puquio, 142, 231n8, 182, 185, 370, 383

Qhapaq ñan. See *Capac ñan*

Qoyllur Rit'i, 53, 66n3, 268, 284, 387

Quechua language: grammar, 50–52; witness validation in, 28

Reciprocal appropriation, 28–31

Reciprocity: generalized, 10, 268, 341, 346, 370, 385–89; grammatical, 29; between humans and nonhumans, 13, 28–29, 34, 82, 339, 346–47, 387–88; of watching, 24–25

Ritual specialist, 24, 28, 32, 35, 55, 62, 67n4, 301, 361n1, 370, 379, 382–83, 390n1, 391n6

Santuyuq, 29–32, 38

Saqsaywaman, 220–**21**, 225, 227

Saywa, 248, 249, 252–53, 256, 258n6

Settlement pattern studies, 86

Shaman. *See* Ritual specialist

Situa (Citua), 242–43, 254

Slingstones, 248, 376

Sonqo, 24, 27, 29, 62

Spondylus, 150–52, 266, 285n1, 321

Staff God, 304–9

Stelae: anthropomorphic, 271, 275, 276, 349–57, 376–**77**, 378, 380; carving of, 342; Formative period, 336–38, 341–42, 356–59; iconography, 349–357, **377**, 380

Stones: carved, 128, 185–91, 194–**95**, 201n14, 217–29, 244, 266, 275, 338–39, 342–43, 349–60,

387; as people, **6**, 23, 27, 213–14, 223–25, 252, 336, 354–55; "seats," 216–17, **218**–19, **220–21**, **222**–30, 232n17, 233n24, 233n25, 233n26, 234n29, 244, 386, 387

Storage facilities. See *Colcas*

Sukanka, 149–50, 152, 155, 159n5

Sunken temple, 348–49, 352, 357

Suntor wasi, 325

Talega, 31

Tanta Carhua, 81–82, 102, 111n3

Textiles, Andean, 31–32, 36–39, 224, 228, 255, 280, 303–9, 356, 383

Tiana, 226

Time, reckoning, 76, 152, 326

Tiwanaku: site of, 335, 340, 342, 347, 349; tunic, 303–6, 309, 322

Tombs: above-ground, 177, **179**, 180, 194–95, 200n9, 246, 249, 256, 297, 302–3, 308–9, 322–23; Andean, general, 297–98; in caves, 185, 199n2; cist, 303, 307–8, 309, 316–**17**, 318–23, 325, 327n4; in houses, 302, 308–9, 321; Late Intermediate period, **100**, 177; multi-chambered, 82, **93**, 309; multi-storied, 309, 311, 318, 322–25, 327n7; Wari, 307–25

Topa Inka, 200n8, 271, 276, 388–89

Transference, principle of, 224, 255, 383

Tripartition, 265–66, 269, **271–72**, 274–83, 286n15, 304

Trophy heads, 311, 317, 385

Tropical forest products, 173, 299

Tutayquiri, 87, 91–92, 95, 102, 104, 109

Ushnu (usnu), 111n3, 129–30, 149–56, 216–19, 232n16–232n23, 239–57, 376, 380, 386; artifacts associated with, 150, 152, 249, 256, 325; evidence of feasting at, 152; rituals performed at, 254–57; as sacrificial site, 219, 244, 254; types of, 244–251

Urcos, **11**

Vessel smashes, ceramic, 311, 317

Viewsheds, 250–52, 269

Vilca. See *Willk'a*

Vilcashuamán, 216–19, 224, 227, 232n14, 241, 244–**45**, 257, 258n3

Viracocha Inka, 175, 225, 242

Vision, significance of in Andes, 12, 27–28, 34, 38, 213, 216, 251–52, 269, 387

Wak'as: as agentive, 7–10, 65–66, 78–81, 85, 91, 197, 268, 301, 340, 382, 387–88; as ancestors, 7, 9, 81, 86, 156, 195–96, 202n19, 255; architectural, 296, 306; clothing of, 9, 12, 255, 274–75, 387; destruction of, 34, 75, 111n5, 152, 214–15, 275, 297, 357, 378–79, 389; egg-shaped, 105–8; gender of, 383–84; in Huarochirí manuscript, 82–84, 91, 112n10; Inka brokerage of, 83–84; as landscape features, 5–6, 7, 59, 85, 183–88; linguistic connotations of, 54–56, 65; as material entities, 5–8, 24, 80–81, 85, 91, 337, 340; as oracles, 9, 23, 35–37, 83, 145, 156, 371, 373, 376–78, 382–83; partible nature of, 5, 80–81, 274, 379, 383; performativity of, 78, 89; as persons, 8–10, 24, 59–60, 183, 340, 379, 382–83; portable, 58, 265–74, 278–84, 301, 337, 378; proto-, 341, 357–59; temporality of, 76–77, 80–85, 108–9, 173; as territorial markers, 86, 106, 337, 381
Wamani, 230n1, 244, 249–53, 258n4. See also *Apu*
Wanakauri. *See* Huanacauri

Wank'a. See *Huanca*
Wari: in Amazonia, 300; capital city, 307–311, 313–18; craft production, 319, 322; D-shaped structures, 298, **308**–11, 313–25; figurines, 285n2; sites, 302–23; tombs, 307–23; wak'as, 296–324
Warpa: effigy vessel, 303–4, 323; sites, 311–14, 322
Wasitira, 24, 34–35
Wat'a, 97, 178–80, 188, 191, 193
Watching, in Andes, 24–25, 34–35, 38, 213, 382
Wawqe (Huaoque), 37, 233n25, 271, 275, 378, 381, 386
Wayna Qhapaq. *See* Huayna Capac
Willk'a (Vilca), 7, 55–58, 67n6

Yanakona, 171, 175, 180, 192, 196, 200n8, 285n6, 373–74, 390n4, 390n5
Yanantin, 221, 381, 387–88
Yauyos, 77, 89, 90–91, 93, 102, 112n7
Yayamama tradition, 342, 384
Ychsma, 127, 134, 146–48
Yungas, 90, 95, 101, 157, 159, 382